DOWNTON ABBEY

THE COMPLETE SCRIPTS

SEASON ONE

A CARNIVAL FILMS/MASTERPIECE CO-PRODUCTION

DOWNTON ABBEY

THE COMPLETE SCRIPTS

• SEASON ONE •

JULIAN FELLOWES

Collins

First published in 2012 by Collins

An imprint of HarperCollins*Publishers*
77–85 Fulham Palace Road
London W6 8JB

www.harpercollins.co.uk

2

Episode 4: written by Julian Fellowes and Shelagh Stephenson
Episode 6: written by Julian Fellowes and Tina Pepler

Photography by Nick Briggs

A Carnival Films/Masterpiece Co-Production

A catalogue record for this book is
available from the British Library

ISBN: 978-0-00-748739-4

Printed and bound in Great Britain by
Clays Ltd, St Ives plc

MIX
Paper from
responsible sources
FSC **FSC™ C007454**
www.fsc.org

Find out more about HarperCollins and the environment at
www.harpercollins.co.uk/green

To Emma and Peregrine, *Downton*'s sternest critics and most fervent supporters.

CONTENTS

NOTE: Dotted lines alongside the script text indicate sections of text that were cut from the original script to make the final edited version.

FOREWORD

It is not given to many to write themselves into a whirlwind on the scale of *Downton Abbey*. I am often asked why it has all happened, and while I try to come up with various reasons, I don't really know the answer. What I do know is that it is a great privilege to be allowed to invent a community and to continue to track their fortunes, through ill wind and good, with the luxury of space and length that only television can give you. Of course none of it would have come to pass without our consistently marvellous crew and our truly extraordinary actors, every one of whom has fleshed out their characters until they are controlling me and not the other way round. I cannot name favourites, except to proclaim that they are all my favourites, and I thank God for them.

This is a chance to see the complete scripts of the first series as they were when they went forward into production. Of course, when any show is filmed, parts of the screenplay will be cut, either before shooting begins or in the edit, but here you are allowed to read the whole script, as it once was. Cuts are sometimes made because the visual realisation of the story renders elements and scenes redundant; then again, some of the cuts are to gain time. Either way, there is, I hope, a certain interest in learning what went and what stayed, and in places, I have added notes to explain the choices and the decisions made.

One thing I can say is that working on *Downton* has been an extraordinary and fulfilling experience in every way. The show, and everything to do with it, has made me feel a very lucky man.

Julian Fellowes

EPISODE ONE

ACT ONE

1 EXT. NORTHERN ENGLAND. DAWN.

At dawn, a steam train travels through this lovely part of England. As the camera moves in, we can see a man, whom we will know as John Bates, sitting by himself in a second class carriage. Above him run the telegraph wires, humming with their unrevealed, urgent messages. The train flies on.

2 INT. VILLAGE POST OFFICE. DAWN.

A postmaster is sorting the letters with his wife when there's a noise. They look at each other.

POSTMASTER: You do it.

Clearly, this is not what she wants to hear. She sits in the corner, puts on a heavy set of headphones and listens.

POSTMASTER'S WIFE: Oh my God.

She starts to write on a telegram form. Then she takes off the headphones as he draws near. She lets him read it.

POSTMASTER: That's impossible. It can't be.

If anything, he's more shocked than she is.

POSTMASTER (CONT'D): I'll take it up there now.
POSTMASTER'S WIFE: Jimmy can do it when he comes in.
POSTMASTER: Better take it now.
POSTMASTER'S WIFE: Don't be stupid. None of them will be up for hours and what difference will it make?

But she sighs and shakes her head with sorrow. The credits begin.

3 EXT. DOWNTON ABBEY. DAWN.

April 1912 — The sun is rising behind Downton Abbey, a great and splendid house in a great and splendid park. So secure does it appear, that it seems as if the way of life it represents will last for another thousand years. It won't.*

4 INT.   ANNA'S AND GWEN'S BEDROOM.

There is a sharp knock on the door.

    DAISY (V.O.): Six o'clock.
    GWEN: Thank you, Daisy.†

She looks across at the other body in the bed.

    GWEN (CONT'D): Anna?
    ANNA: Just once in my life, I'd like to sleep until I
    woke up natural.

She groans and lies back, eyes closed.

....

* I was keen on Highclere to play Downton Abbey from the start, because it is an extraordinary expression of aristocratic confidence, a loud statement of the value of aristocracy. The house was built, or rather, adapted, in the 1830s, at the very beginning of Queen Victoria's reign, by Sir Charles Barry who was working on the Houses of Parliament at the time. Knowing as we did that the series, if it was going to run at all, would trace the decline of this particular class there seemed to be a nice irony in choosing a house that was so confident of their worth and value, and you get that from the first moment you arrive, when you enter the great atrium hall to find the coats of arms of every bride reaching all the way up to the ceiling. Somehow that seemed right, as a comment on Robert's melancholy appreciation that these will prove to be the last days of summer for his kind. These houses were deliberately designed to look monumental, and when you enter any of them, even Blenheim, you will find they are not quite as big as they look from outside, although they are big enough, Lord knows. But Highclere has the added advantage of a very straightforward plan. On the left of the entrance is the small library, followed by the large library, the painted room, the drawing room, the smoking room which we don't use, the staircase, the door to the kitchens, and the circuit is complete with the dining room. Once they've been shown that plan, it becomes a very easy one for the audience to follow. It's the same with the bedrooms; there's a square gallery running round the hall and the bedrooms are off it. So the audience never has to wonder how they got to the library or where precisely is the drawing room. It's all absolutely clear, and that's a big advantage in filming. Basically, these are the rooms we use to show how the Crawleys live, and these are the rooms we film in.

† Daisy, the scullery maid, is up before anyone. Her first job of the day is to wake the other servants.

5 INT. KITCHEN. DAY.

Daisy the scullery maid is raking out the clinker.* Mrs Patmore, the cook, comes in and ties on her apron.

MRS PATMORE: Is your fire still in?

DAISY: Yes, Mrs Patmore.

MRS PATMORE: My, my, will wonders never cease? Have you laid the servants' hall breakfast?

DAISY: Yes, Mrs Patmore.

MRS PATMORE: And finished blacking that stove?

DAISY: Yes, Mrs Patmore.

MRS PATMORE: What about the bedroom fires?

DAISY: All lit, Mrs Patmore.

MRS PATMORE: I suppose you woke them?

DAISY: I don't think so.†

MRS PATMORE: Then take your basket and get started on the fires on the ground floor.

Daisy gets to her feet and lifts the heavy basket.

....

* We built the kitchens and the attics at Ealing Studios because in all of these houses those are the bits that are completely changed, either to be used for other, more modern purposes, or so run down that you'd have to rebuild them anyway. The advantage is that having standing sets at Ealing gives us flexibility. Highclere has other activities going on and we have to fit round those so we have the option of going to Ealing. We've also built Robert's dressing room there, and Mary's bedroom – which is sometimes redecorated to be someone else's. The doors of these rooms are copied from the bedroom doors at Highclere, as well as the windows and, through the glass, we see great panoramic cycloramas of the park. The point of all this brilliant craftsmanship is that we're never completely stuck for something to do.

† One of Daisy's jobs is to creep into the bedrooms – the only time she ever went into the upstairs rooms – and build the fires. This was done for me just once in my life, and I cannot tell you the sense of luxury it conveys. The maid wore gloves, thick felt gloves, so you wouldn't hear as she put the fire together. Everything was done very quietly and then lit, so that when you woke up there was the fire already burning in the grate.

**6 INT. GREEN BAIZE DOOR/GREAT HALL/HALL/LIBRARIES.
DAY.**

*Daisy comes up the grim kitchen staircase and pushes open the
door. Beyond is a different world, with the light from a high
glass dome playing on the pictures in their gilt frames, on
the Turkey carpets, on the rich, shining woods of the
furniture and gleaming floor. In a long, tracking shot, we
follow the maid as she crosses the great hall into the
marble-floored entrance hall, and on into a small library.
She checks the fire. It has not been lit, so she moves on
into the main library, vast, gilded and splendid. The first
footman, Thomas, has just finished opening the shutters and he
passes her without a word, as she kneels and glumly starts to
brush out the grate. We follow Thomas.**

....

* The challenge at the beginning of any series is to give enough information
to follow the whole show but to convey it without it feeling indigestible.
Brian Percival was the director of the first episode, the ninety-minute one,
and is now the father director of the series; he usually does the first block and
the last block, and has become the authority for other directors to refer to, in
terms of the *Downton* style. He came up with an extraordinary shot to
introduce the house and the life being lived in it. Daisy is first seen in the
Ealing set climbing the kitchen staircase, but the top of these stairs is a
replica of the real one at Highclere, so she is then picked up coming out
through the glass screen at Highclere and is taken round the hall and through
the libraries, until we lose Daisy and pick up Thomas so he can conduct us
out of the library, past the drawing room door, through the hall again, past
the staircase and into the dining room. In a single shot the audience has the
whole layout of the ground floor that we're going to use, the way the servants
work within it, where they come in and go out, as well as all the different
tasks that are being undertaken; Brian shows us how there is a pecking order
of command, from top to bottom. And all this information has been given in
three minutes. A marvellous piece of work.

7 INT. DINING ROOM. DAY.

… into the richly furnished dining room. He opens the shutters as his junior, William, comes in with a tray.

    THOMAS: Where have you been?
    WILLIAM: I'm not late, am I?
    THOMAS: You're late when I say you're late.*

William starts to spread a white damask table cloth.

8 INT. DRAWING ROOM. DAY.

Anna and Gwen open the curtains and shutters. Anna turns.

    ANNA: Daisy? Whatever are you doing there, crouching in the dark?

The wretched Daisy is bent over the fire grate.

    DAISY: You weren't here and I didn't like to touch the curtains with my dirty hands.
    GWEN: Quite right, too.
    ANNA: Why didn't you put the lights on?
    DAISY: I dursen't.
    GWEN: It's electricity, not the devil's handiwork. You'll have to get used to it sooner or later.
    ANNA: At Skelton Park, they've even got it in the kitchens.
    DAISY: What for?†

....

* At the beginning we wanted the audience to understand that this was a show essentially about two groups of people living in one house, but with different functions within it, and the first few scenes are about that. They define the chain of command so that when the junior footman says 'I'm not late, am I?' and the senior footman replies 'You're late when I say you're late', we immediately know which one is the more powerful in the set-up.

† This was the moment when electricity was gradually spreading through England. Reasonably sophisticated people could deal with it, but it was still sufficiently new that there were people (in this case Daisy) who were alarmed. The point was that few really spotted its significance. Even Robert shows later he couldn't see the point of having it in the kitchens. Of course, by the time the second series starts, in 1916, things have moved on and the whole house has been electrified.

And the maids, so crisp and clean in their outfits, plump the cushions and dust and tidy and make the kitchen maid, still hard at it in the ashes, feel very small indeed.

9 INT. DOWNSTAIRS PASSAGE. DAY.

The august figure of Mrs Hughes, the housekeeper, walks down a passage in her black dress, keys at her belt. She pauses by an open door and goes in.

10 INT. DINING ROOM. DAY.

The fire is alight. William is finishing the table while Thomas sets out the dish holders on the sideboard and fits their oil lamps. Mrs Hughes stands for a moment.

MRS HUGHES: It's musty in here. Open a window.

Thomas stares at her.

MRS HUGHES (CONT'D): It's all right, Thomas. I'm not countermanding Mr Carson's orders. I suppose I can ask for a window to be opened without your calling the police.

Thomas is not convinced but he opens the window.*

MRS HUGHES (CONT'D): William, go and tell Mr Carson that breakfast is ready.

11 INT. CARSON'S PANTRY. DAY.

Carson, the butler, sits in his magnificence. He wears an apron for his early duties. The silver safe is open nearby and three candlesticks are on his table. William knocks.

WILLIAM: Breakfast is ready, Mr Carson.
CARSON: Ah, William. Any papers yet?

....

* I was rather sorry when this was cut because when Mrs Hughes says, 'It's all right, Thomas. I'm not countermanding Mr Carson's orders', what she means is that she understands Thomas is not under her direct control, so again the audience would have been given the sense that there is a very complicated precedence among these people. In fact, the female staff, apart from the kitchen workers, were under the housekeeper, the male staff answered to the butler, and the kitchen was controlled by the cook. It's not therefore just a simple case of there being the family and the servants. Not by any means.

WILLIAM: They're late.

CARSON: They certainly are. Get the board out, so you can do them as soon as they're here.

William opens a cupboard and takes out a blackened ironing board which he sets up. An iron is heating on the grate.

CARSON (CONT'D): Do you know what's happened to the fourth of the Lamerie candlesticks?

WILLIAM: His lordship took one up with him. He went straight from the dining room to bed.

CARSON: Did he, indeed? I'm trusting you to fetch it back when he's out of his rooms. Why didn't Thomas tell me last night?

WILLIAM: He thought it didn't matter.

CARSON: Everything matters, William. Remember that or you'll never make first footman. Never mind butler. Everything matters.

WILLIAM: Yes, Mr Carson.

12 INT. DRAWING ROOM. DAY.

The maids are finishing as Mrs Hughes looks in.

MRS HUGHES: Is the morning room tidy?

ANNA: Yes, Mrs Hughes.

MRS HUGHES: Good. I want the dining room given a proper going over, today. You can do it after they've had their breakfast.

She catches sight of Daisy, still bent over the grate.

MRS HUGHES (CONT'D): Heavens, girl. You're building a fire, not inventing it. How many have you done?

DAISY: This is my last 'til they come downstairs.

MRS HUGHES: Very well. Now get back to the kitchens before anyone sees you.

Daisy gathers up her things and scuttles out.

13 EXT. DOWNTON PARK. DAY.

The newspaper boy is cycling down the drive towards the house, his satchel slung over his shoulder. As he approaches the kitchen entrance, the camera drifts up the facade to find a lovely young face looking out.

14 INT. MARY'S BEDROOM. DAY.

Lady Mary Crawley, twenty-one, is the family beauty. Lazily, she turns back from the window in her luxurious chamber. A fire crackles merrily in the grate. She walks to the bed and pulls at the bell rope.

15 INT. SERVANTS' HALL. DAY.

The whole household is at breakfast, as the bell rings.

THOMAS: And they're off.*
MRS HUGHES: No rest for the wicked.

She glances up at the line of bells. So does Mrs Patmore.

MRS PATMORE: Lady Mary. Are the tea trays ready?

There is a constant sense of small rivalries. Anna gets up.

ANNA: All ready, Mrs Patmore. If the water's boiled. Could you give us a hand to take the other two up?

A lady's maid, in a black dress with no apron, snorts.

O'BRIEN: I've got her ladyship's to carry.
GWEN: I'll help.

She goes too as there is a noise at the back door.

CARSON: The papers. At last. William.

16 INT. BACK DOOR. DAY.

William opens the door and the labrador, Pharaoh, comes in. The paperboy is just getting back on his bike.

WILLIAM: You're late.
BOY: I know. But…
WILLIAM: But what?
BOY: You'll see.

And he is gone. William, puzzled, goes back in.

....

*Thomas: 'And they're off.' What we are doing here is giving a sense of an unbreakable routine, a life lived by bells, bells that kick off the upstairs life, bells that summon them to various tasks, and the servants have to try and get their breakfast down before the bells start to ring. They know that once the working day begins, it doesn't end until everyone goes to bed.

17 INT. CARSON'S PANTRY. DAY.

*A newspaper is laid out on the filthy board. An iron comes
down on it. William is at work. Carson looks in.*

  CARSON: Do the *Times* first. He only reads that at
  breakfast. And the *Sketch* for her ladyship. You can
  manage the others later, if need be.

He walks away as William turns the page. He is stunned.

18 INT. SERVANTS' HALL. DAY.

*Carson's pantry is off the passage leading to the Servants'
Hall. The butler walks back and sits at the table.*

  DAISY: Why are their papers ironed?
  MRS PATMORE: What's it to you?
  O'BRIEN: To dry the ink, silly. We wouldn't want his
  lordship to have hands as black as yours.*

*She gets up and goes as another bell rings on the board above
their heads. And another. And another. And another.*

  WILLIAM: Mr Carson.

He is standing holding the paper. Carson looks round.

  WILLIAM (CONT'D): I think you ought to see this.

19 INT. KITCHEN. DAY.

*Now the room is bustling. Mrs Patmore is putting eggs and
bacon into some chafing dishes. Mrs Hughes is with her.*

  MRS HUGHES: I can't make myself believe it.
  MRS PATMORE: Me neither.

Thomas looks round the door.

  THOMAS: His lordship's dressed.

This immediately increases the tension.

....

* Ironing newspapers is a cliché in a way because everyone knows it was done;
but on the other hand a lot of people still think they were ironed to make
them flat, as opposed to being ironed so that the ink would dry. It is
sometimes quite fun to correct these common misapprehensions.

MRS PATMORE: William! Please stop talking and take this
tray. And mind the burners are still lit.
WILLIAM: Yes, Mrs Patmore.

He picks up the laden tray. Thomas questions him.

THOMAS: Is it really true?
WILLIAM: 'fraid so.

Thomas shares this with the cook who shakes her head.

MRS PATMORE: Nothing in life is sure.

20 INT. DINING ROOM. DAY.

*Carson looks at his watch as William hurries in. On the
sideboard, the burners beneath the dish-holders have been
lit. William places the silver dishes on them.*

CARSON: You're cutting it fine.
WILLIAM: Yes, Mr Carson.

*They exchange a look as Carson straightens the newspaper by
the place at the head of the table.*

21 INT. GALLERY/STAIRCASE/GREAT HALL. DAY.

*A door opens. Robert walks out of his dressing room. With a
growl of delight, Pharaoh bounds over to bid his master good
morning, and to follow him. Robert, Earl of Grantham, is
handsome and clever, but his life isn't as uncomplicated as
one might think. He walks along the gallery and on down the
massive staircase into the great hall. Now we see it in all
its glory. This could only be the palace of an English
nobleman. He hesitates. Does he seem troubled? He goes
into the dining room.*

22 INT. DINING ROOM. DAY.

Now the butler stands alone by the sideboard.

ROBERT: Good morning, Carson.
CARSON: Good morning, m'lord.
ROBERT: Is it true? What they're saying?
CARSON: I believe so, m'lord.

*Robert takes up a plate. Watched by Carson, he lifts the
lids and helps himself to breakfast.*

ROBERT: I'm afraid we'll know some people on it. Lady Rothes for one. We only saw her a few weeks ago. I don't suppose there are lists of survivors, yet?

CARSON: I understand most of the ladies were taken off in time.

ROBERT: You mean the ladies in first class?

He looks at the butler who acknowledges this.

ROBERT (CONT'D): God help the poor devils below decks, on their way to a better life. What a tragedy. He sits, shaking open the paper. On the third page, is a picture of the familiar four-funnelled liner, *Titanic*.*

Mary enters with her sister, Edith, twenty. The upstairs echo of the rivalry among the servants, is the relationship between Mary and Edith. They hurry to look over his shoulder.

EDITH: When Anna told me, I thought she must have dreamed it.

MARY: Do we know anyone on board?

She goes to help herself to breakfast. Edith joins her.

ROBERT: Your mother knows the Astors — at least she knows *him*. And we dined with Lady Rothes last month. There are bound to be more.

....

*The challenge of an opening episode, as I keep saying, is to give the audience enough information so that they can follow the show. The reason I chose the sinking of the *Titanic* to begin with, was because the *Titanic* is an iconic disaster. There are very few people who've never heard of the *Titanic* and most of us have a fairly accurate idea of when it took place, which is just before the First World War. By sinking two off-screen characters on the *Titanic* it is a shorthand way of saying we are in England and it is just before the First World War. These characters are not living in Queen Victoria's reign, but during the aftermath of the long Edwardian summer, in that seemingly placid period just before the war would shake everything up. The audience knows all this because the script contains one word, *Titanic*, or indeed from the moment when Robert opens the newspaper and they see those familiar four funnels. You don't have to spend lots of time explaining. This one incident tells them what they need to know. As it happens, I was later asked to write the mini-series of *Titanic*, but, in case anyone is interested, that was a complete coincidence.

EDITH: I thought it was supposed to be unsinkable.

ROBERT: Every mountain is unclimbable 'til someone climbs it. So every ship is unsinkable until it sinks.

The door opens again. This time it is his youngest daughter, Lady Sybil, seventeen, who comes in with an envelope.

SYBIL: Good morning, Papa.

He nods, pointing at the yellow square.

ROBERT: What's that?

SYBIL: Just arrived. A telegram. I told the boy to wait, in case there's an answer.

Robert takes it, slits it open and reads. He is quite still for a moment, then he stands abruptly and leaves the room. The girls stare at their father's unfinished plate.*

23 INT. BEDROOM PASSAGE. DAY.

As Robert appears, a door opens. O'Brien comes out.

ROBERT: Is her ladyship awake?

O'BRIEN: Yes, m'lord. I'm just going to take in her breakfast.

ROBERT: Thank you.

He knocks gently, speaking as he does so.

ROBERT (CONT'D): May I come in?

....

* The daughters are deliberately defined quite differently from the start. Mary is fairly hard, a bit snobbish and even selfish, but not essentially a bad person. She is reasonably decent inside and she is prepared to accept the new; she is not digging in her heels. Edith is not an originator and so she just goes along with what is happening. If she had lived in the fifteenth century she'd have covered her hair and spent half the day on her knees. While the youngest, Sybil, is essentially a rebel. She doesn't accept limitations, immediately identifies with new causes, including women's rights, and she is enthused by the sense of change in the air. The characters were cast accordingly and I think all three have delivered. The great thing about defining the sisters means that you get a different mood out of all of them. Otherwise there is a danger that you have something generic called 'the daughters' and not much more. You have to make it clear from the start that they are going to have contrasting responses to everything and, in this case, the actresses built on that.

24 INT. CORA'S BEDROOM. DAY.

*Cora, Countess of Grantham, is in bed. She's pretty, in her forties, and American. She's reading a paper and looks up.**

CORA: Isn't this terrible? When you think how excited Lucy Rothes was at the prospect. Too awful for any words.

But her husband doesn't really respond.

CORA (CONT'D): Did J. J. Astor get off? Of course that new wife of his is *bound* to have been rescued...

Still, Robert will not join in. She tails off.

ROBERT: I've had a telegram from George Murray. One of his partners is in New York...

....

*The Granthams are fictional. I have read in the newspapers that Cora is based on Mary Leiter or May Goelet or Consuelo Vanderbilt or Cornelia Bradley-Martin or any of the other famous American 'Buccaneers', but all this is nonsense. She is entirely made up. Although Mary Leiter (who married Lord Curzon) was the daughter of a self-made man, a dry goods manufacturer, and in that sense she is closer to Cora than, say, Consuelo Vanderbilt, who could be seen as an American aristocrat because her money was in its third generation. The fact is a lot of American girls arrived in the 1880s and 1890s, with the express purpose of marrying into the aristocracy. The fashion began to die out by the Great War and there aren't many American-heiress brides in the late teens or after, because basically, by the twenties, most of them wanted to marry rich Americans and stay on Long Island for that Gatsby life. Freezing to death in some castle in Staffordshire was no longer considered the fun it had seemed thirty years before. In fact, that was part of the inspiration for the show. When Gareth Neame (Executive Producer) asked me whether or not I wanted to write it and, in his words, whether I would go back into *Gosford Park* territory for television, I was reading a book about these American girls called *To Marry an English Lord*, by Gail MacColl and Carol McD. Wallace, rather a funny book, actually, which has since been reissued because of *Downton*. And it did occur to me that we all know about May Goelet and Cornelia Bradley-Martin and many others who arrived and married slightly impoverished peers, rescuing their houses in the process, but we don't really know much about what happened to them later, because they were mostly still there in the twenties and thirties and forties, struggling with the new century and sharing the war effort. I thought it would be interesting to see one of these characters twenty years down the line, so in a way Cora was the first character I imagined. But, as I say, she isn't based on anyone specific.

CORA: Yes?

ROBERT: Apparently James and Patrick were on board.

This is astonishing. Terrible. She puts down the paper.

CORA: What? They can't have been. They weren't going over 'til May.

ROBERT: Then they changed their plans. They're definitely on the passenger list.

Cora is aghast. With a knock, O'Brien enters carrying a tray. She places it across Cora's legs, starting to tidy.

CORA: Thank you, O'Brien. That'll be all for the moment.

O'Brien doesn't need to be told twice. She retreats. Cora and Robert stare at each other. Can this be happening?

CORA (CONT'D): But surely they must have been picked up?

ROBERT: Doesn't look like it.

CORA: What? Neither of them? My God.

She is weeping now. Then a thought occurs to her.

CORA (CONT'D): You must tell Mary. She can't hear it from anyone else.

His face tells us that he knows his duty.

END OF ACT ONE

ACT TWO

25 INT. MARY'S BEDROOM. DAY.

Anna and Gwen are on either side of the bed, finishing off the counterpane. O'Brien is in the doorway.

O'BRIEN: Neither of them were picked up. That's what he said.

ANNA: Mr Crawley *and* Mr Patrick?

O'BRIEN: That's what he said. Her ladyship was the colour of this cloth.

GWEN: Well, it's a terrible shame if it's true.

O'BRIEN: It's worse than a shame. It's a complication.

She goes. Anna and Gwen pick up some linen, a candlestick and a water carafe and follow.

26 INT. BACK STAIRCASE/HALL. DAY.

The three maids are coming down into the back hall.

GWEN: What do you mean?
O'BRIEN: What do you think? Mr Crawley was his lordship's cousin and heir to the title.
GWEN: I thought Lady Mary was the heir.
O'BRIEN: She's a girl, stupid. Girls can't inherit. But now Mr Crawley's dead. And Mr Patrick was his only son. So what happens next?*
ANNA: It's a dreadful thing.
BATES (V.O.): Hello?

The man from the train is below them. With a suitcase.

BATES: I've been waiting at the back door. I knocked but no one came.
O'BRIEN: So you pushed in.
BATES: I'm John Bates. The new valet.

....

* This is really the crux – and the most controversial element – of the plot of this episode and, really, of the rest of the series. Robert's estate, that is Downton Abbey and more or less everything else he owns, is entailed to the earldom. That means they cannot be divided. Whoever inherits the title gets it all. This arrangement was not uncommon then, and was designed to avoid a fortune being endlessly divided into nothingness. In short, it is how the British families retained their status. Of course, for most of them, where the property was entailed there was a son to inherit. But the Granthams have no son. That is the difficulty. I had a particular case in mind, naming no names, of a chap we know who grew up abroad and who was the heir to a great position. The peer only had daughters and this heir was, I think, his second cousin's son. Anyway, he made the decision that he would bring this young man over to live in England, on the estate, to be trained up for the role. The young man arrived, a stranger to England and found himself in this anomalous spot, quite a distant relation who was going to get everything, while there were all the daughters who were close family and who weren't going to get anything. Knowing them and hearing about this first hand, I could see there was dramatic potential in the situation, and that was the original idea for the Matthew Crawley story.

*What makes this surprising is that he walks with a stick and has a noticeable limp. O'Brien stares at him.**

> O'BRIEN: The new valet?
> BATES: That's right.
> O'BRIEN: You're early.
> BATES: Came on the milk train. Thought I could use the day to get to know the place. And start tonight.
> ANNA: I'm Anna, the head housemaid.
> O'BRIEN: And I'm Miss O'Brien, her ladyship's maid.
> BATES: How do you do?

He holds out his hand. Anna shakes it. O'Brien does not.

> O'BRIEN: You'd better come along with us.

He shares a look with Anna as he goes.

27 INT.   KITCHEN.   DAY.

Mrs Hughes is questioning Bates, watched by O'Brien, Mrs Patmore and the rest. They're amazed.

> MRS HUGHES: But how can you manage?

His answer is direct and even challenging.

> BATES: Don't worry about that. I can manage.
> MRS PATMORE: Because we've all got our own work to do.
> BATES: I can manage.

....

* My wife, Emma, was the one who originally said why not make Bates lame? That was a good idea for me because it meant that he could never be a straightforward valet. (a) He couldn't be an extra footman which valets were expected to be, and that would become part of the plot. (b) It means that somehow Robert and he share some experience that is behind the unusual decision to allow him to hold the position. That put a kind of emotional narrative and some mystery into this particular strand of the story which of course pays off when Robert is persuaded first that he has to sack Bates, and then when Robert changes his mind. All of it is somehow tied up with Bates having been Robert's servant when they were serving in the South African War, or as we call it now, the Boer War. I have never really clarified quite what happened that bonded them so tightly. There was a moment when I did come up with a back story to explain it, but it seemed a bit banal so I cut it, and we have deliberately kept it vague. Maybe one day I will spill the beans.

CARSON: All right, Mrs Hughes. I'll take over, thank you. Good morning, Mr Bates, and welcome.

But he has not seen the stick until the others break back, giving him a full view. He's taken aback, but recovers.

CARSON (CONT'D): I hope your journey was satisfactory?
BATES: It was fine. Thank you.
CARSON: I am the butler at Downton. My name is Carson.
BATES: How do you do, Mr Carson.
CARSON: And this is Thomas, first footman. He's been looking after his lordship since Mr Watson left. It'll be a relief to get back to normal. Won't it, Thomas?

But Thomas is not sure he wants to go back to normal and even Carson is not sure this change will be 'normal.'

CARSON (CONT'D): I assume everything's ready for Mr Bates's arrival?
MRS HUGHES: I've put him in Mr Watson's old room, though he left it in quite a state, I can tell you.
MRS PATMORE: But what about all them stairs?
BATES: I keep telling you, I can manage.

The awkward moment registers. Anna comes to the rescue.

ANNA: Of course you can.
CARSON: Thomas, take Mr Bates to his room and show him where he'll be working.

Thomas and Bates go off together.

CARSON (CONT'D): Thank you, everyone.

The company disperses back to their tasks.

O'BRIEN: Well. I can't see that lasting long.
CARSON: Thank you, Miss O'Brien.

He goes, leaving her flattened.

28 INT. SERVANTS' STAIRCASE. DAY.

Bates briefly pauses at the foot of the ninety-seven stone steps as Thomas moves on ahead... Bates follows.

29 INT. SERVANTS' ATTICS. DAY.

Thomas watches from the door as Bates puts his case on the bed. The room is modest but adequate. Bates looks round.

BATES: Oh yes. I shall be comfortable here. Why did the last chap leave?

THOMAS: Nobody knows. Just took off. Came down one morning, said cheerio, and that was it. Some of his lordship's cufflinks went missing at the same time, but nothing was done about it.

BATES: Why not?

THOMAS: They don't like scandal and he was clever not to take too much. Come on.*

30 INT. LIBRARY. DAY.

Mary is completely stunned. She is alone with her father.

MARY: But I thought he wasn't going until next month.

ROBERT: And he didn't write to say they were leaving earlier?

....

* The core concern in this way of life, which was shared by many employers and which we can easily understand, was that it meant having people living in your house that you didn't know. For this reason, under the Black Code in the eighteenth century, any crime against a master or mistress by a servant was savagely punished as it came under the heading of petty treason. In this it was the same as when a wife murdered her husband; that was also petty treason and it almost invariably carried the death penalty. When a servant murdered their employer, they could expect no mercy. At one stage, the statutory punishment was being burnt to death or something equally horrific. It was such a risk, you see, letting these strangers into your home, there was no lock between you, and what did you know of them, apart from some reference from another stranger? On a more basic level, the general fear was theft. Today, when someone is sacked from an office, they are often escorted to the door of the building; there was similar thinking then, that when you sacked a servant, they must be kept under surveillance until they'd left the house, because once they'd lost their job they would immediately fill their pockets with spoons and be off. In fact, the worst thing for a servant was to be suspected of theft. Once you'd been sacked for stealing your career in service was finished, and so it was enormously important that you should never be suspected of dishonesty.

MARY: We weren't in each other's pockets.
ROBERT: No.

A horrid thought strikes her.

MARY: Does this mean I'll have to go into full mourning?
ROBERT: My first cousin and his son are almost certainly
dead. We will all be in mourning.

Robert is very moved by what has happened. Mary is not.

MARY: No, I mean with the other thing. After all, it
wasn't official…
ROBERT: If you're saying you do not wish to mourn Patrick
as a fiancé, that is up to you.
MARY: No one knew about it, outside the family.
ROBERT: I repeat, it is up to you.
MARY: Well, that's a relief.

*Which shocks her father. The truth is, Robert loves his
children but he doesn't really know them.**

31 INT. ROBERT'S DRESSING ROOM. DAY.

*The dressing room is neat, lined with mahogany doors, with
dressing brushes and bibelots laid out on a chest of drawers.
The large bed is always made up, but unslept in. Thomas
closes a wardrobe door.*

THOMAS: There's some cedar-lined cupboards in the attic,
for things that aren't often worn. Travelling clothes
and such. Mr Watson used it to rotate the summer and
winter stuff. I'll show you later.
BATES: What about studs and links? Do I choose them? Or
does he?
THOMAS: Lay them out unless he asks for something in
particular. These are for a ball, these for an ordinary
dinner, these only in London…

....

* In my head, Mary thought she was prepared to marry Patrick in order to
keep Downton and everything else in the family. The question is, would she
have married him if it came to it? I suspect she would have, because I think
she is sufficiently worldly in her values. But I also believe she would have
regretted it, because of her finer side which she keeps largely repressed.

BATES: I'll get the hang of it.
THOMAS: Yeah, you'll have to.

Bates has wandered over to a vitrine beneath the window.

THOMAS (CONT'D): Snuff boxes. He collects them.
BATES: Beautiful. It's lucky Mr Watson didn't help himself.
THOMAS: He knew they wouldn't let it go if he had. He was canny like that.

Bates stares down at the glittering geejaws.

BATES: Funny, our job, isn't it?
THOMAS: What d'you mean?
BATES: The way we live with all this. A pirate's hoard within our reach. But none of it's ours, is it?
THOMAS: No. None of it's ours.

32 INT.   UPSTAIRS PASSAGE.   DAY.

Thomas meets O'Brien, who is carrying some linen.

O'BRIEN: Well?
THOMAS: I can't believe I've been passed over for Long John Silver.
O'BRIEN: You should have spoken up when you had the chance. Don't make the same mistake next time.
THOMAS: Who says there'll be a next time?

But Mrs Hughes is in the passage now.

MRS HUGHES: Is this a public holiday no one's told me of?

They go about their business, but O'Brien winks at Thomas.

33 EXT.   GARDENS.   DOWNTON ABBEY.   DAY.

Cora and Robert are walking the dog.

CORA: I think she's quite right.

He does not comment.

CORA (CONT'D): It was a family understanding, that's all.
There's no need to present her as second hand goods because of a private arrangement.
ROBERT: If you say so. She was certainly reluctant to go into mourning.

He raises his brows to signify his disapproval.

> CORA: Well, she'll have to. We all will. O'Brien's
> sorting out my black now and I've told Anna to see what
> the girls have, that still fits.

But mourning is not what she has been thinking about.

> CORA (CONT'D): Of course this alters everything.

She has spoken with real finality, but he says nothing.

> CORA (CONT'D): You won't try to deny it? You'll
> challenge the entail *now*? Surely?*
> ROBERT: Can't we at least wait until we know they're dead
> before we discuss it?
> CORA: Don't talk as if I'm not brokenhearted, because I
> am.

But she still has something to get off her chest.

> CORA (CONT'D): Of course I've never understood why this
> estate has to go to whomever inherits your title —
> ROBERT: My dear, I don't make the law.
> CORA: But even if I did, why on earth was *my* money made
> part of it?
> ROBERT: I cannot go over this again. My father was
> anxious to secure Downton's future and —
> CORA: Your father was anxious to secure my cash! He
> didn't wait a month before he made me sign it over!
> ROBERT: If we'd had a son, you'd never have noticed.
> CORA: Don't be unkind.
> ROBERT: I'm not. I'm just stating a —

....

* This was the other half of the contentious entail plot. Would people
understand that Cora's fortune has been incorporated within the estate,
making it part of the whole that must pass to the heir to the title? As Violet
says later, the old Earl, Robert's father, would have assumed his healthy
young American daughter-in-law would have a son, and he was protecting
the family from Cora's running off and taking her money with her. This sort
of thing was done at the time, but it certainly seems unfair to our eyes. To be
honest, I am not sure whether the audience did ever grasp the detail of this
element, but they seemed to understand that Cora was going to lose her own
money to the new heir, as well as the estate. That's all that matters.

CORA: It was bad enough that Patrick would get everything, but at least he was going to marry Mary —

The sight of Carson walking towards them calms her down.

ROBERT: What is it?
CARSON: The Dowager Countess is in the drawing room.
ROBERT: I'll come now.
CARSON: She asked for *Lady* Grantham.

This is a surprise to both husband and wife.

CORA: I wonder what I've done wrong this time.

She doesn't bother to exclude the butler.

CARSON: Oh, and the new valet has arrived, m'lord.
ROBERT: Has he? Thank you, Carson.

Carson hesitates.

ROBERT (CONT'D): What is it?
CARSON: I am not entirely sure he will prove equal to the task but your lordship will be the judge of that.

He turns back to the house. Cora and Robert register this.

CORA: I'd better go.
ROBERT: Tell her about James and Patrick. She won't have heard.

34 INT. DRAWING ROOM. DAY.

Violet, Countess of Grantham, stands by the fire, dressed from head to toe in black, the first character to be so.*

VIOLET: *Of course I've heard!* Why else would I be here?
CORA: Robert didn't want you to read it in a newspaper and be upset.
VIOLET: He flatters me. I'm tougher than I look.

Cora's expression implies that this would be hard.

VIOLET (CONT'D): I'm very sorry about poor Patrick of course. He was a nice boy.

....

* We wanted a decent entrance for Maggie Smith's character and so we see her now for the first time, dressed entirely in black, like the Fairy Maleficent at the Princess Aurora's christening.

CORA: We were all so fond of him.

VIOLET: But I never cared for James. He was too like his mother and a nastier woman never drew breath.

Which puts paid to any worries about excessive grief.

CORA: Will you stay for some luncheon?

VIOLET: Thank you.

Cora walks towards the bell-pull by the fire.

CORA: I'll let Carson know.

VIOLET: I've already told him. Shall we sit down?

Violet has business to discuss.

VIOLET (CONT'D): You agree this changes everything.

For once, Cora is surprised. She does agree.

CORA: My words entirely.

VIOLET: Do you know the new heir?

CORA: Only that there is one.

VIOLET: He's Robert's third cousin once removed. I have never, to my knowledge, set eyes on him.

They both know what this conversation is about.

CORA: Of course, if I hadn't been forced to sign that absurd act of legal theft by your late husband!

Violet flashes for a moment, then steadies herself.

VIOLET: My dear, I haven't come here for a fight.

Cora is silent. Why has her mother-in-law come?

VIOLET (CONT'D): Lord Grantham wanted to protect the estate. It never occurred to him that you wouldn't have a son.

CORA: Well, I didn't.

VIOLET: No. You did *not*.

Obviously, this has been a source of quarrel before now.

VIOLET (CONT'D): But when Patrick had married Mary and your grandson been hailed as master, honour would have been satisfied. Unfortunately, now —

CORA: Now a complete unknown has the right to pocket *my* money along with the rest of the swag!

VIOLET: What does Robert say?

CORA: Nothing yet. He's too upset.

VIOLET: Good. Don't let him come to a decision until we can be sure it's the correct one.

At this Cora starts to huff, but Violet raises her palm.

VIOLET (CONT'D): The problem is, saving your dowry would break up the estate. It'd be the ruin of everything Robert's given his life to.

CORA: And he knows this?

VIOLET: If he doesn't, he will.

CORA: Then there's no answer.

Cora is now truly fascinated. Which the other woman sees.

VIOLET: Yes there is, and it's a simple one. The entail must be smashed in its entirety and Mary recognised as heiress of all.

CORA: There's nothing we can do about the title.

VIOLET: No, she can't have the title. But she can have your money. And the estate. I didn't run Downton for thirty years to see it go, lock, stock and barrel, to a stranger from God knows where.

At last Cora speaks in a voice of wonder.

CORA: Are we to be friends, then?

Violet hesitates. She would not go quite that far.

VIOLET: We are allies, my dear. Which can be a good deal more effective.

35 INT.   SERVANTS' HALL.   DAY.

It is lunchtime. The camera passes Mrs Patmore, Daisy and the kitchen staff eating in the kitchen, and arrives in the Servants' Hall, where Carson addresses Bates.

CARSON: Downton is a great house, Mr Bates, and the Crawleys are a great family. We live by certain standards and those standards can at first seem daunting.

BATES: Of course —

CARSON: If you find yourself tongue-tied in the presence of his lordship, I can only assure you that his manners and grace will soon help you to perform your duties to the best of your ability.

BATES: I know —

ROBERT (V.O.): Bates! My dear fellow!

Robert is in the doorway. The stunned company struggles to its feet. Whereupon he notices he has interrupted them.

ROBERT: I do apologise. I should have realised you'd be at luncheon.
CARSON: Not at all, m'lord.
ROBERT: Please sit. Sit, everyone. I just want to say a quick hello to my old comrade in arms. Bates, my dear man. Welcome to Downton.

But Bates has struggled to his feet and now Robert sees that he is disabled. He takes his hand.

ROBERT (CONT'D): I'm so sorry to have disturbed you all. Please forgive me.

He goes. The table is silent, with everybody's eyes fixed on the newcomer. He shrugs slightly, looking round.

BATES: You never asked.

O'Brien catches Thomas's eye. Their look is not friendly.

END OF ACT TWO

ACT THREE

36 INT. KITCHEN. DAY.

Mrs Patmore and the kitchen maids are working flat out.*

MRS PATMORE: Thomas, take that up!

The footman loads a pie onto a tray with Daisy's help.

MRS PATMORE (CONT'D): Leave that, Daisy! He's a grown man. I suppose he can lift a meat pie. Now, put the apple tart into the low oven!

Daisy smiles up at Thomas as he hurries out. Mrs Patmore sees a bowl on the side.

....

* Mrs Patmore is really only interested in what she is doing. She doesn't take a wide view of whether it is a just world or not, she's simply concerned about having enough flour – and the right flour – to cook with, but she does have very high standards. She is an excellent cook, not a plain cook at all, and despite the odd disparaging reference from Violet, her ex-employer, she is valued by the Granthams. The status she has achieved for herself is therefore enough and she doesn't challenge the system. Like Mrs Hughes (and not like Carson), she does not worship the family, she just gets on with it.

Of course the cook had a real relationship with the mistress in that the menus were checked and discussed between them and so on, but this was not like being housekeeeeper and *nothing* like the position of the lady's maid, so when Cora comes down to the kitchen it is a fairly big event and Mrs Patmore is a bit nervous. In popular culture, the cook was expected to be bad-tempered anyway. This was usually blamed on their living in great discomfort. The kitchens were hot and stuffy and, even though the ceilings were often high in order to take the smoke and fumes above the heads of the workers, nevertheless they spent their days next to the steaming ranges. The thing about cooking, which again I hope we have conveyed, was that it went on all the time because there were so few short cuts and labour-saving devices. When you are making everything from the horseradish sauce through to the biscuits the cooking was never ending. That is something that our takeaway, throwaway generation finds difficult to conceive of. The cook got out of bed, got dressed and started cooking and she kept cooking until basically the servants had had their last feed and that was it. Actually, in the series, we never make it clear who cooks the servants' food. In some houses the senior kitchen maid, Daisy in this instance, would do more of the cooking for the servants, but nevertheless the main cook was still ultimately responsible, as she was for the catering upstairs. This would consist of three or four large meals every day, if you include tea which was course a big thing, then.

In real life, Mrs Patmore would not have made the cakes in a house like Downton Abbey because that was more the business of the still-room maid – but we don't have a still room maid among the cast. We just thought it was one more character than we could service. In reality, at Highclere, a still-room maid would have made the jams and cakes and so on, as well as laying out the breakfast trays for the married women. In some houses there was also a pastry chef, who would take care of the baking side of things, but we don't have a pastry chef, either. In fact, in a really big house like Chatsworth or Wilton or Blenheim, there would have been a great variety of cooks. But in terms of a drama narrative there is a limit to how many people you can balance in the air at once, and we may have exceeded our limit as it is.

MRS PATMORE (CONT'D): And take that away. Mr Lynch shouldn't have left it there.
DAISY: What is it?
MRS PATMORE: Salt of Sorrel. I asked him for some to clean the brass pots. But there's no time until the luncheon, so put it somewhere careful. It's poison.

Daisy picks it up, surveying the many waiting dishes.

DAISY: It seems a lot of food, when you think they're all in mourning.
MRS PATMORE: Nothing makes you hungrier or more tired than grief. When my sister died, God rest her soul, I ate my way through four platefuls of sandwiches at one sitting and slept round the clock.
DAISY: Did it make you feel better?
MRS PATMORE: Not much. But it passed the time.

Daisy takes a step towards the scullery.

MRS PATMORE (CONT'D): Oh my Lord, what was this chopped egg supposed to be sprinkled on?

She has picked up a bowl of egg from the table.

DAISY: Was it the chicken?
MRS PATMORE: It was. Take it upstairs now.
DAISY: I can't go in the dining room.
MRS PATMORE: I should think not! Find Thomas or William. Tell them what to do.

Daisy still hesitates.

MRS PATMORE (CONT'D): For heaven's sake. Get a move on, before they get back from church!

37 EXT. DOWNTON CHURCH. DAY.

People in black are emerging, among them a sober-looking lawyer, George Murray, who is walking with Robert.

ROBERT: Well, we've given them a memorial in London and a memorial here. I don't know what else we can do.
MURRAY: I think it's gone off pretty well, all things considered. I prefer memorials to funerals. They're less dispiriting.
ROBERT: We could hardly hold a funeral without the bodies.

MURRAY: It was right to bury Mr Crawley in Canada. In fact I hear the Canadians are making quite a thing of the *Titanic* cemetery.

ROBERT: It seems strange to have buried James without Patrick.

MURRAY: They may still find some trace of him.

ROBERT: After three months? I doubt it. No, I'm afraid Patrick was food for the fishes long ago.

Robert sighs. It is very distressing.

MURRAY (CONT'D): I'm surprised at the number they found. You'd think the sea would have taken more of them.

ROBERT: They didn't all drown apparently. They froze to death in their life jackets. Hundreds of corpses, men, women and children, bobbing on the surface of the ocean.

He shakes his head in sorrow.

38 EXT. GARDENS. DOWNTON. DAY.

Robert and Murray approach the house. The smarter members of the congregation walk behind, including the girls.

ROBERT: So, Murray, what have you to tell me about the lucky Mr Crawley? Nothing too terrible, I hope.

MURRAY: I've only made a few enquiries but, no, there's not much to alarm you. Matthew Crawley is a solicitor, based in Manchester —

ROBERT: Manchester?

MURRAY: Manchester. His special field is company law.

ROBERT: Really?

MURRAY: His mother is alive and he lives with her. His father, obviously, is not. He was a doctor.

ROBERT: I know. It does seem odd that my third cousin should be a doctor.

His prejudice is unconscious. Murray is slightly offended.

MURRAY: There are worse professions.

ROBERT: Indeed.

39 INT. BASE OF THE SERVICE STAIR. DAY.

Daisy waits, until she spies William coming down.

> DAISY: Do me a favour. This should have been sprinkled
> on the chicken.
> WILLIAM: But isn't there more to go up?
> DAISY: Please. It won't take a moment.
> WILLIAM: Give it here.

Daisy hands over the bowl and he turns to go back up.

40 EXT. GARDENS. DOWNTON. DAY.

Robert and Murray approach the entrance to the great house.

> MURRAY: We ought to talk about the business of the
> entail.
> ROBERT: Shall we do it after luncheon?
> MURRAY: Can we tackle it now? There's not much to be
> said on the subject.

Robert can see these words are not a good sign.

> MURRAY (CONT'D): As you know, on your death the heir to
> the title inherits everything, except for the sums set
> aside for your daughters and your widow.
> ROBERT: Yes.
> MURRAY: Owing to the terms of her settlement, this will
> include the bulk of your wife's fortune.
> ROBERT: It has been our sole topic of conversation since
> the day the ship went down.
> MURRAY: Of course it must seem horribly unjust to Lady
> Grantham, but that is how the law stands.
> ROBERT: Is there really no way to detach her money from
> the estate? Even to me, it seems absurd.
> MURRAY: Your father tied the knot pretty tight. I'd say
> it's unbreakable.
> ROBERT: I see.
> MURRAY: The consolation must be that if you did extract
> the Levinson money, Downton would collapse.
> ROBERT: You mean it could only be achieved by massive
> selling.
> MURRAY: It would be impossible for your heirs to remain
> here.

A bitter thought strikes Robert. He turns with a wry smile.

ROBERT: I can hardly question that. Since *I* could not have stayed here if I hadn't got hold of the Levinson money in the first place!

His emotions have unwittingly broken out. They've reached the house and Robert strides inside, leaving the lawyer to make his own way in. Mary, Edith and Sybil are walking behind them. Edith makes a point of wiping her eyes.

MARY: Really. Do you have to put on such an exhibition?
SYBIL: She's not.
MARY: *I* was supposed to be engaged to him for heaven's sake not you, and *I* can control myself.
EDITH: Then you should be ashamed.

Without waiting for a reply, she walks inside.

41 INT. KITCHEN. DAY.

Daisy comes back in, still holding a bowl.

MRS PATMORE: Come on, girl, get a move on!

She passes Daisy, carrying a hot serving dish.

MRS PATMORE (CONT'D): Oh, and don't tell me you've not sent up the egg!

Daisy looks down at the bowl she's carrying and stops dead. Without a word, she spins and races out the way she came.

42 INT. BASE OF THE SERVICE STAIR. DAY.

Daisy is trembling with terror when Gwen appears.

DAISY: Oh, God, help me! Please, God, help me.
GWEN: What on earth's the matter?
DAISY: Just run upstairs to the dining room and find William, I beg you.
GWEN: I can't do that now
DAISY: You've got to. I'll be hanged if you don't.
GWEN: What?

Daisy is moaning with fear, when they hear a voice.

WILLIAM (V.O.): Daisy? Is that you?

He comes round the bend in the stair, holding the bowl.

   WILLIAM: Is it the chicken in a sauce? Or the plain
   chicken with sliced oranges?

Daisy almost faints with relief and joy.

   DAISY: Oh, thank you, blessed and merciful Lord. Thank
   you.

She runs up to him, and swaps the bowls.

   DAISY (CONT'D): The chicken in the sauce.

A rather bemused William nods and goes back up.

   DAISY (CONT'D): I'll never do anything sinful again I
   swear it! Not 'til I die!

She hurries back to the kitchen, leaving a puzzled Gwen.

43 INT. HALL. DAY.

*Robert is in the hall with Murray. The other guests are
starting to walk past them, nodding and smiling sadly, and
enter the dining room.*

   CORA: Lord Grantham says you're not staying, after all?
   MURRAY: You're very kind, Lady Grantham, but I must get
   back to London.
   CORA: But you'll stay for luncheon?
   MURRAY: Thank you, but no. I'll eat on the train. In
   fact, if you'd be so good as to ask for the motor to be
   brought round.
   CORA: I thought you wanted the afternoon to talk things
   through?
   MURRAY: I think we've said everything we have to say.
   Haven't we, my lord?

He looks over for confirmation.

   ROBERT: For the time being, yes. Thank you, Murray.
   You've given me a good deal to think about.

Is this hopeful? The girls are loitering to one side.

   CORA: Mary, try to get everyone into the dining room.
   And Edith, make sure old Lord Minterne sits down.

44 INT. CARSON'S PANTRY. DAY.

Carson is decanting port. He has stretched gauze across a silver funnel and now he lights a candle to place behind the flow of wine as he pours. Mrs Hughes is watching him.

MRS HUGHES: They've all gone then?

CARSON: They have, thank the Lord.

MRS HUGHES: What about the lawyer?

CARSON: He was the first away. Didn't even stay for the luncheon.

MRS HUGHES: I wish they'd make their minds up. Gwen's put clean sheets on the Blue Room bed. Now she'll just have to strip it again.

CARSON: Can't you leave it for the next guest?

MRS HUGHES: Only if you don't tell.

Which makes them both laugh.

MRS HUGHES (CONT'D): So, has it all been settled?

CARSON: No, I don't know that anything's been *settled*. There's a fellow in Manchester with claims to the title, I gather. But it's all a long way from settled.

MRS HUGHES: You mustn't take it personally.

CARSON: I do take it personally, Mrs Hughes. I can't stand by and watch our family threatened with the loss of all they hold dear.

MRS HUGHES: They're not 'our' family.

CARSON: They're all the family I've got!

To our surprise, and hers, he's almost shouting.

CARSON (CONT'D): I beg your pardon.

MRS HUGHES: Do you ever wish you'd gone another way?

He looks at her. What does she mean? She shrugs.

MRS HUGHES (CONT'D): Worked in a shop? Or a factory? Had a wife and children?

CARSON: Do you?

MRS HUGHES: I don't know. Maybe. Sometimes.*

There is a knock at the door and Gwen appears.

 GWEN: William's laid tea in the library but her ladyship
 hasn't come down.
 MRS HUGHES: Oh, she'll be tired. Take a tray up to her
 bedroom.
 CARSON: Is Thomas back?
 GWEN: Not yet, Mr Carson.

She goes. Carson looks at Mrs Hughes.

 CARSON: He asked to run down to the village. I didn't
 see why not.
 MRS HUGHES: I suppose they do realise this is a job and
 not just the chance to put their feet up?

She sighs. And so does he.

SCENE — NO DIALOGUE OF THOMAS WALKING THROUGH THE VILLAGE

45 INT.   LIBRARY.   DAY.

Robert is alone by the fire staring into the flames, when Edith comes in, closing the door behind her.

 EDITH: Are you all right, Papa?
 ROBERT: I suppose so. If being all right is compatible
 with feeling terribly, terribly sad.
 EDITH: Me too.

He opens his arms and hugs her.

 ROBERT: We loved Patrick, didn't we?
 EDITH: Oh, Papa.

* Here is the distinction between Carson, who is completely unchallenging of the system, in fact who loves the system and finds comfort in it, and derives his own sense of self worth from it, as opposed to Mrs Hughes. I don't mean she is persecuted or wretched and she is certainly not a revolutionary, but she is not in love with the whole set-up either. I don't think she dislikes the Granthams, I think she quite likes Robert and Cora, but she doesn't feel the need to kiss their feet and if tomorrow she had to go off and be someone else's housekeeper that would be fine. Where this helps us, the difference between them I mean, is that with every situation below stairs you've got these completely contrasting approaches to the way of life.

She is crying again, quite genuinely.   He pats her back.

   ROBERT: Well, well.   Life goes on.

She pulls herself together, wiping away her tears.

   EDITH: What did Mr Murray have to say?
   ROBERT: Only that I have some very difficult decisions
   ahead.
   EDITH: You must do what you think right.
   ROBERT: I may not have an option.
   EDITH: No, I only mean… you should do what you feel is
   your duty.   Not just what's best for Mary.

He looks at her.   She realises how bald her statement was.

   EDITH (CONT'D): Or Sybil.   Or me.   We'll manage.
   ROBERT: Of course you will.

But she has given herself away a little, all the same.

46 INT.   CORA'S BEDROOM.   DAY.

*Gwen is leaving.   The tea tray she has brought is on the
table.   O'Brien helps Cora into a relaxing teagown.*

   O'BRIEN: It's iniquitous.   They can't expect you to sit
   by silent, as your fortune is stolen away.*
   CORA: Can't they ?
   O'BRIEN: His lordship would never let it happen.

....

* All of these scenes where we deliberately present the information upstairs
and follow it with the discussions about it downstairs are really illustrating
one of the central truths of this way of life which is that the servants always
knew more about the family than the family knew about the servants. They
might be quite familiar with their lady's maid and valet, and the butler, too,
but seldom much beyond that. Even the cook, who was a senior figure,
would have great areas of his or her private life about which their employees
knew nothing, and once you get to the housemaids, footmen, hall boys,
kitchen maids, most employers would hardly know their names. We try to
show this with Edith speaking to Daisy and having to check, 'Daisy, isn't it?'
or when Mrs Hughes is talking to Cora about Gwen, 'one of the housemaids,
m'lady'. We are reminding the audience that, before they get too cosy about
the whole thing, and despite the fact that most of the members of the family
are quite nice, there was nevertheless great inequality in this world.

But Cora will say nothing on this topic. She stretches out on a daybed, taking up a book. O'Brien pours some tea.

CORA: How's Bates working out?
O'BRIEN: Well... I don't like to say.

Cora looks at her, over the book.

O'BRIEN (CONT'D): Only it seems unkind to criticise a man for an affliction, m'lady.

Cora still does not comment. O'Brien presses her case.

O'BRIEN (CONT'D): Even if it means he can't do his job.

At this, Cora does focus on what her maid is saying.

47 INT.   LIBRARY.   DAY.

Robert's writing.   Pharaoh lies by the fire.   The door opens.

BATES: Mr Carson said you wanted me, m'lord.
ROBERT: Yes, Bates, I thought I'd have a bath before I change tonight. I'll come up before the gong.
BATES: Very good, m'lord.

He would go, but Robert stops him.

ROBERT: So how are you settling in?
BATES: Very well, I think. Unless your lordship feels differently.
ROBERT: No complaints?
BATES: If I had any, I should take them to Mr Carson, m'lord. Not you.
ROBERT: You're probably right.

He chuckles at being put in his place. But he does need to reassure himself about Bates.

ROBERT (CONT'D): And the house hasn't worn you out? With the endless stairs and everything?
BATES: I like the house. I like it as a place to work.

Robert nods. He has been slightly emboldened by their talk.

ROBERT: What happened?
BATES: It's only the old wound. After I left the army I'd a spot of bother and, just when I'd got through that, about a year ago my knee started playing up.

With a wry laugh, he gestures with his stick.

BATES (CONT'D): A bit of shrapnel was left in or
something, and it moved. But it's fine. It's not a
problem.

But Robert is clearly troubled, which he tries to lighten.

ROBERT: We've seen some times, haven't we, Bates?
BATES: We have, m'lord.
ROBERT: And you'd let me know if you felt it was all too
much for you?
BATES: I would. But it won't be.

48 EXT. THE PARK. DAY.

Thomas is walking up the drive, in the beautiful park.

49 EXT. KITCHEN COURTYARD. DAY.

Thomas comes in through the gates.

O'BRIEN (V.O.): And where have you been?

O'Brien sits on a low window ledge. She is smoking.

THOMAS: The village. To send a telegram if you must
know.
O'BRIEN: Ooh, pardon me for living.

But she offers him a fag. These two are friends.

O'BRIEN (CONT'D): Well, Murray didn't stay long.
THOMAS: Does her ladyship know how they left it?
O'BRIEN: No. They talked it all through on the way back
from the church.
THOMAS: If I was still his valet, I'd get it out of him.
O'BRIEN: Bates won't say a word.

She rolls her eyes at the absurdity of this.

THOMAS: He will not. I'd bet you a tanner he's a spy in
the other direction.

She shudders, and he looks at her, questioning.

THOMAS (CONT'D): I wanted that job. We were all right
together, his lordship and me.
O'BRIEN: Then be sure to get your foot in the door, when
Bates is gone.

This is rather a big assumption.

> THOMAS: We can't get rid of him just because he talks behind our backs.
> O'BRIEN: There's more than one way to skin a cat.

She gives him a wink.

50 INT. MARY'S BEDROOM. NIGHT.

Anna is dressing Mary's hair for dinner, watched by Edith and Sybil. They are all three in black evening clothes.

> ANNA: Perhaps she misunderstood.
> MARY: No. It was quite plain. O'Brien told her Bates can't do the job properly. Why was he taken on?
> ANNA: He was Lord Grantham's batman when he was fighting the Boers.
> MARY: I know that, but even so.
> SYBIL: I think it's romantic.
> MARY: I don't. How can a valet do his work if he's lame?
> ANNA: He's not very lame. There.

She's finished. She takes up a few items to wash.

> ANNA (CONT'D): Anything else before I go down?
> MARY: No. That's it. Thank you.

The maid goes. Mary grimaces at her skirt.

> MARY (CONT'D): Oh, I hate black.
> SYBIL: It's not for long. Mama says we can go into half mourning next month. And back to colours for September.
> MARY: It still seems a lot for a cousin.
> EDITH: But not for a fiancé.

This produces a momentary silence.

> MARY: He wasn't really a fiancé.
> EDITH: No? I thought that was what you call a man you're going to marry.
> MARY: I was only going to marry him if nothing better turned up.
> SYBIL: Mary! What a horrid thing to say!
> MARY: Edith would have taken him, wouldn't you?
> EDITH: Yes. I'd have taken him. If you'd given me the chance, I'd have taken him like a shot.

The awkwardness of this prompts Sybil to calm things down.

SYBIL: Might something better turn up?
MARY: We'll have to wait and see.
EDITH: We'll have to wait and see if he comes to the boil.
MARY: He will. Don't you worry.
EDITH: He hasn't yet.
SYBIL: Who? Who hasn't?

Mary continues to address her spikier sister.

MARY: Things are different for me, now.
EDITH: How do you know? Has Papa told you things are different? Suppose he can't make them different?
MARY: He can and he will. It's not like when it was all going to Patrick. *Papa* won't give everything to a man we've never even *heard* of.
EDITH: And you're happy to catch him in that way?
MARY: I don't care how I catch him.
SYBIL: In what way? Who? What's changed? What things are different?

But Mary and Edith know what they're talking about.

END OF ACT THREE

ACT FOUR

51 INT. KITCHEN PASSAGE. NIGHT.

Carson is walking along the passage as Thomas tries to get his attention.

THOMAS: I just think you should know it's not working, Mr Carson. It's been going on for three months now and it's not working.
CARSON: Do you mean Mr Bates is lazy?
THOMAS: Not lazy, exactly. But he just can't carry. He can hardly manage his lordship's cases. You saw how it was when they went up to London for the memorial. He

can't help with the guests' luggage neither, and as for
waiting at table, we can forget that.
CARSON: And what do you want me to do?
THOMAS: It's not for me to say. But is it fair on
William to have all the extra work?

Carson does not comment but he takes the point.

THOMAS (CONT'D): I don't believe you'd like to think the
house was falling below the way things ought to be.
CARSON: I would not.
THOMAS: That's all I'm saying.

Carson sighs. He is not a comfortable man.

52 INT. MARY'S BEDROOM. NIGHT.

Sybil's by the door. Mary still sits at the dressing table.

SYBIL: I'm going down. Coming?
MARY: In a moment. You go.

Sybil walks over to the table, worried.

SYBIL: I know you're sad about Patrick, whatever you say.
I know it.
MARY: You're a darling.

She takes her sister's hand and kisses it.

MARY (CONT'D): But you see, I'm not as sad as I should
be. And that's what makes me sad.

With a melancholy smile, she releases Sybil's hand.

53 INT. GALLERY. NIGHT.

*Sybil comes out of Mary's door and walks down the gallery to
the staircase, when she sees Edith, standing there.*

SYBIL: What's the matter?

Edith is startled, then she recovers.

EDITH: Nothing.

*Sybil finds what her sister was looking at. Among a group of
silver-framed photographs on a chest is one of a smiling,
young man, not handsome but pleasant-looking.*

SYBIL: Poor Patrick.

EDITH: Yes.   Poor darling Patrick.

For the first time, she sounds warm and genuine, as the tears start to course down her cheeks. Sybil hugs her.

SYBIL: You're the poor darling. I know how you'll miss him.

EDITH: More than he'd miss me.

SYBIL: Nonsense. He was devoted to you.

EDITH: Do you think so?

SYBIL: Of course. He loved us all, and we loved him.

Naturally, this is not what Edith wanted to hear.

EDITH: Not Mary. She never cared for him. Not really.

SYBIL: That isn't true.

EDITH: You heard her. She's more upset about wearing black than she is about him dying. I just hope —

SYBIL: What?

EDITH: I hope one day she learns what it feels like to be unlucky.

SYBIL: Oh dearest, you don't mean that.

But as Edith dries her tears, it looks as if she does.

54   INT.   ROBERT'S DRESSING ROOM.   NIGHT.

Robert is in white tie. Bates is brushing his tail coat.

ROBERT: Thank you.

Bates bends to pick up something on the floor.

ROBERT (CONT'D): I'll do that.

BATES: No.

He has spoken quite sharply. Robert waits.

BATES (CONT'D): No thank you, m'lord. I can do it.

ROBERT: I'm sure.

BATES: I hope so. I hope you are sure.

Robert sighs. He's clearly troubled about the situation.

ROBERT: Bates, we have to be sensible. I won't be doing you a favour in the long run if it's too much for you. No matter what we've been through, it's got to *work*.

BATES: Of course it has, sir. I mean m'lord.

His slip has reminded Robert of their history.

ROBERT: Do you miss the army, Bates?

BATES: I miss a lot of things. But you have to keep moving, don't you?

ROBERT: You do, indeed.

BATES: I'll show you, m'lord. I promise. I won't let you down. We've managed so far, haven't we?

His supplication is moving. After a moment, Robert nods.

ROBERT: Yes, we have. Of course we have.

55 INT. CORA'S BEDROOM. NIGHT.

Cora is dressing for dinner, putting a few finishing touches to her appearance. With a knock, Robert comes in. O'Brien takes the discarded underwear and leaves.

ROBERT: You look very nice.

CORA: Thank you.

Cora waits for him to speak but he doesn't.

CORA (CONT'D): Did Murray make matters clearer?

ROBERT: Yes. I'm afraid he did.

But he will not be drawn. She pins on a brooch.

CORA: By the way, O'Brien says Bates is causing a lot of awkwardness downstairs. You may have to do something about it.

ROBERT: She's always making trouble.

CORA: Is that fair when she hasn't mentioned it before now?

ROBERT: I don't know why you listen to her.

CORA: It is quite eccentric, even for you, to have a crippled valet.

ROBERT: Please don't use that word.

CORA: Did he tell you he couldn't walk when he made his application?

ROBERT: Don't exaggerate.

CORA: But doesn't it strike you as dishonest not to mention it?

ROBERT: I knew he'd been wounded.

CORA: You never said.

ROBERT: You know I don't care to talk about all that.

She waits but there is no explanation forthcoming.

> CORA: Of course I understand what it must be like, to
> have fought alongside someone, in a war.
> ROBERT: Oh? You understand that, do you?
> CORA: Certainly I do. You must form the most tremendous
> bonds, even with a servant —
> ROBERT: Really? Even with a servant?

His sarcasm is infuriating. She's only trying to help.

> CORA: Oh Robert, don't catch me out. I'm simply saying I
> fully see why you want to help him.
> ROBERT: But?

She shrugs, slightly. It is difficult for her, too.

> CORA: Is this the right way, to employ him for a job he
> can't do? When he needs special treatment at every turn?
> Is it any wonder if the others' noses are put out?
> ROBERT: I just want to give him a chance.

The trouble is she may be right.

> ROBERT (CONT'D): I'm going down.
> CORA: I won't be long.

He leaves.

56 INT. DRAWING ROOM. NIGHT.

Violet is looking out of the window as Robert comes in.

> ROBERT: Mama, I'm sorry. Nobody told me you were here.

She smiles at him, shielding her eyes with a fan.

> VIOLET: Such a glare. I feel as if I were on stage at
> the Gaiety.
> ROBERT: We're used to it. I do wish you'd let me install
> it in the Dower House. It's very convenient. The man
> who manages the generator could look after yours as well.
> VIOLET: It's no good. I couldn't have electricity in the
> house. I wouldn't sleep a wink. All those vapours
> seeping about.
> ROBERT: Even Cora won't have it in the bedrooms. She did
> wonder about the kitchens, but I couldn't see the point.

Violet listens politely. She has come with an agenda.

VIOLET: Before anyone joins us, I'm glad of this chance for a little talk. I gather Murray was here today.

ROBERT: News travels fast. Yes, I saw him. And he's not optimistic that there's anything we can do.

VIOLET: Well, I refuse to believe it.

ROBERT: Be that as it may, it's a fact.

VIOLET: But to lose Cora's fortune, too —

ROBERT: Really, Mama. You know as well as I do Cora's fortune is *not Cora's fortune any more!* Thanks to Papa, it's part of the estate and the estate is entailed to my heir! *That's it! That's all of it!*

VIOLET: Robert, I don't mean to sound harsh —

ROBERT: You may not mean to, but I bet you will.

VIOLET: Twenty-four years ago you married Cora, against my wishes, for her money. Give it away now, and what was the point of your peculiar marriage in the first place?

ROBERT: If I told you she'd made me very happy, would that stretch belief?

VIOLET: It's not why you chose her, above all those girls who could have filled my shoes so easily.

ROBERT: Marriage is like life. Things change.

VIOLET: They haven't changed for me.

ROBERT: If you must know, when I think of my motives for pursuing Cora, I'm ashamed. There is no need to remind me of them.

VIOLET: Don't you care about Downton?

ROBERT: What do you think? I have given my life to Downton. I was born here and I hope to die here. I claim no career beyond the nurture of this house and the estate. It is my third parent and my fourth child. Do I care about it? Yes. I *do care!*

He is uncomfortably aware his voice has risen because they are no longer alone. The door has been opened by Thomas in the hall, and Cora enters with her daughters.

CORA: I hope I don't hear sounds of disagreement.

VIOLET: Oh, is that what they call discussion in New York?

MARY: I'm glad you're fighting. I'm glad somebody's putting up a fight.

SYBIL: You're not really fighting Granny, are you, Papa?

ROBERT: Your grandmother only wants to do what's right. And so do I.

Carson is at the door.

  CARSON: Dinner is served, m'lady.

Robert gives his arm to Violet, Cora to Mary and the other two follow as a pair.

57 INT.   THE SERVANTS' HALL.   NIGHT.

Gwen's laying the table for the servants' dinner.   The other maids sit round, reading and sewing.   Bates is reading.

  DAISY: Does anyone else keep dreaming about the *Titanic*? I can't get it out of my mind.
  GWEN: Not again. Give it a rest.
  ANNA: Daisy, it's been three months. It's time to let it go.
  DAISY: But all them people, freezing to death in the midnight, icy water.
  O'BRIEN: Oh, you sound like a penny dreadful.
  GWEN: I expect you saw worse things in South Africa. Eh, Mr Bates?
  BATES: Not worse. But pretty bad.
  DAISY: Did you enjoy the war?
  BATES: I don't think anyone enjoys war. But there are good memories, too.
  ANNA: I'm sure there are.
  GWEN: Mr Bates, would you hand me that tray?

She has spoken quite innocently as Bates is right by a tray of forks. He stands and picks it up but as he takes a step towards Gwen he stumbles and the tray falls with a clatter.

  BATES: Blast.
  ANNA: I'll do it.

She stoops and gathers the forks in no time. But O'Brien watches his humiliation with a wry expression.

  O'BRIEN: I expect you've got some bad memories, too? Eh, Mr Bates?

Before he can answer, Carson looks in.

  CARSON: The ladies are out. We've given them coffee and his lordship's taken his port to the library. Anna, Gwen. Go up and help clear away. Daisy, tell Mrs Patmore we'll eat in fifteen minutes.

The gathering is broken up.

58 INT. DINING ROOM. NIGHT.

Thomas and William are stacking the plates and glasses onto trays as the women come in to help. Gwen picks up a plate.

GWEN: I keep forgetting. Do these go next door or back to the kitchen?
THOMAS: Those go back. But the dessert service and all the glasses stay in the upstairs pantry.
WILLIAM: Put it on here.

She does. He picks up the tray and goes out.

59 INT. SERVERY. NIGHT.

This little room is next to the dining room, containing sinks and cupboards for the best china and glass. As Thomas puts his tray down, he sees O'Brien watching from the door.

THOMAS: What is it?
O'BRIEN: Her ladyship's told him she thinks Mr Bates ought to go. She said to me: 'If only his lordship had been content with Thomas.'
THOMAS: Did she really?

Anna comes in with a tray.

ANNA: What are you doing up here?
O'BRIEN: It's a free country.

Anna starts to unload the glasses onto the side. Then takes a jug and puts a small amount of water into each one.

O'BRIEN (CONT'D): Why do you always do that?
ANNA: Stops the red wine marking before Daisy has a chance to wash up.

She looks at the pair of them hovering.

ANNA: Well, I'm going for my dinner. You two can stay here plotting.

60 INT. SERVANTS' PASSAGE. NIGHT.

Bates is trying to open a door in the kitchen passage. He carries boots, and his stick is making things awkward.

ANNA (V.O.): Let me.

She has come upon him unawares.

BATES: There's no need.

She looks at him, understanding his predicament.

ANNA: Mr Bates, anyone can have their hands full.

She holds the door for him. For once, his guard is down.

BATES: Thank you.
ANNA: We'd better get moving, or they'll start without
us.
BATES: Just let them try.

He chuckles. By now, Anna is definitely a friend.

61 EXT. DOWER HOUSE. DAY.

The Dower House is an attractive villa in the park.

62 INT. DRAWING ROOM. DOWER HOUSE. DAY.

Watched by Cora, Violet is reading a letter.

VIOLET: So the young Duke of Crowborough is asking
himself to stay.
CORA: And we know why.
VIOLET: You hope you know why. That is not at all the
same. What does Robert say?
CORA: Not much. Except Crowborough's had plenty of
chances to speak before now if he'd wanted to. But
Robert's being so stubborn about everything at the
moment.

Violet queries this with a look.

CORA (CONT'D): You've heard about his new valet?
VIOLET: My maid told me.
CORA: It's really too tiresome that he won't see sense.
VIOLET: On that or anything else.
CORA: Amen.
VIOLET (CONT'D): You realise the Duke thinks that Mary's
prospects have altered.
CORA: I suppose so.
VIOLET: There's no 'suppose' about it.

She has risen and now she glances approvingly into a glass.

VIOLET (CONT'D): Of course this is exactly the sort of opportunity that will come to Mary, if we can only get things settled in her favour. Is Robert coming round?
CORA: Not yet. To him, the risk is we'd succeed in saving my money but not the estate. He feels he'd be betraying his duty if Downton was lost because of him.
VIOLET: Well, I'm going to write to Murray.
CORA: He won't say anything different.
VIOLET: Well, we have to start somewhere. *Our* duty is to Mary.

Cora does not disagree, even if she is not optimistic.

VIOLET (CONT'D): What do the other girls say? Do they know about Crowborough?
CORA: Not yet. Why?
VIOLET: I used to think Edith had a soft spot for Patrick… It won't please her to see Mary a duchess.
CORA: Oh, no. Edith liked Patrick. We all did. But there was no more to it than that.

With a look of pity, Violet hands the letter back.

VIOLET: Well, give him a date for when Mary's out of mourning. No one wants to kiss a girl in black.

She knows her business, this one.

63 INT. MARY'S BEDROOM. DAY.

The screen is filled with the image of Mary, in ravishing shades of pink and mauve and lilac.

EDITH (V.O.): Do stop admiring yourself. He's not marrying you for your looks.

The other two girls are with Mary who sits before a glass.

EDITH: That's if he wants to marry you at all.
MARY: He will.
SYBIL: You look beautiful.
MARY: Thank you, Sybil, darling.

Casually, she blows Sybil a kiss. Cora appears.

CORA: We should go down. They'll be back from the station any moment.

Her daughters file out past her. But she stops Mary and removes a flower from her hair.

CORA (CONT'D): Let's not gild the lily, dear.

Mary says nothing. She stops as her mother speaks again.

CORA (CONT'D): And Mary, try to look surprised.

64 INT. SERVANTS' HALL. DAY.

Carson is addressing his team, who seem tidy and prepared.

CARSON: Are you all ready? Very well. We will go out to greet them.
DAISY: And me, Mr Carson?
CARSON: No, Daisy. Not you. Can you manage, Mr Bates? Or would you rather wait here?

Bates is walking out with the others. He stops patiently.

BATES: I want to go, Mr Carson.
CARSON: There is no obligation for the whole staff to be present.
BATES: I'd like to be there.
CARSON: Well, it's certainly a great day for Downton, to welcome a duke under our roof.

At this, O'Brien rolls her eyes at Thomas. But he is taken up. He mutters to his underling, William.

THOMAS: Remember to help me with the luggage. Don't go running off.
BATES: I'll give you a hand.
THOMAS: Oh, I couldn't ask that, Mr Bates, not in your condition.

This sentence poses as care but it is of course an insult. Bates moves off. Thomas turns to Carson.

THOMAS (CONT'D): How long do we have to put up with this, Mr Carson? Just so I know.

65 EXT. DOWNTON ABBEY. DAY.

The servants file out of the kitchen court to the entrance where they form a line as the car arrives. Mrs Patmore and her staff spy from behind a screen of bushes. Cora emerges with the girls, followed by Pharaoh, who greets Robert as he gets out of the car. He's with a most superior-looking fellow, Philip, Duke of Crowborough.

ROBERT: Welcome to Downton.
CROWBOROUGH: This is so kind of you, Lady Grantham.
CORA: Not at all, Duke. I'm delighted you could spare the time. You know my daughter Mary, of course.
CROWBOROUGH: Of course. Lady Mary.

He gives a secret smile to Mary, who is thrilled.

CORA: And Edith. But I don't believe you've met my youngest, Sybil.
CROWBOROUGH: Lady Sybil.
SYBIL: How do you do.

He has taken the girl's hand with a slight bow and she blushes. She is really charming. And Mary intervenes.

MARY: Come on in. You must be worn out.

Then he remembers something and turns back to her mother.

CROWBOROUGH: Lady Grantham, I've a confession to make which I hope won't cause too much bother… My man was taken ill just as I was leaving —
ROBERT: Oh well, that won't be a problem, will it Carson?
CARSON: Certainly not. I shall look after His Grace, myself.
CROWBOROUGH: I wouldn't dream of being such a nuisance. Surely, a footman —

He stops and looks at Thomas.

CROWBOROUGH (CONT'D): I remember this man. Didn't you serve me when I dined with Lady Grantham in London?
THOMAS: I did, Your Grace.

Crowborough looks back smiling at Robert and Carson.

CROWBOROUGH: There we are. We will do very well together, won't we…?
THOMAS: Uh, Thomas, Your Grace.

CROWBOROUGH: Thomas.

He turns back to Mary. The servants bow and curtsey as the guest passes them. Until O'Brien hooks Bates's stick with her foot and he, taken unawares, falls. He knows who did it, but when he glances at her, she looks away.

ROBERT: Bates? Are you all right?
BATES: Perfectly, m'lord. I apologise.

With the help of Anna and William, he gets to his feet. The incident is over. O'Brien is already on her way back to the house. The footmen take the luggage in. The car drives off.

ANNA: Hold still.

She starts to brush the dust off Bates's coat.

ANNA: That's better.

She smiles, but now her warmth has the wrong effect.

BATES: Please don't feel sorry for me.

But of course she does.

END OF ACT FOUR

ACT FIVE

66 INT. GALLERY. DAY.

The Duke is in the door of a bedroom where Thomas unpacks.

CROWBOROUGH: Is it all straightforward?
THOMAS: Yes, thank you, Your Grace.

Now we see that Mary is also watching from the gallery.

MARY: What shall we do? What would you like to do?

He pretends to ponder this as he walks away from the room.

CROWBOROUGH: I'd rather like to go exploring.

MARY: Certainly. Gardens or house?

CROWBOROUGH: Oh, the house I think. Gardens are all the same to me.

MARY: Very well. We can begin in the hall which is one of the oldest —

She is walking towards the staircase but this is not it.

CROWBOROUGH: No. Not all those drawing rooms and libraries…

MARY: I'm not certain I understand.

CROWBOROUGH: What about the parts of the house which no one sees?

MARY: The kitchens, you mean?

CROWBOROUGH: Even the kitchens must be full of people at this time of day.

MARY: Well, what then?

CROWBOROUGH: I don't know… the secret passages and the attics…

She's puzzled by his approach. But after a second she nods.

MARY: It seems a bit odd, but why not? I'll just tell Mama —

CROWBOROUGH: No, don't tell your Mama.

MARY: But there's nothing wrong in it.

CROWBOROUGH: No, indeed. I'm only worried the others might want to join us.

This is very bold. And naturally she is delighted.

67 INT. ATTICS. DAY.

William comes up the stairs, carrying the Duke's cases. He is observed by Mrs Hughes, on her rounds.

MRS HUGHES: Thomas should have done that. If he's so keen to be a valet.

WILLIAM: I don't mind.

He stops before a door but both his hands are full.

MRS HUGHES: I'll do it.

She opens the door of a luggage room, where cases are neatly stacked on both sides. She watches from the door.

68 INT. MORNING ROOM. DAY.

Cora is alone with Robert, who strokes Pharaoh, idly.

CORA: Mary's settling him in.
ROBERT: Cora, don't let Mary make a fool of herself.

This is rather worrying for the anxious mother.

ROBERT (CONT'D): By the way I'm going up to London next week.
CORA: Do you want to open the house?
ROBERT: No, no. I'll take Bates and stay at the club. I won't be more than a day or two.

Naturally, she is interested.

CORA: I see. Are things progressing?
ROBERT: What 'things'?

He looks at her, knowing what she wants him to say.

ROBERT (CONT'D): It's just a regimental dinner.

Which is frustrating and makes her angry.

CORA: It's a pity Bates spoilt the arrival this afternoon.
ROBERT: He didn't spoil anything. He fell over.
CORA: It was so undignified. Carson hates that kind of thing.
ROBERT: I don't care what Carson thinks.

Robert is wrong-footed when the door opens on Carson.

CARSON: A message from the Dowager Countess, m'lady. She says she won't come to tea but she'll join you for dinner.

Cora and Robert exchange a glance.

ROBERT: Carson, I hope you weren't embarrassed this afternoon. I can assure you the Duke very much appreciated his welcome.
CARSON: I'm glad.
ROBERT: Is Bates all right?
CARSON: I think so, m'lord.
CORA: It must be so difficult for you, all the same.

Carson silently acknowledges this, bows and goes.

ROBERT: Don't stir.

69 INT.   SERVANTS' ATTICS.   DAY.

Mary and Crowborough are giggling as they explore.

MARY: Do you realise this is the first time we've ever been alone?*

CROWBOROUGH: Then you've forgotten when I pulled you into the conservatory at the Northbrooks'. How sad.†

MARY: No, I haven't. But it's not quite the same with twenty chaperones hiding behind every fern.

CROWBOROUGH: And are you glad to be alone with me, m'lady?

MARY: Oh dear. If I answer truthfully, you'll think me very forward…

She looks up, expecting a kiss, but he keeps opening doors.

MARY (CONT'D): I don't think we should pry. It feels rather disrespectful.

CROWBOROUGH: Oh, nonsense. It's your father's house, isn't it? You've a right to know what goes on in it.

....

* This situation would have been quite tough for Mary and girls like her. Even today, it can be difficult for a woman to promote and prosecute a romance if she isn't getting much help from the man, but in those days it was effectively an art for a woman to take the initiative. It wasn't that you couldn't do anything, but you couldn't do much, without risking being labelled 'loose' or 'fast' and all those other words. I remember an old aunt of mine telling me about her preferred method of man-catching in her early years. When she went to a house party she used to take with her a selection of books on very different topics. If she liked a man in the party, she would wait until the last night and then she'd engage him in conversation on one of these subjects, announcing: 'I've got a book upstairs on this very thing which I must lend you.' She would give him the book the following morning, when they were all leaving, and of course as a gentleman he was obliged to return it. He would then come to her family's house in London and they would be back in touch, but, as people say now, what a palaver (although it did eventually result in her ensnaring a husband she adored). I think Michelle plays the scene when she goes up into the attics with Crowborough particularly well. She is not comfortable, but at the same time she has to take what advantage she can of the opportunity to be alone with him.

† I have some old friends called Northbrook and I usually put their name somewhere in almost every script, for a bit of good luck. You will find them in *Separate Lies* and *Mary Poppins*, and many others.

He has come to a door at the end of the passage.

CROWBOROUGH (CONT'D): Where does this lead?
MARY: To the men's quarters. With the lock on the
women's side. Only Mrs Hughes is allowed to turn it.
CROWBOROUGH: Mrs Hughes and you.

He turns the key and goes through. He opens another door.

CROWBOROUGH (CONT'D): And this?
MARY: A footman, I imagine.

*He glances at the name card on the door: 'William'. He loses
interest and looks at the next: 'Thomas'. He goes inside and
starts opening the drawers of a modest chest, rummaging,
looking under the clothes inside.*

MARY (CONT'D): Should you do that?
CROWBOROUGH: I'm… I'm making a study of the genus
'footman.' I seek to know the creature's ways.

She laughs. There is a noise.

MARY: Someone's coming.
CROWBOROUGH (V.O.): There's nothing to be afraid of.

*But instead of coming out, he shuts the door, leaving her
stranded. Round the corner walks Bates. He approaches her.*

BATES: Can I help you, m'lady?
MARY: We were just exploring…

She feels foolish. The door opens and Crowborough appears.

BATES: Were you looking for Thomas, Your Grace?
CROWBOROUGH: No. As Lady Mary says, we've just been
exploring.
MARY: I don't know when I was last up here…

Bates opens the door by which they are standing.

BATES: Would you care to explore my room, m'lady?

*Mary is hideously embarrassed. She is entirely in the wrong
and she knows it. This is grossly improper of her.*

MARY: Of course not, Bates. I'm sorry to have bothered
you. We're just going down.

Watched by Bates, they walk away together.

CROWBOROUGH: Why did you apologise to that man? It's not his business what we do.
MARY: I always apologise when I'm in the wrong. It's a habit of mine.

70 INT. LIBRARY. DAY.

Robert is standing with Carson in front of him.

ROBERT: Who's complained? Thomas?

But Carson doesn't want to give anyone away.

CARSON: The plain fact is Mr Bates, through no fault of his own, is not able to fulfil the extra duties expected of him. He can't lift, he can't serve at table, he's dropping things all over the place. On a night like tonight he should act as a third footman. As it is, m'lord, we may have to have a *maid* in the dining room.

Robert cannot help smiling at Carson's stricken face.

ROBERT: Cheer up, Carson. There are worse things happening in the world.
CARSON: Not worse than a maid serving a duke.

Robert wishes this was a joke but it isn't.

ROBERT: So you're quite determined?
CARSON: It is a hard decision, your lordship. A very hard decision, but the honour of Downton is at stake.
ROBERT: Don't worry, Carson. I know all about hard decisions, when it comes to the honour of Downton.

He kneels down and strokes Pharaoh.

71 INT. LUGGAGE ROOM. DAY.

William puts the cases on to a rack.*

MRS HUGHES: You mustn't let Thomas take advantage. He's only a footman, same as you.
WILLIAM: It's all right, Mrs Hughes. I like to keep busy. Takes your mind off things.
MRS HUGHES: What things have you got to take your mind off?

He doesn't volunteer the answer. But she knows.

MRS HUGHES (CONT'D): If you're feeling homesick, there's no shame in it.
WILLIAM: No.
MRS HUGHES: It means you come from a happy home. There's plenty of people here who'd envy that.
WILLIAM: Yes, Mrs Hughes.

He goes. She walks out and shuts the door behind her.

72 INT. ROBERT'S DRESSING ROOM. NIGHT.

Robert is dressed. Bates is tidying.

BATES: Will that be all, m'lord?
ROBERT: Yes… that is, not exactly.

Bates hovers, puzzled. Robert doesn't know how to begin.

ROBERT (CONT'D): Have you recovered from your fall this afternoon?
BATES: I'm very sorry about that. I don't know what happened.
ROBERT: The thing is, Bates…

He hesitates. Bates knows what's coming and is silent.

ROBERT (CONT'D): I said I would give you a trial and I have.

Bates waits, which makes Robert more awkward.

ROBERT (CONT'D): If it were only up to me…

He pauses and then unwillingly stumbles on.

ROBERT (CONT'D): There's this question of a valet's extra duties…

....

* We were almost obliged to drop this scene through lack of time, and eventually we shot it in the guests' ironing room at Highclere, a very interesting interior apparently converted from a chapel, which is to be found high up, almost among the attics, presumably why its original purpose was abandoned. We don't normally film in that part of the house, but of course we knew about this beautiful room with all the pine cupboards that would have been allocated to the visiting maids and valets. We hadn't planned to film in it but there was suddenly space in the day for this scene to be shot and we needed an instant set. So the unit rushed up there with a camera.

BATES: You mean waiting at table when there's a large party?
ROBERT: That. And carrying things. And…

He tails off. This is agony for both men.

ROBERT (CONT'D): You do see that Carson cannot be expected to compromise the efficiency of his staff?
BATES: I do, m'lord. Of course I do.

He is a desperate man. Quite desperate.

BATES (CONT'D): Might I make a suggestion? That when an extra footman is required the cost could be taken out of my wages —

Robert cannot bear what he is doing to this fellow.

ROBERT: Absolutely not. I couldn't possibly allow that.
BATES: Because I'm very eager to stay, m'lord. Very eager, indeed.

His eyes are filling but he manages to pull back.

ROBERT: I know you are. And I was eager that it should work…
BATES: You see, it is unlikely that I'll find another position.
ROBERT: But, surely, in a smaller house, where less is expected of you?
BATES: It's not likely.
ROBERT: I mean to help until you find something.
BATES: I couldn't take your money, m'lord. I can take wages for a job done. But that's all.

But Robert says nothing to alter the situation.

BATES (CONT'D): Very good, m'lord. I'll go at once.
ROBERT: There's no need to rush out into the night. Take the London train tomorrow. It leaves at nine. You'll have a month's wages, too.

For a moment it looks as if Bates will object.

ROBERT (CONT'D): That I insist on.

Bates nods and goes to the door.

ROBERT (CONT'D): This is a bloody business, Bates, but I don't see any way round it.

BATES: I quite understand, m'lord.

He goes. And Robert hates himself.

73 INT. DINING ROOM. NIGHT.

The family, Violet and the Duke finishing dinner with a savoury, waited on by Carson, Thomas and William.

CORA: I'm afraid we're rather a female party tonight, Duke. But you know what it's like trying to balance numbers in the country. A single man outranks the Holy Grail.

CROWBOROUGH: No, I'm terribly flattered to be dining *en famille*.

EDITH: What were you and Mary doing up in the attics this afternoon?

SYBIL: I expect Mary was just showing the Duke the house. Weren't you?

Sybil has come to the rescue, which earns Mary's gratitude. But Violet also sees that Edith is making trouble.

VIOLET: Are you a student of architecture?

CROWBOROUGH: Absolutely.

VIOLET: Then I do hope you'll come and inspect my little cottage. It was designed by Wren.

CROWBOROUGH: Ah.

VIOLET: For the first Earl's sister.

ROBERT: The attics?

EDITH: Yes. Mary took the Duke up to the attics.

ROBERT: Whatever for?

CORA: Why was this, dear?

MARY: We were just looking around.

EDITH: Looking around? What is there to look at but servants' rooms? What was the real reason?

VIOLET: Don't be such a chatterbox, Edith.

CORA: I think we'll go through.

Firmly, she leads the way out. Edith starts again.

EDITH: I still don't understand —

MARY: Will you hold your tongue!

Robert and Crowborough stand as the ladies leave the room.
Carson shuts the door on her harsh, hissed whisper. He
brings the decanter of port over to Robert and offers both men
a cigar. Then he leaves with the two footmen. Robert
gestures to the Duke.

    ROBERT: Move up.

Which Crowborough does. Robert passes the port to him.

    ROBERT (CONT'D): Did you find anything very interesting
    in my attics?
    CROWBOROUGH: Only your daughter, sir. And I'd taken her
    up there with me.

Which makes Robert smile a little.

74 INT. SERVANTS' HALL. NIGHT.

The servants' dinner is laid. The staff sit about. Daisy
lingers near Thomas. Mrs Patmore is in the doorway. Thomas
and William are with them.

    THOMAS: How long do you think they'll be? I'm starving.*
    CARSON: Have you settled the ladies?
    THOMAS: Yes, Mr Carson.
    CARSON: Then it won't be long once they go through.
    DAISY: Do you think he'll speak out? Do you think we'll
    have a duchess to wait on? Imagine that!
    MRS PATMORE: *You* won't be 'waiting' on her, whatever
    happens.
    CARSON: There is no reason why the eldest daughter and
    heiress of the Earl of Grantham should not wear a
    duchess's coronet with honour.
    MRS HUGHES: Heiress, Mr Carson? Has it been decided
    then?
    CARSON: It will be, if there's any justice in the world.

....

* Servants' eating hours varied from house to house. As with so many aspects
of this way of life, there were not the hard and fast rules that people now like
to talk about. In some houses the servants ate before the family, at about
seven o'clock when the family was coming down after dressing. They'd be
given a drink before dinner (at least they'd have a drink after the First World
War, though not before) and then the servants' feed would happen. It wasn't
very long, about half an hour, after which dinner would be served in the

He looks up at the board. The dining room bell is still.

>MRS HUGHES: We'll know soon enough.
>MRS PATMORE: What are you doing, Anna?

Anna is bringing in a plate of hot food for a laid tray.

>ANNA: I thought I'd take something up to Mr Bates, him
>not being well enough to come down. You don't mind, do
>you, Mrs Hughes?
>MRS HUGHES: I don't mind. Not this once.
>CARSON: Take him whatever he might need.

Carson is obviously embarrassed. He addresses the company.

>CARSON (CONT'D): Mr Bates is leaving without a stain on
>his character. I hope you all observe that in the manner
>of your parting.
>WILLIAM: I don't see why he has to go. I don't mind
>doing a bit of extra —

....

Continued from page 60:

dining room. That's what we did in *Gosford Park*. In other houses they would
eat at the other end of the proceedings and in fact, when we were filming
Gosford Park, there was a wonderful chap on the set as an advisor called
Arthur Inch. He had been a butler for many years and, before that, a
footman. He's dead now, I'm sad to say, but he was a lovely chap and he knew
everything there was to know about this way of life. He had spent years
under both regimes, eating his dinner before the family and eating it
afterwards. He much preferred the latter, even if he was ravenous by the time
it came, because then the day's work was essentially done. If there was a great
ball or something, things might be different as everyone stayed on duty, but
on a normal night, when your employees were reasonable people, they let the
staff go after dinner was done, finished their own drinks and went to bed.
The maids and valets still had to go up and undress them, but for everyone
else the day was done and you could relax, and that's how we do it at
Downton. It was quite late. They would sit down to dinner at ten thirty or
eleven, and it must have required quite an adjustment from the young
members of the staff, most of whom had come from farms and shops where
they had their supper at half past six, but they would bridge the gap with tea.
This would take place at about five and it would finish with the dressing gong.
The valets and maids would then hurry upstairs, but it was also a marker for
the kitchen staff and the footmen that upstairs dinner was on the way.

THOMAS: It's not up to you. I'll take care of his lordship tonight, shall I, Mr Carson?
CARSON: Not when you're looking after the Duke, you won't. I'll see to his lordship, myself.

Which annoys Thomas.

75 INT. ATTICS. NIGHT.

Anna, with her tray, is outside Bates's door which is ajar.

76 INT. BATES'S ROOM. NIGHT.

She comes round the door. Bates is slumped forward, his head in both his hands, crying. Silently, she retreats.

77 INT. ATTICS. NIGHT.

Anna walks a little way away.

ANNA: Mr Bates! Are you there?

She draws nearer and knocks. The door opens. Bates stands there. He has rubbed away the tears but his eyes are red.

ANNA (CONT'D): I brought something up. In case you were hungry.
BATES: That's very kind.

He takes the tray from her. Neither of them moves.

ANNA: I'm ever so sorry you're going.
BATES: I'll be all right.
ANNA: Of course you will. There's always a place for a man like you.

Which is a compliment. He is gentler now.

BATES: Oh yes. Something'll turn up.
ANNA: Tell us when you're fixed. Just drop us a line. Else I'll worry.
BATES: Well, we can't have that.

He smiles sadly but he doesn't promise. He shuts the door. The door closes. Anna walks down the corridor.

END OF ACT FIVE

ACT SIX

78 INT. DINING ROOM. NIGHT.

The candles burn low. Robert and Crowborough are still there. The cigar smoke swirls and coils around them. Robert rises.

ROBERT: We must go through and let the servants get in here.
CROWBOROUGH: I should be grateful if we could stay for just a minute more. I have something to ask you.

Robert nods and sits down again.

CROWBOROUGH (CONT'D): I was terribly sorry to hear about your cousins.
ROBERT: You said. Did you know them?
CROWBOROUGH: Not well. I used to see Patrick Crawley at the odd thing.

He hesitates. There is a sort of tension in the air.

CROWBOROUGH (CONT'D): I imagine it will mean some adjustments for all of you… To lose two heirs in one night… It's terrible.
ROBERT: Indeed. It was terrible.
CROWBOROUGH: Awful. But then again, it's an ill wind…

He half smiles at Robert who is not making this easier.

CROWBOROUGH (CONT'D): At least Lady Mary's prospects must have rather improved.
ROBERT: Have they?
CROWBOROUGH: Haven't they?

Robert gives himself another glass of port as he looks at the greedy fortune-hunter. Is it right that Downton should be broken up and destroyed for this nonentity? It is not.

ROBERT: I will not be coy and pretend I do not understand your meaning, though you seem very informed on this family's private affairs.

Now it is Crowborough's turn to be silent.

ROBERT (CONT'D): But you ought perhaps to know that I do not intend to fight the entail. Not any part of it.

CROWBOROUGH: You can't be serious.

ROBERT: It pains me to say it, but I am.

CROWBOROUGH: You'll give up your entire estate? Your wife's money into the bargain, to a perfect stranger? You won't even put up a fight?

He is too angry to be discreet.

ROBERT: I hope he proves perfect but I rather doubt it.

CROWBOROUGH: Ha. It is an odd thing to joke about.

ROBERT: No odder than this conversation. So there you have it. But Mary will still have her settlement, which you won't find ungenerous.

CROWBOROUGH: I'm sorry?

ROBERT: I mean only that her portion, on her marriage, will be more than respectable. You'll be pleased, I promise.

An expression of concern crosses the younger man's face.

CROWBOROUGH: Oh, heavens. I hope I haven't given the wrong impression...

ROBERT: You know very well the impression you've given.

CROWBOROUGH: My dear Lord Grantham —

ROBERT: Don't 'my dear Lord Grantham' me! You knew what you were doing when you came here. You've encouraged Mary, all of us, to think —

CROWBOROUGH: Forgive me, but I came to express my sympathies and my friendship. Nothing more. Lady Mary is a charming person. Whoever marries her will be a lucky man. He will not, however, be me.

ROBERT: I see. And what was it that you asked me to stay behind to hear?

Crowborough and Robert lock eyes.

CROWBOROUGH: I... I forget.

79 INT. HALL. NIGHT.

Robert walks on through, without a backward glance, but Crowborough hesitates, then starts towards the staircase. He takes one of the candles on the table by the staircase, and lights it.

MARY (V.O.): Aren't you coming into the drawing room?

She is standing in the shadows. Waiting.

CROWBOROUGH: I'm tired. I think I'll just slip away.
Please make my excuses.
MARY: I'm afraid I've worn you out. Tomorrow, we can
just —
CROWBOROUGH: I'm leaving in the morning.

He stares at her. They both know what this means.

CROWBOROUGH (CONT'D): Good night. Oh, you might tell
that footman...
MARY: Thomas.
CROWBOROUGH: Thomas. You might tell him I've gone up.

He goes.

EDITH: So he slipped the hook.

She is in a doorway, watching. A smile plays on her lips.

MARY: At least I'm not fishing with no bait.

*She walks past her sister towards the drawing room. But
there are tears on her cheeks which she wipes away angrily.*

80 INT. CROWBOROUGH'S BEDROOM. NIGHT.

Thomas hangs a dressing gown in a wardrobe.

THOMAS: I don't *believe* that!

*What is strange is that he's clearly speaking to a social
equal. Who turns out to be the Duke of Crowborough.*

CROWBOROUGH: Well, believe what you like. He won't break
the entail. The unknown cousin gets everything and
Mary's inheritance will be the same as it always was.
THOMAS: How was I to know? When the lawyer turned up, I
thought —
CROWBOROUGH: You couldn't have known and you were right
to send the telegram. But it's not going to come off.
THOMAS: So what now?
CROWBOROUGH: You know how I'm fixed. I must have an
heiress, if I have to go to New York to find one.
THOMAS: What about me?

This is amazing. Thomas kneels to remove Crowborough's shoes.*

> CROWBOROUGH: You... you will wish me well.
>
> THOMAS: You said you'd find me a job if I wanted to leave.
>
> CROWBOROUGH: And do you?
>
> THOMAS: I want to be a valet. I'm sick of being a footman.
>
> CROWBOROUGH: But I have a valet. I thought you were trying to get rid of the new one here.
>
> THOMAS: I've done it. But I'm not sure Carson's gonna let me take over.

He approaches the Duke.

> THOMAS (CONT'D): And I want to be with you.

They embrace.

> CROWBOROUGH: I can't see it working. We don't seem to have the basis of a servant—master relationship?

He kisses his fingers.

> THOMAS: You came here to be with me.

....

* Thomas is of course an interesting character in that his predicament is one that few of his contemporaries would even acknowledge existed. He is a homosexual, which makes him defensive and hostile but also makes him, to a degree, to me anyway, sympathetic. He is a villain in the first series, less so in the second, probably less so in the third actually, but his real role is to be gay, and being gay in 1912 was very, very difficult. I think there are plenty of younger people out there who don't understand that it was actually illegal at that time, a crime, and a man could risk prison by expressing his attraction to someone else. Of course, people can say there is still sexual behaviour that is illegal, but it is pernicious. Here, by contrast, we have a grown man who wants to be allowed to enjoy a relationship with another consenting adult, and for this, in 1912, he could go to prison. I think the enormity of that injustice is interesting and makes Thomas somehow sympathetic because of it.

Incidentally, Crowborough wouldn't have been the first gay peer to marry money in order to rescue his family financially. Aristocracy in decline is a subtext of the whole show and an heiress was quite a popular way out of disaster. The truth is, that life may seem magnificent and even enviable, but, in many cases, by the start of the First World War, it was resting on sand.

CROWBOROUGH: Among other reasons. But one swallow
doesn't make a summer.
THOMAS: Aren't you forgetting something?

His voice has got quite nasty. But Crowborough smiles.

CROWBOROUGH: What? Are you threatening me?

Thomas's silence appears to confirm that he is.

CROWBOROUGH (CONT'D): Because of a youthful dalliance? A
few weeks of madness in a London Season? You wouldn't
hold that against me, surely?
THOMAS: I would if I have to.
CROWBOROUGH: Who'd believe a greedy footman against the
word of a duke? If you're not very careful, you'll end
up behind bars.
THOMAS: I've got proof.

The Duke opens a drawer and brings out a bundle of letters.

CROWBOROUGH: You mean these?

*Thomas lunges, but Crowborough's quick. He hurls them into
the fire and holds Thomas in an arm lock. The letters burn.*

CROWBOROUGH (CONT'D): I'm grateful. My mother's always
telling me never to put anything in writing and now,
thanks to you, I never will again.
THOMAS: How did you get them, you bastard?
CROWBOROUGH: Don't be a bad loser, Thomas. Go to bed.
Unless you want to stay.

*With a withering look, the footman leaves. But Crowborough
doesn't mind. He's on to the next adventure.*

81 INT. MRS HUGHES'S SITTING ROOM. NIGHT.

Mrs Hughes is sitting by her fire when Carson looks in.

CARSON: I think I'll turn in.
MRS HUGHES: No big announcement, then?
CARSON: No. Nor likely to be. He's off on the nine
o'clock train.
MRS HUGHES: He never is! And when we've had a turkey
killed for tomorrow's dinner!
CARSON: Thomas says he's packed already.
MRS HUGHES: I wonder what she did wrong.

CARSON: She did *nothing* wrong! Not from the way his lordship was talking.

MRS HUGHES: So His Grace turned out to be graceless?

But Carson doesn't find these things funny.

CARSON: Goodnight, Mrs Hughes.

MRS HUGHES: Goodnight, Mr Carson.

82 INT. CORA'S BEDROOM. NIGHT.

Robert and Cora are in bed.

CORA: If you knew that was your decision why put Mary through it?

ROBERT: I didn't know it *was* my decision, my *final* decision, until tonight. But I find I cannot ruin the estate and hollow out the title, for the sake of Mary, even with a better man than that.

CORA: I try to understand. I just can't.

ROBERT: Why should you? Downton is in my blood and in my bones. It's not in yours. And I can no more be the cause of its destruction than I could betray my country.

She feels a mixture of admiration and irritation.

ROBERT (CONT'D): Besides, how was I to know he wouldn't take her without the money?

CORA: Don't pretend to be a child because it suits you.

ROBERT: Do you think she would've been happy with a fortune-hunter?

CORA: She might've been. I was.

This admission of the unspoken brings Robert up short. After a beat, he sits on the bed and takes her hand.

ROBERT: Have you been happy? Really? Have I made you happy?

CORA: Yes. That is, since you fell in love with me.

She is playing with him a little, but she does love him.

CORA (CONT'D): Which if I remember correctly was about a year after we married.

ROBERT: Not a year. Not as long as that.

He raises her hand to his lips. Then…

ROBERT (CONT'D): But it wouldn't have happened for Mary.
CORA: Why not?
ROBERT: Because I'm *so* much nicer than the Duke of Crowborough.
CORA: I'll be the judge of that.

These two are well suited. She lowers the lamp wick, blows it out and settles down.

CORA (CONT'D): But don't think I'm going to let it rest, Robert. I haven't given up by any means.
ROBERT: I must do what my conscience tells me.
CORA: And so must I. And I don't want you to think I'll let it rest.

With a sigh, he blows out his lamp.

83 INT.   HALL.   DAY.

Carson is crossing the hall when he sees Robert.

CARSON: Would it be acceptable for Bates to ride in front with Taylor? Otherwise, it means getting the other car out. He and His Grace are catching the same train.
ROBERT: Perfectly acceptable. And if His Grace doesn't like it, he can lump it.

Carson almost smiles as he goes off to sort this out.

84 EXT.   DOWNTON ABBEY.   DAY.

Crowborough is leaving. He stands with Cora at the door.

CROWBOROUGH: You've been so kind, Lady Grantham.   Thank you.
CORA: Goodbye, Duke.

Her voice is cold. She holds out her hand stiffly.

CROWBOROUGH: You'll make my farewells to your delightful daughters?
CORA: They'd have been down if they'd known you were leaving so soon.
CROWBOROUGH: Alas, something's come up which has taken me quite by surprise.
CORA: Obviously.

Robert now emerges from the main door, with Pharaoh.

CROWBOROUGH: Well, Grantham, this has been a highly enjoyable interlude.
ROBERT: Has it? And I feared it had proved a disappointment.
CROWBOROUGH: Not at all, not at all. A short stay in your lovely house has driven away my cares.

He catches Thomas's eye as the latter is strapping on the luggage. The other servants are in attendance. Taylor, the chauffeur, stands by the open door.

TAYLOR: We ought to go, m'lord. If His Grace is to catch the train.

Robert walks over to Bates, who is by the car.

ROBERT: Goodbye, Bates. And good luck.
BATES: Good luck to you, m'lord.

Crowborough has climbed in. The chauffeur shuts the door and gets in, as does Bates. The car is moving off, when —

ROBERT: Wait!

The car stops. Robert runs forward, opening Bates's door and pulling the case off the valet's lap.

ROBERT (CONT'D): Get out, Bates.
CROWBOROUGH: I don't want to be late.

Robert ignores him, holding the door. A shocked Carson runs forward to close the door after Bates. Taylor drives off.

ROBERT: Get back inside. And we'll say no more about it.

Bates takes his case and goes. Robert looks at his butler.

ROBERT (CONT'D): It wasn't right, Carson. I just didn't think it was right.

On the steps, Cora looks on this with resignation and goes inside. Carson shepherds the other servants away. Thomas and O'Brien are in a rage. Anna is delighted. The others are mainly just curious.

85 EXT. CRAWLEY HOUSE. MANCHESTER. DAY.

A large, suburban villa. The postman walks down the path.

86 INT. CRAWLEY DINING ROOM. MANCHESTER. DAY.

This is a pleasant room. A handsome woman in her fifties, Isobel Crawley, is eating breakfast with her son, Matthew, who reads a paper. A maid carries in letters on a salver.

    MAID: First post, ma'am.
    ISOBEL: Thank you, Ellen.

She takes them, holding one out to Matthew. He opens it and reads. He looks astonished.

    MATTHEW: It's from Lord Grantham.
    ISOBEL: Really? What on earth does he want?

He scans the letter a little more.

    MATTHEW: He wants to change our lives.

They digest this extraordinary remark together.

END OF EPISODE ONE

EPISODE TWO

ACT ONE

1 INT/EXT. MOTOR CAR/CRAWLEY HOUSE. DOWNTON. DAY.

Matthew and Isobel Crawley are being driven by Taylor. The car turns into a gate.

TAYLOR: Here we are, ma'am. This is Crawley House.*
MATTHEW: For good or ill.

Isobel gives him a sharp look as the car comes to a halt and Taylor gets out. They speak in lowered tones.

MATTHEW (CONT'D): I'm still not sure we've done the right thing. Why are we here?
ISOBEL: For the thousandth time, we're here because you will inherit a great position for which you are completely unprepared. Would you rather arrive in twenty years' time as an ignorant stranger?

Taylor opens her door, and she climbs out. Matthew gets out and joins her on the far side, as Taylor unstraps the bags.

MATTHEW: I still don't see why I couldn't just refuse it.
ISOBEL: There is no mechanism for you to do so! You *will* be an earl. You *will* inherit the estate. Of course you can throw it away when you have it, that's up to you.†
MATTHEW: And do you approve?
ISOBEL: Whether I approve is neither here nor there. It will happen.

....

* I had a struggle here, because putting names outside houses is quite modern. They had nailed a huge plaque on the gates saying 'Crawley House', very cheerily, but I didn't see it until the rushes. So it had to be removed by the special effects department. If you look carefully you can see slightly wobbly stones in the gate pier.

A butler, Alfred Molesley, has come out of the front door but he hangs back, seeing they are talking. Now Matthew turns to him.

MATTHEW: Can I help…?
MOLESLEY: I'm Molesley, sir. Your butler and valet.
MATTHEW: I thought we were to be looked after by Ellen and Mrs Bird.
MOLESLEY: Lady Grantham employed me, sir.
MATTHEW: Mr Molesley, I'm afraid —
ISOBEL: May I introduce ourselves? I am Mrs Crawley and this is my son, Mr Matthew Crawley.
MOLESLEY: I'll just give Mr Taylor a hand with the cases.
MATTHEW: I can —
ISOBEL: Thank you, Molesley.

Molesley and Taylor start to carry the bags inside. Isobel and Matthew walk behind them. He lowers his voice.

MATTHEW: I won't let them change me.
ISOBEL: Why would they want to?
MATTHEW: Mother, Lord Grantham has made the unwelcome discovery that his heir is a middle class lawyer and the son of a middle class doctor.
ISOBEL: *Upper* middle class.

....

† The whole business of Matthew's being the heir. It was very important that this would be credible. There was a certain kind of story-telling imperative that would have quite liked the heir to be a window cleaner from Solihull, picking up the salt cellar and saying what's this?, but we just felt it would be unbelievable at that particular time, if not so much now. However, this didn't mean the heir had to be a super-toff. In those days it would have been perfectly credible for the younger son of an earl to take up a position in the army, perhaps, and then for his son to do something else, until they would gradually grow, as a family, into the professional world. They wouldn't have had much private income, as the system in England leaves the younger sons to shift for themselves. And so by the time you've got to third cousins like Robert Grantham and Matthew's father, the junior branch is sufficiently distant not even to be quasi-aristocratic. They are respectable *haut bourgeois*.

*She's rather miffed by his description.**

> MATTHEW: He wants to limit the damage by turning me into one of his own kind.
>
> ISOBEL: When you met him in London, you liked him.

They have reached the front door and they go inside.

2 INT. LIBRARY. DAY.

Robert is at his desk. His wife is with him.

> ROBERT: They must be here by now. I've sent Mary down to greet them.
>
> CORA: I simply do not understand why we had to rush into this.
>
> ROBERT: Matthew Crawley is my heir.
>
> CORA: But Patrick was your heir. He never lived here.

....

* Isobel has grown up in the world of medicine and become a nurse in the Boer War, one of the first moments when you had that kind of civilian response to a war which would become much more ordinary in the First World War. Up to the Crimea, on the whole war was something that the army was doing over there, and the idea that we were all in it together hadn't really taken root. They were patriotic, of course, but the civilians didn't really see they had a role to play. That was essentially a twentieth-century thing. But anyway, Isobel became a nurse, which meant she'd had nursing training. You will notice that she didn't become a doctor. I thought that would be over-egging it a bit because, although there were women doctors by the end of the nineteenth century, they were pretty few and far between and they had a tough struggle to make themselves heard.

Matthew, therefore, comes from an intellectual and knowledge-based society. He hasn't grown up killing things and checking the bridle and girth. I suppose the fundamental philosophy of *Downton* is essentially that pretty well all of the men and women in the house, whatever their role there, are decent people. We have one or two who fall below that marker but mainly they are trying to do their best. Of course we need conflict, but to me it's not enough just to have nasty people versus nice people, which is why the *Downton* disagreements usually depend on both points of view being reasonable. The audience will hopefully they have their sympathies and take the side of one character or the other, but I also hope they will sometimes change their minds.

ROBERT: Patrick was in and out of this house since the day he was born. You saw how many of the village turned out for the service.
CORA: But nothing's settled yet.
ROBERT: Yes, it is settled, my dearest one, whether you like it or not.
CORA: I wouldn't say that. Not while your mother breathes air.

This makes him smile.

3 INT. DRAWING ROOM. CRAWLEY HOUSE. DAY.

Matthew and Isobel are with a maid, Ellen.

ISOBEL: Oh, Ellen, this is much better than I thought it would be. You have done well.

Molesley comes in, carrying a small attaché case.

MOLESLEY: Would you like this in here, ma'am, or taken up to your room?
ISOBEL: In here, thank you. So, are you the whole of our new household?
MOLESLEY: There's a local girl, ma'am. Beth. She's to double under housemaid and kitchen maid.*
MATTHEW: This is ridic —

....

* The maids would almost certainly be local girls since service was generally seen as a rite of passage. They would be chosen by the housekeepers and mistresses of the local houses, who would visit the schools to see the leaving girls, with the great houses getting first shout, and when they had been chosen, these ones would be seen as having won the prizes. The farmers, the shop keepers, the businessmen from the nearby towns would court the maids of the great houses, because they'd had a training, almost like a finishing school, in sewing and cooking and clothes, and they were mostly very competent by the time they had worked for a few years in service. In other words, they were considered excellent wife material. If you see photographs of great households with masses of maids, almost all of them are young because, as a rule, they only worked into their middle twenties, before leaving to marry. It was kind of a ten-year career really, from about fifteen to twenty-five. In this show, they are northern, because *Downton Abbey* is set in Yorkshire.

ISOBEL: Thank you very much, Molesley. And do you know Downton well?

MOLESLEY: I grew up in the village, ma'am. My father's still here, but he's widowed now. That's why I wrote to Mr Carson.

Matthew looks at his mother with an expression that makes her anxious they should be alone before he speaks.

ISOBEL: Might we have some tea?

MOLESLEY: Very good, ma'am.

The man goes, shutting the door. They are alone.

MATTHEW: Well, he can go right now.

ISOBEL: Why?

MATTHEW: Because we do not need a 'butler' — or a 'valet', if it comes to that. We've always managed perfectly well with a cook and a maid and they cannot expect us —

Isobel turns on her son quite severely.

....

Continued from page 77:

The footmen were more likely to have travelled to find work. William is local and so is Molesley, who started out as a footman and has been promoted, but Thomas, for instance, and later Jimmy, have both grown up elsewhere. Certainly, the senior servants, the valets, the ladies' maids, the housekeeper, the chauffeur, were often from different parts of the Kingdom. We don't have the generator men, figures of some mystery at the time as they understood electricity which was a frightening concept, because we just thought it was one too many but they and the butler, particularly, would often travel far afield. These were big careers and seen as such, and the employers would generally advertise in *The Lady* which was read by the entire servant class when in search of a job. As for casting, we asked Jill Trevellick not to worry when it came to whether or not an actor could do a Yorkshire accent. They could come from anywhere and I remember I said I wanted someone Irish because I knew I wanted to deal at a certain point with Irish politics. Our Irishman would turn out to be Tom Branson, the chauffeur. Phyllis Logan came in for the housekeeper and Mrs Hughes immediately became Scottish which she wasn't before. We had already agreed that it was one of those roles that could be filled by someone from any part of the country.

ISOBEL: What they expect Matthew, is that we won't know
how to behave. So if you don't mind, I would rather *not*
confirm their expectations!
MATTHEW: I have to be myself, Mother. I'll be no use to
anyone, if I can't be myself. And before they — or you —
get any ideas, I will choose my own wife.
ISOBEL: What on earth do you mean?
MATTHEW: Well, they're clearly going to push one of the
daughters at me. They'll have fixed on that when they
heard I was a bachelor.*
MOLESLEY: Lady Mary Crawley.

*She is standing in the doorway in a riding habit. She must
have heard. Both Crawleys are extremely flustered.*

....

* This was widely seen as a desirable outcome in these situations, if it could
possibly be arranged; the bloodlines would be mixed together and justice was
seen to be done. Of course, by the 1890s, unlike other European countries,
we didn't really go in for arranged marriages. The system here was for your
daughters to participate in what came to be known as the London Season
and young men from a similar background would meet them. In effect what
you said to your children was: You must choose from within this gene pool,
but within the pool you can please yourself. That was the rule of thumb.
Obviously there were a few great prizes every year, the elder sons of great
families, and there were the heiresses, although, until the American girls
arrived, there were not many of those because of the English system, which
meant that the girls got nothing if there was a boy. That's why the American
heiresses were such a bonus, because American rich people made all their
children rich and so to have an American heiress it wasn't necessary that her
siblings were dead and she had no brother. Consuelo Vanderbilt, who
became Duchess of Marlborough, had two brothers but that didn't stop her
bringing a huge fortune into the Churchill family. This would never happen
in an English dynasty. By definition, if an heiress was English, her family
would have more or less died out, which meant they were often bad breeders,
whereas an American heiress carried no such stigma – they came from
perfectly healthy stock. In all this, breeding was a pretty key element, and
unless your estate was in need of rescue, it was better to marry into a family
like that of the Duke of Abercorn, a famously fertile tribe, where every one of
them produced enormous families. If you married a Hamilton from the
Abercorn branch, you had a pretty strong chance of healthy descendants.
   That said, in the highest echelons there was still a certain amount of
nudging involved. Very few duchesses at that time had not been born at the
very least the daughter of an earl. And so, inevitably, when someone did

MARY: I do hope I'm not interrupting.

ISOBEL: Lady Mary —

MARY: Cousin Mary, please. Mama has sent me down to welcome you and ask you to dine with us tonight. Unless you're too tired.

ISOBEL: We would be delighted.

MARY: Good. Come at eight.

She is about to leave.

ISOBEL: Won't you stay and have some tea?

MARY: Oh, no. You're far too busy, and I wouldn't want to push in.

Her slight emphasis on the word 'push' tells us she heard Matthew's speech. She walks out, leaving them stunned.*

4 EXT. CRAWLEY HOUSE. DOWNTON. DAY.

Mary has been helped onto her side-saddle by the head groom Lynch, who mounts as Matthew comes out. She ignores him.†

MARY: Lynch, I think we'll go back by the South Lodge.

LYNCH: Very good, m'lady.

MATTHEW: Lady Mary, I hope you didn't misunderstand me. I was only joking.

MARY: Of course. And I agree. The whole thing is a complete joke.‡

The two horses move off. Matthew has begun badly.

....

Continued from page 79:

appear who was beautiful and the daughter of an earl and very nice, on the whole she had the pick of the room. Nevertheless, as I have said, as a system it was less constraining than those in a lot of the continental countries.

We are told that Mary had been pushed towards first Patrick, who went down on the *Titanic*, and then towards Matthew. Of course my own theory, which is expressed by Anna the maid, is that Mary probably would not have gone through with it with Patrick. It is one thing to entertain the idea of marrying for social reasons, but when the reality of letting someone into your life and your bed starts to take shape, it is quite a different matter.

* One reason for this scene was to show that Matthew, although he's a clever fellow, has curious spots of blindness when it comes to other people's feelings.

5 INT. SERVANTS' HALL. DOWNTON. EVE.

There are the remains of a tea, bread, butter, jam, on the table. O'Brien is cleaning a bracelet, while Anna mends the trimming on a bodice. Gwen is there, eating, and William and Daisy. Thomas reads his newspaper. Bates drinks tea.

THOMAS: So what do you think we'll make of them?

O'BRIEN: I shouldn't think much. She hasn't even got a lady's maid.

ANNA: It's not a capital offence.

BATES: She's got a maid. Her name's Ellen. She came a day early.

O'BRIEN: *She's* not a lady's maid. She's a housemaid who fastens hooks and buttons when she has to. There's more to it than that, you know.

There is a voice from the kitchen calling Daisy. But Thomas is showing her a cartoon in the paper, which absorbs her.

....

† This scene is annoying because somehow the riding habit got put on wrongly. When a woman was riding side-saddle she wore breeches and boots under the skirt of her habit to protect her legs but these were concealed by the habit. In period drama on television you will often see petticoats fluttering away and stockinged legs as the skirt flies up, which is all complete nonsense. Bare or stockinged legs would be rubbed raw of skin within five minutes. Women wore perfectly normal breeches and boots and so the skirt of the riding habit was essentially a coat which was designed to break open at the waist if she fell, so she would not be dragged. But of course the wrapover part of it was meant to go underneath, against the horse, and for some reason here it was put on backwards. When Matthew comes out and Mary is in the saddle, you can actually see her breeched leg. We were told off for this by several viewers and quite right, too.

‡ I felt that it wasn't enough for them just to be introduced. There had to be some electricity in the meeting. If Mary could take against Matthew at the very beginning then obviously it made the ensuing journey more interesting. In Hollywood, this used to be called 'meeting cute' which meant some comic mishap would start the whole thing off wrongly. Any Tracy/Hepburn or Day/Hudson movie will show you what I mean.

ANNA: We'll want some very precise reporting, when
dinner's over.

WILLIAM: Are we to treat him as the heir?

O'BRIEN: Are we heck as like. A doctor's son from
Manchester? He'll be lucky if he gets a civil word out
of me.

ANNA: We're all lucky if we get a civil word out of you.

*Before O'Brien can think of a suitably withering reply,
Carson pauses at the door, carrying a thick brown paper
bundle. It seems to hold a booklet or something similar.*

CARSON: Gwen. Parcel for you. Came by the evening post.

GWEN: Thank you, Mr Carson.

THOMAS: Have you seen 'em yet, Mr Carson?

CARSON: By 'them' I assume you mean the new family?
In which case, no. I have that pleasure to look forward
to.

His position is clear. He goes as Mrs Patmore looks in.

MRS PATMORE: Daisy? Did you hear me call? Or have you
gone selectively deaf?

DAISY: No, Mrs Patmore.

MRS PATMORE: Then might I remind you we are preparing
dinner for your future employer! And if it goes wrong,
I'll be telling them why!

*Daisy scuttles off as the gong sounds, and the others head for
the stairs.*

6 INT. MARY'S BEDROOM. DOWNTON. NIGHT.

Cora is with her daughter. They're both in evening dress.

MARY: But why are they here at all? When you're going to
undo it?*

....

* Mary is really affronted by the fact that everything is going to pass to a
stranger instead of coming to her, and her position is not at all unreasonable
to a modern audience. In fact, to our generation, it is the law that seems
unreasonable in denying any inheritance rights to someone simply because
she's female. We find that extraordinary. I think many in the audience would
be genuinely amazed to discover that it is still the case.

CORA: Your father's not convinced it can be undone.
MARY: But you'll still *try*?
CORA: Granny and I are willing to try.
MARY: And Papa is not?

Her stunned disbelief is actually rather touching.

CORA: We'll bring him round. You'll see. We're trying
to find a lawyer who'll take it on.

Mary is quite heartened to hear this.

CORA (CONT'D): So, what are they like?
MARY: She's nice enough. But he's… very full of himself.
CORA: Why do you say that?

Mary hesitates, and then decides against the truth.

MARY: Just an impression. Let's go down and you can
decide for yourself.

7 INT. HALL. DOWNTON. NIGHT.

*In the Great Hall, the family is assembled and Carson has the
servants lined up. Thomas holds the inner glass door open
for the Crawleys to enter. Behind him, at the other end of
the outer hall, William has closed the front door behind the
Crawleys and Robert has stepped into the outer hall to greet
them.*

ROBERT: Hello, again. It's a pleasure to meet you at
last, Mrs Crawley.
ISOBEL: We're delighted to be here. Aren't we, Matthew?
MATTHEW: Delighted.

*His mother is determined to present herself as comfortable
with the situation. He rather less so. After they have
entered the Great Hall, the footmen drop back to their places
in the line, and Cora steps forward.*

CORA: Welcome to Downton.
ISOBEL: Thank you. You've been so kind.

Matthew turns to the line of servants, with a laugh.

MATTHEW: What a reception committee!

He regrets his gag when nobody says anything. Isobel is
anxious to cover his gaucheness. She turns to Carson.

    ISOBEL: Yes. Thank you...
    ROBERT: This is Carson. We'd all be lost without him.

The butler's steely mien does not alter.*

    ISOBEL: Thank you, Carson. For making us feel so
    welcome.

Matthew catches Mary's eye and he would be tempted to make a
joke of their predicament, but she looks away.

    ROBERT: Mama, may I present Matthew Crawley and Mrs
    Crawley? My mother, Lady Grantham.

....

*The butler was really the head of the household, but only the male staff were specifically under his command, the footmen, the hall boys and so on, even if he had a kind of watching brief for the whole operation. A housekeeper was in charge of the female staff, that is all the housemaids, but it was anyone's guess if she was in the charge of the lady's maid because the lady's maid had the ear of the mistress so in that area they had to walk fairly gingerly. The other big trouble spot could be the cook, because the cook, male or female, was in charge of the kitchen staff, so technically the housekeeper couldn't really give orders to a kitchen maid although there was no question that she was considerably her superior in rank. But then there was an odd detail in that the housekeeper was in charge of the stores and the cook in a great house never had a key to the store cupboard. Instead, she would have to ask the housekeeper for the ingredients to do her own job. This situation famously resulted in many passionate battles, as one can easily imagine.

The housekeeper and the butler usually ate with the rest of the servants, but in some houses, though not at Downton, together with the valet and the ladies' maid, they would leave after the main course and go to the housekeeper's room to eat their pudding separately. We thought of doing this, but on reflection it felt like a bridge too far. Even so, what I hope we still get is that sense of a complicated pecking order: the butler, the cook, the housekeeper, the ladies' maids and the valets, would comprise what was known as the Upper Ten. Why they were called the Upper Ten and the rest were called the Lower Five nobody knows, because there were usually far more than five of the maids and footmen and so on, and there were often fewer than ten of the seniors, but anyway that's how it was. And whatever the technical rank of the rest, people deferred to the butler.

Isobel steps forward and takes Violet's hand.

ISOBEL: What should we call each other?
VIOLET: We could always start with Mrs Crawley and Lady Grantham.*

Cora decides to head off any further trouble.

CORA: Come into the drawing room and we can make all the proper introductions. Thank you, Carson.
ROBERT: Yes, Carson. Thank you for making them feel so welcome.

He is exasperated by the butler's coolness. Violet shares a look with Carson to make it clear they're on the same side.

8 INT. DINING ROOM. DOWNTON. NIGHT.

Dinner has just begun, Carson still as stiff as a board. Thomas and William are taking round the first course.

ROBERT: Do you think you'll enjoy village life? It will be very quiet after life in a city.
VIOLET: Even Manchester.
ISOBEL: I'm sure I'll find something to keep me busy.
CORA: You might like the hospital.

This earns her a dagger-like glance from Violet.

ISOBEL: What sort of hospital is it? How many beds?
VIOLET: Well, it isn't really a hospital —
ROBERT: Don't let Doctor Clarkson hear you. He thinks it's second only to St Thomas's.
CORA: It's a cottage hospital, of course, but quite well equipped.
ISOBEL: Who pays for it?

....

* Violet would never be rude to Mrs Crawley in an obvious way. If you said why were you so rude to her, she'd say 'Rude? I wasn't rude', because it is part of her self-image that she always behaves perfectly. Here, I think she is simply sending out a clear message that just because the law has placed them in this, to her rather invidious, position, it doesn't mean they're all going to cosy down by the nursery fire. Violet is quite sure this is never going to happen and after this exchange, so are we.

VIOLET: Oh, good. Let's talk about money.*

Robert ignores his unhelpful and snobbish mother.

ROBERT: My father gave the building and an endowment to
run it. In a way he set up his own memorial.†
ISOBEL: But how splendid.
ROBERT: And Mr Lloyd George's new insurance measures will
help.

*During this, Carson notices William's sleeve is coming apart
at the shoulder seam. He is not pleased.*

VIOLET: Please don't speak that man's name, we are about
to eat.

During this, Thomas has stopped at Matthew's left.

....

* It is a truism that the upper classes never talk about money, but like many truisms it is not really true, or at least it is misleading. The British aristocracy is, and always has been, aware that their way of life and their presentation generally depends on sufficient funds being available. This has led them into curious marriages and business arrangements, many to be later regretted, times without number. As I have observed elsewhere, they may never talk about it, but they never think about anything else.

† Before the great changes of the 1870s and 1880s, local health, schooling and everything else was run by the families of the great estates. The daughters of the house and the daughters of the agent and the daughters of the vicar would all go down and teach geography and letters and numbers and religious instruction. It was a bit haphazard but not entirely inefficient and, rather depressingly, the percentage per capita of literacy was if anything higher at the turn of the century than it is now. The syllabus was not wide. The emphasis was on providing the children with the necessary equipment to earn their living. They had to be literate, they had to be numerate, and they needed good handwriting, another detail that is lost to this generation. But I didn't really want a school, which would be difficult to manage in terms of the narrative strands for young pupils, whereas a hospital seemed to me to be a good way of creating a dynamic within the village so that we would not be solely dependent on the activity in the house. It would also provide the chance of some rebellion for Isobel who, with her medical training, would be able take a superior position to the Crawleys. I always feel a little sorry for Richard Clarkson, the doctor, so wonderfully played by David Robb, because the stories continually depend on his misdiagnosing everything.

THOMAS: I will hold it steady and you can help yourself, sir.

The implication being that Matthew does not know how to be served by a footman. Isobel winces, Violet smirks.

MATTHEW: Yes. I know. Thank you.

The girls exchange looks. Mary gives a gracious smile.

MARY: You'll soon get used to the way things are done here.

MATTHEW: If you mean I am accustomed to a very different life from this, then that is true.

Naturally, the simplicity of his reply wrong-foots Mary.

SYBIL: What will you do with your time?

MATTHEW: I've got a job in Ripon. I've said I'll start tomorrow.

This is a total bombshell. To family and servants, alike.

ROBERT: A 'job'?

MATTHEW: In a partnership. You might have heard of it. Harvell and Carter.

ROBERT: The lawyers?

MATTHEW: They need someone who understands industrial law, I'm glad to say, although I'm afraid most of it will be wills and conveyancing and other, lowly activities.

He smiles around, but this has not made things any better.

ROBERT: You do know I mean to involve you in the running of the estate?*

....

* Matthew's career is a secondary strand in the series because I don't think we're terribly interested in it. But it was important to contrast the American and middle-class work ethic with the aristocratic assumption that unless you are going to have a career as a diplomat or in Parliament, you should stay at home and manage the rent roll. Matthew wants to work and this allows Cora, as an American, to sympathise with him, while Robert is bewildered. It's not because Robert is lazy. He just doesn't understand why working on the estate and overseeing it isn't enough, while Matthew doesn't want to become dependent on his rich and grand relation. He wants some money in his trousers that he's earned himself. It is a typical *Downton* plot, in that one hopefully sympathises, to a degree, with both sides.

MATTHEW: Oh, don't worry. There are plenty of hours in the day, and of course I'll have the weekends.

ROBERT: We'll discuss this later. We mustn't bore the ladies.

VIOLET: What is a 'weekend'?

She feels she has been transported to an alien planet.

9 INT. KITCHEN. DOWNTON. NIGHT.

Mrs Patmore is in the thick of her main work event of the day and is increasingly irritated by the rest of them.

DAISY: Why shouldn't he be a lawyer?

O'BRIEN: Gentlemen don't work, silly. Not *real* gentlemen.

ANNA: Don't listen to her, Daisy.

MRS PATMORE: No! *Listen to me!* And get those kidneys up to the servery before I knock you down and serve your brains as fritters.

DAISY: Yes, Mrs Patmore.

She scurries away with the tray.

ANNA: I wonder what that Mr Molesley makes of them.

WILLIAM: Mr Bates, you know Mr Molesley, don't you?

BATES: I do. We were footmen together. In a house near Stafford. Before the South African War.

THOMAS: Poor old Molesley. I pity the man who's taken that job.

BATES: Then why did you apply for it?

Thomas is caught out, but he bounces back.

THOMAS: I thought it might help me to get away from you, Mr Bates.

He looks round the company, satisfied with his response.

THOMAS (CONT'D): And I didn't know then that Mr Crawley wasn't a gentleman.

MRS HUGHES (V.O.): Might I ask who is serving the savoury?

She is in the doorway. Thomas and William hurry out.

10 INT. HALL. DOWNTON. NIGHT.

The ladies leave the dining room together. Cora walks with
Isobel on their way to the drawing room.

CORA: How do you find Molesley?
ISOBEL: He seems very willing.
CORA: We felt combining the roles of butler and valet was
  more suitable for a house of that size. Don't you agree?

Isobel smiles her agreement. She is out of her depth.

ISOBEL: I am so interested to see the hospital.

Violet is walking just behind them with Mary.

VIOLET: Ooh, well, you would be. With your late husband
  a doctor.

She makes it sound roughly equivalent to a plumber's mate.
Isobel understands this, and defies it.

ISOBEL: Not just my husband. My father and brother, too.
  And *I* trained as a nurse during the war.
VIOLET: Fancy.
ISOBEL: I'd love to get involved somehow.
VIOLET: You could always help with the bring-and-buy sale
  next month, that would be *most* appreciated.

They've reached the drawing room door, held by Thomas.

11 INT. DINING ROOM. DOWNTON. NIGHT.

The men are alone drinking Port. Robert's still bewildered.

ROBERT: How will you manage it?
MATTHEW: Like many others, I shall bicycle to the
  station, take a train there and back, and bicycle home.*

This is astonishing to Robert. And disappointing.

ROBERT: But I've brought you to Downton so the people
  here will know you.

....

* Some of this was cut, but I think it's interesting for the audience to see what
they missed. Here we have Matthew talking about bicycling to the station
which is quite unnecessary as we see him do it. When you're writing
something you often forget that it's going to be told visually, and so there are
things that don't need to be said.

MATTHEW: They will know me. They have many years to get to know me, before any change of leadership. But I'm afraid I must keep busy.

ROBERT: And you can't be busy at Downton?

MATTHEW: I can and I will be. But it won't keep me busy enough.

12 INT. SERVANTS' HALL. NIGHT.

Daisy, Anna and Bates listen to Thomas, as William comes in. Anna has her sewing things. The hall boys are laying the table. William sits at the piano and starts to play.

THOMAS: She's a match for the old lady. She wasn't going to give in.

CARSON (V.O.): What 'old lady' are you referring to, Thomas?

He stands in the doorway, magnificent. William stops.

CARSON (CONT'D): You cannot mean her ladyship the Dowager Countess. Not if you wish to remain in *this* house.

THOMAS: No, Mr Carson.

CARSON: William, are you aware the seam at your shoulder is coming apart?

WILLIAM: I felt it go a bit earlier. I'll mend it when we turn in.

CARSON: You will mend it *now*. And you will never again appear in public in a similar state of undress.

WILLIAM: No, Mr Carson.

CARSON: To progress in your chosen career William, you must remember that a good servant at all times retains a sense of pride and dignity, that reflects the pride and dignity of the family he serves.*

This has silenced the company. William is crushed.

CARSON (CONT'D): And never make me remind you of it again.

He leaves. The sigh of relief is almost audible.

DAISY: I'll do it. And cheer up. We've all had a smack from Mr Carson.

She takes the coat and picks up a needle from the table. Anna glances at the despondent William.

ANNA: You'll be a butler, yourself, one day. Then you'll do the smacking.
WILLIAM: I could never be like him. I bet he comes from a line of butlers that goes back to the Conqueror.
BATES: He learned his business and so will you. Even Mr Carson wasn't born standing to attention.
THOMAS: I hope not for his mother's sake.

In the laugh that follows, William notices Daisy smiling at him. He finds it surprisingly encouraging.

13 INT. CORA'S BEDROOM. DOWNTON. NIGHT.

Robert and Cora are in bed. She is trying to read.

ROBERT: But if he must work, it should be politics. He could build on it when he goes to the Lords.
CORA: He trained for the law.
ROBERT: Well, I don't know what the local people will make of it.
CORA: I can't see why he has the right to your estates *or* to my money. But I refuse to condemn him for wanting an honest job.
ROBERT: Really, Cora. Just because you dislike my mother, there's no need to turn into Mark Twain.

He blows out his lamp and settles down for the night.

END OF ACT ONE

....

* '… a sense of pride and dignity, that reflects the pride and dignity of the family he serves'. I think we've forgotten this side of being a servant because the PR for service, as a job, was not good for the generation who grew up after the Second World War. They saw it as a servile career and an improper one, doing things that people ought to do for themselves. But with any kind of labour, it is necessary for an employee to feel that there is some honour in what they're doing and for the employer to be aware of this. At least if you want the workers to be happy. That was true of the great households. In those days, to work in these palaces was something to be proud of, you were at the top of the tree in that career, someone to be reckoned with. If you went into the pub and you were working at Blenheim, you were something. You were not, after all, working at the Rectory.

ACT TWO

14 INT. CARSON'S PANTRY. DAY.

A new day. Carson is checking the account books, when William appears, carrying an envelope.

 WILLIAM: This was at the back door.
 CARSON: Thank you, William.

The footman goes as he opens the letter. One glance is enough to make him stand, take his hat and hurry away.

15 EXT. DOWNTON VILLAGE. DAY.

Bates is walking back through the village when, across the road some way ahead, he sees Carson hurrying along. He vanishes into the pub. Bates is rather surprised. He walks on, past a sign announcing the cottage hospital.

16 INT. WARD. VILLAGE HOSPITAL. DAY.

Isobel is in a ward, with Doctor Richard Clarkson.

 CLARKSON: It's kind of you to take an interest.
 ISOBEL: I'm afraid it's a case of the warhorse and the drum. You know my late husband was a doctor?
 CLARKSON: I do. I'm familiar with Doctor Crawley's work on the symptoms of infection in children.
 ISOBEL: My father was also in medicine, Sir John Turnbull, and my brother is Doctor Edward Turnbull.*

He acknowledges her provenance.

 ISOBEL (CONT'D): Even I studied nursing during the South African War.

....

* I was sorry they cut the reference to Isobel's father and brother, although it wasn't a surprise when they did. The Front Office for any film or television production can get a bit nervous when characters talk about people who aren't then represented in the drama as they tend to think it muddles the audience. But I disagree. I believe it is this sort of casual detail that creates a sense of the world beyond.

*They have come to a bed which is screened off. A young woman
is being helped away by a nurse. Isobel looks enquiringly at
her companion. Clarkson lowers his voice.*

> CLARKSON: Very distressing. A young farmer, John Drake,
> a tenant of Lord Grantham's. He came in today. It's
> dropsy, I'm afraid.*
> ISOBEL: May I see him?

*Clarkson is surprised but he moves back the screens. A young
man of about thirty is sitting up against pillows, his skin
grey, his legs twice their normal size. He looks up.*

> ISOBEL: I hope you're not too uncomfortable, Mr Drake.

*But the patient cannot speak, and instead only wheezes muffled
words until he starts to cough violently and when he takes
away the handkerchief, it's thick with blood.*

17 EXT. VILLAGE HOSPITAL. DAY.

Isobel and the Doctor are together.

> ISOBEL: Is the dropsy of the liver or the heart?
> CLARKSON: Everything points to the heart. There is a
> good deal of fluid around it.
> ISOBEL: You mean an effusion.

....

* I was very keen that Isobel should not simply be a great lady rolling
bandages, but instead someone with real medical knowledge. So in her very
first episode we have the plot of John Drake. The name is in fact lifted from
the father of one of my son's school friends. The wretched contents of our
address book have had to endure watching television on Sunday night and
finding their own names jumping out of the screen at them.

I was interested by the dropsy plot, because dropsy sounds like a
nineteenth-century disease when it isn't, in fact, but I enjoyed all the medical
stuff. I have a friend, Alasdair Emslie, who is a doctor and I would write to
him, explaining that I needed an illness where, say, someone is perfectly all
right on Tuesday, dying on Wednesday and on Thursday they're playing
cricket. He then replies that this could happen in a case of myeloencephalitis,
or whatever, and that in fact this particular disease has a six-hour span. I
would write it and send the script to him and he would reply that, no, she
would never say he was too cold and she'd have to use a stick to apply the
liniment and not a fork. I'd then correct the details and hand it in.

CLARKSON: Forgive me. I keep forgetting I am talking to a medical expert.

The touch of irony is not lost on Isobel.

ISOBEL: What will happen to his wife?
CLARKSON: She may try to keep the farm on. Grantham is not a harsh landlord. But her children are young…
ISOBEL: What can I do to help?

Clarkson hesitates.

ISOBEL: If I'm to live in this village, I must have an occupation. Please. Let me be useful.
CLARKSON: It will take a lot to keep him comfortable. If you could look in from time to time, and relieve my nurses I should be very grateful.

18 INT.   DRESSING ROOM.   CRAWLEY HOUSE.   DAY.

Molesley's staring out of the window, as Bates comes in. He looks round, leaning on his stick. Nothing is out of place.

BATES: Very tidy, I must say.
MOLESLEY: That's how he leaves it.

Molesley shrugs. He is clearly despondent.

MOLESLEY (CONT'D): He chooses his clothes himself. He puts them out at night and hangs the ones he's worn… I get to take the linen down to the laundry, but that's about all.
BATES: That's all?
MOLESLEY: I'll do this, he says, and I'll take the other and I'll tie that. And I'm just stood there like a chump watching a man get dressed. To be honest, Mr Bates, I don't see the point of it.*
BATES: Don't tell Thomas. He's jealous enough already.
BATES: What about the butlering?
MOLESLEY: The food's on the sideboard, and he keeps the wine on the table so he can pour it himself. It's like an all-day breakfast.

19 EXT. GARDENS. DOWNTON. DAY.

Robert is walking with Violet.

ROBERT: I thought you didn't like him.

VIOLET: Well, so what? I have plenty of friends I don't like.

ROBERT: Would you want Mary to marry one of them?

VIOLET: Why do you always have to pretend to be nicer than the rest of us?

ROBERT: Perhaps I am.

VIOLET: Then pity your wife whose fortune must go to this odd young man, with his 'weekends' and 'jobs'. If Mary were to marry him then all would be resolved.

They've reached the house. Thomas stands to attention.

20 INT. ANNA'S AND GWEN'S BEDROOM. DOWNTON.
NIGHT.

Anna comes in. Gwen has been reading something and now she hurriedly stuffs it into a folder along with other papers.

ANNA: What have you got there?

She starts to undress.

GWEN: Nothing.

ANNA: What kind of nothing? You haven't got an admirer?

GWEN: I might have. Why shouldn't I?

....

* Matthew has a resistance to a level of luxury which he suspects is unmanly. He has someone washing his smalls and helping him into his coat and he feels it must be wrong. But we (I hope) don't quite agree because we know this is someone's work. And so, just as we thought that Robert was in the wrong in objecting to Matthew wanting a career, so now we think Matthew is slightly in the wrong. Why should he deprive Molesley of his living? Part of this way of life means being a creator of jobs, a local employer. Once again, in the *Downton* way, at a certain point you're slightly on the side of one character but when you hear the other argument you could change sides.

Molesley in the hands of Kevin Doyle became wonderfully melancholic and of course I started to write for that because this is what happens when people develop a character. The story here should make the audience aware that when people work for you, you mustn't take away their dignity, whatever it is they're doing. For me, that is the mistake that Matthew is making, which would – and does eventually – horrify him.

ANNA: Don't tell Mrs Hughes or she'll bring the vicar
round to have you exorcised.
GWEN: How are we supposed to find husbands if we're never
allowed to see any men?
ANNA: Perhaps she thinks the stork brings them. What's
he like?

Gwen is puzzled until Anna nods at the folder.

GWEN: Oh. He's… all right.
ANNA: Don't trust me then.

*During this, Anna, then Gwen, change into nightdresses, wash
with a jug and basin on a table, and climb into bed.*

ANNA: Lady Mary's in for a surprise. Thomas was in the
library when old Violet came in from the garden. Seems
they want to fix her up with Mr Crawley.
GWEN: Well, it makes sense. And she was going to marry
Mr Patrick.
ANNA: Would she have, though? When it came to it?
That's the question.

And she blows out the candle.

21 INT. HALL. CRAWLEY HOUSE. DAY.

*As Matthew enters, Molesley steps in to take his coat but
Matthew shrugs it off and hangs it up. His mother arrives.*

ISOBEL: There you are, dear. I was hoping you'd be home
in time.
MATTHEW: In time for what?
ISOBEL: I have been paid the compliment of a visit.

Her eyes give him a warning.

22 INT. DRAWING ROOM. CRAWLEY HOUSE. DAY.

*Violet, in a marvellous hat, sits with an equally elegant
Cora. The others enter. Molesley is serving tea.*

CORA: Good afternoon, Cousin Matthew. We were just
saying how charming this room is now.

VIOLET: It always seemed rather dark when my mother-in-
law lived here, but then she made everything dark.*

*Violet chuckles. She laughs pleasantly. Molesley has
brought a plate over.*

MOLESLEY: Sir.
MATTHEW: No, thank you.
MOLESLEY: A cup of tea, sir?
MATTHEW: It's all right. I'll help myself.

He goes to the tea table to fetch one. Violet takes pity.

VIOLET: So, Molesley, how does it feel to be home again?
Your father must be glad you're back.†
MOLESLEY: He is, your ladyship.
VIOLET: Might I give you this cup? Then we really must
be going.

Molesley takes Violet's cup. They walk into the hall.

ISOBEL: Thank you.
CORA: You'll think about it?

Isobel nods, as they all follow Violet out.

....

* With these characters, you can often only suggest their back story because
you haven't got time to do more, and I thought that if Violet, who always
looks as if she's in control of everything, had endured a nightmare mother-
in-law, there would be a suggestion that she might understand what it is not
to be behind the wheel; to have to deal with someone when she couldn't get
them out of the way. In fact, we have one or two other references to this
demonic, previous Lady Grantham who drove the young Violet mad.

† This, the local roots of many servants, was a significant part of life on a
country estate as opposed to working in a London house. In the capital there
was a tremendous turnover in this job and in fact, surprisingly, in the 1880s,
the average time for a London footman to stay in a house was eighteen
months. This can partly be explained by the fact that you couldn't often get
promotion within the same house. As a rule, you had to go somewhere else
to move up. But the real difference, when it came to the country house, was
that many of the servants would have been born in the area, which meant
that they and their employers had a certain shared history. With the
exchange between Molesley and Violet, we are suggesting an easiness, where
everyone knows and accepts the rules.

23 INT. SERVANTS' HALL. DOWNTON. DAY.

The servants are also having tea. Anna's trying to get a mark out of a shirt while O'Brien discusses the new family.

> O'BRIEN: He's only a third cousin. What does that mean? I might be 'third cousin' to the King.
> BATES: Or a trapeze artist.
> ANNA: Or a mass murderer.
> O'BRIEN: All right.

She hates their teasing. Anna turns to show Gwen the stain.

> ANNA: What do you think that is?
> GWEN: I don't know. Milk?

Anna sniffs it.

> ANNA: I'll try it with some water and see what happens.

She stands and leaves, taking the shirt with her.

24 INT. DRAWING ROOM. CRAWLEY HOUSE. DAY.

Isobel, Matthew and Molesley are back.

> MATTHEW: Thank you. We can manage now.

Molesley, defeated, goes and they are alone.

> MATTHEW (CONT'D): What was all that about? And why were they spooning over Molesley?
> ISOBEL: They weren't 'spooning'. They were trying to be nice, because you were so rude to him.
> MATTHEW: What?
> ISOBEL: They thought you'd made him look a fool, and they were right. Now, never mind that. I need help with your father's books.

He's upset but he's missed his moment to challenge her.

25 INT. KITCHEN. DOWNTON. DAY.

Anna is alone in the kitchens, working at the shirt with a damp cloth, when she hears a noise from one of the larders. She walks to the door. Carson is filling a bag, which he drops at the sight of her. Fruit, meat and bread roll out.

Carson acknowledges Anna.

CARSON: I thought no one was here.

He bends down and gathers up the contents into the bag.

ANNA: Can I help, Mr Carson?
CARSON: No, no, thank you, Anna.

But he is agitated as he takes the bag and hurries away.

26 INT. WARD. VILLAGE HOSPITAL. DAY.

Isobel is sitting with Drake, sponging off his swollen legs which are weeping straw-coloured fluid. Clarkson looks in.

CLARKSON: Hard at work, I see.
ISOBEL: May I borrow your stethoscope, Doctor? Just for a moment.

He is a little taken aback but he gives it to her. She now addresses the patient, John Drake.

ISOBEL (CONT'D): May I?

He nods weakly and she listens to his chest. She gestures for the doctor to come away and speak to her.

CLARKSON: I must compliment you, Mrs Crawley. When you made your offer, I thought you might be a 'Great Lady Nurse' and faint at the sight of blood. But I see you're made of sterner stuff.
ISOBEL: It's definitely the heart. It's almost too quiet to hear at all.
CLARKSON: I'm afraid so.
ISOBEL: I've been thinking about the treatments that are available.

Clarkson isn't quite sure he is pleased by this.

ISOBEL (CONT'D): Considerable success has been achieved in the last few years by draining the pericardial sac of the excess fluid and administering adrenaline —
CLARKSON: Mrs Crawley, I appreciate your thoroughness…
ISOBEL: But you're unwilling to try it.
CLARKSON: Injection of adrenaline is a comparatively new procedure.

ISOBEL: It was a while ago now, but I saw my husband do it. I know how.*

CLARKSON: Please, Mrs Crawley. Don't force me to be uncivil. We would be setting an impossible precedent. When every villager could demand the latest fad in treatment, for each new cut and graze.

ISOBEL: I would remind you we are not talking of a cut or a graze, but of the loss of a man's life and the ruin of his family.

CLARKSON: Of course. And I don't mean to be flippant. But I beg you to see that it is not… reasonable.

Isobel is anything but convinced.

27 INT. SERVANTS' HALL. DOWNTON. DAY.

They're having tea. O'Brien holds forth as Anna returns.

O'BRIEN: I'm sorry but I have standards.

During this Anna is speaking to Bates in a low voice.

ANNA: I've just seen something ever so odd.

BATES: What sort of odd?

O'BRIEN: And if anyone thinks I'm going to pull my forelock and curtsey to this Mr Nobody from Nowhere —

CORA (V.O.): O'Brien!

Cora is in the doorway. They scramble to their feet. O'Brien is slower than the others. She stares at Cora.

CORA: Were you discussing Mr Crawley?

O'BRIEN: Yes, m'lady.

CORA: Is it your place to do so?

O'BRIEN: I've got my opinions, m'lady. Same as anybody.

Now Mrs Hughes has appeared, flustered by Cora's presence.

....

* For this story, I wanted a condition where there was a new treatment which a local doctor would probably resist, whereas Isobel has come from a big city, where medicine is inevitably slightly more up to the minute. Manchester wouldn't be ahead of London, but it certainly would be ahead of Downton, and so you have Clarkson resisting the injection of adrenaline which had only started to be the accepted treatment for dropsy quite a short time before this.

MRS HUGHES: Can I help your ladyship?

CORA: This is the button *we're* missing from my new evening coat. I found it lying on the gravel.

Mrs Hughes takes the button, puzzled by the atmosphere.

CORA (CONT'D): But I was shocked at the talk I heard as I came in. Mr Crawley is his lordship's cousin and heir. You will therefore please accord him the respect he's entitled to.

O'BRIEN: But you don't like him, yourself, m'lady. You never wanted him to come here. I remember distinctly —

CORA: You're sailing perilously close to the wind, O'Brien. If we're to be friends, you will not speak in that way again about the Crawleys or any member of Lord Grantham's family. Now I'm going up to rest. Wake me at the dressing gong.

O'Brien gives a slight nod. Cora goes.

THOMAS: I don't think that's fair. Not here in the Servants' Hall.

O'BRIEN: I agree. If she was a real lady she wouldn't have come down here. She'd have rung for me, and given me the button. That's all.

THOMAS: This isn't her territory. We can say what we like, down here.

MRS HUGHES: Who says?

THOMAS: The law. And Parliament. There is such a thing as free speech.

MRS HUGHES: Not when I'm in charge.

Thomas has annoyed her.

MRS HUGHES (CONT'D): Don't push your luck, Thomas. Now. Tea's over. Back to work. You'd better take this.

She hands the button to the lady's maid. The others go, leaving Anna and Bates with O'Brien. She laughs bitterly.

O'BRIEN: Friends? Who does she think she's fooling?
We're not friends.
ANNA: No?
O'BRIEN: No. And you're not 'friends' with the girls
neither. We're servants you and me. And they pay us to
do as we're told. That's all.*

With a bleak expression, she stalks out.

28 INT. DRESSING ROOM. CRAWLEY HOUSE. NIGHT.

Matthew is trying to knot the white tie. Molesley hovers.

MOLESLEY: May I —?
MATTHEW: I can manage. Where have I put my cuff links?

Molesley darts forward with a pair to fasten them.

MOLESLEY: I thought these would make a change.
MATTHEW: I want my usual ones.

*Molesley turns back to the link box, but Matthew gets there
before him and takes out a pair which he inserts.*

MATTHEW: I know I'm a disappointment to you, Molesley,
but it's no good. I'll never get used to being dressed
like a doll.
MOLESLEY: I'm only trying to help, sir.
MATTHEW: Of course. And if I've offended you, I
apologise. But surely you have better things to do?
MOLESLEY: This is my job, sir.
MATTHEW: Well, it seems a very silly occupation for a
grown man.

*He takes the tail coat and shrugs it on, then goes to the
door. But he is a nice man. He has no wish to be offensive.*

MATTHEW (CONT'D): Look, I'm sorry if I —

Molesley stands. Matthew doesn't know how to finish it.

MATTHEW (CONT'D): I'm sorry.

....

* One of the reasons for this scene is that I'm absolutely convinced this way of
life, like any way of life for that matter, had its own rules, and in order for it to
be bearable people had to accept those rules and live by them. Cora, as an
American and to an extent an outsider, doesn't always observe the rules.

29 INT. MARY'S BEDROOM. NIGHT.

Anna finishes Mary's hair, with Edith and Sybil watching.

SYBIL: Why are you so against him?

MARY: Aside from the fact he's planning to steal our inheritance?

EDITH: *Your* inheritance. It makes no difference to Sybil and me. We won't inherit, whatever happens.

Edith is on the bed. Seeing a letter in a book she pretends to read the book, but really reads the letter. Mary shrugs.

MARY: He isn't one of us.

SYBIL: But Cousin Freddie's studying for the bar, and so is Vivian MacDonald.

MARY: At Lincoln's Inn. Not sitting at a dirty little desk in Ripon. Besides, his father was a *doctor*.

SYBIL: There's nothing wrong with doctors. We all need doctors.

MARY: We all need crossing sweepers and draymen, too. It doesn't mean we have to dine with them.*

....

* What I was trying to do here was to introduce the notion that most people, even among the upper classes and to an accelerating degree, did have to earn their living. In a lot of historical fiction it's as if everyone was the eldest son but any great family had a lot of members who were not left great fortunes. There were whole areas of gainful employment that were acceptable to junior members of such a family, the church, the army, the navy, and, to a certain extent, the law. One of the things about the Indian army was that it paid properly, unlike the Grenadiers, or other smart regiments, which required a private income. When the money started to dry up with the agricultural depression of the 1880s, it was bad news for those dependent on handouts. Of course looking at it now, retrospectively, we can see the modern world in a way beginning in the 1880s, when things were still done in the old way but financial realities were beginning to bite.

Deliberately I have made Mary quite snobbish. I felt it would be unrealistic and even sentimental to have the entire family devoid of any social awareness and so what I hope we've achieved is different manifestations of it. Robert is not a snob but he doesn't challenge the structure of the world in which he lives; Sybil, on the other hand, consciously rejects all of its values. Edith does what she is told and Mary has that kind of non-extreme snobbery which means she could enjoy meeting many different types but she doesn't question her own social superiority. In this scene, you get the relative positions of the girls.

CORA (V.O.): Whom don't we have to dine with?

She has come into the room, dressed for dinner. Anna gathers the discarded clothes and leaves.

EDITH: Mary doesn't care for Cousin Matthew.
CORA: Sybil, be a dear and fetch my pink evening shawl.
O'Brien knows which one. And Edith, can you see that the drawing room is ready?

The sisters know they have been dismissed, and go.

CORA (CONT'D): I'm glad to catch you alone —
MARY: You've driven the others away.

Cora laughs.

CORA: Oh, perhaps I have. Pretty.

She admires some flowers as she gathers her thoughts.

CORA (CONT'D): The point is, my dear, I don't want you, any of you, to feel you have to dislike Matthew.
MARY: You disliked the idea of him.
CORA: That was before he came. Now he's here, I don't see any future in it. Not the way things are.
MARY: But you and Granny are going to overturn all that.
CORA: Suppose we can't?
MARY: I don't believe a woman can be forced to give away all her money to a distant cousin of her husband's. Not in the twentieth century. It's too ludicrous for words.
CORA: It's not as simple as that. The money isn't mine any more. It forms a part of the estate.
MARY: Even so, when a judge hears —
CORA: For once in your life, will you just *listen*!

She has shouted at her daughter, shocking them both.

CORA (CONT'D): I believe there is an answer which would secure your future and give you a position…
MARY: You can't be serious.
CORA: Just think about it.
MARY: I don't have to think about it. Marry a man who can barely hold his knife like a gentleman?

Cora laughs.

CORA: Oh, you exaggerate.
MARY: You're American. You don't understand these things.

A real insult from a daughter. Cora comes back, fighting.

> CORA: Really, Mary, anyone would think he'd turned *you* down.
> MARY: Don't be ridiculous.

But her tone suggests Cora may be on to something.

> MARY (CONT'D): Have you mentioned this to Granny? Did she laugh?
> CORA: Why would she? It was her idea.

30 INT. BACKSTAIRS. DOWNTON. EVE.

Carson is coming downstairs. Anna going up.

> CARSON: Anna, I'm glad I've caught you.

She waits patiently while he gets his nerve up.

> CARSON (CONT'D): When I was… collecting that food earlier… for his lordship.
> ANNA: Yes, Mr Carson?
> CARSON: I hope you didn't feel the need to mention it to anybody?

Anna hesitates. She never actually told Bates, but…

> CARSON: When his lordship makes donations — to charity, you understand — he doesn't like notice taken of it.

He goes downstairs and she continues up, seriously puzzled.

END OF ACT TWO

ACT THREE

31 INT. KITCHEN. NIGHT.

William is waiting as Daisy loads a tray. He is reading a book, which is making him smile.

> DAISY: What've you got there?
> WILLIAM: A book of the new dance steps. My Mum sent it.
> DAISY: Let me see.

He shows her a page with drawings of a couple dancing the
Grizzly Bear. They study the foot pattern, curiously.

DAISY (CONT'D): Go on, then.

William holds the book and starts to execute the steps, but
somehow he gets them wrong, trips himself up and crashes into
the table. Daisy roars with laughter.

DAISY: Whatever will they think of next?
MRS PATMORE: They'll think there's a hyena loose in my
kitchen.

She has stolen up on them.

DAISY: Sorry, Mrs Patmore.

32 INT. DINING ROOM. DOWNTON. NIGHT.

William enters the dining room, where the two families are at
dinner. There is a slightly stiff atmosphere.

ISOBEL: I thought the hospital a great credit to your
father's memory.

She smiles at Robert, which he receives pleasantly.

ISOBEL (CONT'D): But I'm afraid the good doctor and I did
not see eye to eye.
VIOLET: You amaze me.
ISOBEL: He's treating one of your tenants, John Drake,
for dropsy, but he seems reluctant to embrace some of the
newer treatments.
ROBERT: Drake is a good man and far too young to die, but
I suppose the doctor knows his business.
VIOLET: Not as well as Mrs Crawley, apparently.

But Robert wants things to go well. He changes the subject.

ROBERT: By the way, if you ever want to ride, just let
Lynch know and he'll sort it out for you.
MARY: Oh, Papa. Cousin Matthew doesn't ride.
MATTHEW: I ride.

Her insolence is irritating, but she is a match for him.

MARY: And do you hunt?

This time, of course, she has assessed him accurately.

MATTHEW: No. I don't hunt.

VIOLET: I dare say there is not much opportunity in Manchester.

MATTHEW: Are you a hunting family?

MARY: Families like ours are always hunting families.

ROBERT: Not always. Billy Skelton won't have them on his land.

MARY: But all the Skeltons are mad.*

MATTHEW: Do you hunt?

MARY: Occasionally. I suppose you're more interested in books than country sports.

MATTHEW: I probably am. You'll tell me that's rather unhealthy.

MARY: Not unhealthy. Just unusual. Among our kind of people.

Which is flattening. The others are uncomfortably aware that the dinner has turned into a duel. Carson leaves.

33 INT. SERVERY. NIGHT.

Carson comes in. Mrs Hughes is there, rearranging china. Daisy loads trays of dirty plates from the previous course.

MRS HUGHES: I'm changing round the dessert services. We always seem to use the Meissen and never the Spode.†

....

* I wanted the many watching who were not hunting people to understand the ordinariness of the culture of country sports at this time. To our forebears in 1912, farming and shooting and hunting and estate management were all manifestations of a way of life where there were many different roles but a single morality. I didn't want to stumble into the great argument, but it was important to me to get this across. I remember there was some pressure to give dialogue to a character to justify hunting, and for someone else to attack it. But at this time, hunting, and everything connected to it, was seen as ordinary and I do feel that one of the things you have to watch in period writing is to put modern prejudices into period situations.

† One of the servants' jobs, and particularly the housekeeper's, was this endless rotation of sheets and china and sets of this and that, to make sure that everything was used and everything was looked after. The family, in that, as in so many things, was living on a pie crust in a state of blissful ignorance while all the necessary work was being done largely without their knowledge. I think that is a key part of this world.

CARSON: We're missing a sugar sifter. I know I put three out.

MRS HUGHES: I was talking to Anna earlier —

Carson stands as if he'd been shot.

CARSON: Why? What's she been saying?

Mrs Hughes stops her work, taken aback by his tone.

MRS HUGHES: Whatever's the matter?

CARSON: What did Anna say?

MRS HUGHES: Only that she thinks Thomas is bullying William.

Carson is immensely relieved. He nods.

CARSON: She may have a point. I'll keep an eye out. Ah. Here it is.

The sifter was behind some dishes. He takes it and leaves.

34 INT. DINING ROOM. DOWNTON. NIGHT.

As Carson returns, Mary is still taunting Matthew.

MARY: Do you ever read Greek mythology?

MATTHEW: Why?

MARY: I've been studying the story of Andromeda. Do you know it?

The others know Mary. They sense something is coming.

MATTHEW: Why?

MARY: Her father was King Cepheus, whose country was being ravaged by storms and, in the end, he decided the only way to appease the gods was to sacrifice his eldest daughter to a hideous sea monster. So they chained her naked to a rock, and —

VIOLET: Really, Mary. We shall all need our smelling salts in a minute.

MATTHEW: But the sea monster didn't get her, did he?

MARY: No. Just when it seemed he was the only solution to her father's problems, she was rescued.

MATTHEW: By Perseus.

MARY: That's right. Perseus, son of a god. Rather more fitting, wouldn't you say?

MATTHEW: That depends. I'd have to know more about the princess and the sea monster in question. Perhaps they were well suited.

He looks at her with a challenge in his eyes. They don't like each other, these two, but there is something sexual happening between them. Which she feels as much as he.

MARY: Oh, I don't think so. Not at all.

The family continues to eat, this time in silence.

35 INT. SERVANTS' HALL. NIGHT.

Several of them are there. Daisy flicks through William's book, while William plays the piano in the background.

DAISY: I wish I could dance like that.
THOMAS: Like what?

He snatches the book and stares at the page.

THOMAS (CONT'D): Don't you know the Grizzly Bear?*
BATES: As if you do.
THOMAS: Certainly, I do. Miss O'Brien, shall we show them?
O'BRIEN: Not likely.
THOMAS: William! Give us a tune. Come on, Daisy.

William's annoyed to be forced to play but Anna nods and he does. Thomas seizes the amazed girl and starts to dance.

MRS PATMORE: Daisy, stop that silly nonsense before you put your joints out. See to the range and go to bed.

She is watching from the door. A breathless Daisy prepares to obey but, as she lets go of Thomas, she smiles at him.

DAISY: Thank you. That was beautiful.

....

* The new dances were the beginning of a kind of drip, drip, drip of the modern world creeping into these men's and women's consciousness. Because in a way music is one of the things that has changed our society more than almost anything else. Today, popular music has the power to alter our behaviour completely, and it began then.

Thomas rather enjoys the whispered compliment. *

36 EXT. DOWNTON. NIGHT.

Robert and Cora are at the door as Matthew walks Violet across the gravel. Isobel is already climbing into the car.

VIOLET: I'm sorry Mary was rather sharp, this evening.
MATTHEW: I doubt that Cousin Mary and I are destined to be close friends.

She is sad about this, but she has to agree for now.

MATTHEW (CONT'D): I don't blame her. Her father's home and her mother's fortune are to be passed to me. It's very harsh.†
VIOLET: Of course, in Spain or Portugal, Mary would be her father's heir.

He nods, but does not argue, which interests her.

VIOLET (CONT'D): What would you say if the entail were set aside in Mary's favour?
MATTHEW: I should try to accept it with as good a grace as I could muster.

....

* Unrequited love is quite a big theme of this show. Lots of the characters are in love with the wrong people, not just among the family, but also with the servants, as I think unrequited love is often a product of the work situation. That is, when you mix up a lot of men and women in close physical proximity, and you keep them working together day after day, you will inevitably have emotional entanglements. In an ordinary courtship, in the outside world, then unrequited love is less inevitable. The young man comes to call with an invitation to dinner, and if the young lady doesn't want to go then that's the end of that. But when, like at Downton (or any factory or office block), you have people being brought together constantly, whether or not they would rather avoid the encounters, then I'm afraid unrequited love is often a by-product. In this instance we're talking about Daisy being in love with Thomas the footman who of course is gay. She is not aware of this, and it is worth remembering that although, here, most of the older household suspect he is, in those days it wouldn't be anything like common knowledge.

† Matthew doesn't at all blame Mary for resenting him. Here it is her own grandmother, Violet, who wishes Mary would shut up and get on and marry him. In other words, the situation obliges almost everyone to behave in the opposite way to their natural instincts.

VIOLET: Would you? Good evening, Taylor.
TAYLOR: Good evening, m'lady.

He stands by the open door, bringing conversation to an end.
She climbs in, followed by Matthew.

37 INT. CARSON'S PANTRY. NIGHT.

Carson is putting the silver that was used at dinner into his
safe. He looks at a candlestick as Mrs Hughes enters.

MRS HUGHES: I'll say goodnight, Mr Carson.
CARSON: Look at that scratch. I'll have to get it sorted
out when they're up in London.

He holds out the candlestick. She stares at it.

MRS HUGHES: You can hardly see it.
CARSON: But I'll know it's there.
MRS HUGHES: Are you all right now? Only you seemed a
little upset earlier.
CARSON: I'm sorry about that. I'm just —

He was caught off guard, and almost confided in her. He takes
up his pipe and starts to light it.

CARSON (CONT'D): I'm a bit tired.
MRS HUGHES: And no wonder. Did the dinner go well?
CARSON: Well enough. Although they won't make a match
between them, if that's what they're thinking.
MRS HUGHES: Lady Mary doesn't like him?
CARSON: Why *should* she like the man she's been passed
over for? And why has she been? That's what I'd like to
know.
MRS HUGHES: It's the law.
CARSON: Then it's a wicked law.

38 EXT. KITCHEN COURTYARD. DOWNTON. DAY.

At a table in the yard, O'Brien has Cora's evening coat,
wrapped in linen, as she sews the button on. Thomas fiddles
with a clock. He has oil and screwdrivers and cloths. They
are both smoking surreptitiously.

O'BRIEN: Why does Mr Carson let you do that?
THOMAS: Because my Dad was a clock-maker. Anyway, this
is from the Morning Room. It isn't a good one.

O'BRIEN: Did you really ask Mr Carson for the job with the Crawleys?

She gives a snort of derision, which he finds unfair.

THOMAS: I'm sick of being a footman.
O'BRIEN: I'd rather be a footman than wait on someone who ought to be a footman, himself.*
THOMAS: But he shouldn't have told Bates.

He glances at her as he continues to poke inside the clock.

THOMAS (CONT'D): How are things with Lady G.?
O'BRIEN: Same as usual.
THOMAS: Yes, my lady, no, my lady, three bags full.
O'BRIEN: I'd like to give her three bags full. Preferably on a dark night.
THOMAS: Will you hand in your notice?
O'BRIEN: And let her ruin me with a nasty reference? Oh, I think *not*.

O'Brien bites the thread fiercely as the clock chimes.

39 INT. DRAWING ROOM. DOWER HOUSE. DAY.

Doctor Clarkson is with Violet.

CLARKSON: I don't want to exaggerate. She's been very generous in many ways.
VIOLET: Generous? To instruct you in your own practice?
CLARKSON: She may even have a point. But it does not seem to me realistic —

....

* In a way O'Brien's struggle is still with us. Is it easier to deal with people who are born great than with people who have made themselves great. Because when people make themselves great then in a way they are an indictment of everyone else who has *not* become great. If it's possible then why haven't you done it? Whereas if you live in a world where people's greatness is determined by birth, then it's not your fault that you haven't done anything to bring it about. That was just the way the cookie crumbled. Oddly, really, even today, you will find a curious hostility to self-made money that doesn't exist towards inherited fortunes. Morally of course it ought to be quite the reverse but it isn't, and there's no doubt that, particularly in this country, success can provoke tremendous fury for no real reason.

VIOLET: Nor is it! Put an end to her meddling! I am
your President and I say get rid of her.
CLARKSON: What does Lord Grantham think?

She thinks for a moment how to suggest Robert's agreement.

VIOLET: He's as shocked as I am that she's attempting to
teach you to suck eggs. Tell her you don't need her help.
CLARKSON: Won't that be awkward? I gather she's planning
to stay in the village for the foreseeable future.
VIOLET: No one can foresee the future, Doctor. Not you,
not I, and *certainly not* Mrs Crawley.

40 EXT. THE PARK. DOWNTON. DAY.

Robert is with Matthew, surveying the house from a hill.

ROBERT: You do not love the place yet.
MATTHEW: Well, obviously it's —
ROBERT: No. You don't love it. You see a million bricks
that may crumble, a thousand gutters and pipes that may
block and leak, lead that will shrink, and stone that
will crack in the frost.
MATTHEW: But you don't.
ROBERT: I see my life's work.*
MATTHEW: Was it ever in danger?
ROBERT: Many times. My dear Papa thought the balloon
would go up in the 1880s.
MATTHEW: What saved it?

Robert looks at him for a second before he answers.

ROBERT: Cora. I often wonder what the good Isaiah
Levinson would have thought, when he built that first
emporium in Cincinnati, if he knew that the fruits of his
toil would save a seat of unearned privilege.
MATTHEW: For the benefit of a man who does not share his
blood.

Robert chooses not to answer this.

....

* Personally, I do believe that this life is only possible to live in a positive and
fulfilling way if you believe in it. The harshest fate, then or now, is to inherit
a great name, a great fortune and a great house, when you have no desire to
live that life. It is just a smothering weight around your neck and I have seen
men almost broken by it.

MATTHEW (CONT'D): So, it's safe now.

ROBERT: It is healthy. Nothing in life is safe.

He walks towards the house with his almost-son.

41 INT. DRAWING ROOM. CRAWLEY HOUSE. DAY.

Isobel is sealing an envelope when Molesley enters.

ISOBEL: I have an errand for you, and it will be quite an imposition.

MOLESLEY: Very good, ma'am.

ISOBEL: Tomorrow, I want you to travel to Manchester, to this address, and to put this letter into the hands of Doctor Gordon. He will give you a package in return.

She is almost defiant enough to frighten the butler.

42 INT. SERVANTS' HALL. DOWNTON. DAY.

Anna is cleaning some satin ball slippers with breadcrumbs. Bates comes in, carrying a hunting coat. He looks round.

BATES: Where is everyone?

ANNA: They've gone down to the village. Some travelling salesman's set up at the pub for the afternoon.

He sits and starts to clean the brass buttons, by means of a split card to protect the material beneath them.

BATES: Alone at last.

He's joking, but is there a trace of a blush on her face?

BATES (CONT'D): We shouldn't be without both footmen. Does Mr Carson know?

ANNA: Mrs Hughes does. She's gone with them. They won't be long.

He nods at the ballroom slipper she is working on.

BATES: So, you see to the girls *and* you're supposed to be head housemaid. You should put in for a raise.

ANNA: What d'you mean 'supposed to be'?

He laughs. He really does like her, no question. They are interrupted by the sound of a bell ringing.

BATES: What's that?

Anna jumps up to look at the bell board. It's the front door. They are both caught out by this.

BATES: I said they shouldn't have let both footmen go.
ANNA: Well, you'll have to answer it. Mr Carson wouldn't like a maid answering the front door.
BATES: He'd be afraid they'd think it was a doctor's surgery.

He has already risen. He walks towards the main hall.

43 EXT. ENTRANCE. DOWNTON. DAY.

A smooth character, Charles Grigg, stands there, looking like a travelling salesman. He pulls the bell again.

44 INT. HALL. DOWNTON. DAY.

Bates opens the door.

BATES: I'm sorry to have kept you waiting, sir.
GRIGG: So that's why it took you so long.

He casts a sneering look at Bates's stick.

GRIGG (CONT'D): I'm here to see Lord Grantham.
BATES: Is he expecting you?
GRIGG: No. But he'll be very interested in what I have to tell him.
BATES: His lordship is not at home, but if you will leave your name, I —
GRIGG: Don't be all high and mighty with me. I don't know who you are, but you're certainly not the butler, so don't make out you are.
BATES: How do you know?
GRIGG: Because Charlie Carson's the butler round here.
BATES: Does your business concern him?
GRIGG: It might do.
BATES: If you will excuse me for one moment, sir.

Bates walks over to the hovering Anna who's heard all this.

BATES (CONT'D): Fetch Mr Carson as fast as you can. Use the front door.

She nods and hurries off. Bates turns to the visitor who has by now followed him into the hall.

BATES (CONT'D): If you'd like to follow me, sir —

He turns towards the service stair.

GRIGG: Oh, no. If you think you're tucking me away
somewhere, you've got another thing coming.
BATES: But you'll be more comfortable, sir —
GRIGG: Sorry, chum.

*He turns to the left and walks into the library. Bates, in a
quandary, follows him, glancing around.*

45 INT. LIBRARY. DAY.

*Grigg strolls through the small library into the main one,
surveying it all with a lordly air. He takes up a position
in front of the chimneypiece.*

GRIGG: Oh aye. I'll not mind waiting here.
SYBIL (V.O.): Bates?

*She's in a riding habit in the arch dividing the two
libraries. She is staring at the man.*

BATES: This gentleman is an acquaintance of Mr Carson,
m'lady.
SYBIL: What is he doing in here?
BATES: He says he has urgent business with his lordship.
GRIGG: Urgent.
BATES: I've sent for Mr Carson to come at once.

He gives a clear message with his eyes.

SYBIL: Then I'll stay with you. In case explanations are
needed.

Bates mimes 'Thank you.'

46 EXT. PARK. DOWNTON. DAY.

*Robert is walking home. Carson is visible some way away.
Robert sees Anna racing down the drive, waving at Carson.
She reaches him.*

ANNA: You're needed at once in the library.

47 INT. HALL. DOWNTON. DAY.

Robert has come through the front door into the outer hall when he hears a noise. He is surprised.

GRIGG (V.O.): How long are you expecting me to wait. I'm a very busy man, you know.

BATES: If you could just be patient for a little longer, sir.

48 INT. LIBRARY. DOWNTON. DAY.

Robert enters, puzzled.

GRIGG: Ah!

ROBERT: May I ask who this is? And what precisely is going on?

There is the sound of running feet and Carson bursts in.

CARSON (V.O.): Mr Bates, what are you…

Carson sees Lord Grantham.

CARSON (CONT'D): I am sorry, your lordship. Mr Bates you may go now.

ROBERT: Please stay where you are. Nobody's going anywhere.

This has defeated Carson's anxiety to clear the room.

ROBERT (CONT'D): Do I take it you know this man?

GRIGG: Don't try and deny it.

CARSON: No, I won't deny it. I do know him, m'lord, but not what he is doing in the library.

BATES: I tried to stick him downstairs, out of sight, Mr Carson, but he wouldn't come.

This makes Carson pause, as Anna comes round the door.

CARSON: Thank you. That was thoughtful.

ROBERT: But who is he?

GRIGG: Will you tell him, or shall I?

CARSON: His name is Charles Grigg. We worked together at one time.

GRIGG: Oh, I'm a little more than that, aren't I, Charlie? We're like brothers, him and me.

CARSON: We are *not* like brothers.

Anna looks over to Carson, standing to attention, silent.

GRIGG: We were an act. On the halls.
ROBERT: You were on the stage? Carson, is this true?

He is genuinely astonished.

CARSON: It is, m'lord.
GRIGG: The Cheerful Charlies. That's what they called
us.

Grigg has taken out an old flyer out. Now he unfolds it.
There they are. The Cheerful Charlies. Carson says nothing.

GRIGG: We did quite well.
CARSON: Until you couldn't keep your hands out of the
till.
ANNA: Would you like us to go, Mr Carson?
CARSON: You know it now. You might as well bear witness
to my shame.
BATES: Not 'shame' —
CARSON: *Shame!*

His shout has silenced them all, even Robert and Sybil.

CARSON (CONT'D): He turned up in the village with no
warning some days ago, on the run, asking for somewhere
to hide. And, of course, for money.
ROBERT: God in heaven.
CARSON: He's wanted for some petty crime, of which he is
certainly guilty.
GRIGG: Steady on.
CARSON: He threatened to expose my past, to make me a
laughing stock in this house, and in my vanity and pride,
I gave him what he wanted.
GRIGG: You did not.
CARSON: I put him in an empty cottage and fed him from
the kitchens. I couldn't buy food in the village. It
would raise too many questions. I stole. I am a thief.
She saw it.

He nods at Anna.

ANNA: I'd never…
CARSON: And now my disgrace is complete. My lord, you
have my resignation.

He looks like a tragic hero on his way to the scaffold.

ROBERT: Really, Carson. There's no need to be quite so
melodramatic. You're not playing Sydney Carton.
SYBIL: Why did you give up the theatre?
CARSON: He was arrested for theft, and sent down.
GRIGG: I was innocent.
CARSON: After that, I decided on a change of career and
chose service.

Robert turns to face Grigg, but the latter is unrepentant.

ROBERT: So, why have you come here? If he's done
everything you asked of him?
GRIGG: Because he hasn't. He wouldn't give me any money.
CARSON: If I had, how could I prevent his returning to
Downton once it was spent?

Robert, calm and immensely impressive, approaches Grigg.

ROBERT: My dear Mr Grigg —
GRIGG: Oh, nice to see someone round here's got some
manners.
CARSON: Hold your tongue!
ROBERT: I'll tell you what is going to happen. When I
have given you twenty pounds, you will leave Downton
immediately. And we'll never set eyes on you again.
GRIGG: I'll have to see about that.
ROBERT: If you return to the area, I will personally
ensure your conviction for theft and blackmail —
GRIGG: Just a minute...
ROBERT: You will serve from five to ten years in His
Majesty's custody.

Grigg is furious at his predicament.

GRIGG: You think you're such a big man, don't you? Just
because you're a lord, you think you can do what you like
with me.
ROBERT: I think it because it is true.

He takes two large white ten pound notes from his wallet.
Grigg hesitates, then takes them.

GRIGG: You'll not always be in charge, you know. The day
is coming when your lot will have to tow the line, just
like everyone else.

ROBERT: Perhaps. But, happily for Carson, that day has not come yet.*

In another moment, Grigg has gone. Bates and Anna look at each other and follow him. But Carson hesitates.

CARSON: I take it my resignation has not been accepted?
ROBERT: My dear fellow, we all have chapters we would rather keep unpublished.

Carson makes to go, but Robert can't control his curiosity.

ROBERT (CONT'D): To be honest, Carson, I'm rather impressed. Did you really sing and dance and everything? In front of an audience?
CARSON: I did.
ROBERT: Do you ever miss it?
CARSON: Not in the least, m'lord.

He is very disdainful as he goes. Sybil holds the flyer. Robert takes it with a smile and puts it in his pocket.

49 INT. SERVANTS' HALL. EVE.

The others are having a tea break before the dressing gong.

ANNA: Poor Mr Carson. We'll have to treat him like a god for a month to calm his nerves.
BATES: He'll be afraid this'll change the way we think of him.
ANNA: Then we mustn't let it.
BATES: Oh, but it will. The Cheerful Charlies?

He gives her a look and she cannot help laughing.

BATES (CONT'D): For all his talk of dignity, we know his story now.
ANNA: And admire him *more* because of it.
BATES: Maybe. But it will change how we think of him. It always does.

Something sad in his eyes catches her attention.

....

* The point of Robert's response here was really was to make it clear that we are in the last days of when it was true. And it was going to be very hard for that generation of aristocrats that they would outgrow and outlive their own power.

ANNA: I don't see why. I shouldn't care what I found out
about you. Whatever it was, it wouldn't alter my opinion
one bit.
BATES: But it would. It certainly would.

*Before they are aware of how much they have revealed, there
is a crash. They look at each other.*

BATES (CONT'D): Blimey. No more surprises please.

50 INT. KITCHEN. DOWNTON. EVE.

Daisy is picking up the pieces of a large china bowl.

MRS PATMORE: Stupid girl! Who's going to pay for it?
Can you tell me that?
DAISY: I didn't do nuffin, honest.
MRS PATMORE: Honest? The day you're honest will be the
day Queen Mary takes up polo!
DAISY: She put it down wrong on the table and it just
fell. I didn't do nuffin.

She hurries past Anna and Bates, with the pieces.

BATES: The Scourge of Tyranny is never far away.

END OF ACT THREE

ACT FOUR

51 INT. DRAWING ROOM. DOWER HOUSE. DAY.

Violet and Cora are together.

VIOLET: We're running out of options. The lawyers I
write to only huff and puff. They echo Murray, and say
nothing can be done…
CORA: Or they don't want the bother of opposing him.
VIOLET: Precisely.
CORA: I wish Mary wasn't so confident that it could all
be put right.
VIOLET: Meanwhile, we have to watch that dreadful woman
parade about the village as if she owned it.

CORA: I think she means well.

VIOLET: *Meaning* well is not enough. Poor Doctor Clarkson. What has he done to deserve that termagent?

CORA: I'm afraid he's in for an uncomfortable afternoon.

VIOLET: Why?

CORA: On my way here, I saw her go into the hospital. She looked extremely determined.

Violet rises.

VIOLET: Not as determined as I am.

52 INT. CLARKSON'S OFFICE. VILLAGE HOSPITAL. DAY.

Isobel is with Clarkson, who looks weary.

ISOBEL: I have the adrenaline here in my hand. Will you really deny the man his chance of life?

CLARKSON: I just wish it was a treatment I was more familiar with.

ISOBEL: And will that serve as your excuse when he dies?

He looks at her for a sombre moment. Then he nods, goes to the door and calls out for a nurse.

CLARKSON: Can you prepare Mr Drake for his procedure, please? Thank you, nurse. I will need a needle, an empty syringe, and another standing ready filled with this.

He hands over the adrenaline, looking back at Isobel.

CLARKSON (CONT'D): Well, Mrs Crawley, I have a feeling we will sink or swim together.

53 INT. WARD. VILLAGE HOSPITAL. DAY.

Drake is sitting up, greyer than ever. His wife is with him with terror in her eyes, as they listen to Clarkson.

CLARKSON: Mr Drake, your heart is not functioning properly and, as a result, your pericardial sac is full of fluid. We call this tamponade. I am proposing, first, to withdraw the fluid, and then to inject the adrenaline to stimulate the heart and restore normal activity.

MRS DRAKE: Is it dangerous, Doctor?

CLARKSON: I cannot tell you it is not. The draining may stop the heart, and the adrenaline may not be able to re-start it.

ISOBEL: Mrs Drake, the choice is simple. If your husband endures this procedure he may live. If he does not, he will die.

The wretched woman trembles, but before she can speak, there is a noise from beyond the screens.

VIOLET (V.O.): Let me pass! I must see the doctor, at once!
CLARKSON: Your ladyship.

She comes sweeping round the screens.

VIOLET: Just as I thought. Please, Doctor Clarkson, tell me you will not permit this amateur to influence your professional opinion.
ISOBEL: *Amateur?*
MRS DRAKE: Your ladyship —
VIOLET: My dear woman do not allow them to bully you. They'll not disturb the peace of your husband's last hours. Not if I can help it.

Violet's words do the trick. Mrs Drake's mind is made up.

MRS DRAKE: But that's just it, m'lady. I don't want them to be his last hours. Not if there's a chance…

She nods towards Clarkson.

MRS DRAKE (CONT'D): Please, doctor. Do what you must.

The nurse takes a pad of chloroform and holds it to the man's face. The doctor feels the ribs, and pushes the needle with the syringe attached into Drake's chest.

VIOLET: As President of this hospital, I must warn you that I shall bring this to the attention of the Board at the first opportunity.
CLARKSON: Steady.

Mrs Drake is crying.

CLARKSON (CONT'D): Nice and steady.

He pulls on the syringe. Violet tries again.

VIOLET: As President of this hospital, I must…

*But Clarkson ignores her. He withdraws the syringe and a
yellow liquid is seen. For a moment, Drake looks as if he
were dead.*

    VIOLET: Have you no pity?
    CLARKSON: Adrenaline. Quickly, quickly. His heart's
    stopped.

*The nurse gives Clarkson the second syringe, which he now
attaches to the needle still in Drake's chest.*

    CLARKSON (CONT'D): Ready?

*The man is in extremis. Clarkson thumps it in. For a
moment, all is stillness. Then, suddenly, colour floods back
into Drake's face. The nurse removes the cloth, as Clarkson
takes his stethoscope and listens. He nods to Isobel and the
nurse. Now Drake blinks and opens his eyes.*

    DRAKE: Oh my dear.

*He has survived it. His voice is normal. As he takes his
wife's hand, Isobel challenges the raging face of Violet.**

54 INT. LIBRARY. DOWNTON. EVE.

Doctor Clarkson is with Robert and Matthew.

    ROBERT: You don't have to worry. She may be President,
    but I'm the Patron and you're quite safe with me.
    MATTHEW: My mother was right, then? The man's life was
    saved?
    CLARKSON: I like to think we were *both* right. But I'm
    not sure Lady Grantham will be so easily convinced.

....

* What I wanted was a very traumatic operation, performed on a man who is
literally hovering between life and death, which would produce an immediate
response so that, having required a very frightening decision to go through
with it, there would be an instant and clear improvement. The treatment for
dropsy, which is very, very dramatic in the terrifying mechanics of draining
off the lungs, does have this effect. The colour at once floods back into the
face. Here, Mrs Drake has to make this terrible decision with Violet deeply
disapproving, but her bravery and courage are rewarded.

ROBERT: Then we must strengthen the argument. Cousin
Isobel wants something to do. Very well. Let's make her
Chairman of the Board. She'd like that, wouldn't she?
MATTHEW: Certainly, she would.
ROBERT: Then my mother will have to listen to her.

This is very puzzling for the good doctor.

CLARKSON: But I thought you were —
ROBERT: You thought I didn't want Mrs Crawley involved?
CLARKSON: So I was led to believe.
ROBERT: Doctor, Mama has many virtues, but not all.
MATTHEW: Which of us does?
ROBERT: She's been the absolute ruler there for long
enough. It's time for some loyal opposition.
CLARKSON: If you're quite certain, my lord.

He hesitates, then thinks better of it and shuts his mouth.

ROBERT: What were you going to say?
CLARKSON: At the risk of being impertinent: On your own
head be it.

55 EXT. DOWNTON. DAY.

*Robert and Matthew are talking. Thomas is holding Matthew's
bicycle for him.*

ROBERT: About your scheme for restoring the estate
cottages.
MATTHEW: You don't mind my interfering?*
ROBERT: My dear fellow, I brought you here to interfere.
In fact, why don't you stay for dinner and we'll talk
about it? We'll send down to Molesley for your clothes.
MATTHEW: Better not. My mother's expecting me. But in
fact, I've been meaning to speak to you about Molesley.
ROBERT: Oh?
MATTHEW: Would you find me ungrateful if I dispensed with
his services?

....

* Matthew's journey in this show, and it is quite a long one, is to educate
Robert in the ways of the modern world, and help him to see that benevolence
is not enough, that business management and common sense must also be
part of it. Here, Matthew starts him off by helping him to see the point of
restoring the cottages.

ROBERT: Why? Has he displeased you in some way?

MATTHEW: Not at all. It's simply that he's superfluous to our style of living.

ROBERT: Is that quite fair? To deprive a man of his livelihood, when he's done nothing wrong?

MATTHEW: Well, I wouldn't quite put it —

ROBERT: Your mother derives satisfaction from her work at the hospital, I think? Some sense of self worth?

MATTHEW: Certainly.

ROBERT: Would you really deny the same to poor old Molesley?

Matthew feels himself slipping off the moral high ground.

ROBERT (CONT'D): And when you are master here? Is the butler to be dismissed? Or the footmen? How many maids or kitchen staff will be allowed to stay? Or must every one be driven out?

The young man has lost this argument.

ROBERT: We all have different parts to play, Matthew. And we must all be allowed to play them.

He is not angry, but he is firm.

56 INT.   CARSON'S PANTRY.   NIGHT.*

Carson reads and smokes his pipe. Mrs Hughes looks in.

MRS HUGHES: I've told William to lock up.

He nods his thanks, but she lingers in the doorway.

MRS HUGHES (CONT'D): Are you feeling better? In yourself? I thought you might be coming down with something. But you seem a bit improved tonight.

CARSON: I'm sorry if I've been edgy.

....

* This scene was filmed, but it was cut in the edit. However, it may seem familiar and that is because it was revived and re-shot the following year, for Episode Seven in the second series. The feeling was that, while it played no part in any specific narrative (and so could easily be moved), it was too important for the back story of Carson's love for Mary not to be included somewhere.

MRS HUGHES: Things'll work out. You'll see. Lady Mary will marry some rich lord and be as happy as a pixie, no matter who gets Downton.

CARSON: I hope so.

MRS HUGHES: Though I can't pretend to share your enthusiasm for her. I think she's an uppity creature.

CARSON: You didn't know her as a child. She was a guinea a minute then. I remember once when she came in here, she can't have been more than four or five. 'Mr Carson,' she says. 'I've decided to run away and I wonder if I might take some of the silver to sell.'

He laughs at his own memory.

CARSON (CONT'D): Well, I said. That'd be awkward for his lordship. Suppose I give you sixpence to spend in the village instead? 'All right,' says she. 'But you must be sure to charge me interest.'

MRS HUGHES: And did you?

CARSON: She gave me a kiss in full payment.

MRS HUGHES: Then she had the better bargain, which doesn't surprise me.

CARSON: Oh, I wouldn't say that.

But she is smiling as he stands to blow out the lamp.

57 INT. GALLERY/STAIRCASE/HALL. DOWNTON. DAY.

A bright afternoon. The three girls emerge from a bedroom, wearing hats and gloves, ready for an excursion.

EDITH: Has the car been brought round? We should go. It's almost three.

SYBIL: I bet Granny wears black.

EDITH: Why must we all go to the hospital?

MARY: I'm afraid Papa wants to teach Granny a lesson. Poor Granny. A month ago these people were strangers. Now she must share power with the mother and I must marry the son.

EDITH: You won't marry him, though, will you?

MARY: What? Marry a sea monster?

Which sets them all off. They descend the staircase.

SYBIL: We shouldn't laugh. That was so unkind.

EDITH: But he must marry someone.

Mary catches sight of her sister's face.

MARY: Edith? What are you thinking?
EDITH: You know I don't dislike him as much as you do.
MARY: Perhaps you don't dislike him at all.
EDITH: Perhaps I don't.

Something about this annoys Mary but she throws it off.

MARY: Well, it's nothing to me. I've bigger fish to fry.
SYBIL: What fish?
EDITH: Are we talking about EN?
MARY: How do you know that? Have you been poking around in my things?
EDITH: Of course not.

Although she has. They've reached the hall now.

SYBIL: Come on. Who is he? It's not fair if you both know.
MARY: You won't be any the wiser, but his name is Evelyn Napier.

Edith salutes as she walks.

EDITH: The *Honourable* Evelyn Napier. Son and heir to Viscount Branksome.
MARY: Who wants an old sea monster when they can have Perseus?

And she walks out through the door to the waiting Taylor.

58 INT. MRS HUGHES'S SITTING ROOM. DAY.

Mrs Hughes is getting ready when Carson looks in.

CARSON: If you're going to the ceremony, I thought we might walk together.
MRS HUGHES: Certainly, I'm going. I want to see the old bat's face when they announce it. I must try not to look too cheerful.

At the sound of the word, he looks up sharply.

MRS HUGHES (CONT'D): Or shouldn't I talk like that in your presence?
CARSON: Do you find me very ridiculous, Mrs Hughes?
MRS HUGHES: What?

CARSON: Am I a joke? Putting on airs and graces I've no right to?

MRS HUGHES: What's brought this on?

CARSON: Nothing. Except at times I wonder if I'm just a sad old fool.

Mrs Hughes has been adjusting her hat in the glass, but now she turns to give him her full attention.

MRS HUGHES: Mr Carson, you are a man of integrity and honour, who raises the tone of this household by being part of it. So no more of that, please. Now, wait while I fetch my coat.

She scurries off, leaving Carson thoughtful and alone.

59 INT. SERVANTS' HALL. DAY.

William is talking to Daisy. Around them, the other servants are setting off in overcoats and hats.

WILLIAM: I wondered if you'd like to walk with —

DAISY: Is Thomas going?

WILLIAM: I think everyone is.

DAISY: Sorry, What were you saying?

WILLIAM: Nothing. Doesn't matter.

He leaves as Mrs Patmore appears.

MRS PATMORE: Put that in the larder before you go, and never mind your flirting.

DAISY: I wasn't flirting. Not with *him*.

She finds the idea outlandish, which puzzles the cook.

MRS PATMORE: William's not a bad lad.

DAISY: He's nice enough. But he isn't like Thomas.

MRS PATMORE: No. He is *not*.

60 INT. DRESSING ROOM. CRAWLEY HOUSE. DAY.

Matthew is being dressed in a morning coat by Molesley.

MOLESLEY: Cuff links, sir?

MATTHEW: Those are a dull option for such an occasion. Don't you agree?

Molesley can't believe what he's hearing.

MOLESLEY: Might I suggest the crested pair? They seem
more appropriate, if you don't mind my saying.
MATTHEW: They're a bit fiddly. I wonder if you could
help me.
MOLESLEY: Certainly, sir.

He puts them in, then holds the coat open quite jauntily.

MATTHEW: I see you got that mark out of the sleeve. How
did you do it?
MOLESLEY: Oh, I tried it with this and I tried it with
that, until it yielded.
MATTHEW: Very well done.
MOLESLEY: Thank you, sir.

He is almost grinning.

61 EXT. DOWNTON VILLAGE. DAY.

*People are going into the hospital. Carson and Mrs Hughes
arrive just after Bates.*

CARSON: You go in, Mrs Hughes. I want a quick word with
Mr Bates, here.

The housekeeper goes in with the others.

CARSON: Mr Bates. I must thank you. Both for what you
did, and for keeping silent afterwards. It was kind of
you. And Anna.
BATES: It was nothing.
CARSON: I hope you don't judge me too harshly.
BATES: I don't judge you at all.

Something in his tone makes the other man look at him.

BATES (CONT'D): *Believe me*, I have no right to judge you.
Or any man.

62 INT. HALL OF THE HOSPITAL. DAY.

*Violet, Isobel and Clarkson step up onto a dais. The crowd
is below them. Some patients are there, including Drake,
still in a wheelchair but transformed. His wife is with him.
Cora whispers to Robert, nodding at the audience.*

CORA: Why are you doing this? And why so many witnesses?
Is it just to punish your mother?

ROBERT: Not 'punish.' I'd say it was to teach her a lesson.

Violet stands, ramrod straight, as Clarkson speaks.

CLARKSON: Ladies and gentlemen, welcome, to this happy event. The investiture of our first Chairwoman, Mrs Reginald Crawley, who has graciously agreed to share the duties of our beloved President, the Dowager Countess of Grantham. Our little hospital must surely grow and thrive, with two such doughty champions united as they are by the strongest ties of all, family and friendship.

Violet and Isobel glare at each other with thinly disguised loathing.

END OF EPISODE TWO

EPISODE THREE

ACT ONE

1 EXT. DOWNTON ABBEY. DAY.

The house catches the morning sun. Bates comes out of the kitchen courtyard and walks away, as briskly as he can.

2 INT. POST OFFICE. DOWNTON. DAY.

Bates comes into the shop.

POSTMISTRESS: There you are, Mr Bates. It's in. Came this morning.

She hands over a 1913 version of Exchange and Mart.

BATES: They said it would. But that isn't quite the same thing.

As he is leaving, he bumps into Gwen by the door. She is carrying a package and, for some reason, is flustered.

BATES (CONT'D): Hello. I could have posted that for you.
GWEN: I prefer to do it myself.
BATES: I'll wait outside.

3 EXT. VILLAGE. DOWNTON. DAY.

Bates and Gwen are walking back together.

BATES: I've got a secret, too.

He smiles as he holds the rolled up magazine. She is nervous of confirming her own secret. She just nods.

BATES (CONT'D): You're all in for a surprise.
GWEN: A nice one, I hope.
BATES: Very nice, yes. Very, very nice.

They walk on.

4 INT. ANNA'S AND GWEN'S BEDROOM. DAY.

Anna is standing on a chair, moving things around on top of a cupboard. She is investigating an immensely heavy box.

GWEN (V.O.): What are you doing?

Anna is so surprised by this that she almost falls. She
steadies herself. Gwen is standing in the doorway.

ANNA: If you must know, I'm trying to find some space on
top of the cupboard to make life easier.

Gwen relaxes. But she is not off the hook.

ANNA (CONT'D): So what's in it, then?
GWEN: What?
ANNA: A bleedin' great packing case that weighs a ton.
That's what!

She pats the box. Gwen looks almost shifty.

GWEN: Can't you just leave it?
ANNA: No. I can't. And you'll tell me right now.
Unless you want me to ask Mrs Hughes about it.

Gwen thinks, then motions to Anna to get off the chair.

5 EXT. GARDENS. DOWNTON. DAY.

Cora is walking. She turns the corner of the path to find
Mary sitting, reading a letter.

CORA: Anything interesting?
MARY: Not particularly.

She folds the page and puts it away.

MARY (CONT'D): It's from Evelyn Napier. You met him with
the Delderfields, last November, at Doncaster races.
CORA: Is that Lord Branksome's boy?*
MARY: It is.
CORA: Do you like him?
MARY: I don't *dis*like him.
CORA: And what's he writing about?
MARY: Nothing much. He's out with the York and Ainsty
next week, and the meet is at Downton, so he wants some
tea when he's here.
CORA: Where's he staying? With friends?

....

* Evelyn Napier is a character I like; he pops up in two or three episodes,
mainly being decent and good, but never showy. Brendan Patricks plays him
with diffidence and skill, and I find him very beguiling. I am not sure we've
seen the last of him, actually.

MARY: He says he's found a pub that caters for hunting.

CORA: Oh, we can improve on that. He must come here. He can send the horses up early if he wants.

MARY: He'll know why you're asking him.

CORA: I can't think what you mean. His mother's a friend of mine. She'll be pleased at the idea.

MARY: Not very pleased. She's dead.

CORA: All the more reason then. You can write a note, too, and put it in with mine.

MARY: Shall I tell him about your friendship with his late mother?

CORA: I'm sure you of all people can compose a letter to a young man, without any help from me.

6 INT.   ANNA'S AND GWEN'S BEDROOM.   DAY.

The two women are staring at a new typewriter on the table.

ANNA: How much did it cost?

GWEN: Every penny I'd saved. Almost.

ANNA: And is this the mystery lover?

Gwen acknowledges the truth with a raised eyebrow.

GWEN: I've been taking a correspondence course in typing and shorthand. That's what was in the envelopes.

ANNA: Are you any good?

GWEN: Yes, I am, actually.

She blushes with a slight smile, proud of herself.*

....

* One of the most important aspects of this period was the shifting view of women's roles. They were on the edge of deep and profound change, which would become apparent almost as soon as the war began. Like any popular movement, the whole question of women's rights didn't break the surface of the water until there was already a good deal of support. Until then, the number of career openings for women was very small; for working class women it was service or work in the factories, for middle class women there was almost nothing beyond being a governess and for upper class women there wasn't even that. I did feel we needed the issue to be represented within the house. The idea that everyone was happy to be in service, and content with the pecking order, was gradually being recognised as false, but of course, as with everything, there were plenty who would resist the new ideas. Here, some of the servants are quite sympathetic to Gwen's ambitions, others feel affronted that in a way it's as if she's saying they're not good enough.

ANNA: But what's it for?

GWEN: Because I want to be a secretary.

ANNA: What?

GWEN: I'm bored with being in service. I'm not saying it's wrong or anything like that, but I'm bored with it. It's not for me. I want to join a business and earn some money and not… be a servant.

Anna is digesting this when the door flies open on O'Brien. The maids stand together, blocking the view of the table.

O'BRIEN: Her ladyship wants the fawn skirt that Lady Mary never wears. The seamstress is going to fit it to Lady Sybil but I can't find it.

ANNA: I'll come in a minute.

O'BRIEN: They're waiting now.

ANNA: One minute. I'm just changing my cap and apron.

She can't of course move without revealing the typewriter. O'Brien goes. As she speaks, Anna fetches a frilly cap and apron for the afternoon and pins them on. So does Gwen.

ANNA (CONT'D): Have you told anyone? What did your parents say?

GWEN: I can't tell them 'til I've got a job. Dad'll think I'm a fool to leave a good place. And Mum'll say I'm getting above myself. But I don't believe that.

She looks at her fellow maid defiantly.

ANNA: Nor do I.

7 INT. LIBRARY. DOWNTON. DAY.

Violet and Cora are with Robert, who's reading the paper.

CORA: It's not of my doing. It's all Mary's own work. But I think we should encourage it.

ROBERT: Branksome's a dull dog but I don't suppose that matters.

CORA: Did you know his wife had died?

ROBERT: He only ever talks about racing.

But, for Violet, it's time to get down to business.

VIOLET: Cora's right. Mary won't take Matthew Crawley, so we need to get her settled before the bloom is quite gone off the rose.

CORA: Is the family an old one?

VIOLET: Older than yours, I imagine.

ROBERT: Old enough.

CORA: And there's plenty of money.

VIOLET: Really?

ROBERT: Mama, you've already looked him up in the stud books and made enquiries about the fortune. Don't pretend otherwise?

Violet draws herself up and becomes very grand, indeed.

ROBERT (CONT'D): Are you afraid someone will think you American if you speak openly?

VIOLET: I doubt it would come to *that*.

CORA: Shall I ring for tea?

Her son checks the clock on the chimneypiece and stands.

ROBERT: Not for me. I'm meeting Cripps at five. Bramley wants to move one of the feeding pens and he needs a decision. I'll see you at dinner.

With a brisk nod at the two women, he goes.

CORA: You don't seem very pleased.

VIOLET: I'm pleased. It isn't brilliant but I'm pleased.

CORA: So?

VIOLET: I don't want Robert to use a marriage as an excuse to stop fighting for Mary's inheritance.

CORA: It won't make any difference.

VIOLET: You can't be sure. She'll be well set up, with a reasonable position. She won't be hungry.

CORA: It won't make a difference. I don't think he has the slightest intention of fighting as it is. The price of saving Downton is to accept Matthew Crawley as his heir. And, as far as he's concerned, that's that.

VIOLET: What about you?

CORA: I don't dislike Matthew. In fact, I rather admire him.

VIOLET: And is that sufficient reason to give him your money?

CORA: Of course not, but —

VIOLET: Then there's no more to be said. Are we having tea? Or not?

Cora goes to pull the bell rope. There will never be more than an armed truce between them.

8 EXT. DOWNTON VILLAGE. DAY.

Edith is walking in the village towards the Crawleys' house when she's overtaken by Matthew on a bicycle. He stops.

MATTHEW: I'd offer you a lift, if I could.
EDITH: It was you I was coming to see.
MATTHEW: Then your timing is matchless. I'm just off the train.

She smiles, falling into step as he wheels the bicycle.

EDITH: The other day at dinner, Cousin Isobel was saying you wanted to see some of the local churches.
MATTHEW: She's right. I do. I want to know more about the county generally, if I'm to live here.

Now comes the rehearsed moment. She takes a breath.

EDITH: Well, I thought I might show you a few of the nearer ones. We could take a picnic and make an outing of it.
MATTHEW: That's very kind.
EDITH: Nonsense. I'll enjoy it. It's too long since I played the tourist.
MATTHEW: It would have to be a Saturday. The churches work on Sunday, and I work all the weekdays.
EDITH: Then Saturday it is. I'll get Lynch to sort out the governess cart and I'll pick you up at about eleven.

Matthew has a date with his cousin. He's trapped.*

9 INT. SERVANTS' HALL. DOWNTON. NIGHT.

Thomas, William and Daisy are staring at the typewriter.

DAISY: How does it work?

....

* This is one of our first plots in which poor Edith is bound to fail. Because Mary is moving on she feels she might have a chance with Matthew, and like many of Edith's ideas, it's perfectly reasonable. For him to marry the second daughter rather than the elder would have solved the situation just as well, the bloodlines would have both been served and everyone would have been content. But we have established a pattern whereby, for Edith, it is usually unlikely to work out. I'm afraid I know people like that.

WILLIAM: Easy. You just press the letters and they print on the paper.

He does this. The others look.

THOMAS: Not that easy. You've smudged it.
WILLIAM: I have not.
CARSON (V.O.): Get back. Please.

He is with Mrs Hughes and O'Brien. They stare at the offending object.

O'BRIEN: They were trying to hide it, so I knew it was wrong.
CARSON: Where's Gwen now?
THOMAS: Doing the dining room with Anna. They'll be finished soon.
CARSON: Then I'll wait.
MRS HUGHES: With all due respect, Mr Carson, Gwen is under my jurisdiction.
CARSON: Indeed she is, Mrs Hughes, and I have no intention of usurping your authority. I merely want to get to the bottom of it.
WILLIAM: Why shouldn't Gwen have a typewriter, if she wants one?
THOMAS: Mind your own business.
GWEN (V.O.): What's that doing here?

She is standing in the doorway with Anna.

MRS HUGHES: Ah, Gwen, come in.
GWEN: Why's that down here? Who's been in my room? They had no right.

Mrs Hughes steps forward to quash this revolution at once.

MRS HUGHES: Now, see here. In the first place none of the rooms in this house belong to you. And in the second, I am in charge of your welfare and that gives me every right.*
ANNA: This is you, isn't it?

....

* Mrs Hughes is essentially a reasonable woman, but even she feels that this is overstepping the mark. Gwen is challenging her authority, which she has not deserved.

She is addressing O'Brien who says nothing.

CARSON: All we want to know is why Gwen wants a
typewriter and why she feels the need to keep it secret.
ANNA: She wants to keep it private, not secret. There's
a difference.
BATES: Amen.

He has joined the group and stands in the door.

GWEN: I've done nothing to be ashamed of. I've bought a
typewriter and I've taken a postal course in shorthand.
I'm not aware that either of these actions is illegal.
MRS HUGHES: Will you tell us why? Preferably without any
more cheek.
GWEN: Because I want to leave service. I want to be a
secretary.

The bomb has dropped.

MRS HUGHES: You want to leave service?
O'BRIEN: What's wrong with being in service?
GWEN: Nothing's wrong with it. And there's nothing wrong
with mending roads, neither, but it's not what I want to
do.
CARSON: I should remind you there are plenty of young
girls who'd be glad of a position in this house.
GWEN: And when I hand in my notice, I shall be happy to
think one of them will be taking my place.
O'BRIEN: What makes you think we'll wait until then?
ANNA: Are you hiring and sacking now, Miss O'Brien? I
thought that lay with Mr Carson and Mrs Hughes.
CARSON: Enough of this. I'm going to ring the dressing
gong, and we'll have no more talk of it tonight.
GWEN: Can I have my machine back now?
CARSON: Very well. But I wish I was sure you know what
you're doing.

She does not answer him but takes the machine and leaves.*

MRS PATMORE: Daisy? What's happened to you? I said you could go for a drink of water, not a trip up the Nile.

She is in the doorway and the girl files out past her. The others drift out, until Anna is alone with Bates.

BATES: You spoke up well in there.
ANNA: She is taking a risk, though. Mr Carson's right.
BATES: Maybe. But it's her risk to take.
ANNA: I suppose you're right.

They start to walk to the service staircase.

ANNA (CONT'D): Anything planned? For your half day tomorrow?
BATES: I might take a train into Leeds.
ANNA: What for?
BATES: No reason in particular. Come on, we'd better get moving or they'll be dressing themselves and we can't have that. They might find out they can manage without us.

With a laugh he starts up the stairs.

10 INT. MARY'S BEDROOM. NIGHT.

Edith is dressed. Anna is finishing off Mary.

ANNA: Which churches will you show him?
EDITH: I can't decide. Kirby, possibly. Or perhaps Easingwold.
MARY: You don't think you're being a bit obvious?
EDITH: Coming from you, that's rich.

There is a rustle in the doorway and their mother enters.

CORA: There was a letter from Mr Napier in the evening post.

....

* Gwen's situation here is, and should be, a complicated one. By her saying 'I want more than this', she is, in a way, indicting the others for not wanting more. But why should they want more? Are they wrong to be content in their work? Are they in the right or is she? This makes the fight between Gwen and Carson a *Downton*'esque one because both sides are perfectly reasonable. Of course Anna and Bates are essentially on Gwen's side.

MARY: Did he accept?

CORA: Not yet.

EDITH: Maybe he thought it too obvious.

This annoys Cora as much as Mary.

CORA: Apparently he'll have a friend with him. They're travelling straight to the meet from London, and they're planning to stay at the Worsley Arms that night.

MARY: Who is this friend?

CORA: An attaché at the Turkish Embassy.

She squints slightly at the page she holds in her hand.

CORA (CONT'D): A Mr Kemal Pamuk. He's the son of one of the Sultan's ministers and he's here for the Albanian talks.

MARY: What's that?

EDITH: To create an independent Albania. Don't you read the papers?

MARY: I'm too busy living a life.

CORA: Since Turkey's signature is vital Mr Napier's been given the job of keeping him happy until the conference begins. And Mr Pamuk is eager to try an English hunt.

EDITH: So that's that, then.

CORA: Not at all. I shall invite this Mr Pamuk to stay here as well. Who knows? A little hospitality in an English house may make all the difference to the outcome.

EDITH: You hope.

CORA: And Mary, you will ride out with them.

MARY: Oh, Mama, must I? My boots are at the menders and I haven't ridden for weeks.

CORA: Anna, please see that Lady Mary is fully equipped to go hunting.

ANNA: Yes, your ladyship.

Cora walks out of the room, on her way to the staircase.

11 EXT. STREET IN A LARGE TOWN. DAY

Bates is holding the magazine he collected earlier. He checks the address and walks into a shop.

12 INT. SHOP. DAY.

This is an odd place with artificial limbs and crutches on display. A man is working at a bench in the corner. *

    MAN: Yes?

    BATES: I saw this advertisement. For a limp correcter.

    MAN: Yes.

    BATES: What does it do exactly?

    MAN: It corrects limps.

He is waiting for Bates to get to the point.

    BATES: Does it work?

    MAN: Well, as I make it and I advertise it, is it likely I'd say no?

    BATES: Could I see one?

....

* Bates's leg story actually comes out of one of my activities when I was an actor. I used to eke out my living by giving lectures on domestic history – 'Anne Boleyn, Witch or Victim', 'The Intrigues of Marie Antoinette', that sort of thing – and I would present these talks in places like Palm Beach or Naples, Florida, or the Colony Club in New York. One of them concerned the private life of Lord Byron. I have always been interested in Keats's theory of 'negative capability' and his belief that the true artist is a vessel that is filled by their own creative talent, that, in other words, they're not terribly interesting as people, and certainly you often find that it is the lesser artist, the movie stars rather than the great classical actors, the writers of thrillers, the popular singers, who are actually more rewarding as characters. As an illustration of this, Byron was not nearly as great a poet as Keats but he lived an extraordinary life and I was haunted for years by the machines that his mother, Mrs Byron, had employed to cure his club foot and straighten his leg. They were instruments of torture, but Byron endured them because when you are different there seems to be a kind of imperative to conquer your difference and become the same as everyone else. The great moral triumph of being different, so brilliantly illustrated by the Paralympics, is to accept your difference which of course empowers you, but there is, I suspect, often a period that you have to go through when you're trying to be the same before you can get to that. I didn't want Bates to be too much of a saint on a monument. He's settling in, he likes Anna more and more and understandably he wants to get rid of his limp. After all, we know it is recent, a war wound that flared up a few years earlier, and he wants to go back to normal. He is also brave enough to subject himself to considerable pain in his efforts.

*Without a word, the man goes into a back room as Bates stares
rather uneasily at the instruments on display.*

MAN: Here we are.

*He is back with a box and now he takes out a kind of caliper,
with iron struts and straps and an adjustable foot platform
at the bottom. It looks extremely uncomfortable.*

MAN (CONT'D): You adjust this to the right height to
minimise your limp. You tighten these gradually, as
tight as you can stand, and, as the leg straightens, the
foot lowers to the floor. You'll need special shoes.
What size are you? And which leg is affected?
BATES: Ten. And it's the right.

*The man goes to fetch a box, while Bates stares at the
machine. He struggles not to wince as he looks at it.*

BATES (CONT'D): How long does it take?
MAN: How long is a piece of string?
BATES: But it really works?
MAN: I'm not saying it's easy. And you can't slack.
Every day, all day, if you mean business.

*He has arrived with a box containing the shoes. Bates stares
at the vicious implement, biting his lip.*

BATES: All right. How much?

13 EXT. CRAWLEY HOUSE. NIGHT.

The windows of Crawley house are lit.

14 INT. DRAWING ROOM. CRAWLEY HOUSE. NIGHT.

Isobel is reading a letter.

ISOBEL: She asks if we can both dine on Saturday. There
are two young men staying, so you won't be so outnumbered
for once.
MATTHEW: What men?
ISOBEL: A Turkish diplomat called… something I can't read
and 'Lord Branksome's charming son.' Who's to be flung at
Mary, presumably.
MATTHEW: When it comes to Cousin Mary, she is quite
capable of doing her own flinging, I assure you. Must we

go? I've got the whole day with Edith. I could use a
night off.
ISOBEL: I think we should.

*She opens another letter, scanning it. When she speaks she
does so without lifting her eyes from the paper.*

ISOBEL (CONT'D): And you're all set to go church
visiting?
MATTHEW: Apparently. I didn't seem to have much option.
ISOBEL: I'm afraid it's my fault. She asked what your
interests were, and I just blurted it all out. I hope
you're not annoyed.
MATTHEW: Not at all. Why should I be?
ISOBEL: No reason.

But she knows more than her son about Edith's intentions.

15 INT. BEDROOM PASSAGE. DAY.

*It's early and Anna is carrying riding boots, a riding habit,
a top hat and veil. She sees Gwen.*

ANNA: Ah. Open the door of the Blue Room, can you? I'm
going to lay it out in there. Then when she gets up it's
ready.

Gwen has opened the door of a bedroom and they go in.

16 INT. BLUE ROOM. DAY.

*This is a handsome, spare bedroom. Anna chatters on as she
spreads the things out on the bed.*

ANNA: I couldn't find her breeches anywhere. So I asked
Mr Bates and he looked among his lordship's riding
clothes. There they were.

Still Gwen is silent. The garments are laid out.

ANNA (CONT'D): I only hope to God I've got everything.
Hat, I'll do here. Gloves and crop are in the hall.

There is the sound of a sob and she turns. Gwen is crying.

ANNA (CONT'D): Gwen? Whatever's the matter?

Gwen just shakes her head, crying in good earnest now.

ANNA (CONT'D): Come on. You can tell me. Has someone been teasing you?

Gwen shakes her head but still cries. There is a step in the passage and Bates looks round the door. He is carrying a tweed suit on his arm. He sees the source of the crying.

BATES: What's up?

ANNA: She's upset.

GWEN: Oh, I'm just being silly. You should get that brushed.

BATES: He won't be up for another half an hour. Now, what is it?

GWEN: I suppose I've just realised that it's not going to happen.

BATES: What isn't?

GWEN: Oh, none of it. I'm not going to be a secretary. I'm not going to leave service. I doubt I leave *here* before I'm sixty.

ANNA: What's all this?

GWEN: You saw their faces, and they're right. Oh, look at me. Can you see me in an office? Sitting in the boardroom, taking down dictation?

ANNA: Why shouldn't you?

Gwen is not crying now. Instead, she is in despair.

GWEN: Because I'm the daughter of a farmhand and I'm lucky to be a maid. I was born with nothing, and I'll die with nothing.

BATES: Don't talk like that.

GWEN: Why not?

BATES: Because it's not true. Because you can change your life if you want to.

GWEN: Really?

BATES: Yes. Sometimes you have to be hard on yourself, but you can change it completely. I know.

He winces slightly, as if at a sudden stab of pain.

ANNA: Mr Bates? Are you all right?

BATES: Take her upstairs. Dry her off.

17 INT. BEDROOM PASSAGE/BACKSTAIRS. DAY.

They emerge. Anna and Gwen go one way and Bates heads for the backstairs. He rests for a moment, breathing deeply, then he lands heavily on the landing and cries out in pain.

MRS HUGHES (V.O.): Mr Bates? What's the matter?

She is coming up at the same time and is only now in sight.

BATES: Nothing. Not a thing. I'm fine.
MRS HUGHES: Let me help you down to the next landing.
BATES: I am perfectly all right, thank you, Mrs Hughes.
MRS HUGHES: Are you sure? You're as white as a sheet.
BATES: That's my wonderful complexion, inherited from my Irish mother.

With a forced chuckle, he goes on down.

END OF ACT ONE

ACT TWO

18 INT. KITCHEN. DAY.

Trays are rushed in by Thomas and William. Daisy snatches off the dirty glasses and replaces them with waiting clean ones. Mrs Patmore ladles stirrup cup from a steaming tureen and kitchen maids cut up fruit cake as fast as they can.

MRS PATMORE: Take it, take it! Don't dawdle!

The footmen hurry away from the mad, frantic workplace.

19 EXT. THE MEET AT DOWNTON. DAY.

As the laden footmen glide smoothly out of the front door, Robert, Cora and Sybil walk among the riders chatting. Thomas and William, supervised by Carson, carry the trays of stirrup cup and cake for riders and followers. Mary, looking superb in a habit that fits like a glove, stares at the crowd. The head groom, Lynch, is mounted beside her.

LYNCH: Can you see them, m'lady?

MARY: Not yet. Oh, wait a minute. Here's Mr Napier.

A pleasant-looking man, Evelyn Napier, comes trotting over.

MARY (CONT'D): I was beginning to give up on you. We're moving off.

EVELYN: We were fools not to accept your mother's invitation and send the horses down early. As it is, my groom only got here an hour or two ago, and my mount's as jumpy as a deb at her first ball.

MARY: What about Mr Pamuk? I gather if he takes a tumble, you'll be endangering world peace.

EVELYN: Not only that. His father's a bigwig at the Ottoman Court, so if I don't get him home safe and sound I know I'll be beheaded by proxy.

MARY: Isn't it a risk to take him hunting?

EVELYN: Don't worry about Kemal. He knows what he's doing on a horse.

MARY: Where is he?

EVELYN: Fussing. He's rather a dandy. You should have heard him ask about the clothes for what he persists in calling a 'noble house.'

MARY: I can see him now. A funny little foreigner with a wide, toothy grin and hair reeking of pomade.

EVELYN: I wouldn't quite say that. Here he is now.

Mary looks up and her jaw drops. Riding towards her is one of the handsomest, sexiest men she has ever seen in her life. He stands in his stirrups and doffs his silk hat.*

KEMAL: Lady Mary Crawley, I presume?

MARY: You presume right.

....

* We had to find a very good-looking actor to play the Turk as we needed the audience to believe that Mary would be sufficiently overcome to abandon her principles. The problem with good looks, when they are important to a narrative, is that men and women seldom agree about what constitutes a good-looking member of their own sex. In this instance we felt it was more important that women should find Pamuk attractive and I remember settling that beforehand with Jill Trevellick, our casting agent, who recommended Theo James, and happily she was right. Most women did think him extremely good-looking. If men find him handsome, too, then so much the better.

KEMAL: Sorry to be so dishevelled. We've been on a train
since dawn and we had to change in a shed.
MARY: You don't look dishevelled to me.
EVELYN: I think we're going.

The hunt is moving off. Mary turns to the groom.

MARY: Lynch, you don't have to stay with me.
LYNCH: His lordship asked me to.
MARY: It's a waste of your day. Help Mr Napier's man get
their things back to the house.
LYNCH: His lordship said…
EVELYN: Don't worry. I'll look after her.
LYNCH: But his lordship —
KEMAL: We'll make it our business to keep her from harm.
I promise.

And before Lynch can say another word, they have gone.

20 INT. CARSON'S PANTRY. DAY.

Carson, Thomas and William are cleaning silver.

CARSON: You can dress Mr Pamuk, Thomas. Mr Napier's chap
will bring the luggage over this morning, so you've time
to get sorted out.
THOMAS: Why doesn't he have his own man?
CARSON: Mr Napier's valet was to see to both, but it's a
lot to ask when they won't be here before six.
THOMAS: I thought he was supposed to be in England to
prevent a war.
CARSON: Not single-handedly.
THOMAS: Even so. He can't be up to much if he doesn't
have his own valet.
WILLIAM: It might be different if you're a Turk. I've
heard lots of things are different when you're a Turk.

He speaks the comment more innocently than Thomas hears it.

THOMAS: That's a thought.
CARSON: Get into the pattern, Thomas. You're not
polishing an apple.

But Thomas's mind is on other possibilities.

21 EXT. OPEN COUNTRY. DAY

The hunt is in full cry, dangerous and glamorous and
frightening. Mary gallops along in the crowd, then pulls up
*as she sees Kemal on the crest of a hill.**

> MARY: I hope the day is living up to your expectations.
> KEMAL: It is exceeding them in every way.

The look he gives her is unmistakable.

> MARY: Where's Mr Napier?
> KEMAL: He's gone over the bridge. Look.

He points to a group including Napier on the road.

> KEMAL: And what about you? Will you follow him? Or come
> over the jump with me?
> MARY: Oh, I was never much one for going round by the
> road.
> KEMAL: You believe in living dangerously, then?
> MARY: Of course. What did the Frenchman say? *L'audace,*
> *toujours l'audace.*

He smiles at this. They are kindred spirits.

> KEMAL: Stay by me and we'll take it together.

They set off down to the stream which they clear easily.†

....

* Inevitably, with this sequence, we had a few complaints about the wrong bridles and that sort of thing. Apparently no one would have hunted on a skewbald in those days, but on the whole, I was pleased with the hunt. The one thing I was very keen on was that we should not show hunting as it is usually depicted in films, where the horses fly across green meadows in sunny, high summer with the trees heavy with leaf. They even got it wrong in *Tom Jones*, which is a wonderful film. So, here we made quite a point of shooting the scene early in the schedule, when the trees were bare and while we were in fact still in the hunting season.

† I was particularly impressed with Michelle Dockery's mastery of the art of riding side-saddle. She has a little help from a (marvellous) double in a few of the shots, but nevertheless what she did achieve in a comparatively short time was extraordinary. She wanted to make it look good and she certainly did. Theo also served us well and he was just as keen to get the riding right.

22 INT. CHURCH. DAY.

Matthew and Edith are in the nave of a church.

EDITH: I wish we could talk a little more about you.
What was it like? Growing up in Manchester?

But Matthew doesn't even hear her. He's looking around.

MATTHEW: Does it say anything about the Lady Chapel
screen?*

Edith sits and opens the little brochure wearily.

EDITH: The screen dates from the early sixteenth century.
The pomegranates commemorate Queen Catherine of Aragon
and the fleurs de lys represent the Virgin Mary.
MATTHEW: Two women who had a lot to put up with.
EDITH: The side aisles were added in the fourteenth
century by Bishop Richard de Warren.
MATTHEW: Yes, you can see that in the treatment of the
stone.
EDITH: It's wonderful to think of all those men and women
worshipping together through the centuries, isn't it?
Dreaming and hoping, much as we do, I suppose.

Matthew nods absent-mindedly. He is hardly listening.

MATTHEW: Is the screen a Cromwell casualty?
EDITH: I dare say.
MATTHEW: I wonder how Mary's getting on.

No comment could be less to Edith's taste than this.

EDITH: All right, I should think. Why?
MATTHEW: I just wondered. Will she stay with the hunt
the whole day?
EDITH: Oh, you know Mary. She likes to be in at the
kill.

She doesn't like Mary. Matthew's tone is more ambivalent.

....

* I had to adjust all of Edith's dialogue about the screen and the other details
concerning the church's interior once we had settled on which church we
were actually going to use. I was sent the brochure and I had to rewrite the
scene to fit that particular nave.

MATTHEW: Where shall we go next?

EDITH: Not home?

MATTHEW: Oh, not yet. We've time for one more at least before we lose the light.

EDITH: I underestimated your enthusiasm.

Sighing, she limps out to the trap, on her tired feet.

23 EXT. DOWNTON. EVE.

The three riders amble down the drive towards the house with its blazing windows, in the fading light.

24 INT. HALL/BACKSTAIRS PASSAGE. DOWNTON. EVE.

Napier, spattered in mud, like the others, from head to toe, is removing his second boot with the bootjack in the outer hall, as Mary and Kemal walk away in their stockinged feet into the Great Hall. While the others are talking, Thomas whispers to Carson.

THOMAS: Is that one mine?

Robert and Cora have arrived.

ROBERT: Home is the hunter. Home from the hill.
Heavens. You have been in the wars.

Carson has organised a square of drugget to receive the muddy boots and clothes. He waits with Thomas as Napier's valet starts to remove his master's coat and Anna tends to Mary.

MARY: Papa, this is Mr Pamuk. My father, Lord Grantham.

KEMAL: How do you do, my lord?

ROBERT: Did you have a good day?

KEMAL: Couldn't have been better.

Carson takes Thomas over to Pamuk after his moment with Robert is over and Robert has turned to Evelyn who's coming through.

CARSON: This is Thomas, sir. He will be looking after you.

KEMAL: Oh, I thought —

He looks over to Evelyn who shrugs as he hears Mary speak.

MARY: You remember Mr Napier.

CORA: Of course. How are you?

EVELYN: It's so kind of you to have us, Lady Grantham.

MARY: And this is Mr Pamuk.

CORA: How do you do?

During this, Pamuk has used the jack for his boots and given his coat to Thomas, so he stands in his shirtsleeves. Her eyes register his beauty, which amuses Robert.

ROBERT: Now, what would you like? Something to eat?

MARY: Baths first, then eggs in our rooms. Once we've shed our outer garments.

As soon as she came in, Anna held a boot-pull for her and took her muddy coat. There's a mass of movement throughout.

THOMAS: Your cases are upstairs, sir. If you'd like to follow me.

As he and Pamuk walk past, he glances over to a slightly open door where O'Brien, Gwen and Anna are all craning to see the visitor. His look of delight to O'Brien says it all. Behind the door, the women pull back.

GWEN: He doesn't look Turkish at all.

ANNA: Well, he doesn't look like any Englishman I've ever met, worse luck. I think he's beautiful.

The door opens to reveal Carson.

CARSON: Is there some crisis of which I am unaware?

O'BRIEN: No, Mr Carson.

CARSON: I cannot think of another reason why you should congregate here.

ANNA: No, Mr Carson.

They turn and head back down towards the kitchens.

25 INT. ROBERT'S DRESSING ROOM. NIGHT.

Bates is helping Robert dress for dinner.

ROBERT: Have you seen our visitor? Quite a treat for the ladies.

BATES: Indeed, m'lord.

ROBERT: Are they settled in all right?

BATES: I believe so. Mr Napier's valet seems a competent fellow, and Thomas knows what he's doing.

ROBERT: Why doesn't the gorgeous Turk have his own chap?

BATES: Apparently his man speaks no English, so Mr Pamuk decided to leave him in London.

ROBERT: Probably very wise. I hope Thomas doesn't mind.

BATES: You know Thomas, m'lord. He has to have a grumble, but I gather he cheered up when he saw the gentleman.

Robert makes no comment, but he gives Bates a humorous look, which Bates returns, then without warning, he winces.

ROBERT: Bates? Is anything wrong?

BATES: Nothing at all, m'lord. Is that strap too tight?

He adjusts the strap on the back of the white waistcoat.

26 INT. KEMAL PAMUK'S BEDROOM. NIGHT.

Thomas stands near Kemal who is also getting into his white waistcoat. Thomas steps forward.

THOMAS: Shall I adjust it, sir?

He tightens the band round the back of Kemal's waist, letting his hands linger.

KEMAL: Now I'm relying on you to see that I go downstairs properly dressed. I'm a stranger to England and English ways.

THOMAS: Don't worry, sir. I've got sharp eyes for anything out of order.

This amuses Kemal who smiles warmly at the footman.

KEMAL: Then I put myself entirely in your hands.

THOMAS: You do right, sir.

Thomas misinterprets Kemal's tone which, in his defence, could easily seem flirtatious. He hands Kemal a tie.

THOMAS (CONT'D): I should love to visit Turkey.

Kemal is slightly surprised by this remark, which we register. But he is feeling friendly.

KEMAL: It's a wonderful country.

He starts to tie his white bow tie, but he fluffs it.

    KEMAL (CONT'D): My man always does this. Can you?

Thomas steps in and takes over the tie. Now the two men stand close, face to face. Thomas is in bliss.

    THOMAS: I'm very attracted to the Turkish culture.
    KEMAL: Then I hope your chance will come to sample it.

Unfortunately, Thomas hears this as a direct invitation. He lifts his hand from the tie to Kemal's cheek.

    THOMAS: I hope so, too.

Kemal moves away sharply. His voice is entirely different.

    KEMAL: You forget yourself.

Thomas has misjudged. He could be in big trouble.

    THOMAS: I'm sorry, sir. I thought —
    KEMAL: That will teach you not to believe what the English say about foreigners.

He is standing very still, staring at the servant.

    KEMAL (CONT'D): I ought to report you.
    THOMAS: I think you must have mistaken —
    KEMAL: I mistook nothing. But I will make you an offer.

Thomas waits to hear his fate.

    KEMAL (CONT'D): Later tonight, I may need your help with the geography of the house. I'll know more when you help me undress.
    THOMAS: The geography?
    KEMAL: I'm not sure yet, but I may wish to pay someone a visit. If that is the case you'll help me, and I will say nothing about your behaviour.*

Thomas doesn't know whether to be relieved or jealous.

....

* Thomas's pass here is another beat in the ongoing homosexual narrative. For me, a key element which makes Thomas slightly sympathetic, at any rate to most of us, is the danger that was involved for anyone trying to live life then as a gay; you really were always in danger, every overture could end in ruin. Here we need him to fail, because he must be forced to show Mary's bedroom to a stranger, or how else would Kemal be able to find it?

27 INT. DINING ROOM. DOWNTON. NIGHT.

The Granthams, their daughters, Violet, the Crawleys, Evelyn and Kemal Pamuk are all in the middle of dinner.

VIOLET: I don't understand. Why would she want to be a secretary?

MATTHEW: She wants a different life.

VIOLET: But why? I should far prefer to be a maid in a large and pleasant house, than work from dawn 'til dusk in a cramped and gloomy office. Don't you agree, Carson?

CARSON: I do, m'lady.

MARY: Why are we talking about this? What does it matter?

CORA: It matters whether the people who live and work here are content.

SYBIL: Of course. We should be helping Gwen if that's what she wants.†

ISOBEL: I agree. Surely we must all encourage those less fortunate to improve their lot where they can.

VIOLET: Not if it isn't in their best interests.

ISOBEL: Isn't the maid a better judge of that than we?

This is aimed at Violet as a direct challenge.

MARY: What do you say, Mr Pamuk? Should our housemaid be kept enslaved or forced out into the world?

KEMAL: Why are you English so curious about each other's lives? If she wishes to leave and the law permits it, then let her go.

....

Continued from page 156:

But still it is a reminder of the injustice meted out to homosexuals at that time. You could try your luck with a maid and the worst thing that could happen would be for her to turn you down, but a gay pass could mean prison. A friend of mine overheard a group in a restaurant talking about this episode and a woman said: 'Do you think people really did go to bed with the footman when they were staying in a house party?' And one of the others replied, 'Oh my dear, it was part of the job description.' I loved that.

† When it comes to Gwen's goals, Sybil is extremely sympathetic, Edith doesn't see the point and Mary couldn't care less either way, which, for me, sums up the sisters very aptly.

VIOLET: Perhaps the law should not permit it, for the
common good.
ISOBEL: So you hanker for the days of serfdom?
VIOLET: I hanker for a simpler world. Is that a crime?
KEMAL: I too dream of a simpler world. As long as we can
keep our trains and our dentistry.

He laughs towards Mary on his left. She whispers.

MARY: I wish I shared your enthusiasm. Our dentist is
horrid.
KEMAL: Why go to him?
MARY: Oh, he treated all of us when we were children.
You know how the English are about these things. But he
smells of carbolic and mint and he has blunt fingers like
fat glove-stretchers.*
KEMAL: Well, the next time you feel a twinge you must
come to Istanbul.
MARY: Wouldn't the journey be painful?
KEMAL: Sometimes we must endure a little pain in order to
achieve satisfaction.

*There is a startling invitation here. Evelyn, on her other
side, is aware of this exchange though he cannot hear it.*

EVELYN: Lady Mary rode very well today.
ROBERT: Why did you send Lynch back?
MARY: I had my champions to left and right. It was
enough.

Again, the smile she bestows is for Kemal not Evelyn.

ROBERT: Did you enjoy the hunt, Mr Napier? Mary tells me
you had a tremendous run.
EVELYN: It was like something out of a Trollope novel.

But his discomfort at what he is witnessing is clear.

....

*This observation comes entirely from my own history. The dentist of my
childhood had been my mother's and because he had treated her and her
sisters, there was absolutely no question that he would not treat us.
Unfortunately, by then he was a crusty old man with thick horrible fingers
and no grasp of any of the new methods, so everything he did was agony. In
those days, the emphasis for the English was only on the health of one's
teeth. To mind whether they looked good was just vain silliness, and so we
were all condemned to have teeth like old gardening tools.

CORA: What about you, Mr Pamuk. Was the day a success?
KEMAL: Oh yes, Lady Grantham. I can hardly remember a better one.

The look that he shares with Mary shows it isn't over yet.

28 INT.   DRAWING ROOM.   DOWNTON.   NIGHT.

Carson, Thomas and William are serving the guests from a side table holding coffee and various after dinner drinks.

ROBERT: Mary's got more suitors tonight than the Princess Aurora.
VIOLET: But will she judge them sensibly?
ROBERT: No one's sensible at her age. Nor should they be. That's our job.

Mary wanders over towards Evelyn and Matthew.

MATTHEW: Was it fun to be back in the saddle?
MARY: Yes. Although I'll pay for it tomorrow.
MATTHEW: Would you ever come out with me?

His friendliness has taken her by surprise.

MATTHEW (CONT'D): Or aren't we friends enough for that?

He has put her on the spot with this. She smiles slightly.

MARY: Oh, I think it might be —

But Kemal is trying to catch her eye from across the room.

EVELYN: That run reminded me of a day last month up in Cheshire —

Kemal is nodding towards an open door.

EVELYN (CONT'D): We came down the side of a hill —
MARY: Excuse me.

She hurries away towards Kemal. Evelyn breaks off.

MATTHEW: It seems we must brush up on our powers of fascination.
EVELYN: I was a fool to bring him here.
MATTHEW: Don't you like him?
EVELYN: I like him very much. But so does everyone else, unfortunately.

Edith has arrived to speak to them.

MATTHEW: I hope I didn't wear you out today.
EDITH: Not at all. I enjoyed it. We must do it again.
MATTHEW: Next time let's take my mother. She was so
jealous, she made me promise she could come with us.
EDITH: Of course.

*She answers brightly but her campaign has failed. During
this, Mary has slipped away through the open door.*

29 INT. MORNING ROOM. DOWNTON. NIGHT.

Mary comes in to find Kemal alone, waiting for her.

MARY: What is it?
KEMAL: Is this picture really a della Francesca?
MARY: I think so. The second Earl bought back several
paintings from his Grand Tour and —

*As she approaches the picture, he suddenly pulls her into his
arms and kisses her passionately. She breaks away.*

MARY (CONT'D): Mr Pamuk —
KEMAL: Let me come to you tonight. Please.
MARY: I can't think what I've said that has led you to
believe —
KEMAL: Please. I don't know when we will meet again, so
let it be tonight. *L'audace. Toujours l'audace.*

She looks at him in silence, gathering her strength.

MARY: Mr Pamuk, I will not repeat your words to my
father, since I should hate to see you cast out into the
darkness. But can we agree to consider them unsaid?
Now, if you'll excuse me, I shall rejoin my mother and
sisters.

*She leaves him, but he is not completely cast down. Instead
he smiles softly, whispering, this time to himself.*

KEMAL: *L'audace. Toujours l'audace.* It seems the game
is not over yet.

30 INT. GALLERY. NIGHT.

Kemal, in a dressing gown, looks over to confirm he's at the right door. Thomas nods. Kemal turns the handle.

31 INT. MARY'S BEDROOM. NIGHT.

Kemal comes round the door. Mary seems so young with her loose hair hanging down, lit by a candle, nothing more. She looks up, suddenly, as she hears the door open.

MARY: You must be mad.
KEMAL: I am. I'm in the grip of madness.
MARY: Please leave. At once. Or I'll —

She hesitates.

KEMAL: Or you'll what?
MARY: I'll scream.
KEMAL: No, you won't.
MARY: I'll ring the bell, then.
KEMAL: Who's on duty now? The hall boy? Will you let him find a man in your bedroom? What a story!

Mary stands. Kemal's confidence is infuriating.

MARY: Do you have any idea what you're asking? I'd be ruined if they even knew we'd had this conversation. Let alone if…
KEMAL: What? Don't worry. You can still be a virgin for your husband.
MARY: Heavens. Is this a proposal?
KEMAL: Alas, no. I don't think our union would please your family.
MARY: I'm afraid not.
KEMAL: Or mine.

Mary's rather put out. She thought she was the grand one. Now he smiles, roguishly, playing his next card.

KEMAL (CONT'D): But a little imagination, a phial of blood hidden beneath a pillow. You wouldn't be the first.*
MARY: You and my parents have something in common.
KEMAL: Oh?
MARY: You believe I'm much more of a rebel than I am. Now, please go.

But instead he approaches and draws her down on to the bed. She talks on, but she is beginning to babble.

MARY (CONT'D): I'm not what you think I am. If it's my mistake, if I've led you on, I'm sorry, but I'm not.

She is unnerved by him, rattled, and he can sense her resistance is failing. He is getting to her.

....

* This exchange between Kemal – 'I don't think our union would please your family… or mine' – was to illustrate the arrogance and lack of imagination in this type of Englishwoman. Mary would assume that anyone would be absolutely thrilled by having her as a daughter-in-law. The idea that there was a rival culture which would see her as an unsuitable bride would be astonishing. Michelle does it well. Watch the shadow that crosses her face. In my experience, the English are curiously dense when it comes to recognising any kind of foreign rank. To them, it is better to be an English baronet than a French duke.

In the edit, the Powers made a cut we all came to regret. After commenting that Mary 'could still be a virgin for your husband', which stayed in, Kemal was supposed to say: 'A little imagination, a phial of blood hidden beneath the pillow, you wouldn't be the first.' But this was excised. Despite arguing fairly passionately, I could not convince them the lines were needed. I explained that, without them, it was anyone's guess what Kemal was doing to Mary that would leave her virginity intact. But they were confident that no one would make any untoward connection. 'Nobody will think that,' they said. But everyone thought it. We had letters and calls of complaint, we had indignant Turkish viewers, and no wonder. However, one thing I did realise from this moment and that was the extent to which people were watching the show in detail; some of them would see every episode two, three, four times. All of which meant they assumed that Pamuk must have done something unspeakable which we won't name here. We never came up against another cut that was quite as misleading, but it did mean that when there was a line that made all the difference to the sense of a scene I was a much tougher fighter thereafter.

KEMAL: You're just what I think you are.

MARY: No. I've never done *anything* —

He stops her mouth with his finger, cutting off her speech.

KEMAL: Of course not. One look at you tells me that.

He moves to kiss her, only removing his finger when he can replace it with his own lips. Despite herself she responds.

KEMAL (CONT'D): Oh, my darling.

MARY: But won't it hurt? Is it safe?

She is desperately nervous. He takes her face in his hands.

KEMAL: Trust me. And I promise you a night you will never forget.*

He draws her towards him for another kiss.

END OF ACT TWO

ACT THREE

32 INT.   ANNA'S AND GWEN'S BEDROOM.   DOWNTON.   DAWN.

Anna is asleep. Gwen is next to her. A female hand slides over Anna's mouth and clamps it shut. Her eyes fly open.

MARY (V.O.): Sssh!

Anna looks over and sees Mary, hair tumbled, in a negligee. She nods slightly and Mary removes her hand. With an impassioned look, Mary tiptoes out and Anna follows her.

....

* Young women like the Crawley sisters were brought up in so circumscribed a fashion, with everything they said or did or wore being laid down by Mama, that overpowering physical attraction often came as a complete surprise. It was the one thing you hadn't been trained to deal with. These days, things are very different, but Mary would have been so shielded, from the school room to the ball room, that nothing could have prepared her for this situation. In fact, there are several stories from that time where passion did overturn lives. But then, I suppose it still does.

33 INT. SERVANTS' PASSAGE. DOWNTON. DAWN.

*They are together in the passage. Anna is deeply shocked.**

> ANNA: *What?*
> MARY: He's dead. I think he's dead. No, I'm sure he's dead.
> ANNA: But how? Why?
> MARY: We were together and…

She breaks off. Surely this is clear enough.

> MARY (CONT'D): He's dead.
> ANNA: In your room.

Mary nods. This is deeply shocking. These characters are not living in our world. Anna makes a decision to help.

> ANNA (CONT'D): We've got to get him back to his own bed.
> MARY: How? It's in the bachelor's corridor, miles from my room.
> ANNA: Could we manage him between us?

Mary shakes her head impatiently.

> MARY: He weighs a ton. I can't shift him at all. We'll need at least one other. What about Bates?
> ANNA: He couldn't lift him. William can't keep a secret and Thomas wouldn't try to. And there's no point in asking Mr Carson. He'd pass out from the shock.
> MARY: Well, we've got to do something.
> ANNA: What about your sisters?

Mary shakes her head firmly.

> MARY: Sybil's too young. And Edith would use it against me for the rest of my life and beyond.

* Some viewers may be surprised at the close relationship between Mary and Anna but the position of a body servant was a unique one. Lots of people were extremely fond of their butlers and their housekeepers (though seldom the cook), but there is something about the man or woman who is dressing and undressing you, running your bath and drying your back, that involves trust and inevitably leads to intimacy. These were often the servants who stayed on as gentlemen's gentlemen or lady companions when all the others had gone, because there could be a real friendship there. The plain truth is, you couldn't have someone in your bedroom holding your underpants for you if you didn't like them.

ANNA: Then who else has as much to lose as you, if it
ever gets out?
MARY: Not Papa. Please don't say Papa. I couldn't bear
the way he'd look at me.
ANNA: No, not his lordship…

34 INT. MARY'S BEDROOM. DOWNTON. DAWN.

*Cora covers her face with her hands in horror. Kemal's
naked, dead body is sprawled among the sheets.*

CORA: What happened?
MARY: I don't know. A heart attack, I suppose. Or a
stroke. Or… He was alive and suddenly he cried out. And
then he was dead.
CORA: But why was he here at all? Did he force himself
on you?

*Mary hesitates. Silently, she shakes her head. If anything,
this is even more shocking than the death. Cora breathes for
a moment, to steady her nerves.*

CORA (CONT'D): Well… we can talk about that later. Now,
we must decide what to do for the best.
ANNA: There's only one thing we can do.

She stares at Cora who is beginning to understand.

CORA: I couldn't. It's not possible.
MARY: If you don't, we will figure in a scandal of such
magnitude it will never be forgotten until long after
we're both dead.
CORA: But I —
MARY: I'll be ruined, Mama. Ruined and notorious, a
laughing stock, a social pariah. Is that what you want for
your eldest daughter? Is it what you want for the family?

Cora looks at her child so differently now.

CORA: We must cover him up.

35 INT. BEDROOM PASSAGE. DOWNTON. DAWN.

*A door opens and the women come out, looking about. Anna
carries Kemal's legs, while behind her Mary and Cora have an
arm each over their shoulders. The corpse is in his own
dressing gown. The thin light of dawn seeps in.*

CORA: Hurry. The servants will be up soon.

ANNA: We've got time.

Kemal's head lolls sideways against Cora's neck and she cries out. Mary hisses at her.

MARY: Mama!

CORA: Sorry.

They move on. As they pass, a door opens from the back stairs. Daisy leans out to investigate the noise she just heard. In the distance, along the passage, the women are turning the corner. Anna and Cora are out of sight, but Mary, with the arm of the corpse over her shoulder, is just visible. Daisy watches dumbstruck until they vanish.

36 INT.   KEMAL PAMUK'S BEDROOM.   DAWN.

He is in bed. Anna hangs the dressing gown behind the door, while Mary arranges Kemal in a believable position, weeping as she does so. The eyes are open despite her efforts.

MARY: I can't make his eyes stay shut.

CORA: Leave that and come away!

Anna is kinder. She goes to Mary, taking her shoulders.

MARY: He was so beautiful.

ANNA: Her ladyship's right. We must get back to our rooms.

Anna leads Mary to the door but Cora stands in their path.

CORA: I feel now I can never forgive what you have put me through this night. I hope in time I'll come to be more merciful. But I doubt it.

MARY: You won't tell Papa.

CORA: Since it would probably kill him and certainly ruin his life, I will not. But I keep the secret for his sake, not for yours.

MARY: Yes, Mama.

CORA: Anna, I will not insult you by asking that you also conceal Lady Mary's shame. Now, let us go.*

She opens the door and they slip silently out.

37 INT. BEDROOM PASSAGE. DOWNTON. DAWN.

The three women hurry down as far as the door to the backstairs, where Anna slips away, leaving the others.†

....

* When they found a maid or a valet whom they really liked, most employers tried to hang on to them and in many cases, as I have said, when the way of life began to collapse after the war they stayed on as a companion or a man servant. In the series, we contrast the false friendship between Cora and O'Brien, where Cora does not really know the true O'Brien at all (which I have seen), but also the genuine affection between Anna and Mary. This scene is one of the first moments where it is used dramatically. Mary is trying to think of someone who will help her without question, and that person is her maid. Cora is the next choice because she would also be damaged by a scandal. I remember saying to a famous friend who was going through a bad patch in a marriage that it's important only to stray with someone who has as much to lose as you do. The moment they take up with some girl who's happy to feature in a headline, they've had it. And the only person in this house who will lose as much as Mary is Cora, if the family is to become notorious.

† At the time, the Pamuk story was cited by some in the press as completely unbelievable, when in fact it is one plot that is entirely rooted in truth. I heard the story many years ago, when my wife and I were staying with some friends in the country. Our host had come upon the diary of a great aunt and there he read her account of an incident that took place in about 1895. In this particular house, like Downton, there was a bachelor corridor, but, less usually, there was also a passage set aside for single women, that is young girls, spinsters or widows. One of them had smuggled a man into her room where he proceeded to die of a heart attack in her bed. Naturally she was at her wits' end and, *faute de mieux*, she woke the blameless matron in the next room who was profoundly shocked, but who realised at once that if the story got out they would all be tarred by it. The only way a scandal could be avoided was to deal with the situation, and so she woke the other women along the passage and explained what had happened. Whereupon this gaggle of dowagers and debutantes, one young girl going ahead with a candle to check round every corner, carried the corpse the entire length of the house, and put him into his own bed, where he was found by his valet the following day.

Our friend had rooted out his great grandfather's diary for the same period and it just said that poor nice Mr Thing was found dead by his valet on Sunday morning. So the ruse worked and, even more miraculously, no one talked. As I listened, I remember thinking this tale will come in useful one day. The only thing I added was to make him Turkish.

MARY: She won't betray us.
CORA: I'm sure she won't. It pains me to say it, but
this morning I find that I trust a housemaid more than I
trust my own child.

She moves on, leaving Mary to shift for herself.

38 INT. BEDROOM PASSAGE. DOWNTON. DAY.

*Thomas walks along with a tray of tea and a jug of hot
shaving water. He reaches a door, gives a soft knock, waits
for a second and goes in.*

39 INT. KEMAL PAMUK'S BEDROOM. DOWNTON. DAY.

*Thomas closes the door and turns. The body lies where the
women left it, eyes open, staring. We hear an ear-splitting
crash. Thomas has dropped the lot.*

40 INT. HALL. DOWNTON. DAY.

*Mary descends the stairs. She is dressed simply, in a white
shirt and a black skirt, traces of red around her eyes. The
dining room door opens and Evelyn Napier comes out.*

EVELYN: I imagine you've heard what's happened?
MARY: Yes.
EVELYN: Terrible thing. Awful. *Ghastly* for your
parents. I don't suppose I shall ever make it up to
them.
MARY: It's not your fault.
EVELYN: I brought him here. If it isn't my fault, whose
is it?

Mary would rather not answer this, so she doesn't.

EVELYN (CONT'D): Breakfast's almost finished. Shall I
tell someone you're down?
MARY: No, thank you. I had a tray in my room.
EVELYN: My mother never used to allow trays for unmarried
girls.

He is trying to be light and pleasant.

MARY: Nor does mine. As a rule.

Her tone is sadder and heavier than his.

EVELYN: I was wondering if you might show me the gardens
before I go? We could get some fresh air?
MARY: I won't, if you'll forgive me. I ought to stay and
help Mama.
EVELYN: Of course.

She cannot lift her spirits, no matter how she tries.

EVELYN (CONT'D): I am so sorry about all this. I should
never have inflicted him on you in the first place.

Mary has to defend her chosen lover.

MARY: Please don't say that. We were glad to have him
here. Very glad.
EVELYN: Lynch's taken a message to the local… They'll be
along to collect him in an hour or so. I'll wait until
that's done.

Mary looks at the ground.

EVELYN (CONT'D): I've told your father I'll deal with the
Embassy. There won't be any more annoyance for you.
MARY: Thank you.

Her voice is not steady.

EVELYN: Actually, he was a terribly nice fellow. I wish
you could have known him better. I took him on as a
duty, but I liked him more and more, the longer I knew
him.

*At last Mary looks up, her face streaming with tears, and
Evelyn realises that he is preaching to the converted.*

EVELYN (CONT'D): Perhaps you saw his qualities for
yourself.

*At this Mary breaks down and runs, sobbing, back upstairs.
Evelyn looks after her, speaking under his breath.*

EVELYN (CONT'D): Which, obviously, you did.

Bringing him to an unwelcome conclusion.

41 INT. KITCHEN. DOWNTON. DAY.

William and Thomas, Anna and Gwen have carried down the remains of breakfast, which now they unload with Daisy.

WILLIAM: I had an uncle who went like that. Finished his cocoa, closed his book and fell back dead on the pillow.
THOMAS: I don't think Mr Pamuk bothered with cocoa much, or books. He had other interests.
WILLIAM: I meant you can go just like that. With no reason.
GWEN: That's why you should treat every day as if it were your last.
THOMAS: Well, we couldn't criticise Mr Pamuk where that's concerned.

Something in this disturbs Anna and Daisy.

DAISY: What do you mean?
THOMAS: Nothing. Careful with that.

He picks up his empty tray and goes, followed by William.

GWEN: You're very quiet.
ANNA: There's a corpse upstairs. What would you like me to do? Sing?

Gwen leaves the others to it, walking out into the passage, when she hears her name whispered from the staircase.

SYBIL (V.O.): Gwen?

She looks up. Sybil is standing there with a newspaper.

GWEN: Your ladyship?

Sybil produces a newspaper, open, with a box circled.

SYBIL: I saw this. It came out yesterday. Look. It's for a secretary at a new firm in Thirsk. See.
GWEN: I don't understand. How did you know?

Sybil comes down to the bottom of the staircase.

SYBIL: That you wanted to leave? Carson told my father.
GWEN: And you don't mind?
SYBIL: Why should I? I think it's terrific when people make their own lives. Specially women.

They are forging a bond. Gwen overcomes her amazement and takes the newspaper, staring at a ringed box.

> GWEN: 'A suitable post for a beginner.' What does that mean?
> SYBIL: It means the wages are rock bottom but then you can apply for the next job as an experienced assistant.

Gwen understands this, as she reads.

> SYBIL (CONT'D): And you wouldn't be far from home. For your first position.
> GWEN: We'd have to wait and see if they'd give me an interview.
> SYBIL: Write to them today, and name me as your reference. I can give it without ever specifying precisely what your work here has been.
> GWEN: Is that quite honest?
> SYBIL: Later you can tell them whatever you wish, but first get the job.

She goes back towards the staircase.

> GWEN: M'lady —

Sybil turns.

> GWEN (CONT'D): Thank you.

42 EXT. GARDENS. DOWNTON. DAY.

Evelyn is walking towards Cora. He catches up with her.

> EVELYN: Lady Grantham! I've come to say goodbye. They're bringing the car round to take me to the station.
> CORA: Have you seen Lord Grantham?
> EVELYN: I have, and I've apologised for wreaking havoc on your house.

But she does not judge him harshly. It's not his fault.

> CORA: You've got everything?
> EVELYN: I think so. Your groom's been very kind in helping my chap to organise the horses. And I've taken all of Kemal's belongings.
> CORA: He's… gone now, I understand.
> EVELYN: Yes, he's gone.

Cora ponders this for a moment, as, behind them, the car comes to a halt on the gravel. William and Taylor carry out Napier's and Pamuk's luggage and strap it on the back.

> CORA: Is his mother still alive?
>
> EVELYN: I'm afraid so. Kemal used to talk of her often.
>
> CORA: I should like to write to her if you'd be kind enough to send me the address. She'll have had such hopes for him.
>
> EVELYN: Indeed.
>
> CORA: You build up your dreams for your children. And then... fate just smashes them to pieces.

Evelyn waits. He senses there is something else going on.

> CORA (CONT'D): Have you said goodbye to Mary?
>
> EVELYN: I have.
>
> CORA: Will we be seeing you here again?
>
> EVELYN: Nothing would give me more pleasure, but I'm afraid I am a little busy at the moment...

But Evelyn wants to be honest. He knows what they expected.

> EVELYN (CONT'D): I wonder if I might risk embarrassing you. Because I should like to make myself clear.
>
> CORA: Please.
>
> EVELYN: The truth is, Lady Grantham, I am not a vain man. I do not consider myself a very interesting person.

She listens without contradicting him.

> EVELYN (CONT'D): But I feel it's important that my future wife should think me so. A woman who finds me boring could never love me, and I believe marriage should be based on love. At least at the start.

Cora does not find anything dishonourable in this. *

....

* I think that what one has to remember is that the pursuance of a courtship was quite tough if you weren't getting much help from the girl. Mary can only see Evelyn Napier in contrast to her first mad passion (for Pamuk) and even when she compares him to Matthew, she's not really interested. What was difficult then was to take the conversation to a courtship level, when you had to make do with a walk in the park, or a chat on the sofa after dinner. Today, we're allowed to whisk them off to Paris for the weekend but they weren't.

CORA: Thank you for your faith in me, Mr Napier. Your instincts do you credit. Good luck to you.

She gives him her hand in forgiveness and he walks away across the wide lawn, taking Mary's future with him.

43 INT. LIBRARY. DAY.

Robert is standing by the fire, Pharaoh at his feet, when Carson comes in.

ROBERT: Did Mr Napier get off all right?
CARSON: He did, m'lord. Taylor waited to see he was safely on the train.

Robert nods.

ROBERT: And poor Mr Pamuk has been taken care of?
CARSON: We got Grassbys from Thirsk in the end. They're very good and they didn't mind coming out on a Sunday.
ROBERT: Death has no Day of Rest. Is everyone all right downstairs?
CARSON: Well, you know. He was a handsome stranger from foreign parts one minute, and the next he was as dead as a doornail. It's bound to be a shock.
ROBERT: Of course. Upstairs or down. It's been horrid for the ladies. And for the female staff, I expect.
CARSON: It's particularly hard on the younger maids.
ROBERT: Indeed. Don't let the footmen be too coarse in front of them. Thomas likes to show off, but we must have a care for feminine sensibilities. They are finer and more fragile than our own.

The two men know this at least.

END OF ACT THREE

ACT FOUR

44 INT. SERVICE STAIRCASE. DOWNTON. DAY.

Mrs Hughes comes down the service stairs, carrying boot hooks and a nightdress. She hears a groan and at the base, she sees Bates leaning on a table, sweating with pain.

MRS HUGHES: Mr Bates, I am going to have to insist that you tell me what is the matter.

He straightens up and gives an approximation of a smile.

BATES: I thought it was for Mr Carson to give me orders.
MRS HUGHES: Mr Carson's no better than any other man when it comes to illness. Now tell me what it is and I'll see what I can do.
BATES: It's nothing. Truly. I twisted my bad leg and walked on it too soon. I'll be fine in a day or two.

His manner is deceptive, but she is not entirely deceived.

MRS HUGHES: Well, if it isn't, I'm sending for the doctor.

At this moment, Anna comes along the passage, carrying a pair of shoes. Mrs Hughes holds out the hooks and dress.

MRS HUGHES (CONT'D): You left these behind in the Blue Room, when you were dressing Lady Mary for the kill.
ANNA: I'm sorry, Mrs Hughes.

Anna notices Bates's pallor.

ANNA: Are you all right?
MRS HUGHES: He is not all right and he will not tell me why.
BATES: A man's got to have some secrets.
ANNA: But he can have too many.

She looks into his eyes. He won't give in.

45 INT. DRAWING ROOM. DAY.

Cora is with her three daughters, reading and embroidering, when Violet walks in, followed by Carson.

    CARSON: The Dowager Countess —

She's already in. Carson leaves and closes the door.

    VIOLET: Is it really true? I can't believe it!
    CORA: It's true.
    VIOLET: But last night he looked so well!

She directs this at her granddaughters, without a response.

    VIOLET (CONT'D): Of course it would happen to a
    foreigner. Typical.
    MARY: Don't be ridiculous.

This earns her a sharp look.

    VIOLET: I'm not being ridiculous. No Englishman would
    dream of dying in someone else's house. Especially
    someone they didn't even *know*.*
    SYBIL: Oh Granny, even the English aren't in control of
    everything.
    VIOLET: Well, I hope we're in control of something, if
    only ourselves.
    MARY: But we're not! Don't you see that? We're not in
    control of anything at all!

....

* It is very rewarding to write for Maggie. She never misses a trick and she understands her characters in all their variety. Violet Grantham is many things, tough, snobbish and absolute in her values but she has contrasting qualities, too. Here, for example, she won't let Cora tick off Mary for being rude because she knows the girl is in a state of shock (even if she doesn't know why). In other words, in this scene, she is kind. This almost contradictory trait could seem out of character in lesser hands, but it is not because Maggie has that ability, which only great actors have, of playing different things at once, achieving a layered performance of many colours. She is also free of the compulsion to be liked, and as a result she is totally unsentimental in what she does. She can play great emotion but she is never sentimental. This ability to synthesise the contrary elements of a character makes her work permanently interesting, because it also makes her truthfully unpredictable. I admire that very much.

She has shouted and now she storms out, slamming the door.

CORA: Edith, go and tell Mary to come back at once, and apologise to her grandmother.

But for once Violet is surprisingly sympathetic.

VIOLET: No. Leave her alone. She's had a shock. We all have. Let her rest.

Edith looks at Cora who nods. Edith sits again as the door opens and William comes in with the tea tray.

VIOLET (CONT'D): Ah. Just the ticket. Nanny always said sweet tea was the thing for frayed nerves. Though why it has to be sweet I couldn't tell you.

And she sits, with a grandchild on either side.

46 INT. KITCHEN. DOWNTON. DAY.

Thomas has a hot water jug which Daisy is filling. At a basin, O'Brien uses soda to get marks out of a collar. Mrs Patmore is cooking. Gwen watches.

GWEN: What did you mean, Mr Pamuk lived each day as if it were his last?
THOMAS: What I said.
GWEN: But how did you know?
THOMAS: I can't keep William waiting. Gangway.

He has picked up the hot water jug and heads for the door, but as he passes O'Brien, she speaks under her breath.

O'BRIEN: I'll be asking the same question later. So you'd better have an answer ready.

Thomas winks at her and goes. Mrs Patmore looks over.

MRS PATMORE: Daisy, assuming you have not been hypnotised by Doctor Mesmer, could you oblige me by cutting up them onions? Now?
DAISY: Yes, Mrs Patmore.

Daisy is trembling, knowing her great secret.

MRS PATMORE: Where have you hidden the flour? I can't see it anywhere.
DAISY: It's just there, Mrs Patmore.

MRS PATMORE: Well, fetch it to me then. You're all in a daze today.

Daisy does as she is told. But something in the girl's demeanour has attracted O'Brien's interest.

47 INT. DRAWING ROOM. CRAWLEY HOUSE. EVE.

Isobel is writing. Matthew is with her.

MATTHEW: Do you think we should have gone up there? To see how they are?
ISOBEL: I sent a note, but I thought I'd just be in the way. Why?
MATTHEW: I thought Mary was rather struck with him last night, didn't you?
ISOBEL: It must have been frightful for all of them. But there it is. In the midst of life we are in death.
MATTHEW: On second thoughts, perhaps you were right to stay away.

48 INT. CORA'S BEDROOM. NIGHT.

O'Brien is brushing Cora's hair. Cora is dressed in her night clothes and her bed has been turned down.

CORA: What a horrible, horrible day.
O'BRIEN: You'll be glad to see the end of it.
CORA: Poor Mr Pamuk. I keep thinking of his parents. He had such a brilliant future ahead of him.
O'BRIEN: Death is all we can rely on.

She starts to plait Cora's hair for sleeping.

O'BRIEN: I suppose Mr Napier will have to manage everything.
CORA: I suppose he will.
O'BRIEN: We all thought him a very nice gentleman.
CORA: Yes, he is nice.
O'BRIEN: Will we be seeing a lot of him?

Cora knows what the maid is trying to find out, but it is going to become clear soon. After a beat, she speaks.

CORA: I don't expect so, no.
O'BRIEN: Because we rather hoped Lady Mary might have taken a shine to him.

CORA: It seems not.

O'BRIEN: Oh, well. There are plenty more fish in the sea than ever came out of it.*

Cora stands, weary and sad, and removes her dressing gown.

CORA: I hope there are, O'Brien. I certainly hope there are.

As she goes to the bed, O'Brien watches her.

49 INT. KITCHEN PASSAGE. NIGHT.

Mrs Hughes is walking along when Carson appears. He is carrying a candle.

MRS HUGHES: Are you turning in?

CARSON: Not quite yet. But you go.

She starts to leave.

CARSON (CONT'D): And, Mrs Hughes. I know some of them missed church today. But so did the family. I don't want anyone reprimanded.

MRS HUGHES: I agree. It's been unsettling for everyone. Goodnight, Mr Carson.

She goes one way, he goes the other.

50 INT. BEDROOM PASSAGE. DOWNTON. NIGHT.

Carson is walking down a passage, still carrying his candle. He opens a door and goes into Kemal's bedroom.

51 INT. KEMAL PAMUK'S BEDROOM. NIGHT.

The room is tidy, the bed is stripped, with the blankets folded at one end. He looks around and is about to leave.

MARY (V.O.): Are you looking for something?

....

* Another on-going theme in the series is the sense that the servants are always aware of what's going on and this is truthful. One thing one can say about this world: the servants always knew far more about the family than the family knew about the servants.

He holds up the candle. She is sitting by the window.

CARSON: Your Ladyship?
MARY: Are you looking for something?
CARSON: I just wanted to make sure the room had been
tidied up after the — after the people had left.

She nods, standing and staring at the neat, empty bed.

MARY: Life can be terribly unfair, can't it?
CARSON: It certainly can.
MARY: Everything seems so golden one minute, and then
turns to ashes the next… Can I ask you a question,
Carson?

This Mary is a gentler person than we have seen before.

MARY (CONT'D): Have you ever felt your life was somehow…
slipping away? And there was nothing you could do to
stop it?
CARSON: I think everyone feels that at one time or
another.

But Mary is almost talking to herself.

MARY: The odd thing is I feel, for the first time really,
I understand what it is to be happy. It's just that I
know I won't be.
CARSON: Oh, don't say that, m'lady. Don't raise the
white flag quite yet.

She looks bewildered by his response.

CARSON (CONT'D): You will still be mistress of Downton.
Old Lady Grantham hasn't given up the fight, not by a
long chalk.
MARY: Oh, that. I wasn't thinking about that.
CARSON: And if I may say so, your ladyship, you are still
very young.
MARY: Am I? I don't feel it.

*She smiles, as if to make a joke of it, but Carson is moved
by her sorrow to make a declaration.*

CARSON: We're all behind you, m'lady. The staff. We're
all on your side.
MARY: Thank you, Carson. You've always been so kind to
me. Always. From when I was quite a little girl. Why
is that?

CARSON: Even a butler has his favourites, m'lady.*
MARY: Does he? I'm glad.
ANNA (V.O.): Lady Mary?

The voice is out in the corridor, a little way away. They are silent until Anna comes in, holding a candle.

ANNA (CONT'D): Oh, your ladyship, I thought you might be in —

She has seen Carson, which is a surprise to her.

MARY: Carson and I were just making sure that everything was shipshape and Bristol fashion.

She moves to the door. It is time for the chink to close and class values to reassert themselves.

....

* It was necessary for Mary to be allowed to show her response to the death of Pamuk. Otherwise she would have seemed too hard. And she knows that Carson is always on her side. It wouldn't really matter if she told him she'd murdered their Turkish guest because Carson would immediately justify it, so she is safe in revealing herself. The children of a great house, when they grew up with the servants, tended to have a slightly different relationship with them than people who arrived as adults, and there are many stories of servants forming special bonds with the children of the family. I remember a chap telling me how he was the favourite of his grandfather's first footman who would give him sweets and carry him piggy-back. And before one detects anything sinister in this, I am sure they were, for the most part, friendships born of a perfectly normal human need to have someone to be fond of. In those days, children were freer than their parents to roam below stairs. Bonds would develop and, especially where the servant was unmarried and childless, they could be very strong. Carson loves Mary like a daughter, which she knows and relies on, because he is much less critical than her own parents.

Children in a series are extremely difficult to manage. As they age, you would need to produce a new child roughly every three episodes. This means we can't explore the different relationship that children would have had with the household, which is rather a shame. For instance in proper households they would have called the butler 'Mr Carson'. It would have been considered ill bred for them to call him 'Carson'. They would go down to the kitchens and lounge around, begging the cook to give them the lickings out of the bowl and getting under everyone's feet. I was trying to suggest some of this, and Mary's relationship with Carson is the nearest I could get without having a child in the cast.

MARY (CONT'D): And it is. Goodnight, Carson.
CARSON: Goodnight, m'lady.

She and Anna go. And, after a moment, so does the butler.

52 INT. SERVANTS' HALL. DOWNTON. DAY.

The bells are ringing and the servants peel away.

MRS HUGHES: That's Lady Mary.
ANNA: Send not to know for whom the bell tolls. It tolls
for me.

*With a wry smile she stands and goes. The others leave until
Bates is alone at the table. He starts to move, then sits
back with a groan. Biting his lip, he forces himself up and
hobbles off. From a doorway, Mrs Hughes is watching.*

53 INT. ROBERT'S DRESSING ROOM. DAY.

Bates, in some pain, is helping Robert finish dressing.

ROBERT: What a business! I still can't get over it.
And of all the men on earth — I mean, he looked so fit.
Did you see any signs?
BATES: I didn't have much of a chance to study the
gentleman.
ROBERT: You don't suppose there was something sinister in
it? Every day the papers warn us of German spies, and
they did say his presence was essential for peace in
Albania.
BATES: I doubt that, m'lord. Anyone wanting to poison
his food would have to get past Mrs Patmore.
ROBERT: Blimey, that's a thought. Unless of course she's
a spy herself.

He laughs but Bates doesn't.

ROBERT (CONT'D): No, you're quite right. It's not funny.
Not funny at all.

He stands for Bates to brush his shoulders.

ROBERT (CONT'D): Anyway, I'd better write to the Turkish
Ambassador —

He has glanced at Bates and is silenced by the man's face.

ROBERT (CONT'D): Bates, I wish you'd tell me what's
wrong. You'll be in no trouble. I only want to help.
BATES: I know that, your lordship, and I'm grateful.
Truly. But there's nothing I need help with.

Robert does not try again.

54 INT.   BEDROOM PASSAGE.   DAY.

Robert comes out of his dressing room. Mrs Hughes is there.

ROBERT: Good morning... Mrs Hughes,
MRS HUGHES: Good morning, my lord.
ROBERT: I wonder if you —

He hesitates, glancing back at the dressing room door.

ROBERT (CONT'D): Never mind.

He walks on but she continues to the door.

55 INT.   ROBERT'S DRESSING ROOM.   DAY.

Bates is bent over in agony. He grips the bedstead.

MRS HUGHES: Now will you kindly explain what in heaven is
going on?

*Bates looks up and tries to smile as he stands but the pain
is too great and he gasps.*

BATES: I'm perfectly well, Mrs Hughes. A bit stiff,
that's all.

But this time she shuts the door and sits on the bed.

MRS HUGHES: Just so long as you know I'm not leaving
until you tell me.

He stares at her for a moment. Then he sighs.

BATES: I hope you have a strong stomach.

*She waits as, slowly, he pulls up the leg of his trouser.
The savage, straightening implement is cutting sharply into
his flesh, which is mottled and bleeding and bruised, black
and red and blue, the length of his calf and ankle.*

MRS HUGHES: Oh, my God.

When Bates looks up, to his surprise he finds she's crying.*

56 EXT. GARDENS. DOWNTON. DAY.

Mary is walking on her own when she looks up. Matthew is coming across the lawn towards her.

MATTHEW: Cousin Mary?
MARY: Hello. Are we expecting you?
MATTHEW: No, but I wanted to see you. I looked for you yesterday at church.
MARY: I wasn't feeling up to it. None of us were. Shouldn't you be at work?

MATTHEW: I've sent a message that I'm coming in late.

She smiles a little. This means he has come to see her.

MARY: So, why are you here?
MATTHEW: Only to say that I was very sorry about what happened.

She looks at him. What does he suspect? Nothing of course. How could he suspect anything? And yet…

MARY: We didn't know him at all, really. But…
MATTHEW: Even so. It must have been a horrible shock.
MARY: Yes.
MATTHEW: And he seemed a nice fellow.
MARY: He was. A very 'nice fellow'.

She mimics his words but she feels his understanding.

MATTHEW: So, if there's anything I can do, please ask.

She studies his face and sees his generosity.

MARY: There isn't. But thank you.

....

* I am often asked for favourite scenes in an episode or a series, but this remains one of my all-time favourites. The revelation of Bates's pain, not just physical but emotional, the absolute sympathy and understanding from the woman who knows him, but does not know him, all this is expressed here with the most extraordinary economy by Phyllis Logan and Brendan Coyle in a deeply moving exchange. Really marvellous work.

57 EXT. PARK. DOWNTON. DAY.

At one end of the lake Mrs Hughes and Bates stand solemnly.

BATES: Well, here goes.

MRS HUGHES: Do you think we ought to say a few words?

BATES: What? Good riddance?

MRS HUGHES: That and your promise.

BATES: Very well. I promise I will never again try to cure myself. I will spend my life happily as the butt of others' jokes and I will never mind them.

MRS HUGHES: We all carry scars, Mr Bates, inside or out, and we must all put up with them as best we can. You're no different to the rest of us. Remember that.

BATES: I will try to. That I do promise.

So saying, he bends to pick up the hideous instrument of torture and throws it far out into the water.

MRS HUGHES: And good riddance!

The brace sinks out of sight beneath the surface.

58 EXT. KITCHEN YARD. DAY.

O'Brien is with Thomas, who gestures with his cigarette.

O'BRIEN: So he definitely went in?

THOMAS: I saw him walk through the door.

O'BRIEN: But you don't know if he went back to his own room.

THOMAS: Yes, I do. 'Cos I was the one who found him there the next day.

O'BRIEN: What I mean is: You don't know he went back under his own steam.

THOMAS: I suppose not. But how else would he have done it?

O'BRIEN: That's what they call the Big Question.

A thought occurs to him.

THOMAS: I don't want to get into any trouble over this.

O'BRIEN: Don't worry. You won't. Your secret's safe with me.

END OF EPISODE THREE

EPISODE FOUR

ACT ONE

1 EXT. DOWNTON VILLAGE. DAY.

A hammer smashes down on to a peg in the ground. Men are erecting tents for the stalls. A helter skelter is being tested, while a steam-run pianola fills the Green with raucous music. It is a modest affair, really, but it seems exciting in this village. Anna, Bates and Gwen watch.*

> GWEN: When does it open?
> BATES: Tomorrow afternoon.
> GWEN: Let's get up a party for the evening if Mrs Hughes lets us. After we've had our dinner.
> ANNA: You're right. It doesn't come often and it doesn't stay long.
> GWEN: And what about you, Mr Bates?
> BATES: I don't see why not.

Anna sees Mary loitering on the edge of the Green.

> ANNA: You go on ahead. I'll see you back at the house.

2 EXT. DOWNTON VILLAGE. DAY.

Mary is watching the activity when Anna joins her.

> ANNA: Is everything all right, m'lady?

Which jerks Mary out of her reverie.

> MARY: What? Oh, yes. I was collecting something from Doctor Clarkson for Mama, and I stopped to see how they were getting on.
> ANNA: Has she recovered from…

....

* It was around now that the format of the show was beginning to be settled and, without its becoming an absolute law, we usually have some kind of event, a big dinner party or a hunt or a shoot or a funfair or a trial, at the heart of the episode. Originally this script was written without one which was why we first became aware of the fact that, coincidentally, all the earlier episodes had been centred on a resonant happening. So I went back to the drawing board and put in the funfair, which now plays through the whole of it.

She lifts her eyebrows slightly as they start to walk away.

MARY: If you think she'll *ever* recover from carrying the body of Mr Pamuk from one side of the house to the other, then you don't know her at all.
ANNA: Well, I didn't mean 'recover' exactly. Just, get past it.
MARY: She won't do that, either. When she dies they'll cut her open and find it engraved on her heart.
ANNA: What about you? What about your heart?
MARY: Haven't you heard? I don't have a heart. Everyone knows that.*
ANNA: Not me, m'lady. Still, at least you were lucky with... you know.

Mary instinctively lays her hand on her stomach.

MARY: Oh, yes. I was lucky there. That's me. Lucky as a lark.

But these two are friends now. Across the Green, Isobel and Matthew also watch the fair workers. They wave.

ANNA: I'm glad you think better of Mr Crawley, these days.
MARY: Who says I do?

Mary smiles as they walk on.

3 INT. LIBRARY. DOWNTON. DAY.

Robert is working, with Pharaoh at his feet. Carson enters.

CARSON: You wanted to see the new chauffeur, m'lord.
ROBERT: Yes, indeed. Please bring him in.

Carson nods and a young man, in his thirties, appears. This is Tom Branson. He is attractive and polite. Carson leaves.

....

* After the Pamuk affair Mary has become essentially a different person. She is no longer the cold Ice Queen. She has, in the process, acquired a dimension of physicality which is interesting and good, but it has opened her up and made her more vulnerable than she was before. Michelle understood all that completely of course, and played it very well.

ROBERT: Come in, come in. Good to see you again…
Branson, isn't it?
BRANSON: That's right, your lordship.
ROBERT: I hope they've shown you where everything is?
And we've delivered whatever we promised at the
interview?
BRANSON: Certainly, m'lord.
ROBERT: Good.

Robert finds him rather an interesting character.

ROBERT: How did you first come to be a chauffeur?
BRANSON: My father was a tenant of Mrs Delderfield's and
I was apprenticed to the chauffeur there. But he'd been
a coachman and he didn't have much feeling for cars. In
the end, the mistress asked me to take over.
ROBERT: Won't you miss Ireland?
BRANSON: Ireland, yes, but not the job. She was a nice
lady, but she only had one car and she wouldn't let me
drive it over twenty miles an hour. So it was a bit…
well, boring, so to speak.

Which makes Robert laugh. Branson looks around.

BRANSON: You've got a wonderful library.

The remark does not offend Robert but it does surprise him.

ROBERT: Are you interested in books?
BRANSON: Not in books, as such, so much as what's in
them.

A reading chauffeur? Unusual. Robert thinks for a moment.

ROBERT: You're very welcome to borrow books, if you wish.
BRANSON: Really, m'lord?

He is astonished and delighted. Robert nods.

ROBERT: There's a ledger over there that I make everyone
use, even my daughters. Carson can tell you when the
room's empty.
BRANSON: Do all the servants enjoy the same privilege?
ROBERT: I suppose they could, although I doubt they'd
avail themselves of it. Carson and Mrs Hughes sometimes
take a novel or two. What are your interests?
BRANSON: History and politics, mainly.

ROBERT: Heavens.* Well, when you come back, you should
start looking in that section, there.†

Carson has reappeared at the door.

ROBERT: Branson's going to borrow some books. He has my
permission.
CARSON: Very good, m'lord.

Does Carson approve? Probably not. He looks at Branson.

....

* The Irish troubles were a hot topic throughout this period, much more even
than in the 1970s. We remember the Suffragettes and the emergence of the
unions, but in fact if we'd been alive at that time the front page would have
been dominated by Ireland, so here Branson is bringing those troubles to
Downton. Because, by this stage, the show had developed its own method of
dealing with these things. We don't usually introduce famous characters like
Lloyd George or Curzon or De Valera, but we allow our characters to refer to
political events and scandals and things that were happening.

To achieve this, to make the Crawleys and their servants aware of what
was going on, I had the idea of bringing in an Irish chauffeur who was
political and a republican. He is not active, in the sense of being a freedom
fighter, but he is energetically pro-independence for Ireland. It seemed to me
that such a chap would allow us to talk about the topic without its seeming
contrived. I also thought – although only vaguely when I was writing this
episode – that we might have a cross-class romance at some point and so it
seemed a good idea that he should be young and handsome, whether or not
we actually did anything with it. The actor who plays Branson (Allen Leech)
had worked with me and our producer, Liz Trubridge, on a film I wrote and
directed, called *From Time to Time*. He impressed us both and he had a kind
of gritty, very real sort of good looks, as opposed to the face of a film star,
which is more useful in this kind of drama.

† I was sorry they cut this section, when Robert invites Branson to borrow
books. It was taken from *Below Stairs* by Margaret Powell, whose memoirs of
a life in service have just been reissued, for which I wrote the preface. She
takes a fairly jaundiced view of the world but she was operating in smaller
households than Downton, where she was only one of two or three servants
and they worked like dogs. But, once, she does go to a grander house on a
temporary basis to replace a cook, and there all the servants were encouraged
to borrow books from the library. When I read it, I thought it was rather a
nice touch and quite Robert'ish. Since I knew it was based on truth I was
looking forward to being attacked but in the event it was cut. Naturally,
Carson can't bear the idea.

BRANSON: Is that all, m'lord?
ROBERT: It is. Off you go and good luck.

Branson goes, leaving master and butler alone.

ROBERT: Well. An Irishman with an interest in politics…
Are we mad?
CARSON: I could always bring in fire drill for the staff.
ROBERT: Thank you, Carson.

They share the moment.

ROBERT (CONT'D): He seems quite a bright spark after poor
old Taylor.

Carson is not prepared to volunteer an opinion. Yet.

ROBERT: I always thought he was happy. Why did he want
to leave?
CARSON: I believe it was *Mrs* Taylor, m'lord. She felt
cut off. She wanted to live in a town.
ROBERT: But running a tea shop? I cannot feel that'll
make for a very restful retirement, can you?
CARSON: I would rather be put to death, m'lord.
ROBERT: Quite so. Thank you, Carson.

With a glance at the dog, he returns to his letter.

4 EXT. THE GARDENS. DOWNTON. DAY.

*Cora and Violet are together, drinking tea at a table under a
tree.* *

VIOLET: What about some house parties?
CORA: She's been asked to one next month by Lady Anne
McNair.

....

* This scene had originally been set in the drawing room, but the episode was
largely made up of interiors and so the director understandably took it
outside because the weather was so lovely. But I'm afraid it didn't seem to me
believable that these two would have tea in a place where they were not able
to sit in the shade. Those women avoided the sun like the plague at any time
and just a little hat would not have answered. If they'd found a summer
house it would have been fine, but to have them sitting out in the open, as
they do, made the scene feel modern and odd, to me anyway.

VIOLET: A terrible idea. She doesn't know anyone under a hundred. Find her a house with an unmarried son.
CORA: The Tenbys?
VIOLET: The eldest boy's taken. It was announced last week. Of course, most of the good ones are.
CORA: I might send her over to my aunt. She could get to know New York.
VIOLET: I don't think things are quite that desperate. Poor Mary. She's been very down in the mouth lately.
CORA: She was very upset by the death of poor Mr Pamuk.
VIOLET: Why? It's been three months.

She's genuinely puzzled. Then she remembers herself.

VIOLET (CONT'D): It was sad. But she didn't know him, and one can't go to pieces at the death of every foreigner. We'd all be in a state of collapse whenever we opened a newspaper. Of course, Mary's main difficulty is that her situation is unresolved.

But Cora only looks at her and does not weigh in.

VIOLET (CONT'D): I mean, is she an heiress or isn't she? If only it could be resolved.
CORA: Maybe it *is* resolved. How many times have you written to lawyers only to get the same answer? The entail's unbreakable. Mary cannot inherit. To be fair to Mr Murray he said it from the start.
VIOLET: The truth is, no London lawyer wants to challenge him. They feel they need Murray's permission.

But she is thinking hard.

VIOLET (CONT'D): What we need is a lawyer who is decent and honour bound to look into it, whatever Murray might say. And I… I think perhaps I know just the man.
CORA: I'd hate to go behind Robert's back.

Violet gives her a scornful look.

VIOLET: That's a scruple no successful wife can afford.

5 INT. DRAWING ROOM. CRAWLEY HOUSE. DAY.

Molesley is clearing away Isobel's and Matthew's tea.

ISOBEL: Thank you, Molesley.
MATTHEW: Are you going to the fair while it's here?

MOLESLEY: I shouldn't think so, sir. But I don't mind
it. I like the music.*

Isobel has noticed that his hands are red and sore.

ISOBEL: Goodness. What's happened to your hands?
MOLESLEY: It's nothing, ma'am.
ISOBEL: But it looks very painful.
MOLESLEY: Oh, no, ma'am. Irritating more than painful.
ISOBEL: Are you using anything new? To polish the
silver? Or the shoes?
MOLESLEY: No.
ISOBEL: May I?

She takes his hand and peers at it. Molesley looks awkward.

MATTHEW: Leave him alone, Mother.

Isobel pays no attention.

ISOBEL: It looks like Erysipelas. You must have cut
yourself.
MOLESLEY: Not that I'm aware of.
ISOBEL: We'll walk round to the hospital tomorrow.
MOLESLEY: Really, ma'am…
ISOBEL: I insist.

Matthew and Molesley know there will be no reprieve.

6 EXT. COURTYARD. DOWNTON. NIGHT.

Bates comes out to find William loitering in the shadows.

BATES: A penny for your thoughts.
WILLIAM: You'd be wasting your money.
BATES: It's mine to waste.
WILLIAM: I was just wondering why we get so drawn to
people who have no interest in us. What's nature playing
at?
BATES: If you find the answer to that, lad, you'll put
the poets out of business.

....

* Molesley had acquired by this stage a kind of bruised pride that is
endlessly entertaining. He is not exactly prim, but always slightly on the
defensive.

Which makes William smile a little sadly.

> WILLIAM: But you can't make someone love you, can you?
> BATES: No. And you can't make them *not* love you, either.
> Which can be just as hard.
> WILLIAM: I wouldn't know about that.
> BATES: Not yet, maybe. But you will.

7 INT. KITCHEN. DOWNTON. DAY.

It is a new day. Anna blows her nose. Mrs Patmore is cooking.

> MRS PATMORE: You've got a cold, I want you out of here.
> ANNA: Blimey. I'm beginning to feel like the Ancient
> Mariner.

*Mrs Hughes comes through the door. Anna is pouring some
water from the earthenware filter.*

> MRS HUGHES: Anna, there you are. You know I'm out
> tonight? Because I don't want to come home to any
> surprises.
> MRS PATMORE: That'll be the day.
> ANNA: We thought we might go to the fair later. You'd
> like that, wouldn't you, Daisy?
> MRS PATMORE: You ought to go. She's been that down in
> the mouth, since the death of poor Mr Pamuk —
> DAISY: Don't say that.*
> MRS PATMORE: Well, she has.
> ANNA: We could all walk down after the servants' dinner,
> if —

But she silences herself with another sneeze.

> MRS PATMORE: You won't be walking anywhere.

She glances over to Mrs Hughes.

> MRS PATMORE (CONT'D): She's got minutes to live by the
> sound of it.
> ANNA: It's just a bit of a cold, but —

Again, the sneezing takes over.

....

* Of course the servants don't know why Daisy is 'down in the mouth', but the
audience does. I think it's always interesting to have moments where the
audience knows more than the people on the screen.

MRS HUGHES: Go to bed at once. We can't have you spraying everyone with germs. I'll bring up a Beecham's Powder.
ANNA: Yes, Mrs Hughes.

Anna leaves.

MRS HUGHES: Right. If there's anything you want to ask me, it'll have to be before I go.
MRS PATMORE: What would I want to ask you? I am preparing a meal for Lord and Lady Grantham, and the girls. No one is visiting. No one is staying. What do I need to ask?

Mrs Hughes is not looking for a fight.

MRS HUGHES: Well, that's settled then.

She leaves. Mrs Patmore turns to her resident victim.

MRS PATMORE: What is it?
DAISY: Only I'd rather you didn't mention Mr Pamuk, not by name.

She puts a pot on the draining board

MRS PATMORE: You're an odd one and no mistake. And that pot is not clean. I can tell it from here. Do it again.

Daisy looks at the pot. It looks clean to her.

8 INT. COTTAGE HOSPITAL. DAY.

Isobel and Molesley are with a nurse.

NURSE: I'm afraid Doctor Clarkson's out, delivering a baby. We don't know when he'll be back.
ISOBEL: No matter. If you'll just open the store cupboard, I can easily find what I need.
NURSE: Well, I…
ISOBEL: You can tell the Doctor that you opened the cupboard for the Chairman of the Board. I assure you he will not raise the *slightest* objection.

9 INT. HOSPITAL STORE ROOM. DAY.

Isobel finds the bottle she is looking for.

ISOBEL (CONT'D): This should do it. Tincture of Steel. Ten drops in water, three times a day.

She hands the bottle to him and next she takes out a jar.

ISOBEL (CONT'D): And this is Solution of Nitrate of
Silver. Rub a little in, morning and night.
MOLESLEY: How long before it's better?
ISOBEL: Erysipelas is very hard to cure. We should be
able to reduce the symptoms but that may be all we can
manage. Oh, and you must wear gloves at all times.
MOLESLEY: I couldn't wait at table in gloves. I'd look
like a footman.*
ISOBEL: You may have to.

This is nothing to her, but for him, it's terrible news.

ISOBEL (CONT'D): The tincture and the salve will help.
Try them for a week and we'll see. But I cannot promise
a cure in the near future.

10 INT. MATTHEW'S OFFICE. RIPON. DAY.

Matthew is working in this modest office. A clerk looks in.

CLERK: Someone to see you, Mr Crawley.
MATTHEW: There's nothing in my diary.
CLERK: It's Lady Grantham.
MATTHEW: Well, in that case show her in at once.

He stands walking round the desk.

MATTHEW: Cousin Cora, to what do I owe —

....

* This is one of my favourite lines, which counters a perennial error, when
costumiers put a butler in gloves, as you see in many, many period shows.
Butlers never wore gloves. The reason was really that they never handled the
plates, but it was also a question of status. And footmen only wore gloves to
serve at table. On television you see them carrying suitcases in gloves,
walking down the lawn in gloves, when it was simply to wait at table. An odd
detail, which we did write in originally, was that they didn't wear them at
shooting lunches. Except in very, very grand houses, they would normally
have been in outside clothes. A reference for all this is a film called *The
Yellow Rolls-Royce*, directed by Anthony ('Puff') Asquith, son of the Prime
Minister, the first Earl of Oxford and Asquith. Puff Asquith must be one of
the very few directors in film history who grew up with a butler. In the film
the butler is never seen wearing gloves so I always quote this as an eyewitness
account.

He stops dead.   Violet stands before him, filling the room.

VIOLET: I hope I am not a disappointment.

11 INT.   MRS HUGHES'S SITTING ROOM.   DOWNTON.   DAY.

*Mrs Hughes faces O'Brien across a table, on which is a hat.
O'Brien looks contemptuously at the cheap headgear.*

MRS HUGHES: I thought it might be nice to cheer it up a
bit.

O'BRIEN: Easier said than done.

MRS HUGHES: Perhaps with a flower, or a bit of veil or
something?

O'BRIEN: I can find you a veil if you like.   I hope
you're not expecting me to do it.

MRS HUGHES: Not if you're busy, of course.

O'BRIEN: Good.

She turns to go.   Mrs Hughes decides to punish her rudeness.*

MRS HUGHES (CONT'D): And Miss O'Brien, I've sent Anna to
bed with a cold, so I need you to manage the young
ladies.

....

* O'Brien has less back story than some. We know she was one of several
siblings, and a little more is revealed in the second series, but she has self-
knowledge. When she looks in the glass in the last episode and says: 'Sarah
O'Brien, this is not who you are', there is a sense of the complexity of this
woman. I believe that she revels not in nastiness but in power which is why
she treats Cora as she does. For a servant in a large household the
opportunities to be powerful were limited, and the power of a lady's maid
was principally in manipulating her mistress. I had several purposes for the
character of O'Brien. I wanted to demonstrate, as I have often said, that
servants always knew more about the family than the family knew about
the servants. But I also wanted to show that one can see someone every day
and not know their true self. If they are a good performer one can be
completely deceived. I've witnessed this with film stars and toffs and
millionaires who can apparently be taken in by fairly horrible associates and
never know it. If, socially, you're a great prize it is hard to keep reminding
yourself that people will only be showing you their nicest side. So, here,
Cora does not see through O'Brien and she talks of how fond O'Brien is of
her, which is not true, at least not yet. O'Brien only becomes fond of Cora
out of guilt, but before the guilt she's not fond of anyone in that house
except possibly Thomas.

O'BRIEN: What? All three of them? I'm not an octopus.
Why can't Gwen do it?
MRS HUGHES: Because she is not a lady's maid.*
O'BRIEN: And I am not a slave.
MRS HUGHES: Just do it, Miss O'Brien. *Just do it!*

Her sudden, enraged shout drives the other woman away.

END OF ACT ONE

ACT TWO

12 INT. MATTHEW'S OFFICE. RIPON. DAY.

Matthew is at his desk. Across from him sits Violet.

VIOLET: But surely you're willing to try?
MATTHEW: Of course. But I doubt I'll find anything
Murray has missed.

....

* It was not uncommon for the head housemaid to have duties as a lady's maid. In fact for the daughters of a house to be maided by the head housemaid was quite ordinary because it was not considered appropriate that a woman should be solely employed to maintain a young girl's appearance. There were exceptions to this of course, and when the girl turned eighteen, she might be allowed her own maid. Sometimes nannies would stay on and seamlessly develop from nanny into lady's maid.

If a housemaid had ambitions beyond simply marrying a farmer when she was twenty-five, which was the most ordinary route, then the two jobs that stood at the head of the ladder were lady's maid and housekeeper. Both of these would have started as a housemaid. In some households, if they liked a particular maid, they might send her away for a course in hairdressing, or the woman herself might pay for some training, which would enhance the chances of getting a good job. The point of all this is to remind the audience that service, in those days, could be a real career. And if you were a top lady's maid, a top butler, a top cook you had skills that might eventually take you beyond service, into the catering trade, for example, even possibly running your own hotel, as many did.

VIOLET: I will pay you the compliment that I do not believe you wish to inherit just because nobody's investigated properly.*

MATTHEW: No, but —

VIOLET: Nor can Murray accuse you of making trouble, when you are the one to suffer most from a discovery.

MATTHEW: You're right that I don't wish to benefit, at Mary's expense, from an ignorance of the law.

VIOLET: Thank you. I knew you'd say that. Putting it bluntly, do you think Robert has thrown in the towel, prematurely?

She turns her body and her whole chair swings round.

VIOLET (CONT'D): Good heavens, what am I sitting on?†

MATTHEW: A swivel chair.

VIOLET: Oh, another modern brainwave?

MATTHEW: Not very modern. They were invented by Thomas Jefferson.

VIOLET: Why does every day involve a fight with an American?

MATTHEW: I'll fetch a different one.

VIOLET: No, no, no, no. I'm a good sailor.

She looks at him, firmly, waiting for his answer.

MATTHEW: It will depend on the exact terms of the entail and of the deed of gift when Cousin Cora's money was transferred to the estate.

VIOLET: That is all I ask. To understand the *exact* terms.

It is hard for Matthew not to quake in his shoes.

....

* Violet is not a fool. She is a good judge of character, and although she's quite waspish with him, she knows that Matthew will do what she wants because his own sense of honour will force him to. He will be far more scrupulous than an ordinary lawyer, who might skim it for the fees, without taking any trouble. Matthew must be quite, quite sure there is no doubt about his right to inherit. In that she has judged him correctly.

† This, and the later line about being a good sailor, were inventions of Shelagh Stephenson's, and they really make me laugh. I embellished it because I discovered that the swivel chair was invented by Thomas Jefferson.

13 INT. MRS HUGHES'S SITTING ROOM. DOWNTON. DAY.

Mrs Patmore barges in.

MRS PATMORE: Mrs Hughes, I must protest!

MRS HUGHES: What is it, this time?

MRS PATMORE: When I ask for self-raising flour I mean that it should be self-raising. I do not add the words as a frivolity to amuse myself.

MRS HUGHES: And?

MRS PATMORE: You gave me plain flour, so I have a day's baking to throw out unless I am to serve his lordship with a plate of bricks!

MRS HUGHES: Why didn't you check it was right?

MRS PATMORE: Now, don't start blaming me! Of course, if I were allowed a key of my own to the store cupboard, as any sensible person would give me —*

MRS HUGHES: *Enough!*

Her shout has succeeded in silencing the angry cook.

MRS HUGHES (CONT'D): I will bring the flour.

MRS PATMORE: See that you do.

She goes. Mrs Hughes rests her forehead on the table.

14 INT. SERVANTS' HALL. DOWNTON. DAY.

The staff are having tea. William is with Bates.

WILLIAM: Is Daisy going to the fair tonight? With the others?

BATES: Why don't you ask her? She needs taking out of herself.

....

* As I have said elsewhere, one of the great bones of contention in most of these houses was that the housekeepers had the key to the store cupboard, but the cooks did not. If they wanted something they had to ask the housekeeper and it would be given to them. Many cooks saw the custom as a lack of faith, as if they could not be trusted. The defence of it was that if more than one person had keys it would be impossible to keep a proper record of what was in store, of what was running out and what was not. The housekeeper did all the ordering and so that was the logic behind it, but it drove the cooks mad.

Then he notices that Thomas has been listening to this.

BATES: What's it to you?
THOMAS: Nothing.

At that moment, Daisy appears to pour out a cup of tea.

WILLIAM: Daisy, I was hoping —
THOMAS: Would you like to come to the fair with me,
Daisy? There's a few of us going later on.

All her Christmases have come at once. Her eyes light up.

DAISY: Do you mean it?
MRS PATMORE (V.O.): Daisy! Don't let it get cold!

Daisy hurries away, glowing. William drops into the chair by the piano and starts to play a melancholy tune. Bates leans over to Thomas and speaks under his breath.

BATES: You bastard.*

....

* I like the moment when William is trying to get up his nerve to ask Daisy to go to the fair and Thomas deliberately wrecks the plan. It is a demonstration of power. Thomas is a complicated character, both arrogant and defensive. His status is important to him, but his homosexuality makes him vulnerable. When you are a secret member of a group which is always being derided and condemned but you say nothing, it fosters a fury in you for keeping silent, until crushing others is almost the only revenge available. Thomas hates himself for not speaking up, and this is his revenge for that hatred. It's almost like being secretly Catholic or secretly Jewish or secretly anything where you let yourself collaborate in your own degradation by staying silent whenever it comes up.

I have always wondered if that was the reason why Lord Rosebery, Prime Minister at the end of the nineteenth century, despite being one of the greatest and richest noblemen of his day, introduced death duties. That it was a revenge against his own class for being forced to live a lie because he was gay. All his rank and possessions did not protect him from needing to be dishonest about who he really was, from the moment he woke to the hour he slept. As a result, he set *en train* the destruction of that very society that had forced him to live in a miasma of dishonesty. I think this anger at the world is what we see here in Thomas, but of course it is not what Bates sees.

But Thomas is enjoying himself. He winks at O'Brien.

THOMAS: Can I help it if I'm irresistible?

15 EXT. MOTOR CAR. DAY.

*Cora, Edith and Sybil are being driven home from the village.
Branson sees them into the car.*

CORA: Branson, Lady Sybil and I have some errands in
Ripon tomorrow. We'll leave after luncheon.
BRANSON: Certainly, your ladyship.
EDITH: Why is Sybil having something new and not me?
CORA: Because it's Sybil's turn.
SYBIL: Can it be my choice, this time?
CORA: Of course, darling. As long as you choose what I
choose. Branson, you'll be taking Lady Sybil to Ripon
tomorrow. She'll be leaving after luncheon.
BRANSON: Certainly, your ladyship.
SYBIL: Poor old Madame Swann. I don't know why we bother
with fittings. She always makes the same frock.
EDITH: What do you want her to make?
SYBIL: Something new and exciting. Like those drawings
by Léon Bakst.
CORA: You're not in the Ballets Russes, now, dear.

She pats her child's hand, as she glances at the dashboard.

CORA (CONT'D): Heavens. Look at the time. Not a minute
to change and Granny's invited herself for dinner.
SYBIL: Then she can jolly well wait.
CORA: So women's rights begin at home? I see. Well, I'm
all for that.

They laugh, and so, discreetly, does Branson.

16 INT. CARSON'S PANTRY. DOWNTON. EVE.

*Carson is looking at two bottles of Claret on the table
before him. The wine book is open. Mrs Hughes looks in,
wearing her coat. She has made an effort with her hat.*

MRS HUGHES: I'm just off, Mr Carson.
CARSON: According to the wine book, we should still have
six dozen of this, but I'm beggared if I can find much
more than four.

MRS HUGHES: Look again before you jump to any, nasty conclusions.*

He absorbs this as he looks at her.

CARSON: It's a long time since you last took a night off.

His words have triggered her own thoughts.

MRS HUGHES: Maybe too long. But I think I've dealt with everything.
CARSON: We'll be fine. It's only family.
MRS HUGHES: And Old Violet.

Carson looks at her. He doesn't approve and she knows it.

MRS HUGHES (CONT'D): Her ladyship just told me. You don't think I ought to stay, do you?
CARSON: Certainly not. Be off with you.
MRS HUGHES: Oh. Anna's in bed with a cold. So I'm afraid it's down to you.
CARSON: Go.

17 EXT. DOWNTON VILLAGE. DAY.

The fair is open now. Matthew is at the coconut shy, his bicycle parked nearby. He looks up to find Mary watching him.

MATTHEW: I thought I'd have a go before I went home. How about you?
MARY: I'm only here to send a telegram. And I haven't any money.
MATTHEW: Let me.

He gives a penny to the man. She throws and hits one.

MATTHEW (CONT'D): Well done. You've shown me up.

....

* A butler's duties were many and varied. He would be directly responsible for maintaining the cellar, and he would oversee anything that happened in the dining room, but he would also supervise maintenance of the contents or the fabric, that is any kind of work in the house or on the house, unless there was a clerk of the works employed to manage exterior building. A workman employed in the house would be under the charge of the butler in most households. As testimony to this, I always like to see old Carson making his entries in books and doing all his paperwork.

He takes hold of his bike, thinking for a moment.

MATTHEW: Do you know if your father's doing anything this evening?

MARY: He's not coming to the fair.

MATTHEW: Seriously.

MARY: Having dinner with his family.

MATTHEW: Could I look in afterwards?

MARY: May I ask why?

MATTHEW: Your grandmother paid me a visit this afternoon, and I — well, never mind, but I would like to see him.

MARY: Granny came to see you? Is it all part of the Great Matter?

He smiles but he does not answer. They walk on.

MARY (CONT'D): So are you enjoying yourself yet? In your new life?

Is she making fun of him? She doesn't seem to be.

MATTHEW: Yes, I think so. I know my work seems trivial to you —

MARY: Not necessarily. Sometimes I rather envy you, having somewhere to go every morning.

MATTHEW: I thought that made me very middle class.

MARY: You should learn to forget what I say. I know I do.

She laughs, which he takes as a kind of apology.

MATTHEW: How about you? Is your life proving satisfactory? Apart from the Great Matter, of course.

Things are improving, if they can joke about it.

MARY: Women like me don't have a life. We choose clothes and pay calls and work for charity and do the Season. But we're stuck in a waiting room, until we marry.

MATTHEW: Couldn't you find an occupation?

MARY: How? What do I know? My education was little more than etiquette, prejudice and dance steps.*

....

*This is a speech I was rather proud of, and so I was saddened when it fell to the editor's axe. Still it's a good line, I'll use it somewhere else. In this story, just as Violet has judged Matthew correctly in thinking he will give her the right advice, Matthew judges Mary correctly in thinking that she will be quite sympathetic to the position he's been placed in.

MATTHEW: You could help at the hospital.

MARY: Like your mother? Not really. She has knowledge and training. All I could do is read to patients who weren't listening.

MATTHEW: I've made you angry.

MARY: My life makes me angry. Not you.

They walk on.

18 INT. KITCHEN. DOWNTON. NIGHT.

Mrs Patmore and Daisy are spooning food into serving dishes while Thomas and William wait. Carson hurries in.

CARSON: I never put the Sauterne on ice. Mrs Hughes goes out for one night and we all fall to pieces!

THOMAS: We wondered if we could walk down to the fair, after dinner.

CARSON: I suppose so. But don't be too late.

He hurries through, too busy to concentrate.

THOMAS: Where do you think she's gone?

WILLIAM: None of your business.

MRS PATMORE: Like most of what goes on here. Take it!

She slams a roasting tray clumsily into Daisy's hands, who almost drops the thing, but Thomas leaps in to save her.

THOMAS: Well caught, that man! Though I say it myself.

DAISY: Thanks, ever so.

He winks at her, then takes his tray up and marches out. She is smiling when she catches William looking at her.

DAISY (CONT'D): Yes?

William, hurt, turns away and goes. Mrs Patmore looks over.

MRS PATMORE: Well, you've cheered up a bit.

DAISY: But he's so agile, isn't he? He could have been a sportsman.

MRS PATMORE: Who?

DAISY: Thomas, of course.

MRS PATMORE: Oh, really? And which sport did you have in mind?*

19 INT. STAIRCASE. DOWNTON. EARLY EVE.

Mary is making her way down to dinner, when Robert rounds the staircase above, also on his way down with Pharaoh.

MARY: I ran into Cousin Matthew in the village. He wanted to call on you after dinner. Apparently, Granny's been to see him.

ROBERT: Did you tell him she's coming here this evening?

MARY: I didn't know she was.

ROBERT: When he arrives, do your best to keep her in the drawing room.

MARY: I'd like to see *you* try, if she doesn't want to stay there.

20 EXT. DOWNTON. NIGHT.

Matthew is walking towards the house. He lets himself in through the front door, which is unlocked.

21 INT. HALL. DOWNTON. NIGHT.

First William comes through the dining room door, next Cora, turning in the doorway.

CORA: Don't stay too long. Let them have an early night.

The women start across the hall. Mary is at the back, as the others make their way towards the drawing room.

VIOLET: Sybil darling, why would you want to go to a real school? You're not a doctor's daughter.

....

* What is more interesting than the emotion of love? How it really is almost never based on any kind of logical thinking. Maybe, much later in life, some sensible considerations might play a part in deciding whether to commit your heart to another, but when you're young you simply select people you are physically attracted to, and then invest them with all sorts of qualities which they probably don't possess. Or, if they do, it is completely coincidental. Here we have a classic example of that.

Matthew is in the inner hall behind the glass doors. He does not announce his presence but watches the women as they walk, in particular Mary, the way she moves, the way she turns. Then, in a tight shot, we see her realise he is there. She raises her finger to her lips to prevent him making a move.

SYBIL: But no one learns anything from a governess! Apart from French and how to curtsey.
VIOLET: What else do you need? Or are you thinking of a career in banking?
CORA: Things are different in America —
VIOLET: I know. They live in wig-wams.
CORA: And when they come out of them, they go to school.

Mary has waited until the others have gone into the drawing room. Now, she comes to open the glass door for Matthew.

MARY: If you wait in the library, I'll tell Papa you're here.
MATTHEW: Thank you.

He goes left and she goes right. And William watches.

22 EXT. FAIR. DOWNTON VILLAGE GREEN. EVENING.

Mrs Hughes is standing uncomfortably on the Green watching the activity. She tweaks the veil on her hat.

JOE (V.O.): Elsie?

She turns to find a country man in his fifties, in a suit that looks a little tight, smiling nervously. This is Joe Burns.

JOE (CONT'D): It is Elsie, isn't it?
MRS HUGHES: It is. Though there's very few left to call me that, Joe Burns.

He takes her hand, quite tenderly, and looks into her face.

JOE: I'm flattered that I'm one of them.

23 INT. LIBRARY. DOWNTON. NIGHT.

Robert is with Matthew. Pharaoh lies by the fire. Carson has brought in a tray of whisky, water and a soda siphon.

ROBERT: Where's Thomas?

CARSON: I'm afraid I've let some of the servants go down to the fair, m'lord. I didn't know we'd have any visitors tonight.

ROBERT: Oh, that's all right. They don't have much fun. You should join them.

Carson leaves without replying. Robert lifts the decanter.

MATTHEW: Not too much. And just water.

ROBERT: So, what did you say to Mama?

MATTHEW: I haven't spoken to her since the visit, but I have looked through every source, and I can't find one reason to base a challenge.

ROBERT: I could have told you that.

MATTHEW: I'm not quite sure how to phrase it when I tell *her*.

ROBERT: She shouldn't have put you on the spot like that. It was unkind.

MATTHEW: I'm afraid she'll think I've failed because I don't want to succeed.

ROBERT: She will think that, but I don't. And nor will Cora.

MATTHEW: But of course it's impossible for Mary. She must resent me so bitterly, and I don't blame her.

Surprisingly, Robert finds this speech encouraging.

24 INT. SNUG. THE GRANTHAM ARMS. DOWNTON VILLAGE. NIGHT.

Mrs Hughes and Joe are eating dinner.

MRS HUGHES: It must have been so hard for you when Ivy died.

JOE: Took some getting used to. A farming life can be lonely.

MRS HUGHES: What about your son? Do you see much of him?

JOE: No. That's it. I would have given Peter a share in the farm if he wanted it, but he's joined the army.

MRS HUGHES: Well, I never.

JOE: Oh, he seems happy.

MRS HUGHES: That's the main thing.

JOE: I suppose it is. But it's left me on my own.

It is fairly clear where this is leading.

JOE: So how's life treated you?

MRS HUGHES: Oh, I can't complain. I haven't travelled but I've seen a bit of life, and no mistake. Then again, nothing's joy galore, is it?

JOE: I notice you call yourself 'Mrs'.

MRS HUGHES: Housekeepers and cooks are always 'Mrs'. You know better than anyone I haven't changed my name.

JOE: Well, I know you wouldn't change it to Burns, when you had the chance.

*But he smiles as he says it, and so does she.**

25 EXT. DOWNTON VILLAGE. NIGHT.

Thomas, William, Gwen and Daisy walk along. Daisy hangs on Thomas's arm, which is breaking William's heart.

THOMAS: An evening of mystery. Mrs Hughes out on the tiles, all dolled up like a dog's dinner, then Mr Crawley hurries into the library with his lordship...

GWEN: What are you suggesting?

THOMAS: Who knows? There are more things in heaven and earth, Horatio.

WILLIAM: Who's Horatio?

Thomas shares his contempt with Daisy, who also laughs at William. They've reached the helter skelter.

THOMAS: Come on, Daisy.

He hurries her up the steps.

GWEN: Cheer up. It may never happen.

WILLIAM: It already has. Who is Horatio?

He looks at Thomas and Daisy laughing as they ride round.

....

* Mrs Hughes is the daughter of a Scottish tenant farmer which would be a pretty standard background for a servant then. She's shown talent in her job and she's progressed. One of the hardest aspects of being a senior female servant was that, as a general rule, the top jobs, cook, housekeeper, lady's maid, were only given to unmarried women. Interestingly, the cooks and the housekeepers were given 'Mrs' as a courtesy title but ladies' maids were not. Quite why that distinction was made I could not tell you.

26 INT. SERVANTS' HALL. DOWNTON. EVE.

Bates is there, with a box of collars. O'Brien is sewing.
Branson is reading a paper.

O'BRIEN: You shouldn't have eaten with us. The chauffeur always eats in his own cottage.*

BATES: Steady on. You can cut him a bit of slack on his second day.

BRANSON: I'm waiting to take old Lady Grantham home.

O'BRIEN: Even then, Taylor never ate with us. You're taking advantage of Mrs Hughes's absence.

She goes back to her sewing.

BRANSON: What are you doing?

BATES: Sorting the collars. Removing the ones which have come to an end.

BRANSON: What happens to his lordship's old clothes?

O'BRIEN: What's it to you? Clothes are a valet's perk not a chauffeur's.

Bates checks her, raising his eyebrows to Branson.

BATES: I get some. But most of it goes into the missionary barrel.

BRANSON: I know it's meant to be kind, but I can think of better ways to help the needy than sending stiff collars to the equator.

Bates laughs, as he goes on with his work.

BATES: I thought Anna might have come down for her dinner.

O'BRIEN: And show she's ready to start work again? Not a chance. So I'm to have all three girls to manage plus her ladyship who, naturally, doesn't let up.

BATES: She's still in bed, then?

....

* I like these rules; I always enjoy the fact that the kitchen staff eat together and they don't eat in the servants' hall. They may talk to the others, they may come into the servants' hall for a chat, but they never eat there, any more than the outside staff would have come in for their dinner. And O'Brien is right. The chauffeur would have eaten separately.

O'BRIEN: She is. While I'm sat here, sewing like a cursed princess in a fairy tale, and not down at the fair with the others.

BATES: Have they taken her any supper?

O'BRIEN: Don't bother me with it. I've got enough to worry about.

27 INT. DRAWING ROOM. DOWNTON. NIGHT.

Carson has come in, as the clock chimes on the mantleshelf.

CARSON: Would you like me to ask Branson to bring the car round, m'lady?

VIOLET: Is that the time? Where's Robert? He can't have been drinking port since we left, or he'll be under the table by now.

CARSON: His lordship's in the library.

VIOLET: All alone? Oh, how sad.

CARSON: No, he's —

MARY: We can say goodbye to Papa for you, Granny.

Mary is looking straight at Carson as she speaks.

VIOLET: He's what?

The butler is no match for the dowager. He must answer.

CARSON: He's with Mr Crawley, m'lady.

VIOLET: Cousin Matthew is here? Did you know about this?

CORA: No, but —

VIOLET: Please tell Branson I shall be ready to leave in ten minutes.

She is on her feet as she looks back at Mary.

VIOLET: But not *before*.

And she stalks out.

28 INT. LIBRARY. DOWNTON. NIGHT.

Robert and Matthew are still talking.

MATTHEW: The question is, what do I say to Cousin Violet?

ROBERT: Oh, don't worry about that. I can handle her.

From the hearth, Pharaoh looks up at the door.

VIOLET (V.O.): Really? Well, if you can, you must have learned to very recently.

Violet is standing in the doorway. Mary enters behind her. *

29 INT. KITCHEN. DOWNTON. NIGHT.

Bates arrives. Mrs Patmore is sitting, drinking tea.

BATES: All on your own?
MRS PATMORE: And isn't it a blessed relief.
BATES: I was just wondering if anyone had taken Anna up some supper.
MRS PATMORE: Well, if they haven't, she'll have to starve. I cannot put any more weight on these sad and aching feet tonight.

30 INT. ANNA'S AND GWEN'S BEDROOM. DOWNTON. NIGHT.

Anna's reading in bed, when she hears knocking. She puts down her book, grabs a dressing gown, and goes out.

31 INT. PASSAGE. SERVANTS' QUARTERS. DOWNTON. NIGHT.

She looks down the empty passage towards a closed door.

BATES (V.O.): Anna? Are you there?

She can hardly believe her ears. She hurries to the door.

ANNA: Mr Bates?

....

* When we saw the rushes of this, Matthew didn't stand up when Violet came in. He remained sitting, despite the fact that, at that time, it would have been completely impossible for a man to have stayed in his chair when a woman entered a room. So we had to remount the scene and reshoot the moment. What interested me is that, for my generation, if Maggie Smith walked into the room I would have to stand up, never mind if it were the Countess of Grantham in 1913. There was a similar instance when Matthew approached Mary in the garden and didn't remove his hat or even touch it. These episodes, and others like them, have made me realise that the automatic manners of my youth have gone now. If I'd been asked, before *Downton*, whether most men would still stand if a woman came into a room, I would have said yes, but I wouldn't agree with that today.

BATES (V.O.): Can you open the door?

ANNA: I daren't. No one can open that door, except Mrs Hughes.

BATES (V.O.): Just for a moment. I've brought you something.

Anna hesitates. Then, nervously, she unlocks the door. Bates is standing there with a tray. It has covered dishes, a jug of milk, and a small vase with a flower.

ANNA: I don't know what she'd say.

BATES: I do. But she's out for the evening, and the others are down at the fair.

ANNA: You should have gone with them.

BATES: I was worried you'd be hungry.

ANNA: I thought I'd been forgotten.

BATES: You'd never be forgotten by me.

He says it almost without thinking, and then they both realise the import of his words. She takes the tray.

ANNA: It's so pretty.

BATES: An eye for detail, that's what I'm known for.

Will they kiss? There's a noise on the stairs. Anna starts.

ANNA: You'd better go. But thank you.

BATES: Thank *you*.

Which doesn't really make sense, but it does to him. She closes the door and locks it then hurries back to her room.*

32 EXT. DOWNTON. NIGHT.

Violet comes out with Robert. She is furious.

VIOLET: What I cannot understand in all this is you! You seem positively glad to see Mary disinherited!

ROBERT: You speak as if we had a choice —

VIOLET: Thank you, Branson.

....

* I think they were probably right to cut a chunk of this scene. The statement of Bates's love is so well expressed visually, which is not something you can always anticipate when you're writing something. Here, to see this man standing there with his tray, complete with a flower in its little vase, says more about his feelings for her than dialogue would.

The Earl and Countess of Grantham, whose lives are not as
uncomplicated as one might think.

The servants form a line as the car containing the Duke of Crowborough arrives.

ROBERT: Carson, I hope you weren't embarrassed this afternoon. I can assure you the Duke very much appreciated his welcome.

DUKE OF CROWBOROUGH: But I remember this man. Didn't you serve me when I dined with Lady Grantham in London?

Mary looks up and her jaw drops. Riding towards her is one of the handsomest, sexiest men she has ever seen in her life.

Kemal Pamuk, the son of one of the Sultan's ministers, is in England for the Albanian talks.

DAISY: Do you think he'll speak out? Do you think we'll have a duchess to wait on? Imagine that!

MRS PATMORE: You won't be 'waiting' on her, whatever happens.

GWEN: He doesn't look Turkish at all.

ANNA: Well, he doesn't look like any Englishman I've ever met, worse luck. I think he's beautiful.

ISOBEL: What should we call each other?

VIOLET: We could always start with Mrs Crawley and Lady Grantham.

DR CLARKSON: Mrs Drake, the choice is simple. If your husband endures this procedure he may live. If he does not, he will die.

CORA: Are we to be friends, then?

VIOLET: We are allies, my dear. Which can be a good deal more effective.

SYBIL: Why are you so against him?

MARY: Aside from the fact he's planning to steal our inheritance?

EDITH: *Your* inheritance. It makes no difference to Sybil and me. We won't inherit, whatever happens.

MATTHEW: You must have thought me an awful prig when I first arrived.

ROBERT: Not a prig. Just a man thrust into something he'd never wanted or envisaged, clinging for dear life to his old certainties.

VIOLET: The Grantham Cup is awarded to – *she takes a deep breath to steady herself* – to Mr William Molesley for his *Countess Cabarrus* rose.

MARY: You know what all work and no play did for Jack.

MATTHEW: But you think I'm a dull boy, anyway. Don't you?

SYBIL: Good evening, everyone!

STRALLAN: You're so right, Lady Mary. How clever you are. This is exactly what we have to be aware of.

MRS HUGHES: In many ways I wanted to accept. But I'm not that farm girl anymore. I was flattered, of course, but I've changed.

Thomas, William, Gwen and Daisy at the fair. Daisy hangs
on Thomas's arm, which is breaking William's heart.

The crowd starts to
jostle. There are shouts
and jeers. Branson
approaches Sybil,
who is bubbling with
enthusiasm.

BRANSON: Oh, no. Oh, please God, no!
He takes her up in his arms, as tenderly as a father with his child.

She has brought matters to an end. The chauffeur closes the door and starts the car as Robert retreats to the house.

ROBERT: I'm worn out. Tell Lady Mary and Mr Crawley I've gone to bed.
CARSON: Shall I tell them now, m'lord?

Robert thinks for a moment.

ROBERT: No. Wait until they ring.*

END OF ACT TWO

ACT THREE

33 EXT. DOWNTON VILLAGE. NIGHT.

Joe and Mrs Hughes emerge from the pub into the fair.

MRS HUGHES: I ought to start back. This is very late for me.
JOE: Ah, not yet. It's a long time since I had a girl to show off for, at a fair.

He gives the man a penny and takes up the rings to throw.

JOE (CONT'D): So I take it you never get lonely?
MRS HUGHES: Well, that's working in a big house. There are times when you yearn for a bit of solitude.

He makes his final throw and wins a scarecrow doll.

JOE: Well, something to remind you of me.
MRS HUGHES: I don't need help to remember you.

She chuckles pleasantly, as they stroll on.

....

* Robert realises that Mary and Matthew are alone in the library, and this is (I hope) the first moment where we understand that he hasn't let go of Violet's idea that they might marry. He instructs Carson: 'No wait until they ring' – just in case something might be happening.

JOE: But what… what happens when you retire?

MRS HUGHES: I should think I'll stay here. They'll look after me.

JOE: Suppose they sell the estate?

MRS HUGHES: Suppose there's a tidal wave? Suppose we all die of the plague? Suppose there's a war?*

The other servants watch her laugh, from across the Green, then duck back behind a tent, so she does not see them.

THOMAS: What did I tell you? She's found her Romeo.

GWEN: It might be her brother.

THOMAS: She hasn't got a brother or we'd know it by now. Just a sister in Lytham St Anne's.

DAISY: You know everything, don't you?

He blesses her with a look. William snorts.

WILLIAM: Everything, my foot. You're hiding behind him, but he's not what you think he is.

DAISY: Oh, go home William, if you're going to be such a spoil sport.

WILLIAM: All right. I will.

He turns and marches away, when Gwen calls out.

GWEN: Come back! She didn't mean it! William! Wait for me!

....

* The fact that this way of life will not go on for ever is a theme that trickles through the show. That said, some of the characters don't question it and that is Mrs Hughes's position. Human beings usually assume that the way they live now will see them out and there are periods of history where it's fairly true. What we're not prepared for is absolute change and yet it happens. I remember when I was about nineteen I was at a drinks party and a girlfriend and I were talking to an old lady. She noticed the brooch my companion was wearing and commented that she used to have one just like it, it was her favourite, she said, she loved it. When I asked what had happened to it, she told me it was lost. I was horrified. She stared at me as though I were mad. 'But I lost everything,' she said. It turned out she had been a great lady at the Russian Court before the revolution, and she'd wound up in London after a spell of making hats in Paris. It stuck in my mind because I realised that the concept of total reversal was something I hadn't really addressed before then. I remember wondering how would I manage if I was suddenly stranded in Madrid with nothing. Perhaps I'd drive a taxi. That's what lots of them did.

She hurries after him, as Thomas smirks at Daisy. On the other side of the fair, Mrs Hughes is still with Joe.

MRS HUGHES: I must go. But it's been lovely to see you again, Joe. Really.
JOE: And you know what I'm asking?
MRS HUGHES: You haven't asked anything yet.
JOE: But you know what it is, when I do.

The truth is, she undoubtedly does.

JOE (CONT'D): I'm going to stop here at the pub, 'til I hear from you. Oh, and take your time. I'd rather wait a week for the right answer than get a wrong one in a hurry. Think about it, carefully.
MRS HUGHES: I will. I promise you that.

34 INT. LIBRARY. DOWNTON. NIGHT.

Mary pulls the bell rope. Matthew is still there.

MARY: To break the entail, we'd need a private bill in Parliament?

This seems very ridiculous to her.

MATTHEW: Even then, it would only be passed if the estate was in danger which it's not.
MARY: And I mean nothing in all this.
MATTHEW: On the contrary, you mean a great deal. A very great deal.

He looks at her, but the door opens and Carson appears.

CARSON: You rang, m'lady?
MARY: Yes Carson. Mr Crawley was just leaving. After that you can lock up. Do you know where his lordship is?
CARSON: Gone to bed, m'lady. He felt tired after he put Lady Grantham into the car.
MARY: I bet he did. Thank you, Carson.

The butler goes to fetch Matthew's coat.

MATTHEW: Sorry, I wish I could think of something to say that would help.
MARY: There's nothing. But you mustn't let it trouble you.
MATTHEW: It does trouble me. It troubles me very much.

MARY: Then that will be my consolation prize. Goodnight,
Cousin Matthew.

*She holds out her hand. He takes it and holds it tightly, so
wanting to find the right words. But he can't.*

MATTHEW: Goodnight.

His intensity is disconcerting. She pulls her hand back.

35 INT. HALL. DOWNTON. NIGHT.

Carson holds a coat open for Matthew.

MATTHEW: I hope I haven't kept you up too late. I'm
afraid we've interfered with your dinner.
CARSON: It's been rather a chop-and-change evening
downstairs.
MATTHEW: Lady Grantham got off all right?
CARSON: 'All right' is an optimistic assessment, sir.
MATTHEW: It's very difficult, Carson. For her, for Lady
Mary, for everyone.
CARSON: It is, Mr Crawley. But I appreciate your saying
so.

*This is the nicest thing Carson has ever said to Matthew.**

....

* This scene is about the developing relationship between Carson and
Matthew. The family may not all be happy about the situation, but in the last
analysis Matthew has Crawley blood which makes his claims acceptable. But
they are not acceptable to Carson who does not share the blood-based
culture. In some countries, blood matters at every level of society. I am sure
any Italian would recognise a blood link, however distant, but in England
that tremendous importance of blood seems to be restricted to the upper and
the upper middle class, and the working class, where there is a real sense of
clan. You don't often see it among the middle classes where people move
around a good deal and tend to lose touch with most relations more distant
than a first cousin. This is not true of toffs. They often know their eighth
cousins, co-descendents from some Elizabethan courtier. To the Crawleys,
Matthew is family. But to Carson, he's an outsider who deserves to be seen
off.

36 INT. ANNA'S AND GWEN'S BEDROOM. DOWNTON. NIGHT.

Anna has just climbed into bed, when Gwen arrives, with bread and cheese on a plate, and a glass of water.

ANNA: Are you back? How was it?

GWEN: Fine. I came back with William, after Daisy broke his heart… I brought these up for you, but I see you're taken care of.

ANNA: I am. Very well taken care of.

And she snuggles down, lifting the lids off the dishes.

37 INT. SERVANTS' HALL/SERVANTS' STAIRCASE. DOWNTON. NIGHT.

Mrs Hughes returns from the fair and walks along the passage. O'Brien can be seen in the servants' hall sewing.

O'BRIEN: Well, that's Her Greatness done and dusted for the night.

She bites the thread savagely. There is a sound in the passage. It's Mrs Hughes. Bates enters. William's slumped in a corner.

BATES: William, did you have a good time?

WILLIAM: I'm off to bed.

He stands and walks off. Bates follows him to the stairs.

BATES: Wait. What happened?

WILLIAM: Nothing. It doesn't matter.

Bates would say more but Gwen comes downstairs at that moment, and walks with Bates back to the servants' hall.

BATES: How was your evening, Mrs Hughes?

MRS HUGHES: Very enjoyable, thank you. The others are just behind me, so you can lock up in a minute… Well, I'll say goodnight.

She is about to go as Thomas, Daisy, the maids and the hall boys come in, just in time to see her. She waves goodnight to them as she walks away. Thomas turns to O'Brien.

THOMAS: I was right when I said she was looking sparkly-eyed.

CARSON: I *beg* your pardon, Thomas.

*He has crept up on them. Now he waits, to let his disapproval register, then leaves.**

THOMAS: He can disapprove all he likes. Mrs Hughes has got a fancy man.

He laughs with a sneer, and Daisy laughs with him.

BATES: Don't be nasty, Daisy. It doesn't suit you. And Mrs Hughes is entitled to her privacy.
O'BRIEN: You would say that, wouldn't you?
THOMAS: I reckon there's a job vacancy coming up. Miss O'Brien, do you fancy a promotion?
O'BRIEN: Very droll. If she's got a boyfriend, I'm a giraffe.

38 INT. CORA'S BEDROOM. DOWNTON. NIGHT.

Cora's in bed. Robert is in his dressing gown.

CORA: How was she when she left?
ROBERT: You know my mother. She's not keen on conceding defeat.
CORA: And Mary?
ROBERT: Well, she listened to Matthew, but whether she's accepted it remains to be seen.

Cora nods. Robert sits on the bed, taking his wife's hand.

ROBERT (CONT'D): The question is, have *you* accepted it?
CORA: I think so.
ROBERT: But I don't want you to feel angry towards Matthew.
CORA: I won't. I like Matthew.
ROBERT: Don't think he's cheated Mary. He hasn't.
CORA: To be honest, Robert, Mary isn't the person you —

She stops. She very nearly gave away Mary's secret.

ROBERT: Mary isn't the person I what?
CORA: Never mind.

....

* I always want to remind the audience that Carson is like a ringmaster and his job is to keep the entire staff, in some cases potentially quite unruly people, to keep them all on the straight and narrow. The butler of a great house was a headmaster, a taskmaster, a king.

He takes off his gown and climbs into bed.

ROBERT: It's a shame she won't take Matthew. I think even Carson could put up with 'Mr Crawley' if Mary was his wife.

CORA: We don't know he'd take *her*, now.

This really is an odd thing for Robert to hear.

ROBERT: Why on earth do you say that?

CORA: I'm not convinced they're suited.

ROBERT: Have it your own way. *We're* suited. So let's give thanks for that.

He kisses her and settles down. But Cora lies awake.

39 INT. ATTICS. DOWNTON. NIGHT.

Bates, in his vest, carrying a towel, knocks at a door.

BATES: William?

He opens the door but a sad voice speaks out of the dark.

WILLIAM (V.O.): Leave me alone, Mr Bates. I know you mean well, but let me be.

Is he crying? Bates closes the door gently.

THOMAS: What chance did he have? Up against a champion?

He is smirking by his door. Suddenly Bates seizes him by his waistcoat and bangs him hard against the wall, leaning in.

BATES: Now, listen, you filthy little rat. If you don't lay off, I'll punch your shining teeth through the back of your head!

But Thomas just grins into the face so close to his own.

THOMAS: Is this supposed to frighten me, Mr Bates? Because, if it is, it isn't working. I'm sorry, but it's just not working.

His smile is hard, and Bates is one step from murder.

40 INT. MRS HUGHES'S SITTING ROOM

Mrs Hughes is holding the scarecrow doll won for her at the fair by Joe Burns. She smiles at the memory.

41 INT. KITCHEN. DOWNTON. MORNING.

Breakfast time. The place is a whirl of activity.

MRS PATMORE: Daisy! Chafing dishes! Now!
DAISY: They're right in front of you, Mrs Patmore.
MRS PATMORE: Are you trying to trick me?

*But then she looks hard at the table. The dishes are there.
Mrs Hughes has been watching all this.*

MRS HUGHES: Anna's still not well enough. O'Brien,
you'll have to dress the girls again, this morning.

*O'Brien, laying Cora's breakfast tray, looks outraged. She
whispers to Thomas.*

O'BRIEN: When you think of what we know about Lady Mary,
and here I am, waiting on her hand and foot.
THOMAS: Will we do anything with that?
O'BRIEN: Maybe, but not yet. I'm not sure we've got to
the bottom of it, yet.

*Thomas is distracted by William, who is about to go out with
a serving dish.*

THOMAS: What do you look like? Daisy, what do you think
he looks like?

Daisy hesitates. This makes her uncomfortable.

THOMAS: A tramp. A vagrant. That's what. Do your
buttons up.

For a moment, William doesn't move.

DAISY: Well, go on, then.

*Silently, William puts down the dish, refastens his buttons,
picks up his dish again and leaves. Daisy watches him
uneasily. Then Thomas catches her eye and winks, as he goes
out and she smiles. Gwen and Mrs Hughes have witnessed all
this.*

42 INT. SYBIL'S BEDROOM. DOWNTON. DAY.

Sybil's hair is being arranged by O'Brien.

SYBIL: I'll have it down, today. With just a bow to hold it back.

O'BRIEN: Of course, m'lady, if you want to look like a milkmaid.

SYBIL: That's exactly what I want, thank you, O'Brien. How's Anna?

O'BRIEN: Gwen said she was a bit better.

SYBIL: Good. Ouch.

She has been punished. There is a knock and Gwen comes in.

O'BRIEN: What do you want?

GWEN: I've got a message for Lady Sybil. From her ladyship.

SYBIL: Thank you, O'Brien. I'll manage now.

Without a word, O'Brien puts down the brush and leaves.

SYBIL: Odious woman. What does Mama want?

GWEN: I just said that to get rid of her. This came today.

She brings a letter from her pocket and hands it over.

SYBIL: I *knew* they'd want to see you.

GWEN: S'your reference wot's done it.

SYBIL: 'That's' done it.

They look at each other, brimming with excitement. Then…

GWEN: How'm I going to get there? They won't let me take a day off.

SYBIL: You're going to be ill. They can't stop you being ill.

GWEN: What?

SYBIL: No one has seen Anna for a whole day. They won't notice if you vanish for a couple of hours.

GWEN: I s'pose.

SYBIL: I'll get Lynch to hitch up the governess cart and drive you in. It'll work. I promise.

43 EXT.   THE GARDENS AT DOWNTON ABBEY*

Robert is walking with Mary.

MARY: The only one who never sticks up for me in all this is you. Why is that?

ROBERT: You are my darling daughter and I love you, hard as it is for an Englishman to say the words.

MARY: Well, then…

ROBERT: If I had made my own fortune and bought Downton for myself, it should be yours without question, but I did not. My fortune is the work of others, who laboured to build a great dynasty. Do I have the right to destroy their work? Or impoverish that dynasty? I am a custodian, my dear, not an owner. I must strive to be worthy of the task I have been set. If I could take Mama's money out of the estate, Downton would have to be sold to pay for it. Is that what you want? To see Matthew a landless peer with a title, but no means to pay for it?

MARY: So I'm just to find a husband and get out of the way?

ROBERT: You could stay here if you married Matthew.

MARY: You know my character, Father. I'd never marry any man that I was told to. I'm stubborn. I wish I wasn't, but I am.

44 EXT.   ISOBEL'S GARDEN.   DOWNTON VILLAGE.   DAY.

Isobel is pruning roses. Molesley arrives with a tea tray. His hands are still raw and it has spread up his arms.

ISOBEL: It's no better, is it?

MOLESLEY: Not really, ma'am, no.

ISOBEL: What about the solution I gave you?

MOLESLEY: Doesn't make any difference. If anything, it's worse.

....

* This scene was originally written for Episode Five, but it was later deemed more appropriate to the narrative of Four. It is an example of the 'building blocks' element of constructing a screenplay, which is told by a sequence of separate scenes, each one a moment in the story. By re-ordering them, even after they have been shot, the plot line or a character's development can be altered, and often is.

ISOBEL: And you won't wear gloves?

MOLESLEY: Don't ask me to, ma'am. Please. I've been a footman, but I'm not a footman now.

ISOBEL: Are you busy at the moment?

MOLESLEY: I thought I'd walk up to give my father a hand, ma'am. And you did say it might take a week.

ISOBEL: Very well. But if it's no better by next Wednesday we'll ask the doctor. No point in keeping a dog and not letting it bark.

45 INT. LIBRARY. DOWNTON. DAY.

Cora is with Robert.

CORA: Are you doing anything?

ROBERT: Why?

CORA: I was taking Sybil to choose a new frock but I think I've caught Anna's cold.

ROBERT: I've arranged to show Matthew the cottages we're doing up. It is his idea, and he's getting away early on purpose. I'm no judge of hemlines, anyway.

CORA: I'd better cancel it.

ROBERT: Poor Sybil. Surely she can sort out her own frock at this stage. Branson can take her.

CORA: Hmm. She has such wild ideas.

ROBERT: Sounds intriguing.

CORA: Well, if you don't like what she chooses, don't blame me.

46 INT. SERVANTS' HALL. DOWNTON. DAY.

Bates, O'Brien, Thomas, William and Daisy are in there, when Mrs Hughes appears with Anna. Bates jumps up.

BATES: Does this mean you're better?

O'BRIEN: Don't tell me. Let me guess. She doesn't feel up to starting work.

ANNA: I do. I want to.

MRS HUGHES: Not yet. Try a little mending. But that's enough for now.

She puts the sewing basket down on the table and goes.

ANNA: I wish she'd let me do more.

O'BRIEN: Of course you do.

ANNA: I hate being ill. My mother used to look down on
ill people. She used to say 'Oh, they're *always* ill,' as
if it were their fault.*
THOMAS: *My* mother worshipped disease. If we ever wanted
to get anything out of her, we had to start by pretending
to be ill.

Daisy peals with laughter, infuriating William.

WILLIAM: You talk such rubbish.
DAISY: Don't say that. Tell us more.

Mrs Patmore has appeared, spoon in hand.

MRS PATMORE: Daisy, perhaps you can delay hearing
Thomas's life story, and come and help with the dinner.
DAISY: Yes, Mrs Patmore.

She stands and goes, with a smile for Thomas.

BATES: Welcome back. It wasn't the same, without you.

He talks softly to Anna, but Thomas and O'Brien have heard.

O'BRIEN: Some people are easily pleased.

47 INT. MOTOR CAR. DAY.

Branson is driving Lady Sybil.

SYBIL: Madame Swann's is just off the market place.
BRANSON: Will you have your own way, do you think? With
the frock?

Despite Sybil's liberalism, she is rather taken aback.

....

* Although this scene was cut, I love the dialogue, when Anna says: 'I hate
being ill; my mother used to look down on ill people. She used to say "they're
always ill" as if it were their fault.' And then Thomas replies: 'My mother
worshipped disease – if we ever wanted to get anything out of her we had to
start by pretending to be ill.' In actual fact, Anna's mother is based on my
own mother who always thought ill people were frightful time-wasters. She
used to say: 'Well do ring me up when you're well again', and then put down
the telephone, and I'm afraid I'm rather like her. On the other hand,
Thomas's mother is based on Emma's mother. For my mother-in-law, at the
top of the moral high ground is a little hillock and on that hillock are the ill
people. Poor Emma has to deal with these colliding philosophies.

BRANSON (CONT'D): Only I couldn't help overhearing yesterday and from what her ladyship said, it sounded as if you support women's rights.
SYBIL: I suppose I do.
BRANSON: Because I'm quite political.
SYBIL: Are you? I suppose you support an independent Ireland?
BRANSON: Certainly, I do… As a matter of fact I've brought a few pamphlets I thought might interest you, about the vote.

He has the pamphlets on the seat by him and now he holds them back with one hand, for Sybil to take. Which she does.

SYBIL: Thank you… But please don't mention it to my father. Or my grandmother. One whiff of reform, and she hears the rattle of the guillotine.

He laughs. She's less nervous now, if still surprised.

SYBIL (CONT'D): It seems rather unlikely. A revolutionary chauffeur.
BRANSON: Maybe. But I'm a Socialist, not a revolutionary. And I won't always be a chauffeur.

48 EXT. DOWNTON VILLAGE. DAY.

A few days later, Isobel and a wretched Molesley walk past the quiet, morning fair, on their way to the hospital.

49 INT. COTTAGE HOSPITAL. DAY.

Isobel walks into Doctor Clarkson's office, to find Violet is sitting there. Clarkson looks nervous as he stands.

CLARKSON: Mrs Crawley, how nice.

Isobel and Violet nod coolly at each other.

ISOBEL: You're busy. We can come back.

But by now, Violet has spotted the hovering Molesley.

VIOLET: Molesley? What are you doing here? Are you ill?
CLARKSON: Poor Mr Molesley. How's it going?
ISOBEL: The solution doesn't seem to make it any better.
VIOLET: My imagination is running riot.

She clearly has no intention of going.

MOLESLEY: I've got Erysipelas, m'lady.

VIOLET: Oh, I am sorry.

CLARKSON: Mrs Crawley tells me she's recommended Nitrate of Silver and Tincture of Steel.

VIOLET: Is she making a suit of armour?

CLARKSON: It is the treatment I would have recommended myself. But I take it there's no improvement?

MOLESLEY: Not really.

So saying, he unconsciously turns his hand back and forth as he looks at it. Violet glances down. Then looks again.

VIOLET: And you're sure it's Erysipelas?

CLARKSON: That is Mrs Crawley's diagnosis.

VIOLET: What it is to have medical knowledge.

ISOBEL: It has its uses.

Violet now turns to Molesley.

VIOLET: Mmm. I see your father has been making changes at home.

MOLESLEY: He has. He's got no use for the herb garden now me mother's gone, so he's putting it to grass.

VIOLET: And you have been helping him?

MOLESLEY: I have.

VIOLET: Grubbing out the old Rue hedge?

MOLESLEY: How did you know that?

VIOLET: Because this is not Erysipelas. This is a Rue allergy. If Molesley wears gardening gloves, it'll be gone in a week. You weren't to blame. I know you are *unfamiliar* with the country and its ways.

Isobel says nothing. She is livid at this humiliation.

VIOLET (CONT'D): And you, Doctor, should not rely on a diagnosis from those who are unqualified to make one.

CLARKSON: I stand corrected.

VIOLET: Please don't think we're ungrateful for your enthusiasm, Mrs Crawley, but there comes a time when things are best left to the professionals.*

....

* Of course Isobel has overcomplicated it and, for me, that is often the problem with so-called experts. The moment anyone refers to an 'expert opinion', I always reach for my gun. You just know that too many 'experts' will miss the essentials of the case.

ISOBEL: But I —

VIOLET: *I* may have no training but I'm a great believer in common sense. And now really, I really must go. Good day.

Isobel is forced to accept defeat. Violet is leaving.

MOLESLEY: Thank you, your ladyship.

Violet smiles, thrilled to have won this round.

END OF ACT THREE

ACT FOUR

50 EXT. COTTAGES. DOWNTON ESTATE. DAY.

Robert is inspecting a row of cottages with Matthew. Pharaoh is with them. Building is still in progress.

MATTHEW: They're doing a good job.

ROBERT: I think so. They'll see me out, and, with any luck, you.

MATTHEW: I hope Cousin Violet has recovered from last night.

ROBERT: Whatever she says, my mother is as strong as an ox. And it's high time she let go of her scheme for upsetting everything. Time we all did.

MATTHEW: I can't deny I'm pleased to hear you say it.

ROBERT: Are you beginning to see a future here, then?

MATTHEW: In a way, this latest business has forced me to recognise that I do want Downton to be my future.

ROBERT: I'm glad.

MATTHEW: You must have thought me an awful prig when I first arrived.

ROBERT: Not a prig. Just a man thrust into something he never wanted or envisaged, clinging for dear life to his old certainties.

Matthew laughs.

MATTHEW: I could only see the absurdity of the whole
thing — I'm sorry.

ROBERT: Well, there are absurdities involved, as I know
well enough.

MATTHEW: Possibilities too and I was blind to them. I
was determined not to let it change me, it was absurd.
If you don't change, you die.

ROBERT: Do you think so? I'm not sure. Sometimes I
think I hate change.

MATTHEW: At least we can comfort ourselves this will
still be here.

He slaps the freshly restored cottage wall.

MATTHEW (CONT'D): Because we saved it.

Together, they survey the countryside surrounding them.

51 INT. KITCHEN. DOWNTON. DAY.

*Daisy is scouring a copper bowl with flour and vinegar. Mrs
Patmore drinks tea as pots bubble behind her.*

DAISY: Thomas is lovely, isn't he? He's funny and
handsome, but ever so kind too.

MRS PATMORE: I know you've been upset, Daisy. By poor Mr
Pamuk's death and the rest of it but Thomas is not the
answer.

DAISY: But I never had more fun in my life than I did
last night. And he's got such lovely teeth.

MRS PATMORE: He's not for you, Daisy.

DAISY: 'course not. He's too good for me. I know that.

MRS PATMORE: No. He's not too good.

DAISY: What, then?

MRS PATMORE: He's not the boy for you, and you're not the
girl for him.

DAISY: Isn't that what I just said? And why would he be?
When he's seen and done so much, and I've been nowhere
and done nothing.

MRS PATMORE: Perhaps Thomas has seen and done more than
was good for him.

Daisy is genuinely puzzled. What does Mrs Patmore mean?

MRS PATMORE (CONT'D):… He's not a ladies' man.

DAISY: Well, isn't it a blessed relief? Though I could have told you that. He'd never break a heart without breaking his own.

MRS PATMORE: Daisy, Thomas is a troubled soul.

DAISY: I don't know what you mean, Mrs Patmore.

The cook looks at the innocent face and decides against it.

MRS PATMORE: Oh, nothing. I don't mean anything. Except that if I don't get the ice cream started, they'll be dining at midnight.

She goes to work, leaving the maid in blissful ignorance.

52 INT. EDITH'S BEDROOM. DOWNTON. NIGHT.

Sybil watches Anna dressing Edith for dinner. Anna sneezes discreetly.*

SYBIL: Golly, my corset's tight. Anna, when you've done that, could you be an angel and loosen it a bit?

She turns her back to the maid, as Edith sits down at her dressing table.

EDITH: The start of the slippery slope.

SYBIL: I'm not putting on weight.

EDITH: It didn't shrink in the drawer.†

The door opens and Mary comes in, dressed for the evening.

MARY: Are you coming down?

Sybil breathes out, and smiles at the maid.

....

* Anna sneezes here, because originally the scene was much earlier in the episode, so she had still not gone to bed with her cold. Again an example of how the rhythm of a piece sometimes demands that building blocks be moved around.

† I wanted to remind the public that even though women's clothes were beginning to loosen up a bit – a harbinger of the First World War fashions of the shorter skirt and so on – nevertheless they were still wearing corsets and having the laces tightened by their maids, every day of their lives, young and old alike.

SYBIL: I don't know why we bother with corsets. Men don't wear them, and they look perfectly normal in their clothes.

As she talks, Mary picks up a piece of Edith's jewellery, holds it against her throat and drops it in disgust.

MARY: Not all of them.
SYBIL: Besides, the London designers are following the lead of Mr Diaghilev. I saw a picture of Lady Londonderry in something that could have been a teagown.
MARY: Say what you like, men want to see waists.
EDITH: She's just showing off. She'll be on about the vote in a minute.
SYBIL: If you mean do I think women should vote, of course I do.
EDITH: I hope you won't chain yourself to the railings and end up being force-fed semolina.
SYBIL: Probably not. But don't make fun of them.

Anna starts to unbutton Sybil's dress.

MARY: What do you think, Anna?
ANNA: I think those women are very brave.
SYBIL: Hear, hear.

53 INT. DRAWING ROOM. DOWNTON. NIGHT.

Robert and the family are attended by Carson and Thomas.

ROBERT: How did you get on with your dress-maker? Find anything?
SYBIL: I did. And she says she can have it done by Friday.
ROBERT: I'm sorry I couldn't come, but I didn't want to put Matthew off.
EDITH: Were you pleased with the work on the cottages?
ROBERT: They're making a very good job of them. You must all go and see.
CORA: So you'll restore a few every year from now on?
ROBERT: It was Matthew's idea. Old Cripps was rather reluctant, but I'm pleased we went forward.
EDITH: I suppose it's worth it?
SYBIL: Of course it is. Because of the people who'll live in them.

ROBERT: You'll be glad to hear that Matthew's conscience is much more energetic than mine.*

Suddenly, Mary stands.

MARY: If you'll excuse me, I'm going to bed. I've got rather a headache.
CORA: Of course. Shall I bring you something for it?
MARY: No. I'll be perfectly fine. If I can just lie down.
ROBERT: Goodnight, my —

But Mary has already walked out of the room. Almost without thinking, Robert and Carson exchange a glance.

54 INT. HALL. DOWNTON. NIGHT.

Cora comes hurrying out, but Mary's on the staircase.

CORA: My dear, please wait.
MARY: I've told you, Mama. I just need to lie down.

She turns onto the gallery. Cora hurries after her.

55 INT. MARY'S BEDROOM. DOWNTON. NIGHT.

Cora comes in. Mary is sobbing. Her mother goes to her, kneeling and taking her hands, which only makes her cry more.

CORA: Oh, my darling, what is it?
MARY: You heard him. Matthew this, Matthew that. Matthew, Matthew, *Matthew!*

Cora doesn't quite know what Mary means.

....

* Restoring the cottages is the beginning of another *Downton* theme. We shall see that Matthew is essentially a businessman, he thinks the estate has to be managed properly and he would argue that it is not to anyone's advantage to run it badly. He is not at all opposed to Robert's philosophy when it comes to the estate's tenants, i.e. that he, Lord Grantham, is responsible for their welfare, but Matthew would say that it would help them more to make the place efficient. Robert can't see that. He thinks Matthew is too money-conscious, and that striving for financial efficiency is parsimonious and *bourgeois*. These two philosophies will eventually collide, but they don't collide yet.

MARY: Oh mother, don't you see? *He has a son now.* Of course he didn't argue with the entail. Why would he? When he's got what he always wanted.*

Cora holds her sobbing daughter close.

CORA: Your father loves you very much.
MARY: He wouldn't fight for me, though.
CORA: He wouldn't fight for you because he knew he couldn't win.

Mary steps back. She is annoyed to have been caught out in a moment of weakness. She wipes her eyes fiercely.

MARY: You're no better.
CORA: What?
MARY: You don't care about Matthew getting everything, because you don't think I'm worthy of it.

This is a tough one for Cora, because it's true.

CORA: Mary —
MARY: I wish you'd just admit it. I'm a lost soul to you. I took a lover with no thought of marriage! A Turk! Think of that! Oh, my dear!

She laughs bitterly. She's regained possession of herself.

MARY (CONT'D): Don't worry, Mama. You can go down now. 'Everything will look better in the morning.' Isn't that what you usually say?
CORA: I say it, because it's usually true.
MARY: Go back down. Please. Papa will wonder where you are.

....

* Mary is starting to like Matthew but at the same time she resents this unarguable fact. Her father has always wanted a son. He's put a good face on it, but that is what he longed for and now the heir has arrived. He might have been awful, but he's very nice, a personable, pleasant, young man and, without really noticing, Robert is turning Matthew into his son, downgrading Mary in the process. It is bad enough for Mary that the law gives her no value but for her father to collaborate in it, is very hard to bear. And Robert would never consider that he was hurting Mary in his adoption of Matthew, because he is incapable of challenging the moral precepts of the world into which he was born.

She backs away, hands raised. She wants no more comfort. So Cora walks to the door. Once there, she turns back.

    CORA: Don't quarrel with Matthew.
    MARY: Why shouldn't I?
    CORA: Because one day you may need him.

For a second this is puzzling, then Mary understands.

    MARY: Oh, I see. When I've ruined myself, I must have a powerful protector to hide behind.

Cora will not contradict, since it's an accurate summary.

56 INT. SERVANTS' HALL. DOWNTON. DAY.

William is alone, idly tinkling the piano.

    MRS HUGHES (V.O.): I'd tell you off, but I like to hear you play. Where are they all?
    WILLIAM: Busy, I suppose. Gwen was here but Mr Branson brought in a package and she's gone upstairs.
    MRS HUGHES: Haven't you got anything to do?
    WILLIAM: Yes. I have. Of course I have.

He stands, wearily.

    MRS HUGHES: You mustn't let Thomas get you down. He's just jealous. Everyone likes you better than him.
    WILLIAM: Not everyone.
    MRS HUGHES: Then she's a foolish girl and she doesn't deserve you. Though why am I encouraging you? Forget all that. For ten years at least.

She sounds strict but of course she isn't. He looks at her.

    WILLIAM: You're a kind woman, Mrs Hughes.
    MRS HUGHES: So you'd miss me, when I'm gone?

Is she joking? It's hard to say.

    WILLIAM: I don't know how this house would run without you. I don't, truly.
    MRS HUGHES: Stop flannelling and get on. Before I betray you to Mr Carson.

He goes, but his words have helped her with a decision. In the kitchen Gwen is seen reading a letter.

57 INT. SYBIL'S BEDROOM. DOWNTON. DAY.

Sybil opens a dress-maker's box on the bed. Gwen is rather sombre, but Sybil is too thrilled to notice.

SYBIL: It's arrived!
GWEN: Mr Branson collected it, m'lady. Anna would have brought it up, but she's gone to the village.
SYBIL: Is there anything more thrilling than a new frock?
GWEN: I suppose not, m'lady.

Sybil interprets her dreariness as meaning that Gwen very seldom has a new dress, that her question was thoughtless.

SYBIL: You shall have one, too.

She goes to the wardrobe where a tailored suit hangs.

SYBIL (CONT'D): I thought this might be suitable for your interview.
GWEN: I won't be wearing it, m'lady.
SYBIL: Of course you will. We have to make you look like a successful, professional woman.

But Gwen starts to cry. Sybil is bewildered.

SYBIL (CONT'D): What is it? What's happened?
GWEN: I won't wear it, because I'm not going. They've cancelled the appointment.

She fumbles in her pocket and produces a letter which Sybil takes and reads. Her face falls.

GWEN (CONT'D): They've found someone 'more suited to the post and better qualified.'
SYBIL: This time.
GWEN: Let's face it. There'll never be anyone *less* suited to the post or *worse* qualified than I am.
SYBIL: That isn't true.

Sybil guides Gwen towards the bed where they sit.

SYBIL (CONT'D): You'll see. We're not giving up.

She picks up the suit again and gives it to Gwen, who would protest, but Sybil insists, taking the girl in her arms.

SYBIL (CONT'D): No one hits the bull's eye with the first arrow.

58 INT. MRS HUGHES'S SITTING ROOM. DOWNTON. EVE.

Carson looks in. Mrs Hughes is standing, looking pensive.

CARSON: I've put out the Rundell candlesticks for dinner,
tonight. They're not as nice, but the Lameries need
proper cleaning and the pivot's loose on one of the arms.
It won't be for long.

She nods, but she's too preoccupied to concentrate on this.

CARSON (CONT'D): Oh, I'm sorry. I'll come back later.
MRS HUGHES: No. Stay. Please. I've got something I'd
like to talk about. If you've a minute.

He nods and comes in, taking a chair opposite her.

MRS HUGHES (CONT'D): Before I first came here as head
housemaid, I was walking out with a farmer. When I told
him I'd taken a job at Downton, he asked me to marry
him. I was a farmer's daughter from Argyll, so I knew
the life...
CARSON: And you were tempted.
MRS HUGHES: He was very nice. But then I came here, and
I did well, and I didn't want to give it up. So I told
him no and he married someone else.
CARSON: And he was miserable.
MRS HUGHES: No, he was happy. She was a good woman and
they had a healthy son.
CARSON: So, what happened?
MRS HUGHES: She died. Three years ago. And last month
he wrote asking to see me again. And I agreed. Because,
all this time, I've wondered.
CARSON: Go on.
MRS HUGHES: I met him the other night. We had dinner at
the Grantham Arms and after, he took me to the fair.
CARSON: And he was horrible and fat and red-faced. And
you couldn't think what you ever saw in him.

Mrs Hughes fingers the doll Joe Burns gave her.

MRS HUGHES: He was still a nice man. He is still a nice
man. Well, he was a bit red-faced and his suit was a
little tight, but none of that matters. In the real
ways, he hadn't changed.
CARSON: And he proposed again and you accepted?

She looks at him for a moment before she answers.

MRS HUGHES: In many ways I *wanted* to accept. But I'm not
that farm girl anymore. I was flattered, of course, but
I've changed, Mr Carson.
CARSON: Life's altered you, as it's altered me. And what
would be the point of living if we didn't let life change us?*

She doesn't know how to answer.

CARSON (CONT'D): You won't be leaving, then?

*At that moment, there's a knock on the door, and Anna sticks
her head into the room.*

ANNA: You'd better come. Mrs Patmore's on the rampage.
She wants the key to the store cupboard. You know how
angry she gets that she hasn't got one of her own.
MRS HUGHES: Nor will she have. Not while I'm housekeeper
here.

Anna has gone. Mrs Hughes looks at the butler.

MRS HUGHES (CONT'D): Leaving? When would I ever find the
time?

59 INT. DRAWING ROOM. DOWNTON. NIGHT.

*The family, plus the Crawleys and minus Sybil, are waiting to
go to dinner. Carson's with them. Thomas is at the door.*

CORA: Whatever is holding Sybil up?
MARY: She was banging on about her new frock.

60 INT. SYBIL'S BEDROOM/BEDROOM PASSAGE. DOWNTON.
NIGHT.

*In a series of shots, we see Sybil being dressed by Anna before
a looking glass. We only ever see her from the waist up.*

....

* Most people, at some time in their lives, have to take stock of how much they
have changed. They have to accept that they do not want the things they used to
want, or enjoy the things they used to enjoy, and there is nothing wrong with this.
For me, one of the saddest aspects of the sixties generation is that they often
won't acknowledge that their taste, whether in politics, clothes or music, has not
only evolved, but *should* have evolved. I like Joe and I hope the audience does
because, in a story about whether or not Mrs Hughes is going to marry, we
needed her choice to be difficult. Here, she has been offered a healthy life with a
nice man and if she is going to refuse him, then she'll need a good reason. I
thought the actor, Bill Fellows, understood that and played it very well.

61 INT. DRAWING ROOM. DOWNTON. NIGHT.

ROBERT: We'd better go in without her. Or it's not fair on Mrs Patmore.

VIOLET: Is her cooking so precisely timed? You couldn't tell.

Which irritates Cora. Isobel weighs in on Cora's side.

ISOBEL: I think her food is delicious.

VIOLET: Naturally.

62 INT. STAIRCASE. DOWNTON. NIGHT.

Sybil is running down, but still we only see her top half.

63 INT. DRAWING ROOM. DOWNTON. NIGHT.

MATTHEW: Here she comes.

The door opens and, sure enough, Sybil walks in. She's wearing a flowing pair of emerald green silk trousers.

SYBIL: Good evening, everyone!

She is greeted by a sea of dropped jaws, and varying degrees of incredulity, even if Matthew smiles.

64 EXT/INT. DOWNTON/DRAWING ROOM. DOWNTON. NIGHT.*

Outside the drawing room windows, Branson is spying on this scene. His eyes gleam at the appearance of Sybil…

MRS HUGHES: Mr Branson!

She is standing at the corner of the house by the service courtyard. He springs back from the window and stares at her.

MRS HUGHES (CONT'D): Don't play with fire, Mr Branson. Or you'll get burned.

She knows just what is going on.

END OF EPISODE FOUR

....

* We did film this scene but something went slightly wrong with the way it was shot, and it ended up looking incredibly sinister, like something out of *The Woman in Black*. So it was cut.

EPISODE FIVE

ACT ONE

1 INT. MARY'S BEDROOM. DAY.

Gwen and Anna are making the bed, one on each side. Daisy is laying the fire. She drops the fire irons with a clang. Anna lets out a gasp, then laughs at herself.

  ANNA: You made me jump.

Now lumps of coal fall and roll everywhere.

  GWEN: Daisy, what *is* the matter with you? You're all thumbs.
  DAISY: Sorry…

She scrapes everything together again, looking round.

  DAISY (CONT'D): I hate this room.
  GWEN: Why? What's the matter with it?

*In a flash, we see Daisy's viewpoint on that fateful night, the dead body being carried round the corner by Mary. Daisy did not make out the identities of the other carriers, but Mary's face is caught clearly in a shaft of candlelight. She comes out of her reverie to find Anna looking at her.**

2 INT. DINING ROOM. DOWNTON. DAY.

Robert is finishing his breakfast with all three daughters. The dog, Pharoah, is at his feet. He reads a letter.

  MARY: Who's that from, Papa? You seem very absorbed.
  ROBERT: Your aunt Rosamond.
  EDITH: Anything interesting?

There is, but Robert doesn't want to repeat it.

  ROBERT: Nothing to trouble you with.
  SYBIL: Poor Aunt Rosamond. All alone in that big house. I feel so sorry for her.

....

* The purpose of this moment with Daisy was to make it clear that Pamuk isn't going to go away, to remind the audience of the scandal so that they will know the scandalous death of the Turkish visitor will be hovering in the background for some time yet.

MARY: I don't. All alone, with plenty of money, in a house in Eaton Square? I can't imagine anything better.
ROBERT: Really, Mary, I wish you wouldn't talk like that. There will come a day when someone thinks you mean what you say.
MARY: It can't come soon enough for me.

Robert stands and turns to Carson, who is by the sideboard.

ROBERT: Carson, I'll be in the library. Will you let me know when her ladyship is downstairs?
CARSON: Certainly, m'lord.

Robert gathers up his letters, then sees one he'd missed.

ROBERT: Sybil, darling. This is for you.

She takes the letter and opens it. It contains good news.

3 INT. BEDROOM PASSAGE/SYBIL'S BEDROOM. DAY.

Sybil is walking along, with the opened letter in her hands behind her back.

GWEN: What is it, m'lady?
SYBIL: Look.

She gives Gwen the letter she was reading at breakfast.

SYBIL (CONT'D): I saw another opening for a secretary and I applied.
GWEN: For me? But you never said.
SYBIL: I didn't want you to be disappointed.
GWEN: I thought you'd given up.
SYBIL: I'll never give up and nor will you. Things are changing for women, Gwen. Not just the vote but our lives. We're going to have real lives.

During this, Gwen has read the letter.

GWEN: But it's tomorrow! At ten o'clock! How can it be? Last time we waited for weeks and weeks, and this one's tomorrow!
SYBIL: Then we must be ready by tomorrow, mustn't we?

*Gwen is breathless with excitement.**

....

* Sybil now becomes proactive, she's going to take Gwen to the interview.

4 EXT. CRAWLEY HOUSE. DAY.

The Crawleys' house catches the morning light.

5 INT. HALL. CRAWLEY HOUSE. DAY.

Isobel comes downstairs to find Matthew putting on a coat.

ISOBEL: You're very late this morning.
MATTHEW: I'm not going into the office. I'm taking a
will to be signed in Easingwold, at eleven.
ISOBEL: I thought I'd write to Edith, to settle our
promised church visit.
MATTHEW: If you want.

He checks his appearance in the glass.

ISOBEL: We can't just throw her over, when she made such
an effort to arrange the last one.

She gives him a look, which forces him to return it.

MATTHEW: It's all in your head.
ISOBEL: I don't think so.
MATTHEW: Then she's barking up the wrong tree.
ISOBEL: Poor Edith. I do hope there's a *right* tree for
her, somewhere.*

Molesley has come in. He walks forward to open the door.

MOLESLEY: Ma'am, I was wondering if I might take some
time this afternoon, to help in the village hall.
MATTHEW: Why? What's happening?
MOLESLEY: It's the flower show, sir, next Saturday. I'll
give my father a hand with his stall, if I may.
ISOBEL: Of course you must go.
MATTHEW: And so, I'm afraid, must I.

He grabs a hat, kisses his mother's hand and leaves.

....

* I like the relationship between Matthew and his mother, which in many
details is the work of Dan Stevens and Penelope Wilton. By this stage of
the series, I was writing material that would work with the characters they
had developed. He likes and admires her but he can't see why she always
has to make trouble. I think this is lifelike. By now Matthew identifies
with both families, with his mother but also with Robert. He's the pig in
the middle really.

6 INT. CARSON'S PANTRY. DAY.

A hand carefully replaces an ancient key on a hook. It is Thomas who quickly conceals a bottle of wine behind his back when he hears footsteps. Bates looks in at the door.

BATES: Oh. Is Mr Carson about?

THOMAS: I don't think so. I was just looking for him, myself.

But he does not move. Bates stares at him for a moment and then, with a brisk nod, he goes. Thomas is not comfortable.

7.   EXT.   CORA'S SITTING ROOM.   DAY.

The door opens and Robert enters. Cora is at her desk.

ROBERT: Busy?

CORA: I'm just trying to sort out the wretched flower show but come in.

ROBERT: I've had a letter from Rosamond.

CORA: Don't tell me. She wants a saddle of lamb and all the fruit and vegetables we can muster.

ROBERT: She enjoys a taste of her old home.

CORA: She enjoys not paying for food.

ROBERT: Carson will organise a hamper. Then one of the girls can go down and cable which train it'll be on. But there's something else… Apparently, the word's going round London that Evelyn Napier has given up any thought of Mary. That he's going to marry one of the Semphill girls.

Cora looks at him, before she answers quite carefully.

CORA: So what? We knew it wouldn't work after he stayed for the hunt.

ROBERT: She writes as if, somehow, it reflects badly on Mary.

CORA: Your dear sister is always such a harbinger of joy.

ROBERT: No, as if… as if Mary had somehow been found wanting. In her character.

She looks at him hard, but he knows nothing.

CORA: I don't believe Mr Napier would have said that.

She turns her attention back to the letter she is writing.

ROBERT: Neither do I, really, but —

CORA: She ought to be married. When I was her age, I was a mother. Talk to her.

ROBERT: She never listens to me. If she did, she'd marry Matthew.*

CORA: What about Anthony Strallan?

ROBERT: What about him?

CORA: Well, Maud's been dead for two years so he must be over it by now. And he has to marry again.

ROBERT: Why?

CORA: He's got no children. He needs an heir.

ROBERT: How alluring you make him sound.

CORA: Well?

ROBERT: Anthony Strallan is at least my age and as dull as paint. I doubt she'd want to sit next to him at dinner, let alone marry him.†

CORA: She has to marry someone, Robert. And if this is what's being said in London, she has to marry soon.

She is very definite indeed, which surprises him.

....

* As I have said before, Robert loves his three daughters but he doesn't really know them. He thinks they're all nice girls who will marry nice gentlemen and have nice children. He doesn't realise they're born at a period of change which is bound to affect them all. This doesn't mean they don't get on. In fact in some ways Mary is like his son because she is dynamic and worldly and they have a lot in common but, in the last analysis, I think Mary's cleverer than Robert. I wonder if she'd have taken Patrick when it came to it.

† In the first series, Cora is still playing along with the values she's married into even if, every now and then, you can see she disagrees with them. She sticks up for Matthew's having a job for example, but she has yet to re-connect with her beliefs from before she was a member of the British aristocracy. It is not that her spirit has been broken, but she doesn't feel entitled to rebel. So, she assumes that Mary will marry someone like Robert and everything will go on as before. Robert doesn't disagree with this in principle, but he has a clearer view of the qualities that would interest Mary. And Strallan hasn't got them.

8 INT. SERVANTS' HALL. DAY.

Bates sews buttons, Anna mends the hem of a skirt. O'Brien is unpicking a lace collar. Daisy's cracking walnuts. Thomas reads a paper. William is cleaning candlesticks.

O'BRIEN: You shouldn't do that in here.

WILLIAM: I don't like being in the pantry all alone. And Mr Carson won't mind. He's gone into the village.

THOMAS: He'll mind if I tell him.

Anna glances at the lace the other maid is working on.

ANNA: That's pretty.

O'BRIEN: Do you think so? She wants it put onto a new shirt, but it's a bit old-fashioned, to my taste.

DAISY: Oh no, it's lovely.

O'Brien ignores Daisy. Anna tries to make up for the snub.

ANNA: Have you recovered?

BATES: What from?

ANNA: Daisy had a bit of a turn. When we were in Lady Mary's room. Didn't you?

DAISY: I'm fine, thank you.

She doesn't want to continue this.

THOMAS: What sort of turn? Did you see a ghost?

WILLIAM: Will you leave her alone, if she doesn't want to talk about it?

THOMAS: I've often wondered if this place is haunted. It ought to be.

O'BRIEN: By the spirits of the maids and footmen who died in slavery.

BATES: But not, in Thomas's case, from overwork.

ANNA: Come on, Daisy. What was it?

The room's attention upon her, Daisy shrugs, uneasily.

DAISY: I don't know. I was thinking... First we had the *Titanic* —

O'BRIEN: Don't keep harping back to that.

DAISY: I know it's a while ago, but we *knew* them. I think of how I laid the fires for Mr Patrick, but he drowned in that icy water.

O'BRIEN: For God's sake.

DAISY: Then there was the Turkish gentleman. It just
seems there's been too much death in the house.
WILLIAM: But what's that got to do with Lady Mary's
bedroom?
DAISY: Nothing. Nothing at all.

O'Brien is interested by her nervousness. So is Thomas.

9 EXT. DOWNTON VILLAGE. DAY.

Isobel's in the village. There is activity around the hall.

10 INT. DOWNTON VILLAGE HALL. DAY.

*A hum of activity, with bunting being hung and tables set
out. Molesley sees Isobel, who is approaching the stage.*

MOLESLEY: Afternoon, ma'am.

They turn to what is obviously going to be a display table.

ISOBEL: When do you put that magnificent display of
prizes on show?
MOLESLEY: Not 'til the day, itself.
ISOBEL: I remember a superb cup from last year.
MOLESLEY: The Grantham Cup. It was donated by the late
Lord Grantham. For the Best Bloom in the Village.
ISOBEL: And who won it last year?
VIOLET (V.O.): I did.

She is standing there, as magnificent as usual.

ISOBEL: Well done. And the year before?
MOLESLEY: Her ladyship won that one, too.

Isobel looks at Violet, who nods graciously saying nothing.

ISOBEL: Heavens, how thrilling. And before that?

*Molesley changes the subject, turning to an older man who is
arranging a cloth over a table. Isobel understands.*

MOLESLEY: You've met my father.
ISOBEL: Good afternoon, Mr Molesley. What are you
showing this year?
BILL MOLESLEY: Oh, this and that.
MOLESLEY: Only the finest roses in the village.
ISOBEL: Really? What an achievement.

She invites Violet's opinion, but it is a challenge.

VIOLET: It's a wonderful area for roses. We're very
lucky. We'll see some beautiful examples right across
the show. Won't we, Mr Molesley?
BILL MOLESLEY: If you say so, your ladyship.

He is defeated. Violet joins Cora, and Isobel follows.

ISOBEL: How are you getting on?
CORA: My main job is referee. What with defending the
categories and protecting the judges, I'm completely worn
out by the end.
VIOLET: It's so lovely for me, just to sit back and watch
you do the work, after so many years of having to run it...
Well, I must get back. Goodbye, dear.

With a cool smile, she walks off. Cora lowers her voice.

CORA: She can't *stand* not being President any more.
Every year she haunts the tent like the ghost of
Christmas-yet-to-come.
ISOBEL: I was talking to Molesley about the Grantham Cup.
I gather she always wins it.
CORA: That was the price of peace.
ISOBEL: But suppose she hasn't grown the best bloom?
What happens then? Doesn't it annoy the village?
CORA: Not really. They see it as a charming, old world
tradition, and, to be honest, I simply cannot face
another fight.
ISOBEL: I don't blame you.

But there is revolution in her eyes.

11 INT. BEDROOM PASSAGE. DAY.

*O'Brien comes out of Cora's bedroom, carrying clothes, to find
Thomas staring out of a window. He looks worried.*

O'BRIEN: What's up with you?
THOMAS: Nothing.
O'BRIEN: His lordship's blaming Mr Napier for spreading
gossip about Lady Mary, but it was you, wasn't it?
THOMAS: Why do you say that?

O'BRIEN: Because Napier wasn't in on it. Only four people know he was in her room that night. You, me, Lady Mary and possibly Daisy. And I haven't said nothing to nobody.

THOMAS: I didn't tell about Pamuk. I just wrote that Lady Mary was no better than she ought to be.

O'BRIEN: Who did you write it to?

THOMAS: Only a friend of mine. Valet to Lord Savident.

O'BRIEN: You know what they say about old Savident. Not so much an open mind as an open mouth. No wonder it's all round London.

THOMAS: You won't tell, will you? I'm in enough trouble as it is.

O'BRIEN: Why? What's happened?

THOMAS: I think Mr Bates saw me nicking a bottle of wine.

O'BRIEN: Has he told Mr Carson?

THOMAS: Not yet. But he will when he's feeling spiteful. I wish we could be shot of him.

O'BRIEN: Then think of something quick. Turn the tables on him, before he has the chance to nail you.

12 INT. STAIRCASE HALL. DOWNTON. NIGHT.

Robert spies Sybil who is about to go upstairs.

ROBERT: I thought you were in bed hours ago.

SYBIL: I was writing a note for Lynch. I need the governess cart tomorrow.

ROBERT: Oh?

SYBIL: I'm going into Malton.

ROBERT: Don't risk the traffic in Malton. Not now, when every Tom, Dick and Harry seems to have a motor.

SYBIL: Hardly.

ROBERT: Last time I was there, there were five parked in the market place and another three drove past while I was waiting.

SYBIL: Horrid for the horses.

ROBERT: Get Branson to take you in the car. Neither of us is using it.

SYBIL: I thought I'd pop in on old Mrs Stuart. Will you tell Mama, if I forget?

Sybil is not changing her plans. She kisses him goodnight and goes on up the staircase, with her flickering candle.

13 INT. KITCHEN PASSAGE. DAY.

O'Brien, with breakfast tray, is with Thomas. Daisy enters.

O'BRIEN: You're late this morning.
DAISY: The library grate needed a real going-over. Are any of them down yet?
THOMAS: Lady Sybil's in the dining room.
DAISY: I'll start with her room, then.
O'BRIEN: Daisy?

The maid turns in the passage to face them.

O'BRIEN (CONT'D): You know when you were talking about the feeling of death in the house...
DAISY: I was just being silly.
O'BRIEN: I found myself wondering about the connection between the poor Turkish gentleman, Mr Pamuk, and Lady Mary's room.

Daisy is like one struck. She stammers and licks her lips.

O'BRIEN (CONT'D): Only you were saying how you felt so uncomfortable in there.

O'Brien's mouth is smiling pleasantly. Her eyes are not.

DAISY: Well, I... I've got to get on. I'm late enough as it is.

As she scurries off, the others nod. Daisy knows something.

14 EXT. DOWNTON VILLAGE. DAY.

Mary is walking in the village. Matthew comes round the corner on his bicycle.

MATTHEW: Hello.

Matthew dismounts and starts wheeling the bicycle. Mary is going to snap back, but changes her mind.

MATTHEW (CONT'D): Is everything all right?
MARY: I am about to send a telegram.

She falls into step with him as he walks along.

MARY (CONT'D): Papa's sister is always nagging him to send supplies to London and then we cable her, so her butler can be at King's Cross to meet them. It's idiotic, really.
MATTHEW: Is this Lady Rosamond Painswick?
MARY: You *have* done your homework.
MATTHEW: She wrote to welcome me into the family, which I thought pretty generous given the circumstances.
MARY: It's easy to be generous when you have nothing to lose.

He gives a sympathetic look which almost makes her smile.

MARY (CONT'D): So are you doing any more church visiting with Edith?
MATTHEW: My mother's trying to set something up.
MARY: Watch out. I think she has big plans for you.
MATTHEW: Then she's in for an equally big disappointment.

He gives a knowing look and, again, he has made her laugh.

END OF ACT ONE

ACT TWO

15 INT.   SYBIL'S BEDROOM.   DAY.

Anna and Gwen are working as usual when Daisy comes in.

DAISY: Is it all right to do the fire?
ANNA: Why are you so late?
DAISY: I went back to my room after I'd woken everyone, and I just shut my eyes for a moment… I've been trying to catch up ever since.
ANNA: Have you had any breakfast?
DAISY: Not a crumb.
ANNA: Here.

She takes a small tin from beside the bed, holding it open.

GWEN: You can't take her biscuits.

ANNA: She never eats them. None of them do. They're
just thrown away and changed every evening.

Daisy takes the tin and starts to munch one as she speaks.

DAISY: Thanks. She wouldn't mind anyway. She's nice,
Lady Sybil.

Gwen looks at the clock and sits heavily on the bed.

GWEN: Ooh.
CARSON (V.O.): Gwen? May I ask why you are sitting on
Lady Sybil's bed?

He is in the doorway. Which seems to make Gwen nervous.

GWEN: Well, you see I had a turn... like a burst of
sickness... Just sudden-like. I had to sit down.
ANNA: It's true. She came over queasy.
CARSON: You'd better go and lie down. I'll tell Mrs
Hughes.
GWEN: I don't need to interrupt her morning. I'm sure
I'll be fine, if I can just put my feet up.
CARSON: How many more bedrooms have you still got to do?
ANNA: Just one. Lady Edith's.
CARSON: And you can manage on your own?
ANNA: Well, she's no use to man or beast in that state.

*Gwen stands and goes to the door. She looks back, a little
guiltily, to see Anna finishing the counterpane.*

ANNA (CONT'D): Shoo.

She waves her away. Carson looks round the room, sternly.

CARSON: Daisy? May I ask why you are holding Lady
Sybil's biscuit jar?

Daisy, still swallowing, nearly jumps through the roof.

DAISY: I was just polishing it before I put it back.
CARSON: See that you do.

*He goes, leaving Anna and Daisy to share their relief. Anna
picks up a tray, to take candle and water carafe away.*

16 INT. KITCHEN. DAY.

Mrs Patmore is indignant.

MRS PATMORE: Where is that stupid girl?
MRS HUGHES (V.O.): She's just here.

Mrs Hughes is watching from the door, puzzled.

MRS PATMORE: Why are you hiding?
DAISY: I'm not hiding. I'm stood here.
MRS PATMORE: One more word and you'll be up a chimney
with a brush in your hand.
DAISY: Yes, Mrs Patmore.
MRS PATMORE: Have you done them fires? Because it'd be
ever so nice if they were finished by Christmas.

Daisy scuttles off. Mrs Hughes speaks again.

MRS HUGHES: She wasn't hiding.

17 INT. KITCHEN. DAY.

*Mrs Hughes walks along the corridor towards the kitchen where
Cora is standing with Mrs Patmore and Daisy.*

CORA: But Mrs Patmore, it's such a little thing to ask.
MRS PATMORE: I'm sorry, m'lady, but I can't do more than
my best.

Mrs Hughes has arrived.

MRS HUGHES: Is there some difficulty, your ladyship?
CORA: Dear Mrs Hughes, as you know we're giving a dinner
on Friday for Sir Anthony Strallan —
MRS HUGHES: Yes, m'lady.
CORA: Well, it seems he is particularly fond of a certain
new pudding. It's called Apple Charlotte. Do you know
it?
MRS HUGHES: I'm not sure.
CORA: His sister, Mrs Chetwood, sent me the receipt, and
I'm trying to persuade Mrs Patmore to make it.
MRS PATMORE: And I'm trying to persuade her ladyship that
I have already planned the dinner with her, and I can't
change it now.
MRS HUGHES: Why not?
MRS PATMORE: Because everything's been ordered and
prepared.

Mrs Hughes takes the paper from Cora.

MRS HUGHES: Well, there's nothing here that looks very
complicated. Apples, lemon, butter... I think we've some
Granose Flakes. If not, we can certainly get them —
MRS PATMORE: I cannot work from a new receipt at a
moment's notice!
DAISY: But I can read it to you, if that's the problem.

Predictably, this sets the match to the taper.

MRS PATMORE: *Problem?* Who mentioned a problem? How dare
you say such a thing in front of her ladyship!

Cora's had enough. She raises her hands in defeat.

CORA: Very well. We can try it another time, when you've
had longer to prepare. We'll stay with the raspberry
meringue.*
MRS PATMORE: And very nice it'll be, too.
CORA: I'm sure.

Cora walks away with Mrs Hughes, who stops her at the door.

....

* You often see servants depicted as grovelling, but this was not true at all.
The upper servants, who were masters of their own domain, expected to be
treated with a degree of respect, while cooks were notoriously touchy and for
a cook to talk back would be quite normal. Sometimes cooks were absolutely
impossible but if the food was marvellous people didn't want to let them go.
Usually the master of the house would have little to do with them, but his
wife would frequently require all her diplomatic skills. Each house had its
own way of managing this relationship, which was illustrated for me when we
were making the film *Gosford Park*. We had three former servants advising
us, and one day we were doing the scene where Eileen Atkins, playing the
cook, is asked to accompany Stephen Fry. As she leaves the kitchen, she
instructs a kitchen maid to 'see that those menus go up on her ladyship's tray'.
Immediately one of the advisory board said: 'Oh, no. That's quite wrong.
The menus were always done in her ladyship's boudoir.' Whereupon, a
second advisor contradicted her. 'I don't think so, no, her ladyship would
always come down to the cook's sitting room to do the menus.' At which
point the third one remarked that 'ours went up on the tray'. It made me
realise that people are wrong in thinking everything was governed by
universal rules when it often depended on the ways of an individual house.
At any rate, for Mrs Patmore to refuse to follow a new receipt would not be a
first for Cora.

MRS HUGHES: I'm so sorry about that, m'lady.

CORA: Never mind. I was asking a lot.

Behind them Mrs Patmore is hissing more abuse at her underling.

MRS PATMORE: Oh, yes. Butter wouldn't melt in your mouth, would it? But you'll pay for that! And the hour will not be long in coming!

Cora glances back at the irate cook stamping about.

CORA: Do look after that girl.

MRS HUGHES: Daisy? She's used to it. She'll be all right.

CORA: I wonder. Mrs Patmore looks ready to eat her alive.

DAISY: I was only trying to help.

MRS PATMORE: Oh, like Judas was only 'trying to help' I s'pose, when he brought the Roman soldiers to the garden! Oh, just you watch it, my dear! Just you watch it!

18 EXT. THE PARK. DOWNTON. DAY.

Sybil holds the reins of the little cart as it travels briskly through the park. As she approaches the gate, she looks around and pulls in the horse. After a moment there is a movement and Gwen emerges from behind a bush. She is neatly dressed in the suit Sybil gave her. She climbs in and they set off again. Sybil glances at her approvingly.*

GWEN: I've had to let your skirt down a little, but I can put it back.

SYBIL: No, it's yours… What happens if a maid finds your room is empty?

GWEN: It'd only be Anna and she wouldn't give me away. She's like a sister. She'd never betray me.

SYBIL: Then she's not like *my* sisters.

She turns to the horse.

SYBIL (CONT'D): Walk on.

Sybil and Gwen laugh together as they speed off on an adventure.

....

*This is an important marker moment in the development of Sybil. She is no longer content to sympathise with Gwen's ambitions. She is determined to give her practical help.

19 INT. EDITH'S BEDROOM. DAY.

Anna is making the bed. She has to keep walking round it.

BATES (V.O.): Shall I give you a hand?

He is standing in the doorway. He walks over to the bed.

ANNA: Oh, would you? It takes half the time with two.
BATES: I always feel a bit sorry for Lady Edith.
ANNA: Me too. Although I don't know why. When you think what she's got and we haven't.
BATES: Mr Molesley said she'd made a play for Mr Crawley.
ANNA: 'Made a play' is a bit strong.
BATES: Mrs Hughes said she was after the other heir. Mr Patrick Crawley. The one who drowned.
ANNA: That was different. She was in love with him.
BATES: What happened?
ANNA: She never got a look in. He was all set up to marry Lady Mary.
BATES: Then he was a braver man than I am, Gunga Din.

Which makes both smile a little.

BATES (CONT'D): Sad to think about.
ANNA: It's always sad when you love someone who doesn't love you back. No matter who you are.
BATES: I meant it's sad that he died.

Anna feels slightly caught out.

ANNA: Oh. Yes. Very sad. He was nice.

The bed is finished and the room tidied. She has loaded the tray, and now she takes it up and starts for the door.

ANNA (CONT'D): Well, thank you for that. Much appreciated.
BATES: My pleasure.

She is almost out of the room when he speaks again.

BATES (CONT'D): Perhaps Mr Patrick did love her back but just couldn't say it.
ANNA: Why ever not?
BATES: Sometimes you're not at liberty to speak. Sometimes it wouldn't be right.

And he has passed her and gone about his business.

20 EXT. STREET IN MALTON. DAY.

Sybil sits in the governess cart as Gwen climbs down.

   SYBIL: Don't be too long.
   GWEN: They said ten o'clock, so we should be fine. We'll
   be back before they notice we're gone.
   SYBIL: Good luck.

With a nervous smile, Gwen hurries inside.

21 INT. OFFICES. MALTON. DAY

A secretary leads Gwen along the corridor.

   SECRETARY: Take a seat.

*Gwen sits down. A wall clock shows five to ten. A door
opens, a woman emerges. Gwen leans forward expectantly, but
nothing happens.*

22 INT. DRAWING ROOM. DOWER HOUSE. DAY.

Violet sits ruling the roost. Isobel is paying a call.

   VIOLET: The flower show? I thought I was in for another
   telling off about the hospital.

She smiles pleasantly.

   ISOBEL: No. This time it's the flower show. I've been
   to see old Mr Molesley's garden. His roses are the most
   beautiful I've ever laid eyes on.

Now Violet is beginning to get the idea. Her eyes narrow.

   VIOLET: Go on.
   ISOBEL: You may not know it but I believe the committee
   feels obliged to give you the cup for Best Bloom as a
   kind of local tradition.
   VIOLET: No, No. I do not know that. I thought I usually
   won the prize for the Best Bloom in the Village because
   my gardener had *grown* the Best Bloom in the Village.

She sits back pleasantly, waiting for the next tactic.

   ISOBEL: Yes, but you don't 'usually' win, do you? You
   always win.
   VIOLET: I have been very fortunate in that regard.

ISOBEL: Surely, when Mr Molesley's garden is so
remarkable and he is so very proud of his —
VIOLET: You talk of Mr Molesley's pride. What of my
gardener's pride? Is he to be sacrificed on the altar of
Molesley's ambition?
ISOBEL: All I'm asking is that you release them from any
obligation to let you win. Why not just tell them to
choose whichever flower is best…
VIOLET: But that is precisely what they already know.
And do.

Isobel is tough but Violet is tougher. *

23 INT. OFFICES. MALTON. DAY.

*Gwen is sitting, waiting. She looks anxiously at the
receptionist, who smiles coldly. The clocks shows it is half
past eleven.*

24 INT. OFFICES. MALTON. DAY

*The clock shows ten minutes to one. Gwen comes out of an
office, nods to the secretary and rushes along the corridor.*

25 INT. DRESSING ROOM. DAY.

Bates walks in with a coat over his arm, then he stops.

BATES: I'm sorry, m'lord. I didn't think you'd be in
here.

Robert is bent over the case of snuff boxes.

....

* In supporting the claims of old Mr Molesley, Isobel is making trouble.
Partly because Violet irritates her and Isobel would love to take her down a
peg, but mainly because, like pretty well every newcomer to a village in the
country, she can't leave anything alone. I remember in the village where I
grew up, there was a harvest supper every summer which was organised by
my mother and two or three other women. Then a new artistic couple
arrived, arguing that this was terrible and patronising and of course the
supper had to be run by the villagers, themselves. My mother was perfectly
content to be free of the work but she warned them that the supper would
vanish within three years. They laughed at her, seeing this as proof of her
self-importance and vanity. But in fact it had vanished in two.

ROBERT: Are my eyes deceiving me or is one of these
missing?

Bates walks over and stares down.

BATES: I don't know them well enough.
ROBERT: No. Why would you? But there's a very pretty
little blue one, with a miniature framed in French paste.
It was made for a German prince. I forget who... Unless it
was moved for some reason... but why would it be?

*This is the kind of thing any servant dreads.**

26 EXT. STREET IN MALTON. DAY.

Gwen comes racing out and clambers back up.

GWEN: I'm so sorry, m'lady. But I didn't get in there
until nearly twelve.
SYBIL: We'll just have to hope your secret's safe with
Anna.

She looks across at Gwen, who is bursting with excitement.

SYBIL (CONT'D): So? How did you get on?
GWEN: Oh, m'lady! I think they liked me. I really do!

With a grin, Sybil whips up the horse and they set off.

27 EXT. COUNTRY LANE OUTSIDE A VILLAGE. DAY.

*Sybil and Gwen are walking alongside their horse. They are
both looking fairly tired. They see a man ahead of them.*

SYBIL: Hello. Our horse has cast a shoe. Is there a
smithy nearby?
MAN: You can try old Crump in the next village.

Sybil and Gwen both thank him and they walk along together.

....

* The one thing no servant could afford was to attract even the faintest
suspicion of theft. A career in service really depended on having good
references, and while an employer might swallow a bit of bad temper or a lack
of punctuality, they would never overlook theft. Once you were perceived as
a thief you would not work again. So here, it may only be about a little snuff
box, but Thomas and O'Brien are attempting to ruin Bates.

SYBIL: At least it happened on the way home.

GWEN: They'll be worried about you.

SYBIL: The point is you've got the job.

GWEN: I think I have. I hope I have.

She is still excited as they march onwards.

28 INT. KITCHEN PASSAGE. DAY.

O'Brien comes out of the ironing room, carrying a splendid evening dress. She almost bumps into Anna, who's surprised.

ANNA: Is her ladyship wearing that now?

O'BRIEN: Oh no. This is for Friday night. I thought I'd give it a press while I had the time.

ANNA: You don't know what's happened to Lady Sybil, do you? I've got the changes ready for the other two, but there's no sign of her.

O'BRIEN: Don't you start. I've had Her Majesty on at me all afternoon.

William hears this. He is walking down the passage.

WILLIAM: Mr Carson says he'll fetch the police if she's not back soon.

Which is unsettling. Anna goes. So does O'Brien. William continues on down the passage, almost passing Daisy.

WILLIAM (CONT'D): Hello? What's the matter?

DAISY: Nothing. I've got a lot on my mind, that's all.

WILLIAM: Because I may not be as bright as Thomas, but I'm a good listener.

DAISY: Oh, why can't you leave me alone?

She goes, leaving him with a heavy heart.

29 EXT. VILLAGE SMITHY. EVE.

It is getting dark and the girls are exhausted.

MAN: Sorry, Miss. But Mr Crump's staying over at the Skelton estate tonight. He's working there all week.

SYBIL: Is there anyone else?

MAN: Not that I know of.

Sybil thanks him and they trudge on.

30 EXT. A COUNTRY ROAD. DAY.

*The two girls are trying to get the horse to cross a ford.
Their skirts are in the stream.*

    SYBIL: Come on Dragon, come on! Dragon, if you don't
    move now, I'll have you boiled for glue!

*The horse makes a terrific jerking leap across, dragging the
cart and leaving both of them sitting in the muddy water.
The horse looks back at them with a smile.*

31 INT. CORA'S BEDROOM. NIGHT.

O'Brien is fastening the back of a simple evening frock.

    CORA: But what if she's overturned? What if she's lying
    in a ditch somewhere?
    O'BRIEN: I'm sure she'll be back in the shake of a lamb's
    tail.

*But Cora isn't sure. She moves to her dressing table, where
O'Brien tidies her hair and inserts a diamond ornament.*

    CORA: The truth is they're all getting too old for a
    mother's control.
    O'BRIEN: They're growing up.
    CORA: They've *grown* up. They need their own
    establishments.
    O'BRIEN: I'm sure they'll all get plenty of offers.

Cora looks at her through the glass. Will they?

32 INT. CORA'S BEDROOM. NIGHT.*

O'Brien is still working on Cora's hair.

    CORA: Nobody warns you about bringing up daughters. You
    think it's going to be like *Little Women*, and instead
    they're at each other's throats from dawn 'til dusk.†
    O'BRIEN: Not Lady Sybil, surely.
    CORA: Oh no. Sybil's the family peacemaker. But Mary
    and Edith have been like two rats in a barrel since they
    were little girls.

....

* Scenes 31 and 32 were originally separated by what became Scene 33, but
during the shoot the decision was made to combine them.

She is distracted by her own reflection but this last speech has given O'Brien an idea, and not a kind one.

33 EXT. DOWNTON. NIGHT.

Sybil waits, drained, as Gwen slips away round the side of the house. Then she rings the bell and William appears.

    SYBIL: Can you get someone to send for Lynch?
    WILLIAM: I'll take him round to the stables, m'lady. I'm glad to.

Sybil doesn't argue. She almost falls through the door.

34 INT. ANNA'S AND GWEN'S BEDROOM. NIGHT.

Anna walks in. Gwen is in bed, exhausted.

    ANNA: You look done in. I'll bring you some food up later when we've finished dinner.
    GWEN: I think I've got a temperature.
    ANNA: I expect you have. Where were you?

Gwen is rather deflated by this. Her cover is blown.

    GWEN: You came up, then?
    ANNA: I had to change for the afternoon. I've had Mrs Hughes and all sorts asking how you were. I didn't know what to say. I wish you'd warned me.
    GWEN: Did you cover for me?
    ANNA: What do you think?‡

....

† This story is exploring that strange transition when your children grow into adults and begin to have an independent life of their own. Even in their teens, you know what your sons and daughters are doing and, for the most part, where they are. You take them and you collect them and then, suddenly, you're not quite taking them but you're meeting them off a train, and soon after that you don't know where they are and you ring and find they're in Suffolk but you don't know why. This, for most of us, comes as a shock. Here, Cora has reached that moment with Sybil. She doesn't know where her daughter is.

‡ I think this kind of complicity happened a great deal in these households, as it does in any workplace. Even though Anna is both a moral person and a completely truthful one, it wouldn't occur to her to give Gwen away. This class loyalty, which can be very strong, must often have been tiresome for the employers because they knew that even the members of staff they loved and trusted would cover for less worthy co-workers. It is a human instinct.

She adjusts her cap.

ANNA (CONT'D): I don't suppose this had anything to do with Lady Sybil.

GWEN: Oh, Anna, it was a nightmare. The horse threw a shoe and we tried to find a blacksmith but we couldn't…

Anna is laughing at the account and so, at last, is Gwen.

GWEN (CONT'D): I don't know how I got in without being seen. I'm sure I've left a trail of mud up the stairs.

ANNA: So did you get the job?

GWEN: We'll have to wait and see.

But of course she thinks she has.

35 INT. LIBRARY. NIGHT.

Edith, changed, is writing letters when O'Brien comes in.

O'BRIEN: Sorry to bother you, m'lady, but your mother wanted you to know that Lady Sybil's back. She's changing now, so dinner won't be late, after all.

EDITH: What happened to her?

O'BRIEN: The horse went lame.

Edith nods her thanks. But the maid does not leave, instead she seems to hover. At last Edith looks over.

EDITH: Is there anything else?

O'BRIEN: There *is* something that's been troubling me… You remember that Turkish gentleman? Mr Pamuk? The one who died. All sudden like.

EDITH: Of course I remember.

O'BRIEN: Well… it's Daisy, m'lady.

This name does not strike any bells.

O'BRIEN (CONT'D): The kitchen maid. Only she's been talking recently as if she had ideas about Mr Pamuk's death.

EDITH: What sort of 'ideas'?

O'BRIEN: Well, I've no proof and maybe I'm wrong. But I've a sense she knows something but she won't say what.

Now comes the coup de grâce.

O'BRIEN (CONT'D): Something involving Lady Mary.

At last Edith's interest is captured. Entirely.

EDITH: How absurd. What could she know?
O'BRIEN: That's just it. Whatever it is, she won't say.
Not to us, anyway.
EDITH: Have you spoken to Lady Mary about this?
O'BRIEN: I didn't like to, m'lady. It seemed impertinent
somehow. But I thought someone in the family ought to
know about it.

*O'Brien, of course, is cleverer than any of them. Edith
nods.*

EDITH: Quite right. Bring the girl to my room tomorrow.
After breakfast.

Mary comes in, also dressed for dinner, as O'Brien goes.

MARY: What did she want?
EDITH: Nothing. Just a message from Mama that Sybil's
turned up alive.
MARY: Poor darling. She had to walk for miles. I don't
think I'd have got down, however lame the horse.
EDITH: No. I don't believe you would.

She goes back to her letter.

END OF ACT TWO

ACT THREE

36 INT. EDITH'S BEDROOM. DAY.

Edith is with Daisy and O'Brien. Daisy shaking with nerves.

DAISY: I couldn't say, m'lady. I don't know what Miss
O'Brien means. I didn't see nuffin. Well not much.

The other two women exchange a quick glance.

EDITH: O'Brien, I wonder if you might leave us?

O'Brien goes, annoyed to be shut out of her own plot.

EDITH (CONT'D): Now… it's Daisy, isn't it?*

DAISY: Yes, m'lady.

EDITH: I'm sure you see O'Brien acted as she did because she's concerned.

DAISY: I suppose so, m'lady, but —

EDITH: She seems to think that you are in possession of some knowledge that is uncomfortable for you.

Daisy is silent. She won't agree but she can't lie.

EDITH (CONT'D): Because if that is the case, then I don't think it fair on you.

Daisy looks up. She'd thought she was in trouble.

EDITH (CONT'D): Why should you be burdened with Mary's secret? When there's nothing in it for you but worry and grief? My dear, my heart goes out to you. It really does.

These are the kindest words Daisy has heard in a long time. If ever. Her shoulders start to shake and soon she's weeping. Edith steps in and takes her gently in her arms.

EDITH (CONT'D): There, there. Come and sit down. You've been carrying too heavy a load for too long. Just tell me, and I promise you'll feel better.

37 EXT. DOWNTON VILLAGE. DAY.

Violet is getting down from her carriage. Mary is with her. They walk into the village hall.

38 INT. DOWNTON VILLAGE HALL. DAY.

The flower show. The decorations are complete and people are setting out the stalls with cakes and jams as well as flowers. Matthew and Isobel are admiring Bill Molesley's table. Cora sees Violet and comes over to greet her with a cool kiss on the cheek.

....

* It is impossible for Daisy not to tell the truth here because, for her, to be questioned by a daughter of this great house, would be like our being interrogated by the secret police. She feels completely disempowered. And Edith is forceful and determined in her desire to humiliate Mary. She is a nicer person after the war has changed her, but at this stage, she is still fuelled by a kind of jealous rage.

VIOLET: You seem well prepared.

CORA: They'll add a few flowers in the morning before we open, but I think we're nearly there.

Isobel has approached them.

ISOBEL: Do look at Mr Molesley's display. He's worked so hard.

To Violet, this is loaded. They join Matthew at the stall.

MATTHEW: They're rather marvellous, aren't they?

MARY: Lovely. Well done Mr Molesley.

BILL MOLESLEY: Thank you, m'lady.

Violet looks round the room, firmly.

VIOLET: I think *everyone* is to be congratulated. It's splendid.

ISOBEL: But do look at these roses. Have you ever seen the like?

It's a challenge. Violet meets it head on, turning to Cora.

VIOLET: My dear, Mrs Crawley believes I am profiting from an unfair advantage.

CORA: Oh?

VIOLET: She feels, in the past, I have been given the cup more as a matter of routine than merit.

She smiles blandly. Matthew catches Mary's eye.

MATTHEW: That's rather ungallant, Mother. I'm sure when we see Cousin Violet's roses, it will be hard to think they could be bettered.

ISOBEL: Hard. But not impossible.

VIOLET: You are quite wonderful the way you see room for improvement wherever you look. I never knew such reforming zeal.

ISOBEL: I take that as a compliment.

Violet turns away, murmuring audibly to Mary.

VIOLET: I must have said it wrong.

She moves on, leaving Mary and Matthew together.

MARY: Poor Granny. She's not used to being challenged.

MATTHEW: Nor is Mother. I think we should let them settle it between them.

MARY: So you are interested in flowers?

MATTHEW: I'm interested in the village. In fact I'm on my way to inspect the cottages.

MARY: You know what all work and no play did for Jack.

MATTHEW: But you think I'm a dull boy, anyway. Don't you?

She wouldn't answer him, even if she knew the answer.

MATTHEW (CONT'D): I play, too. I'm coming up for dinner tonight. I suspect I'm there to balance the numbers. Is it in aid of anything?

MARY: Not that I know of. Just a couple of dreary neighbours, that's all.

MATTHEW: Maybe I'll shine by comparison.

Violet across the room calls out.

VIOLET: Mary! We're going.

Mary looks at her companion.

MARY: Maybe you will.

39 INT. SERVANTS' HALL. NIGHT.

Most of the servants are present. Carson looks in.

CARSON: Might I have a word?

They are all silenced by his tone.

CARSON (CONT'D): I want to say something before I ring the gong. I'm afraid it's not very pleasant.

Naturally, you could now hear a pin drop.

CARSON (CONT'D): His lordship is missing a very valuable snuff box. It appears to have been taken from the case in his room. If one of you knows anything about this, will he or she please come to me. Your words will be heard in the strictest confidence. Thank you.

He goes, leaving the household amazed. Then O'Brien speaks.

O'BRIEN: I am sorry, Mr Bates. What an unpleasant thing to have happened.

ANNA: Why are you picking on him?

THOMAS: Because he's the only one of us who goes in there. But don't worry. I'm sure it'll turn up.

BATES: Thank you for your concern.

There is the sound of the gong and they all walk out to attend to their duties, leaving Bates alone with Anna. He is pale.

> BATES (CONT'D): I hate this kind of thing. I hope to God they find it.
> ANNA: Don't be silly. Nobody thinks it's you.
> BATES: No?
> ANNA: Why ever would they?

At this, he looks at her but he does not reply.

> BATES: Better get a move on.

40 INT. MARY'S BEDROOM. NIGHT.

Mary is alone. There is a knock and Cora enters.

> MARY: I'm coming. Do you think this brooch works? I can't decide.
> CORA: It's charming.

She sits carefully on the bed.

> MARY: Oh dear. Is it another scolding?
> CORA: Of course not. You're too grown up to scold, these days.
> MARY: Heavens. Then it's really serious.
> CORA: I'd like you to look after Sir Anthony Strallan tonight. He's a nice, decent man. His position may not be quite like Papa's but it would still make you a force for good in the county —
> MARY: Mama, not again! How many times am I to be ordered to marry the man sitting next to me at dinner?*
> CORA: As many times as it takes.

Her voice is stronger than before.

> MARY: I turned down Matthew Crawley. Is it likely I'd marry Strallan when I wouldn't marry *him*?

....

* That line came from a great aunt of mine who said that things with her had got to the point when she felt that if a man could walk and talk and hadn't actually spilt something down his front, she was expected to marry him. In fact, I had two aunts who were sent out to India on the 'fishing fleet'. One of my great great uncles was the Governor of Bombay and two of my grandfather's sisters were despatched to stay with him, but neither came home with a husband. They were what was known as 'returned empties'. They both got married eventually, but quite late by the reckoning of those days.

Her words contain a veiled compliment to Matthew.

CORA: I am glad you've come to think more highly of Cousin Matthew.

MARY: That's not the point.*

CORA: No. The point is, when you refused Matthew, you were the daughter of an earl with an unsullied reputation. Now you are damaged goods.

Her words are a severe shock to Mary.

MARY: Mama —

CORA: Somehow, I don't know how, there is a rumour in London, that you are not… virtuous.

MARY: What? Does Papa know about this?

CORA: He knows it and he dismisses it. Because, unlike you and me, he doesn't know that it is true.

Again, the plain but shocking statement subdues Mary.

CORA (CONT'D): Let's hope it's unkind gossip. Because if anyone heard about…

MARY: Kemal. My lover. Kemal Pamuk.

Her words are meant as a haughty challenge, but Cora is simply relieved she will not have to speak the name.

CORA: Exactly. If it gets around, and you're not already married, every door in London will be slammed in your face.

MARY: Mama, the world is changing —

CORA: Not that much, and not fast enough for you!

MARY: I know you mean to help. I know you love me. But I also know what I'm capable of, and forty years of boredom and duty just isn't possible for me. I'm sorry.

CORA: I do love you and I want to help.

MARY: I'm a lost cause, Mama. Leave me to manage my own affairs. Why not concentrate on Edith? She needs all the help she can get.

....

* Mary's quite harsh to her mother, but then I think young women are often harsh to their mothers and Mary is not a hypocrite. She may not want the world to know the details of her adventures but she doesn't lie to herself. She never pretends about the events in her past or about Pamuk and, to me, that seems an important part of her character.

CORA: You mustn't be unkind to Edith. She has fewer
advantages than you.
MARY: Fewer? She has none at all.

*Edith's reflection can be seen in the glass of a picture on
the wall. The door is slightly open.*

41 INT. UPSTAIRS PASSAGE. NIGHT.

Edith is standing, listening, at Mary's door.

42 INT. KITCHEN. NIGHT.

*Daisy is pouring bread sauce into a sauce boat. She works in
silence as Mrs Patmore takes up a thick cloth.*

MRS PATMORE: Open the oven.

*Daisy opens the heavy door. Mrs Patmore lifts out the big,
earthenware roasting dish with three large fowl. She turns
and walks into the side of the kitchen table and trips. The
dish falls on the floor and shatters. As she screams, a cat
starts out from the shadows and pounces on the first bird.*

ANNA (V.O.): What's happened?

*She and Gwen appear at the doorway as Daisy tries to drive
away the cat from the first bird.*

MRS PATMORE: It's that bloomin' Daisy! I've said she'd
be the death of me, and now my word's come true!
DAISY: I didn't do nuffin!
ANNA: Here, let me help you.

She wrestles Mrs Patmore into a chair. Gwen kicks the cat.

GWEN: Get away! Get back to the stables! Who let this
thing in here?*

....

* I blush to recount that this incident, when they rescue the chicken from the
cat and take it up to the dining room, comes from my own life. I was giving a
lunch party in Sussex and I walked into the kitchen to find that the cat had
hooked the joint out of the oven in some way and both he and the dog had
both had quite a go at it. I had nothing else to give my guests, so I just cut off
the chewed bits, carved the rest in the kitchen, then took it in and served it
up. I thought at the time, what the eye doesn't see the heart won't grieve over,
so that's what we make them do here.

She picks up the bird which has been chewed, with a great mouthful missing from its breast.

    GWEN (CONT'D): What'll you serve now?
    MRS PATMORE: Why, them o'course. I ain't got nothing
    else.

Gwen looks at Anna and Daisy.

    ANNA: I s'pose they'll be all right. Daisy, give us a
    hand, get that cloth.

Anna, Gwen and Daisy take the three birds, wiping them with a cloth.

    ANNA (CONT'D): Now, fetch the serving dish.

Which Daisy does. Anna arranges the birds, with bits of parsley and cress covering their wounds.

    ANNA (CONT'D): What's the matter with that?
    DAISY: Are you sure? Shouldn't we tell?
    MRS PATMORE: Certainly not.

Thomas has just arrived with a tray of dirty crockery.

    THOMAS: Is the remove ready to go up?

Anna sets the plate of broken birds on the tray.

    ANNA: Here we are. Daisy, give him a hand with the
    vegetables.
    DAISY: They're up in the servery. In the warmer.

Thomas and Daisy leave the others alone.

    GWEN: Well, I'm glad *I* don't have to eat them.
    MRS PATMORE: What the eye don't see, the heart won't
    grieve over.

The three mangled birds are carried along the passage.

43 INT. DINING ROOM. DOWNTON. NIGHT.

The same birds are carved and almost eaten. William clears the plates, one by one. Mary is between Matthew and Sir Anthony, who has Cora on his left and Edith opposite.

    STRALLAN: Hmm, there's no doubt about it. The next few
    years in farming are going to be about mechanisation.
    That's the test and we're going to have to meet it.

Mary is day-dreaming and so fails to respond.

STRALLAN (CONT'D): Don't you agree, Lady Mary?
MARY: Yes, of course, Sir Anthony. I'm sure I do.

She leans over to Matthew who is talking to his other side.

MARY (CONT'D): Are we ever going to be allowed to turn?
EDITH: Sir Anthony, it must be so hard to meet the
challenge of the future, and yet be fair to your
employees.

She has spoken across the table, putting her neighbour out.

STRALLAN: This is the point, precisely. We can't fight
progress, but we *must* find ways to soften the blow.
EDITH: I should love to see one of the new harvesters, if
you would ever let me. We don't have one here.
STRALLAN: I should be delighted.

*During this, Carson has filled their glasses and William has
supplied them with pudding plates. William goes out.*

44 INT. SERVERY. NIGHT.

*Mrs Patmore is there as William comes in. Thomas is waiting
while Anna is loading a tray with dirty crockery.*

WILLIAM: I hope they find that snuff box. What happens
if they don't?
THOMAS: They'll organise a search, won't they? I
wouldn't be Mr Bates. Not for all the tea in China.
ANNA: Wouldn't you, Thomas? I dare say he feels just the
same about you.

*But he smirks towards the door and when Anna walks out with
her tray, she sees O'Brien hovering there.*

ANNA (CONT'D): What's the matter with you?
O'BRIEN: Nothing.

*But she is giggling as she hurries away. Inside the pantry,
each footman carries a large meringue on a round tray,
complete with spoon and fork. Carson looks round the door.*

CARSON: Ready?

Mrs Patmore steps forward with a bowl of sugar and a spoon.

MRS PATMORE: Just a minute.

She sprinkles each pudding liberally.

MRS PATMORE (CONT'D): I don't like to put it on earlier. It sinks in and spoils the effect.

She steps back and the men walk in.

45 INT. DINING ROOM. DOWNTON. NIGHT.

Thomas and William start at opposite ends, on opposite sides. Thomas serves first Cora, then Strallan. As he takes a spoonful, Cora turns to speak to Strallan, obliging the guests round the table to finish their conversations and turn to their other neighbour, which in a fragmented way they gradually do, some more reluctant than others. Mary turns to Matthew as she helps herself, after Strallan.

MARY: Mama has released me, thank God.*
MATTHEW: Sir Anthony seems nice enough.
MARY: If you want to talk farming and foxes by the hour.

Matthew nods. They're getting on well and he's glad.

MATTHEW: I'm rather looking forward to the flower show tomorrow.
MARY: Where Mr Molesley's roses will turn everybody's heads. But if you tell Granny I said so, I'll denounce you as a liar.
MATTHEW: I wouldn't dare. I'll leave that to my fearless mother.

She laughs. They are flirting, whether they know it or not.
....

* At a dinner party like this one, it is still the hostess who decides in which direction her guests will talk. You hear people say you have to talk first to the right, or some such, but this is nonsense. The hostess is the decision maker. If she talks first to the man on her right, every woman talks to the man on her right. If she talks to the left, every woman talks to the left. Then or now, she will usually keep the more interesting fellow for the main course, so it's a slight insult if she speaks to you first, but anyway, when the pudding arrives, the table breaks up and you can chat to whomever you like. This rule continues to be observed over most of England, but not in artistic circles, and a director said to me the other day how stiff it must be. In fact, he was quite wrong. One can go to a dinner in Hampstead and spend an hour in silence because both neighbours are talking in the other direction. That never happens where you observe these rules.

MARY: How were the cottages?

MATTHEW: They're coming on wonderfully. I'd love to show you.

During this William and Thomas have reached the end. No one has eaten, but now Cora lifts her fork. Strallan sees his hostess has technically started and takes a forkful.

STRALLAN: Obviously, it's an act of faith at this stage — Good God!

He has shouted, silencing the table.

STRALLAN (CONT'D): Ugh!

He lifts his napkin and spits his mouthful into it.

ROBERT: What on earth?

At last, Strallan remembers himself.

STRALLAN: I do apologise, Lady Grantham. But I had a mouthful of salt.

CORA: What?

Carefully, she tastes some of the pudding.

CORA (CONT'D): Everyone! Put down your forks! Carson, remove this and bring some fruit, bring cheese, bring *anything* to take this taste away! Sir Anthony, I am so sorry.

Up and down the table, there are different reactions.

ROBERT: Fains I be Mrs Patmore's kitchen maid when the news gets out.

SYBIL: Poor girl. We ought to send in a rescue party.

Edith is still making headway with Sir Anthony.

EDITH: You must think us very disorganised.

STRALLAN: Not at all. These things happen.

But the surprising response is that of Mary and Matthew. In the middle of all this, they catch each other's eye and burst into unstoppable giggles, with Mary clutching Matthew's arm in her struggle to control herself, and stifling her laughter with her napkin.

46 INT. SERVANTS' HALL. NIGHT.

By contrast, Mrs Patmore is sobbing into a handkerchief.
Thomas and William are not there. The others watch.

ANNA: Come on. It's not that bad. Nobody's died.
MRS PATMORE: I don't understand it! It must have been that Daisy! She's muddled everything up before now!
DAISY: But I never —

A sign from Carson silences her.

CARSON: Don't worry, Daisy. You're not in the line of fire, here.
MRS PATMORE: I *know* that pudding! I chose it 'cos I know it!
MRS HUGHES: Which is why you wouldn't let her ladyship have the pudding she wanted. Because you *didn't* know it.
MRS PATMORE: Exactly!

Mrs Hughes glances at Carson. At this, Mrs Patmore suddenly
realises she's made a troubling admission and subsides.

MRS PATMORE (CONT'D): I don't see how it happened.

She weeps again, as Carson catches Bates's eye and inclines
his head towards the door. Bates nods and stands.

BATES: Come on, everyone. Let's give Mrs Patmore some space to breathe.

He starts to send them out as he looks at Anna.

BATES (CONT'D): You, too.
ANNA: I don't think I should leave her.
BATES: Yes, you should. Leave her to Mr Carson. He knows what he's doing.

They go, and the cook and butler are alone together. Carson
kneels and puts some coal on the fire.

MRS PATMORE: Don't do that. Get William or the hall boy to do it. It's beneath your dignity.
CARSON: It won't kill me. Now…

He sits opposite her, on the other side of the fire. After a
moment, he takes her hand and pats it.

CARSON (CONT'D): All in your own good time, I think
you've got something to tell me.

Mrs Patmore looks at him. It's true. She has. *

47 INT. KITCHEN PASSAGE. NIGHT.

*Outside the room, the other servants loiter. Anna makes a
sign to Bates. They draw apart.*

ANNA (V.O): I think I know where that snuff box is.
BATES: Where?
ANNA: Hidden in your room.

For a moment, he is stunned with disappointment.

BATES: You don't think —
ANNA: 'Course I don't, you silly beggar.
BATES: Then…?
ANNA: I bet Thomas'd like it, if they took you for a
thief.

The penny drops.

BATES: Yes. I expect he would.
ANNA: Go upstairs now and find it. And when you have,
you can choose whether to put it in Thomas's room. Or
give it to me, and I'll slip it into Miss O'Brien's.
BATES: You naughty girl.
ANNA: Fight fire with fire. That's what my Mum says.

Which makes him smile, even while he is in peril.

END OF ACT TWO

....

* I love Mrs Patmore. I think Lesley Nicol's performance is fantastic. She is
the kitchen Violet. Maggie Smith delivers the cryptic comments upstairs,
Lesley has the barbed tongue downstairs. In a sense they balance each other,
as Robert and Bates, or Anna and Mary, balance each other. But I suspect
Mrs Patmore is a little more soft-hearted.

ACT THREE

Thomas leads the ladies into the drawing room.

SYBIL: Poor Mrs Patmore. Do you think you should go and
see her?

CORA: Tomorrow. She needs time to recover her nerves. I
knew there was something going on.

EDITH: It seems hard that poor Sir Anthony had to pay the
price.

MARY: Good God!

Mary does an imitation of Strallan which makes Sybil laugh.

EDITH: As for your giggling like a ridiculous schoolgirl
with Cousin Matthew! It was pathetic.

MARY: Poor Edith. I am sorry Matthew's proved a
disappointment to you.

EDITH: Who says he has?

MARY: Matthew. He told me. Oh, sorry. Wasn't I
supposed to know?

This is infuriating to Edith, which Cora sees.

CORA: You were very helpful, Edith, looking after Sir
Anthony like that. You saved the day.

EDITH: I enjoyed it. We seemed to have a lot to talk
about.

*She casts a rather superior look at Mary, who makes a face
and comes closer as they start to hiss at each other.*

MARY: Spare me your boasting, please.

EDITH: Now who's jealous?

MARY: Jealous? Do you think I couldn't have that old
booby if I wanted him?

EDITH: Even you can't take every prize.

MARY: Is that a challenge?

EDITH: If you like.

49 INT. SERVANTS' HALL. NIGHT.

*Carson is listening to Mrs Patmore. She is still crying, but
she is calmer now, and more tragic for it.*

MRS PATMORE: I've known it for a while now. At first, I thought it might pass, you know. Like an headache or an earache. But I know it won't.

CARSON: And it's getting worse?

MRS PATMORE: Oh, yes. I could almost manage for a long time. Knowing the kitchen and where everything was kept. Even with that fool girl.

CARSON: I think you might owe Daisy an apology.

This is a hard one to swallow.

MRS PATMORE: Maybe. I've had a lot to put up with, I can tell you.

Carson chooses to ignore this.

CARSON: And you've not been to a doctor?

MRS PATMORE: I don't need a doctor to tell me I'm going blind.*

She looks at him, her eyes filling again.

MRS PATMORE (CONT'D): A blind cook, Mr Carson. What a joke. Whoever heard of such a thing? A blind cook.

She makes to laugh a little at this absurdity. But Carson only takes her hand in both of his, and squeezes it.

50 INT. HALL. DOWNTON. NIGHT.

Robert leads the men out of the dining room.

ROBERT: I hope our salty pudding didn't spoil the evening for you.

MATTHEW: On the contrary.

ROBERT: I'm glad you and Mary are getting along.

Matthew smiles but does not comment.

....

* Mrs Patmore knows that if her suspicions are correct and she is indeed going blind then her situation is very serious, as she will not be able to work. The Granthams may pension her off but it means a severe drop in income and probably intense loneliness after years spent in a loud and busy kitchen. It might not exactly be ruin, but it will be very, very bad. I think Jim and Lesley play this scene wonderfully. It always makes me cry.

ROBERT (CONT'D): There's no reason why you can't be friends.

MATTHEW: No. No reason at all.

Something in his tone emboldens Robert.

ROBERT: I don't suppose there's any chance that you could sort of… start again?

MATTHEW: Life is full of surprises.

With a laugh, Robert walks through the drawing room doors which have been opened by Thomas, leaving Matthew to follow, side by side, with Strallan and the other guests.

51 INT. DRAWING ROOM. DOWNTON. NIGHT.

Mary and Edith look up as the men enter. With an openly competitive glance at her sister, Edith attempts to catch Strallan's eye, but Mary sets off. From Matthew's point of view, he sees Mary coming across the room towards him, with a warm smile.

MARY: I've been waiting for you. I've found a book on the table over here and I think it's just the thing to catch your interest.

MATTHEW: Really? I was only —

But she has gone to the side of Sir Anthony Strallan and slipped her arm through his, leading him over to the central table.

MARY: Well, I was looking in the library and I…

Matthew, left stranded, is completely flummoxed. He stops. Edith glances at him and then goes herself to the table, to talk to Sir Anthony.

EDITH: I was very taken by what you were saying over dinner about the way we…

But Strallan is not listening. He is entirely engrossed.

STRALLAN: You're so right, Lady Mary. How clever you are. This is exactly what we have to be aware of.

As he speaks, Mary glances triumphantly across at her sister, who drops back. Mary turns to Strallan.

Edith joins Matthew, still standing immobile. She is furious.

> EDITH: It seems we have both been thrown over for a bigger prize.

Matthew does not answer, but then the clock chimes.

> MATTHEW: Heavens, is that the time?
> EDITH: You're not going?
> MATTHEW: The truth is my head's splitting. I don't want to spoil the party so I'll slip away. Will you make my excuses to your parents?

He walks towards the door giving a swift order to William to come and let him out. Across the room, Mary looks up and sees Matthew leaving. She realises what she's done.

> MARY: Excuse me Sir Anthony.

Mary follows Matthew out of the room, all of which is observed by Robert.

52 INT. HALL. DOWNTON. NIGHT.

Mary arrives just as William is shutting the main door.

> MARY: Has Mr Crawley left?
> WILLIAM: Yes, m'lady.
> MARY: But what about the car? Branson can't have brought it round so quickly.
> WILLIAM: He said he'd rather walk, m'lady.
> MARY: It's very windy.
> WILLIAM: He mentioned he had a headache. That the wind would blow it away.
> MARY: Thank you.

William gives a slight bow and returns to the drawing room. Mary hovers, glancing out of the window at the receding figure. The truth is, she doesn't know what she wants.

53 INT. DRAWING ROOM. DOWNTON. NIGHT.

ROBERT: Mary can be such a child.
CORA: What do you mean, darling?
ROBERT: She thinks if you put a toy down, it'll still be
sitting there when you want to play with it again.
CORA: What are you talking about?
ROBERT: Never mind.

He reaches down and strokes her cheek, which pleases her.

54 INT. SERVANTS' HALL. NIGHT.

They are all in there when Carson walks by.

ANNA: Mr Carson?

He stops and comes to the door.

ANNA (CONT'D): We were wondering about that snuff box.
Has it turned up yet?
CARSON: I'm afraid not.

*Thomas and O'Brien share a smirking glance. But they do not
see the look that Anna gives Bates.*

BATES: Well, I think we should have a search.
THOMAS: What?
BATES: It doesn't do to leave these things too long.
ANNA: Mr Carson can search the men's rooms and Mrs Hughes
the women's.

*The smiles have been wiped off Thomas's and O'Brien's faces.
They give a hasty glance at each other.*

ANNA (CONT'D): And it should be right away, now we've
talked of it. So no one has a chance to hide the box.
Don't you agree, Mr Carson?
CARSON: Well... perhaps it's for best. Although I'm sure I
won't find anything. I'll fetch Mrs Hughes.

*He walks out of the room and the others stare at each other.
Then Thomas stands, followed by O'Brien.*

THOMAS: I think I'll just...
O'BRIEN: I'd better check it's tidy.

*They hurry out. Leaving Bates and Anna laughing to the
bewilderment of the rest of the staff.*

55 INT. BACK STAIRS. NIGHT.

Thomas and O'Brien race upstairs.

THOMAS: The bastard's hidden it in my room or yours.
O'BRIEN: Why did I ever listen to you in the first place?

Which seems unjust.

56 INT. MAIDS' PASSAGE. NIGHT.

Mrs Hughes emerges from Gwen's and Anna's room. They stand in the doorway watching as she progresses to the next.

MRS HUGHES: Miss O'Brien?

She pushes open the door to find the room in complete chaos. O'Brien stands in the middle of a stripped bed, with boxes and drawers and clothes all over the place.

MRS HUGHES (CONT'D): My, my. You have been busy.

57 INT. HALL. CRAWLEY HOUSE. NIGHT.

Matthew takes off his coat. Isobel comes out of a door.

ISOBEL: I was expecting you later than this. I'll tell Molesley to lock up.
MATTHEW: Thanks. Goodnight, Mother.

He kisses her and starts up the stairs.

ISOBEL: How was the evening? Did you enjoy yourself?
MATTHEW: Quite. The thing is, for a moment I thought —

He stops, smiling down at his mother who looks up at him.

MATTHEW (CONT'D): Never mind what I thought. I was wrong. Goodnight.

He vanishes onto the landing, leaving her to ponder this.

58 INT. DOWNTON VILLAGE HALL. DAY.

The show is in full swing. Villagers and the servants look at every stall, while Violet, Cora, Robert and the girls walk about. Isobel and Matthew are with them. Mary glances at Matthew but, while he nods in greeting, he says nothing.

SYBIL: How pretty. What's it for?

STALLHOLDER: It's for salt, m'lady. The wide mouth stops
it getting damp.
SYBIL: Why should it get damp?
STALLHOLDER: Because a great many cottages are damp,
m'lady.
SYBIL: Yes, of course. How silly of me.

The party has reached Bill Molesley's stall.

ROBERT: My word, Molesley, splendid roses as usual. Well
done.
BILL MOLESLEY: Thank you, your lordship.
VIOLET: All the stalls are set out very well this year.

But Robert and Cora are impressed by Molesley's offerings.

CORA: This is enchanting. Do we grow it?
BILL MOLESLEY: I doubt you've got that one, your
ladyship. I've only just found it, myself.
CORA: Is it a secret? Or could you tell Mr Brocket?
BILL MOLESLEY: I'd be glad to, m'lady.

His son, Isobel's butler, beams. They move on in a group.

CORA: He should come and see the rose garden. He could
give us some ideas.
ROBERT: Old Molesley's a champion. Or he would be, in a
fairer world.

He gives a meaningful smile to his mother.

VIOLET: Don't you start.
ISOBEL: I'm afraid I've been annoying Cousin Violet on
that score.
VIOLET: If Mr Molesley deserves the first prize for his
flowers, the judges will give it to him.
ROBERT: They wouldn't dare.

He shares this with Cora who certainly agrees with him.

VIOLET: Really, Robert. You make me so annoyed. Isn't
it possible that I should win the thing on merit?
ROBERT: I think the appropriate answer to that, Mama, is
'yes, dear'.

*Violet turns away, but not before she has seen Robert give a
wink to Isobel who smiles. It is all very irritating.*

59 EXT. DOWNTON VILLAGE. DAY.

The servants are walking through the village. O'Brien is
with Thomas.

> O'BRIEN: I don't know why we're bothering. We'll have
> missed the speeches as it is.
> THOMAS: Don't be such a grouch.

Anna is walking with Bates.

> ANNA: You should have punished one of them at least.
> BATES: They know that I know, and that's worth something.

They stroll on.

> ANNA: What do you think will happen to Mrs Patmore?
> BATES: She'll muddle through with Daisy to help her. In
> the long term, we'll have to wait for the doctor to give
> his opinion.
> ANNA: I hope there's something they can do.
> BATES: I hope so, too. But if there isn't, I hope they
> *tell* her there isn't. Nothing is harder to live with
> than false hope.

This is enough to make her strong.

> ANNA: I wish you'd come out with it.
> BATES: With what?
> ANNA: Whatever it is that you're keeping secret.
> BATES: I can't.
> ANNA: You don't deny it, then?
> BATES: No, I don't deny it. And I don't deny you've a
> right to ask. But I can't. I'm not a free man.
> ANNA: Are you trying to tell me that you're married?

She has stopped walking and faces him.

> BATES: I have been married, yes. But that isn't all of
> it.

She will never get a better chance to speak her mind.

> ANNA: Because… Because I love you, Mr Bates. I know it's
> not ladylike to say it, but I'm not a lady and I don't
> pretend to be.

He stares at her, this innocent, good woman, and if he could
only change things he would.

BATES: You are a lady to me. And I never knew a finer one.

There is the rattle of wheels. A farmer draws up in a cart, full of hay. There is room for one on the seat beside him.

FARMER: If you want a lift, I can take one of you, but no more.
BATES: One of the women.
ANNA: No, you must go. Then we can all hurry and meet you there.

He looks at her and speaks his answer for her ears, only.

BATES: Yes you're right. I mustn't slow you down. There's been too much of that already.

Before she can protest, he is up on the board and the cart moves off. Thomas sniffs as they all walk on together.

THOMAS: I might get myself a gammy leg. It seems to be the answer to every problem.

Anna is silent as they quicken their pace.

60 INT. DOWNTON VILLAGE HALL. DAY.

The flower show. Cora has come to find Violet.

CORA: It's time for the prize giving, Mama. Here's the list.
VIOLET: Perhaps you should do it.
CORA: You say that every year.
VIOLET: Perhaps one year you'll take me up on it.
CORA: Perhaps I will.

With a side glance at her daughter-in-law, Violet looks at the paper. At the end, next to 'The Grantham Cup for Best Bloom' she of course finds her own name. As Violet starts reading out the winners and handing over the prizes, among the crush, Sybil sees Gwen, who seems depressed. They whisper.

SYBIL: Have you recovered from our ordeal?

Gwen half smiles, but she's obviously cast down.

GWEN: I got a letter this morning. They must have
written it as soon as I left the office… They are
'pleased to have met me', but I 'do not quite fit their
requirements'… So it was all for nothing.

Sybil takes the maid's hand and gives it a squeeze.

SYBIL: I don't agree.
GWEN: You've been kind, m'lady, and I appreciate it. But
only a fool doesn't know when they've been beaten.
SYBIL: Then I'm a fool, for I'm a long way from being
beaten yet.

*She is absolutely determined and this does cheer Gwen up a
bit. Meanwhile, the names continue, with little bursts of
applause. Across the hall, Mary walks over to Matthew.*

MARY: When you ran off last night, I hope you hadn't
thought me rude.
MATTHEW: Certainly not. I monopolised you at dinner.
I'd no right to any more of your time.
MARY: But you see, Edith and I had this sort of bet.
MATTHEW: Please don't apologise. I had a lovely evening
and I'm glad we're on speaking terms. Now, I should look
after my mother.

*He walks through the crush to get to Isobel who is standing
in front of the stage. Edith comes up.*

EDITH: Why was Cousin Matthew in such a hurry to get away?
MARY: Don't be stupid.
EDITH: I suppose you didn't want him when he wanted you,
and now it's the other way round. You have to admit it's
quite funny.
MARY: I'll admit that if I ever wanted to attract a man
I'd steer clear of those clothes and that hat.
EDITH: You think yourself so superior, don't you?
MARY: Why not? I am.

*She goes to join her parents by the stage. Edith senses
someone's eyes on her and she looks over to find O'Brien
staring. Edith nods slightly, whispering to herself.*

EDITH: Well, *I* think she who laughs last laughs longest.

As Mary arrives, Cora turns to her husband.

CORA: Did that missing box of yours ever turn up?

ROBERT: It was a fuss about nothing. They must've put it back on the wrong shelf when they were dusting. Bates found it this morning.

CORA: Next time, have a proper look before you start complaining. I'm sure the servants were frightened half to death.

ROBERT: Mea culpa.

61 INT. DOWNTON VILLAGE HALL. DAY.

On the stage, Violet has reached the final award.

VIOLET: And now, the Grantham Cup for the Best Bloom in the Village.

She is very confident, but there is Isobel, standing directly in front of her and boring into her with an iron gaze. Violet looks to one side and there is Bill Molesley, with his son. The younger Molesley seems stern, but the old man is just hopelessly hopeful.

VIOLET (CONT'D): The Grantham Cup is awarded to —

She takes a deep breath to steady herself.

VIOLET (CONT'D): To Mr William Molesley for his *Countess Cabarrus* rose.

*There is complete silence. The village is too stunned to clap. Bill Molesley looks as if he'd been turned to stone.**

....

* Violet of course is irritated by the idea that she hasn't won on merit in the past, at the same time acknowledging in this judgement that she's aware of what has gone on. I was accused at the time of copying the scene from *Mrs Miniver*, where Dame May Whitty, as Lady Beldon, makes the same decision. I wasn't conscious of it, but when I re-watched the movie not long ago, it was pretty close, so I suppose it must have been hovering in my brain. Funnily enough, I thought I was inspired by something that happened to my mother when I was growing up. We lived then in a house with the most marvellous climbing roses and we always won the prize for them, year after year, at the village flower show. Someone on the committee suggested that my parents might like to donate a cup and my mother, shamelessly really, volunteered to present a cup for the best climbing rose, knowing she would win it. So they bought a very pretty, large silver cup which I suppose my mother planned to use as the table centrepiece and they gave it to the village. Everyone was very grateful, they were thanked a hundred times, and she never won the prize again.

ISOBEL: Bravo! Well done! Bravo!

As soon as she starts to clap, the audience goes mad,
cheering and stamping and clapping, as Bill Molesley is
pushed up onto the stage. He is crying as he reaches for the
cup, which softens even Violet.

VIOLET: Congratulations, Mr Molesley.
BILL MOLESLEY: Thank you, m'lady. Thank you for letting
me have it.
VIOLET: It is the judge's decision, not mine. But very
well done.

He leaves the stage where his friends mill around him as
Violet rejoins her family.

ROBERT: Bravo, Mama. That must have been a real
sacrifice.
CORA: And bravely borne.
VIOLET: I don't know what everyone is going on about.
It's the judges who decide these things, not me.

Cora is puzzled.

CORA: But I…
VIOLET: All is well, my dear. All is well.

Firmly, she crumples the list and hides it in her reticule,
as the celebrations continue around her.*

....

* Violet, like Maggie in a way, is completely unsentimental so she would hate
for anyone to think that she had read her own name and yet given the first
prize to Mr Molesley out of kindness. She needs them to believe that the
judges made the award, but of course no one, certainly no family member,
does think that because they know that no villager would be brave enough to
challenge the Dowager. I suspect one of the keys to Violet, as Maggie has
developed her, is that she doesn't need praise. It is not one of the things that
motivates her. She doesn't need approval, and in a way that is what gives her
strength. Incidentally, I had written that old Mr Molesley won for a *Papa
Meilland* rose, which was my mother's favourite, but we learned it had not yet
been launched and so I changed it to the *Countess Cabarrus*, a fictional flower,
named after a friend.

62 INT. EDITH'S BEDROOM. NIGHT.

The house is quiet. Edith, dressed for bed, sits at a writing table. She is addressing an envelope. She licks it, closes the flap and puts it down on the blotter where we can read it. 'His Excellency the Turkish Ambassador, 43 Belgrave Square, London, SW.'

END OF EPISODE FIVE

....

* The envelope is correctly addressed to SW with no number, because numbers came later.

EPISODE SIX

ACT ONE

1 EXT. RIPON. DAY.

May 1914. There is a crowd at a rally in this country town.
Among them is Sybil Crawley. A Liberal Parliamentary
candidate speaks from a raised platform.

LIBERAL CANDIDATE: Last June saw Emily Davison crushed to
death beneath the hooves of the King's horse! Will the
summer of 1914 prove as fatal for the hopes of women? It
cannot!

A woman heckles him. She's standing next to Isobel Crawley.

LIBERAL CANDIDATE (CONT'D): This historic by-election has
been the first step of the journey to women's equality.
SECOND HECKLER: If you're so keen on women's rights, let
a woman speak!
THIRD HECKLER: Why stop there? Let's get the dogs up,
and listen to them bark!

The crowd starts to jostle. There are shouts and jeers.
Branson approaches Sybil, who is bubbling with enthusiasm. A
clod of earth strikes him on the chest, but he struggles on.

BRANSON: Are you all right, m'lady?
SYBIL: Isn't it exciting?*
LIBERAL CANDIDATE (CONT'D): Are we to lie down under the
weight of the iniquitous Cat and Mouse Act? So women
are thrown out of prison when the system has nearly
killed them, only to be dragged back inside when they
have regained the strength to fight the forces of
oppression? Mr Asquith tells us he is a Liberal. Well,
so am I. He tells us this law was an act of mercy. I
disagree, but let us give him the benefit of the doubt.
That said, if the fate of women troubles him, then let

....

* This is the moment when Sybil is identified as a rebel, not just a political
rebel, because I never really know how political she is, but from now on we
know that she is not going to lead the life that was ordained for her. Her
natural ally in the house is Branson because he is also living within a system
of which he disapproves. So in that sense they are both in the same moral
position of seemingly upholding values that neither of them support.

us send him a message. Let us send him a message with
this vote, so loud and so clear that he can hear it far
away in London. The people of Ripon demand justice, not
just for the men, but for the women of England, too!
Their hour has come! Soon, they will be in Parliament
representing themselves, but, until then, they must find
champions where they may, and you all may rest assured
that I am one of them!*

*As a missile strikes him, and the mood of the crowd grows
angrier, Isobel hurries over to where Sybil is standing with
Branson. Their dialogue is played against the background of
the continuing speech.*

MAN: You're an idiot.
ISOBEL: Sybil? I think it's time Branson took you home.
SYBIL: Not yet.
ISOBEL: I think so. I applaud your spirit in coming, and
I will applaud your discretion when you leave.
SYBIL: But you do agree with everything he says?
ISOBEL: I do, my dear. But I also know that if anything
happens to you, Branson will lose his place.†
BRANSON: Better safe than sorry, m'lady.

With a smile at Isobel, he pulls Sybil through the throng.

BRANSON: The car's just here.
SYBIL: Women must get the vote, mustn't they, Branson?
Why does the Prime Minister resist the inevitable?

....

* I always think it's rather disheartening for an actor when you have been
given, as here, pages to say in the script but you end up with only a moderate
place in the finished scene. You think: Oh good, I can really do something
with this. But inevitably the programme makers focus on the principal
characters and you're just banging away in the background. As an actor, I
cannot tell you how disappointing it can be when you see the final edit. So
Jamie de Courcey has my sympathy because I thought he was very good.

† I won't say Isobel is more progressive here than we have seen earlier, but by
going to a meeting like this, she is making a statement. It doesn't surprise us
that she is on the side of women's rights, most of us would have seen that
coming from Episode Two when we first met her, but she is a little bit more
proactive in the cause of her beliefs than we might have expected, and of
course as the series progresses will become increasingly so.

BRANSON: Politicians can't often recognise the changes
that are inevitable.

They have reached the car and now they climb in.

2 INT. MOTOR CAR. DAY.

Sybil settles into her seat as they drive along.

SYBIL: I hope you do go into politics. It's a fine
ambition.
BRANSON: Ambition or dream?
SYBIL: Ambition. Definitely. They can't afford to lose
a man like you.

She says this simply, with a laugh, but he is pleased.

BRANSON: If I do, it's not all about women and the vote
for me, nor even freedom for Ireland. It's social
injustice. It's the conditions of the workers and the
gap between the aristocracy and the poor and —
SYBIL: And what?
BRANSON: I'm sorry. I don't mean to speak against his
lordship.
SYBIL: Why not? You obviously don't approve of him.
BRANSON: Not as the representative of an oppressive
class, but he's a good man and a decent employer.
SYBIL: Spoken like a true politician. If a rather
Jesuitical one.

He smiles. They have a relaxed relationship, these two.*
Sybil catches sight of the clock on the dashboard.

SYBIL (CONT'D): Golly. Is that the time?

Now she sees herself in the driving mirror.

SYBIL (CONT'D): What *do* I look like? Would you sneak me
in round the back? I should hate for Papa to see me like
this. Branson, if you want to be in politics, why aren't
you?

....

* In this scene, we begin the romance, but we don't do much more than that.
We simply hint at the fact that there is a natural sympathy between these two
because they are both essentially rebelling against the respective authorities
in control of them.

BRANSON: Oh, no reason, really, m'lady. Just a little thing called money.

She keeps forgetting the distance between them.

3 INT. KITCHEN. DOWNTON. DAY.

Mrs Patmore is with Daisy.

MRS PATMORE: You foolish girl! Is it likely? Would I tell you to start a sauce today that's for tomorrow?
MRS HUGHES (V.O.): You might.

She is in the doorway, watching.

MRS PATMORE: What do you want?
MRS HUGHES: You asked for some baking soda.
MRS PATMORE: Though why I should *have* to ask —
MRS HUGHES: Once and for all, Mrs Patmore, *the housekeeper has the keys to the store cupboard.* That is how these things are managed. I did not invent the rules.
MRS PATMORE: Maybe not. But if you ask me, the rules should change.
MRS HUGHES: Really? And have you any thoughts on the future of the House of Lords while you're at it?

She hands the packet to the cook and walks out.

4 INT. CARSON'S PANTRY. DOWNTON. DAY.

Carson is reading a letter when Mrs Hughes arrives.

MRS HUGHES: Mrs Patmore is very cruel to that poor girl.
CARSON: Mrs Patmore is frightened.
MRS HUGHES: Is she right to be?
CARSON: Well, Doctor Clarkson's confirmed she has cataracts.
MRS HUGHES: What can be done about it?
CARSON: There are treatments, but even the best are uncertain. And she doesn't want to risk losing what sight she still has.
MRS HUGHES: I don't blame her. But it can't go on forever.
CARSON: No…

He sounds depressed as he looks down at the letter.

MRS HUGHES: Oh, dear. Have you had bad news? I shouldn't have bothered you.

CARSON: No, you weren't to know.

He sighs as he puts the letter back.

5 INT. KITCHEN PASSAGE. DOWNTON. DAY.

Sybil is creeping along the passage. She almost runs into William, who's carrying a silver table centrepiece.

WILLIAM: Blimey. Excuse me, m'lady.

SYBIL: William, will you find Anna and tell her I've gone upstairs?

WILLIAM: Very good, m'lady.

She goes up the backstairs but we follow him to:

6 INT. SERVANTS' HALL. DOWNTON. DAY.

Bates, Anna, O'Brien and Thomas are there. Thomas is by the door as William pushes it, spilling Thomas's tea.

THOMAS: You clumsy clodhopper.

WILLIAM: Sorry.

THOMAS: You will be sorry when I've finished with you. Look at this!

BATES: Leave him alone.*

WILLIAM: Anna, Lady Sybil's back from Ripon. She's gone up to her room.

Anna nods and leaves.

O'BRIEN: Why does she waste her precious time on politics?

THOMAS: Hear, hear.

....

* I think the problem for living-in servants was that you were in a very unrelenting situation. Especially when individuals did not get on. In many jobs there are some people you don't much like, whether in an office or a theatre or down on the farm, but most of us go home at the end of the day and get rid of it. The living-in servants did not go home. They went upstairs. So if you were embroiled in a feud, you had no real break from it. Then the hours were so long, apart from your one day off a fortnight you were there all the time, eating together, sitting together. I've tried to show that this was one of the drawbacks of the life.

BATES: Oh, don't you believe in rights for women, Thomas?

THOMAS: What's it to you?

BATES: Well, I know you don't believe in the rights of property.

Thomas looks at him. Is this a threat?

BATES (CONT'D): I think some people might find that interesting.

THOMAS: Who's going to tell them? You?

But Bates just smiles. Thomas glances at O'Brien.

7 INT. KITCHEN PASSAGE/CARSON'S PANTRY. DOWNTON. EVE.

Mrs Hughes is hurrying along. She reaches Carson's door.

MRS HUGHES: Mr Carson, are you all right?

CARSON: Why shouldn't I be?

MRS HUGHES: You've never rung the dressing gong and Mrs Patmore's doing a soufflé for the first course.

CARSON: Oh, my God —

He snatches at his watch, jumps up and hurries out.

8 INT. DRESSING ROOM. DOWNTON. EVE.

Pharaoh watches as Bates holds a tailcoat open for Robert.

ROBERT: Rather unlike Carson. We'd better go straight in to dinner.

BATES: I'll tell Miss O'Brien and Anna.

ROBERT: Any more news of the by-election? Mr Crawley was here earlier. He said his mother had gone to the Liberal rally in Ripon. The vicar's wife took her. Classic.

BATES: I hear it was quite lively.

ROBERT: I dare say the Townies will make the usual stink when the Tory candidate's returned.

BATES: I'm not sure. I heard the Liberal was given a hard time, today. Mr Branson said it was getting out of hand when they left.

Bates has been talking easily as he folds the day clothes.

ROBERT: Typical Branson to be there. I hope he squared it with Carson. Who went with him?

Bates realises he has put his foot in it.

BATES: Uh… I'm not sure anyone went with him, m'lord.
ROBERT: But you just said 'they'. Who was with him?
BATES: I don't like to say.
ROBERT: Bates. Who was with him?
BATES: Lady Sybil.
ROBERT: *Lady Sybil?* Why?
BATES: I should never have mentioned it, m'lord. I thought you knew.
ROBERT: No, I did not know.

9 INT. DINING ROOM. DOWNTON. NIGHT.

The family has just sat down to dinner. Violet is with them.
Carson, Thomas and William are serving.

ROBERT: I gather you went to hear the Liberal candidate today?
SYBIL: There were several speakers, actually, he was the last.
ROBERT: Did he speak well?
SYBIL: I thought so.
ROBERT: But there was quite a brouhaha.
SYBIL: You know what these things can be like —
ROBERT: I do. Which is why I'm astonished you should not feel it necessary to ask my permission to attend.

There is a silence in the room. Robert is very angry.

ROBERT (CONT'D): I assume this was Branson's idea.
SYBIL: No, I —
ROBERT: I confess I was amused at the idea of an Irish radical for a chauffeur, but I see now I have been naive.*
CORA: I told Branson to take Sybil.

....

* Robert has that quality of being entertained by the beliefs of his natural enemies but here, like many in the past, he comes up against the consequence of his broad-mindedness. Flirting with revolution, whether it's a figure like Anthony Crosland, a glass of champagne in one hand and a gun in the other, or Marie Antoinette laughing at a play by Beaumarchais, is always much more dangerous than people realise. Personally, I am firmly convinced that, over the centuries, the lefty toff has done far more damage than any street revolutionary.

ROBERT: What are you saying?*

CORA: Sybil needed to get to Ripon, and I asked Branson to drive her. I thought it was sensible. In case there was trouble.

SYBIL: I want to do some canvassing. The by-election isn't far off, and —

VIOLET: Canvassing?

SYBIL: It's quite safe. You're in a group and you knock on doors —

VIOLET: Yes, I know what canvassing is.

MARY: I think that Sybil is…

VIOLET: What? Are you canvassing, too? Or would you rather take in washing?

MARY: I was only going to say that Sybil's entitled to her opinions.

VIOLET: Not until she is married. Then her husband will tell her what her opinions *are*.

MARY: Oh, Granny.

SYBIL: I knew you wouldn't approve.

ROBERT: Which is presumably why you all hid your plans from me.

10 INT. SERVERY. DOWNTON. NIGHT.

Daisy is clearing away plates. Thomas is loading a tray.

THOMAS: Her ladyship'll have a smacked bottom if she isn't careful.

Daisy snorts with laughter as Carson looks in.

CARSON: Hurry up. I don't want anything else to go wrong tonight… Where's the sauce? Doesn't this have Hollandaise?

DAISY: I'll get it. I won't be a jiffy.

....

* In this moment Robert is angry with Cora for allowing Sybil to go to the meeting and in Los Angeles I was attacked by a journalist for letting him speak sharply to his wife, suggesting that because Robert is a sympathetic figure he should have no faults. But nobody's perfect, and just because a couple get short-tempered with each other does not mean there's anything wrong with the marriage. There is a tendency in fiction to suggest that if a couple is happy there can never be a flaw, and if they're unhappy then they're permanently at each other's throat. Of course, neither is true in real life.

THOMAS: Would you do that for me?
DAISY: I'd do anything for you.

She is gone before he can respond.

11 INT. DINING ROOM. DOWNTON. NIGHT.

As Thomas walks in, things are still sticky.

VIOLET: Does this mean you won't be presented next month?
SYBIL: Certainly not. Why should it?
VIOLET: I doubt I'd expect to curtsey to Their Majesties
in June, if I'd been arrested at a riot in May. But of
course I'm old. Things may be different now.*
CORA: She hasn't been arrested and it wasn't a riot.
EDITH: But it might be next time.
ROBERT: There will not be a next time.†

12 INT. SERVANTS' HALL. DOWNTON. NIGHT.

Bates and Anna are with Branson.

ANNA: Her ladyship's not best pleased at being told off
in public. William said she was looking daggers.
BATES: I'm sorry I started all this.
BRANSON: Oh, it's not your fault. Anyway, he ought to be
glad he's got a daughter who cares.

Thomas leans in through the door.

THOMAS: Her ladyship's ready to leave.
BRANSON: I'll bring the car round.
THOMAS: Are you pleased with yourself?

Before Bates can speak, Branson and Thomas have gone.

....

* Maggie Smith is so rewarding to write for because she always gets the gag
and enhances it. Some actors don't quite manage this, but she invariably
makes everything funnier than it was on the page.

† In this scene, the contrast between the conversation and the rituals of rank,
between the topic of women's rights and the footmen in attendance, suggests
one of the central ironies of *Downton*. We start in an era which seemed
graceful and ordered and peaceful, with liveried servants and men pulling
their forelock as they opened the gate, but in fact all that was a veneer over a
society that was preparing, if often unconsciously, for convulsive change.

ANNA: Silly chump. Why must he be so unpleasant all the time?
BATES: He's nervous.
ANNA: What of?
BATES: He annoyed me, earlier on, and I said something stupid. He thinks I'm planning to tell Mr Carson about the wine.
ANNA: Well, he shouldn't have stolen it then, should he?
BATES: No. But I don't want anyone to lose their job because of me.
ANNA: Even Thomas? Even after what they tried to do to you?
BATES: Even then.

She smiles. She approves of this, really.

13 INT. LIBRARY. DOWNTON. NIGHT.

Robert is reading, with Pharaoh at his feet. Carson enters.

CARSON: I'm sorry to disturb you, m'lord.

Robert waits as Carson closes the door. He holds a letter.

CARSON (CONT'D): I don't know how I missed the gong. I must've been distracted.
ROBERT: Never mind. These things happen.

To Carson's dismay, Robert assumes that was why he came.

ROBERT (CONT'D): While you're here, Carson, I'm afraid I was angrier at dinner than the situation warranted. I hope the servants won't make too much of it.*

....

* These houses on the whole worked if the family had a good relationship with certain key members of staff, and of those the chief was the butler. He was really halfway between the staff and the family, and when you got a good one, who was really on your team, you did everything you could to hang onto him. But this friendship, as it really was in many cases, could only be prosecuted when the employer and the butler were alone. You would not usually include the butler in a conversation with your friends in the drawing room, but once you were alone, then you could enjoy a pretty equal relationship, joking, gossiping, talking things through, so there was an almost secret element to the whole thing. It was the same with a valet or a lady's maid. If you saw your maid in public, it would all be very respectful and does your ladyship want to wear the white or the grey tonight? But when you were in the bedroom getting dressed, then the tone of the conversation would be quite different. I hope we make that clear in the series.

CARSON: Well. They like a story. But they move on quick enough.

ROBERT: I don't want Branson to be upset. I got the wrong end of the stick, and I rather let rip.

CARSON: He'll get over it.

ROBERT: But what *are* we going to do if Lady Sybil turns political? I'm sorry. Was there something else?

Carson glances at the letter, but this isn't the time.

CARSON: No, m'lord. Good night.

14 INT. HALL. DOWNTON. NIGHT.

Carson emerges, just as Cora is at the foot of the stairs.

CARSON: Your ladyship, do you have a moment?

CORA: Of course. What is it?

CARSON: Could we go in here?

He's opened the dining room door and turned on the lights.

CORA: Heavens, how mysterious.

15 INT. DINING ROOM. DOWNTON. NIGHT.

Carson closes the door. Cora waits.

CARSON: I've received a letter, m'lady. From a friend of mine. He's valet to the Marquess of Flintshire.

CORA: I don't envy him.*

CARSON: Lord Flintshire is a minister at the Foreign Office…

CORA: As you know, Lady Flintshire is his lordship's cousin.

CARSON: Of course, of course. The point is, he has dealings with the Turkish Ambassador.

Suddenly, Cora realises what's coming. Carson ploughs on.

CARSON (CONT'D): It seems His Excellency has made him privy to a scurrilous story concerning Lady Mary and… the late Mr Pamuk.†

....

* Lord Flintshire starts off here as an unsympathetic figure, but later he grows more cuddly and by the time we meet him in the Christmas Special of the third series, we, and the Granthams, love him. Which of course is quite illogical.

CORA: May I read this letter?

He holds out the letter. She is like ice as she takes it and starts to read.

CARSON: Is there anything you'd like me to do about it?
CORA: No, thank you. Sometimes, even to deny these things is only to throw paraffin onto the flames.
CARSON: I did try to inform his lordship.
CORA: What?
CARSON: But I couldn't seem to find the right moment.

She can breathe again.

CORA: Quite right. Please leave his lordship to me.

16 INT. KITCHEN PASSAGE. DOWNTON. NIGHT.

O'BRIEN: I'm sorry. The only sure way to get rid of a servant is to have him or her suspected of stealing.

O'Brien is plotting with Thomas.

THOMAS: Aren't you forgetting we've tried that? And it didn't work.
O'BRIEN: But last time, we invented a theft. What we need is to make him a suspect when something's *really* been stolen.
THOMAS: How do we know anything's been stolen?
O'BRIEN: Because you stole it, you noodle.
THOMAS: Oh. You mean the wine.
O'BRIEN: Yes, the wine.
THOMAS: But that's the whole point. Bates knows I took it. He was threatening to tell Mr Carson.
O'BRIEN: Well, he can't, can he? Not if we get to him first.

END OF ACT ONE

....

† This exchange is difficult for Cora because the relationship between the family and the servants was predicated on the family always being in the right. For Carson to know about Mary's wrongdoings is hard. Of course, it doesn't shake Carson's love for her at all.

ACT TWO

17 INT. CARSON'S PANTRY. DOWNTON. NIGHT.

CARSON: Are you telling me you *saw* him take the cellar key?

Carson is talking to Thomas.

THOMAS: Not exactly. But I saw him in here and I thought the key was swinging on its hook.

Carson listens to this without comment.

THOMAS (CONT'D): I just wondered if you'd noticed if any of the wine was missing?

18 INT. CORA'S BEDROOM. DOWNTON. NIGHT.

Cora and Robert are in bed together.

ROBERT: I think I owe you an apology after the way I spoke at dinner.
CORA: Next time you want to treat me like a naughty schoolgirl, you might do it in private and not in front of the servants.
ROBERT: You're right. I'm sorry.*
CORA: Of course, it gave your mother her best evening since Christmas.
ROBERT: Even so, we must try to keep control of Sybil.
CORA: Robert, believe me, Sybil is not your problem.

He ponders this response as she blows out her lamp.

....

* I am always interested by convention and this convention, of female diffidence and subservience, was universally accepted at that period. The man was the master of the house and all that nonsense. But I don't think these rules are ever much of a guide to what went on in private. If you go back to the twelfth century there are accounts of men who were terrified of their wives. One must never forget that human nature has a way of manifesting itself whatever the customs of a particular society may be and anyway, Cora comes from a different conditioning. She is not an aristocrat even by American standards. She has new money and when we do meet her mother, Mrs Levinson is brash and loud and certainly not a Winthrop from Boston.

CORA (CONT'D): We've got to support Mary this year, when
we get to London.
ROBERT: But it's Sybil's first Season. We can't have
Mary stealing her thunder.
CORA: Sybil'll do well enough. It's time Mary was
settled. High time.

He is getting sleepy, so he just accepts this.

ROBERT: Poor old Edith. We never seem to talk about her.
CORA: I'm afraid Edith will be the one to care for us in
our old age.
ROBERT: What a ghastly prospect.

For Edith or for them, he does not make clear.

19 INT. SERVANTS' HALL. DOWNTON. DAY.

A new morning. Bates leaves breakfast as Carson arrives.

CARSON: I wonder if I might have a word with you later,
Mr Bates.
BATES: Of course. As soon as I've finished his lordship.

Carson nods briskly and goes. Anna has overheard this.

ANNA: What's that about?
BATES: Search me.

He leaves, but Anna turns to find O'Brien looking at her.

20 INT. DRAWING ROOM. DOWNTON. DAY.

Mary, in a riding habit, gloves, hat and veil, walks in.

MARY: Mama? Anna said you wanted me.
CORA: Look who's paid us a visit.

*She stands, making the guest stand also. He is none other
than Sir Anthony Strallan. Edith is with them.*

MARY: Sir Anthony. How nice. We all thought we'd driven
you away with that horrible salty pudding.
STRALLAN: No, indeed. But I have been away.
EDITH: He's been in Austria and Germany.
MARY: How interesting.
STRALLAN: Interesting. And worrying.

Cora wants to move things along.

CORA: Sir Anthony is here to show you his new car.
STRALLAN: I've rather taken to driving myself and I have to keep finding destinations to justify it.
MARY: What kind of car is it?
STRALLAN: It's an open Rolls-Royce. I wondered if you might like a spin in it.
MARY: How kind. But, alas, not today. I've had Diamond saddled and he's waiting for me.
CORA: You could ride this afternoon.
MARY: It's arranged now. But thank you, Sir Anthony. Do ask me again.
EDITH: I don't suppose you'd take me.

Strallan is enough of a gentleman to know he's trapped.

STRALLAN: Of course! I should be delighted.

Cora is not best pleased.

21 INT.   CARSON'S PANTRY.   DOWNTON.   DAY.

Bates is standing before Carson.

BATES: What is it that I am accused of?
CARSON: Nobody is 'accusing' you of anything. But there's been a suggestion you were handling the cellar key. Before I take it any further, I want to find out if there's a simple explanation.
BATES: Because some wine is missing.
CARSON: How do you know that?

Bates is not prepared to explain.

CARSON (CONT'D): Right. Well, we'll leave it there for now.

22 EXT.   DOWNTON VILLAGE.   DAY.

Sybil is walking towards the Crawleys' front door.

23 INT.   DRAWING ROOM.   CRAWLEY HOUSE.   DAY.

Isobel is with Sybil.

ISOBEL: No, I shan't be going into Ripon on election night and nor should you. Not again. Yesterday was quite frightening enough. What would your father say?

SYBIL: You know how he hates politics. He says that since he's a peer and we're all women, there isn't a vote in the house to be had, and they should leave us alone.
ISOBEL: Well, he's right that politics can be a rough ride. I support women's rights and I'm glad you do. But you won't help the cause by getting caught in a stampede.
SYBIL: But I do so want to go. To feel part of it if Morgan* wins, and to support him if he loses.
ISOBEL: Very commendable, but my advice is to do it by post.

The door opens and Matthew comes in.

ISOBEL (CONT'D): Hello. What are you doing here?
MATTHEW: I thought I'd get some luncheon off you. I'm taking down a will in the next village at two.
SYBIL: I ought to be going. Don't bother Molesley.

24 INT. HALL. CRAWLEY HOUSE. DAY.

Matthew shuts the door. Isobel has followed them.

MATTHEW: What did she want?
ISOBEL: A partner in crime.
MATTHEW: Did she get one?
ISOBEL: Not this time.

25 EXT. COUNTRY LANE. DAY.

Edith and Strallan are bowling along in his car.

STRALLAN: The Kaiser is such a mercurial figure, one minute the warlord, the next a lovelorn poet.
EDITH: But a poet in need of an empire.
STRALLAN: That's very good. 'A poet in need of an empire.' My late wife always used to say...
EDITH: What did Lady Strallan say?
STRALLAN: Never mind.
EDITH: But I should like to hear it.
STRALLAN: Really? Would you, really?

She nods. He is very touched. As she intended him to be.

....

* Morgan, the Liberal candidate. Named for a friend.

STRALLAN (CONT'D): She used to say Kaiser Bill loved uniforms and medals but he never really connected them with fighting.

He laughs and Edith laughs, too.

EDITH: What was she like?
STRALLAN: Maud? Oh, she was awfully funny. Some people couldn't see it, but she was…

Edith is doing very well.

26 EXT. STABLE YARD. DOWNTON. DAY.

William crosses the yard to the woodsheds with a basket, as Mary arrives, leading her horse.

MARY: Is Lynch anywhere about?*
WILLIAM: I haven't seen him, m'lady.
MARY: My horse is lame.

She stands by the animal. William hesitates.

WILLIAM: I could have a look at him.
MARY: Do you know about horses?
WILLIAM: I grew up on a farm, m'lady.
MARY: Well, if you think you can help.

She stands back and William approaches the animal, handling it confidently and examining its hoof without alarming it.

WILLIAM: He's graveled.
MARY: You mean he's picked up a stone?

....

* Lynch the groom raises an interesting point. You introduce these characters but you don't really know which of them will run. And, with *Downton*, the more we got into it the more I realised that we couldn't hope to cover the outside staff. The nearest to someone living and working outside the house that we had room for was the chauffeur. He is, after all, driving the family around. Originally I had ideas of gardeners and grooms and so on, but there simply isn't the space to develop them. Every now and then the characters will refer to the groom or the head gardener, when horses are brought round or flowers are brought in, and the gamekeeper makes an appearance in the second series but the fact remains we were pushing our luck developing eighteen characters; once you go over about ten it is hard to find the space for them to have any story, so that had to be the limit really.

WILLIAM: No, it's an infection. From dirt getting in.
He must have been shod recently.
MARY: I wouldn't know.
WILLIAM: That's when it starts.
MARY: So, it's not too serious?
WILLIAM: Oh, no. I'll clean it up and put a poultice on.

He starts to lead the horse into its open loose box. Mary watches, eventually leaning on the half door.

MARY: Shouldn't you wait for Lynch?
WILLIAM: He won't mind. He knows I can handle horses.
MARY: Did you look after the horses on your father's farm?
WILLIAM: I did. Best job in the world.
MARY: Then why did you leave it?
WILLIAM: My father wanted me to have a chance of bettering myself.
MARY: As a second footman?

She almost laughs at this preposterous idea.

WILLIAM: It's a good place for me, m'lady.
MARY: Of course it is. I'm sorry.

He has a certain innocent cockiness and it makes her smile. *

....

* Mary's snobbery is essentially unconscious. She doesn't mean to hurt William's feelings, but she cannot imagine how anyone could be bettering themselves as a second footman. She apologises, so I don't mean to make her out to be a bitch, but I think it's important to remember that these things were often quite differently perceived by the locals and the families. The big house was a promised land for the nearby schools. Most of the leaving class, certainly the girls, would go into service but usually it would be in more ordinary situations, where they might be maid-of-all-work to a shop keeper, which would mean the life of a dog because they had to do everything, and even if they went into a rectory with two other maids and a cook, it was a much duller life, with no status attached. But if you were chosen by the Marchioness of Exeter's housekeeper to go and work at Burghley, or the Duchess of Richmond to go and work at Goodwood, then this was an excellent start. And if you gained a good reference, then you were on your way. So William or Daisy, far from being failures by being low in the pecking order, have in fact begun well. If the career had continued after the Second World War in the same way, then William would have ended up as a butler, perhaps in a major house.

27 INT.   CARSON'S PANTRY.   DOWNTON.   DAY.

Thomas, O'Brien and Daisy are in there with Carson.

O'BRIEN: I've seen Mr Bates with a bottle from time to time. I must have thought he was helping you.

CARSON: Why would I order a valet to help with the wine?

O'BRIEN: Well, when you put it like that, of course you wouldn't.

CARSON: So, Mr Bates is taking wine? Why would this be? To drink it?

THOMAS: It's not to clean his boots.

CARSON: Thank you, Thomas.

Thomas makes a sign to Daisy to speak, but she does not.

CARSON (CONT'D): Daisy? Thomas says you have something to add to this.

DAISY: Well…

CARSON: You are not in any trouble, or any danger of trouble.

THOMAS: You remember what you saw?

He urges the girl with his eyes. She takes a deep breath.

DAISY: I may have seen him coming out of the cellar.

CARSON: *May?* Did you or didn't you?

But Daisy will not add to her statement.

O'BRIEN: It's very hard for the girl, Mr Carson. You're frightening her.

CARSON: I'm sorry. Thank you. You may go.

28 INT.   CORA'S BEDROOM.   DOWNTON.   DAY.

O'Brien comes in and puts the tray on the bed.

CORA: Thank you, O'Brien.

O'Brien tidies the coverlet and folds a dressing gown.

CORA (CONT'D): How is everything downstairs?

O'BRIEN: All right I think, m'lady. Though Mr Carson's a bit cast down.

CORA: Oh? Why? What's the matter with him?

O'BRIEN: He's found out something about… well, a person he admires, and it isn't very nice.

Naturally, this confirms Cora's worst fears.

> CORA: Has he said who this person is? Who's proved a
> disappointment?
> O'BRIEN: I don't like to say, m'lady.
> CORA: Please do. If you know.
> O'BRIEN: Oh, I know. It's… Mr Bates.

Cora's relief is almost palpable.

> CORA: Oh, Bates. Why? What's he done?
> O'BRIEN: You should ask Mr Carson, m'lady, it's not my
> place to tell.

29 INT. LIBRARY. DOWNTON. DAY.

Sybil comes in to find her father at his desk.

> SYBIL: Papa, can Branson drive me into Ripon on Friday
> evening?
> ROBERT: I don't think so, no. Not after the last time.*
> SYBIL: Oh, please. There's a meeting of my borstal
> charity. I've missed two and I simply must be there.
> ROBERT: You'd have to take Mary or Edith.
> SYBIL: Don't make me, I beg you. Those meetings are
> deadly at the best of times, and you know what they're
> like when they're bored.
> ROBERT: Why are all your causes so steeped in gloom?
> SYBIL: Because it's gloomy things that need our help. If
> everything in the garden's sunny, why meddle?
> ROBERT: Well, I agree with that. Talking of sunny, are
> you looking forward to your coming Season?
> SYBIL: I am rather… So, it's all right? I can go?

He has been distracted by Pharaoh at his feet. He nods.

> ROBERT: Will you be late?
> SYBIL: I think I'll miss dinner.

....

* Sybil lies to her father in order to go to the political meeting in Ripon, and in a way this is a moment of parturition. Once children conceal their purposes or their social engagements or their plans for the weekend, that is the beginning of their move away from the parental set of values. Before that, God knows they may be rude or challenging, but they don't usually have a private life, a secret agenda. And this is where it begins for Sybil.

ROBERT: Remember to tell Branson to take a sandwich for himself.

30 EXT. GARDENS. DOWNTON. DAY.

Matthew comes round the house to find Mary, reading.

MARY: Hello. What are you doing here?
MATTHEW: I'm in search of your father. Carson thought he was outside.
MARY: He's in the library. What is it?
MATTHEW: Nothing much. I've had an enquiry about one of the farms.
MARY: Oh.

She accepts this, uninterested but friendly.

MATTHEW: So, what's new at the big house?
MARY: Sybil, mainly. She's discovered politics, which of course makes Papa see red.
MATTHEW: She was trying to get my mother to go to something yesterday.
MARY: Tell her to keep out of it, if she knows what's good for her.
MATTHEW: I admire Sybil's passion, though.
MARY: Of course. But then I like a good argument. Papa does not.
MATTHEW: If you really like an argument —
MARY: Yes?
MATTHEW: We should see more of each other.

Which makes her laugh.

31 INT. LIBRARY. DOWNTON. DAY.

SYBIL: So, it's all right? I can go?

He has been distracted by Pharaoh at his feet. He nods.

ROBERT: Will you be late?
SYBIL: I think I'll miss dinner.
ROBERT: Well, remember to tell Branson to take a sandwich for himself.

32 INT. MRS HUGHES'S SITTING ROOM. DOWNTON. NIGHT.

Carson is with Mrs Hughes.

MRS HUGHES: Well, I don't believe it.

CARSON: D'you think I *want* to believe it?

MRS HUGHES: I don't trust Thomas or O'Brien further than I could throw them.

CARSON: And Daisy?

MRS HUGHES: That's the hard one. But surely, Mr Bates…?

CARSON: I agree. But I've had some shocks lately, when it comes to thinking you know people. Some bad shocks. And he knew the wine was missing. How was that?

MRS HUGHES: What are you going to do?

CARSON: I'm not sure yet. I think I might get them all together, light the blue paper and see what happens.

MRS HUGHES: Can I watch?

33 INT. DRAWING ROOM. DOWER HOUSE. DAY.

Violet is standing over Cora, who holds a letter.

CORA: But who's it from?

VIOLET: Susan Flintshire.

CORA: What does she say?

VIOLET: Prepare for the worst. Not the first page. My poor niece never uses one word where twenty will do. Start there. 'I'm sorry to have to tell you…'

CORA: 'I'm sorry to have to tell you that Hugh has heard a vile story about your granddaughter Mary…'

She stops reading aloud, but her eyes flick back and forth.

VIOLET: Sorry? She's thrilled… now, first I must ask — and I want you to think carefully before you answer — is any of it true?

Cora hesitates. Violet breathes deeply, composing herself.

VIOLET (CONT'D): I see. Some of it *is* true. How much?

Again, Cora is defeated.

VIOLET (CONT'D): Oh, dear.

CORA: She didn't drag him.

VIOLET: I wondered about that. Obviously Susan has forgotten the distance between the girls' rooms and the bachelors' corridor.
CORA: She couldn't manage it alone.
VIOLET: So how did she do it?
CORA: I helped her. She woke me up and I helped her.
VIOLET: Well. I've often thought this family might be approaching dissolution. I didn't know dissolution was already upon us. Does Robert know?
CORA: No. And he isn't going to.
VIOLET: Oh.

She nods. This, at least, she agrees with.

CORA: Of course it was terribly wrong. It was *all* terribly wrong. But I didn't see how else —
VIOLET: Please! I cannot listen to your attempts to justify yourself.

Cora stands. It is time to bring the meeting to an end.

CORA: I know this has been very hard for you to hear. And God knows it was hard for me to live through. But if you expect me to disown my daughter, I'm afraid you will be disappointed. Good day.

Violet is as motionless as a statue.

END OF ACT TWO

ACT THREE

34 EXT. BACK COURTYARD. DOWNTON. NIGHT.

Bates is alone, staring at the stars. Anna appears.

ANNA: I thought you must be out here.
BATES: And you were right.
ANNA: I know you're upset.

BATES: Yes. I'm upset. I have worked here for two years and Mr Carson has no difficulty believing the worst of me.
ANNA: I think he has a great deal of difficulty, which is why he hasn't told his lordship yet. Can't you just explain about Thomas?
BATES: Not now. It would sound like a false accusation.
ANNA: You can't take it lying down. Because you're *not* guilty of anything wrong and before it's over I'm going to tell the world.
BATES: Are you? I'm not sure the world is listening.

35 INT. SYBIL'S BEDROOM. DOWNTON. NIGHT.

Sybil walks in to find Gwen turning down her bed.

GWEN: Sorry. I'm a bit late tonight.*
SYBIL: Not to worry. How are you?
GWEN: Bearing up.

She gives what is meant to be a brave toss of her chin, as she continues to fold the coverlet.

SYBIL: It's not the end. You mustn't give up. We'll get there.
GWEN: Forgive me, m'lady, but you don't get it. You're brought up to think it's all within your grasp, that if you want something enough it'll come to you. But we're not like that. We don't think our dreams are bound to come true, because they almost never do.

....

* This scene was a slight disappointment because Gwen should have been turning down the bed for the night. It is a custom that has almost gone now, not in hotels perhaps but in most houses. Even so, when you come up after dinner and your bed has been turned down, there is nothing more luxurious. I put it in as a beguiling detail but somehow there was a misunderstanding and Gwen ended up actually making the bed at what must be quite late at night, as if it had sat there unmade all day. It doesn't really make sense and, when I saw it, I complained like billy-o. They tried to minimise it in the edit, but they couldn't change the action because that is what she's doing.

SYBIL: Then that's why we must stick together. Your
dream is my dream now. And I'll *make* it come true.*

36 EXT/INT. BACK DOOR. KITCHEN PASSAGE. DOWNTON. NIGHT.

Thomas is smoking with O'Brien. They're worried.

THOMAS: Why hasn't he done anything? He's had the story
and the witnesses.

O'BRIEN: 'The witnesses'? What do you think this is? A
murder mystery?

THOMAS: Well, Mr Bates can't accuse me now. It'll sound
as if he's trying to get his own back.

O'BRIEN: If I lose my job over this, I swear to God I'll
swing for you.

She stops talking when William walks past on his way to:

....

* One of the socialist arguments that I understand is the injustice of
entitlement, that a child who has grown up in a prosperous middle- or upper-
class household has a sense of entitlement to a certain way of life. There is an
unconscious assumption, by them and their families, that they will get a job
and lead a life that is reasonably similar to the one they've always known.
And in many, many cases it becomes a self-fulfilling prophecy because these
young men and women are comfortable with prominent people, they are at
ease in the presence of money. They have no fear of success.

But someone from an unprivileged background, even when they are
brilliant and talented, can strive for a sense of belonging, the lack of which
can hold them back and cheat them of maximising their potential. I am not,
as it happens, a fan of the Eleven Plus exam, but one of the achievements of
the grammar schools was to give this sense of entitlement to children from
deprived backgrounds. So that by the time they left school and went on to
university or into jobs, there really was no difference between them and
people who'd gone to the greatest public schools in the country. They were
all on an even playing field.

Privileged people are often slow to understand what an advantage they
have been given, because they have grown up in a world of the possible.
That's what this scene is about.

37 INT. KITCHEN. DOWNTON. NIGHT.

William looks in. Daisy is finishing up.

WILLIAM: Is there any stale bread you're throwing out?
And some salt.
DAISY: Why?
WILLIAM: Well, I thought I'd make a last hot poultice for
Diamond. It'll give him a better night.
DAISY: You big softie. What'll Mr Lynch say?

*She pulls the kettle onto the middle of the stove and starts
to rummage for the bread.*

WILLIAM: Why, he doesn't mind. He says I've got the
touch. He thinks I should pack this in and be a groom.
DAISY: Why don't you?
WILLIAM: My Mum. She was so excited when I came here.
They're proud of me and I'd hate to spoil that.
DAISY: Do you miss them?

*William starts to speak, and then nods his head instead. She
brings the bread and a tin bowl to break it up into.*

DAISY (CONT'D): I never had that in my childhood.
Someone you could always trust.
WILLIAM: I trust them. They trust me. There are no lies
in our house.

She is pouring the boiling water in.

WILLIAM (CONT'D): Thanks. That's enough.

He picks up the bowl, still mixing. She watches him go.

38 EXT. GARDENS. DOWNTON. DAY.

Cora and Mary are walking, when Isobel appears.

ISOBEL: I'm glad to catch you. We have a conundrum at
the hospital, and I would value your opinions.
CORA: Of course.
ISOBEL: We've been treating the mother of your footman,
William Mason.
MARY: What's the matter with her?
ISOBEL: Heart, I'm afraid.
CORA: Why didn't Carson tell us?

ISOBEL: That's the point. She's forbidden us to say anything to her son. She's determined not to worry him and equally fierce that he should not take any extra time off.

MARY: That's ridiculous.

ISOBEL: She's gone home now, but she's still very ill. Clearly the boy should go and see her and I assume you would have no objections?

CORA: Of course not.

ISOBEL: So, do we break a patient's confidence and disobey her orders? Or not?

CORA: We can't. If she's forbidden it.

ISOBEL: I must say I agree with you.

MARY: Well, I'll tell him.

CORA: No, you will not. She has rights too. And there are rules.

MARY: I don't care a fig about rules.

Which earns her a sharp look from her mother. *

39 EXT/INT.   RIPON MARKET PLACE/CAR.   EVE.

Sybil and Branson are driving into the square, where a crowd has assembled beneath the windows of the Town Hall.

BRANSON: Where to from here, m'lady?

SYBIL: What do you mean? We've arrived.

BRANSON: The meeting's in one of these buildings?

SYBIL: This is the meeting. We're here for the counting of the votes.

BRANSON: I don't understand. I thought that…

SYBIL: Don't be silly, Branson. You didn't think I'd miss my very first by-election?

BRANSON: But I don't think his lordship would approve.

SYBIL: Let me worry about him.

....

* Should they disobey his mother's wishes and tell William she's on the way out, or is she entitled to control the knowledge of her own illness? In a way I agree with Isobel. If I were dying and I didn't want my son to know for some reason or other, I would be very angry if someone disobeyed me and told him. On the other hand… Anyway, hopefully it's one of my *Downton* conundrums, where you're never quite sure which side you agree with.

*And she jumps out of the car in a trice. The crowd is dense
and the driver behind him hoots. He must move on.*

BRANSON: I have to park the car! Don't move. Stay where
you are!
SYBIL: Really, Branson. I thought I gave the orders.

With a laugh, she pushes into the crowd.

40 INT. DRAWING ROOM. DOWNTON. EVE.

Pharaoh is by the fire. Thomas is at the door.

THOMAS: Sir Anthony Strallan.

*Robert, Cora, Mary and Edith stand. They are dressed for
dinner, as is Strallan. Cora is slightly flustered.*

CORA: Sir Anthony —?
STRALLAN: Don't worry, Lady Grantham. I haven't got the
date wrong.
ROBERT: What a relief. I could hear Cora wondering if
the dinner would stretch.

Strallan laughs. He is relaxed now.

STRALLAN: No, I'm not really here at all. But I was
driving past your gates on my way to the Callender-
Becketts,* so I thought I'd take a chance. The thing is,
I've got two tickets for a concert in York, next Friday,
and I was just wondering —
MARY: How nice. The only thing is, I —
STRALLAN: No. I was hoping Lady Edith might like to
accompany me.

This is enough to silence them all. Edith is stunned.

EDITH: But I'd love to.
ROBERT: Shouldn't you ask what sort of a concert it is?

....

* These are friends of ours in Cheshire and Sarah Callender-Beckett was
lying in bed, half-watching this episode, and half-reading her book, when
suddenly Strallan announced that he was on his way to the Callender-
Becketts. She nearly fainted. I've subjected quite a few friends to similar
treatment over the years.

STRALLAN: Just Hungry Hundreds stuff, mostly, you know.
Bellini, Rossini, Puccini. I'm not up to anything
complicated.
EDITH: I'd like that very much.
STRALLAN: It's quite a hike, so I'll pick you up at six.
Lady Jervas has asked us for a bite to eat afterwards.
If it's all right with your mother?
CORA: By all means.
STRALLAN: I must run. I hope I haven't spoiled your
dinner.

*With a wave, he is gone, leaving Mary cross and Edith in
Paradise. Robert walks up to Cora and speaks very softly.*

ROBERT: We may have to hire a nurse, after all.*

41 INT. KITCHEN. DOWNTON. EVE.

Mrs Patmore and Daisy tip a mousse out of a mould.

MRS PATMORE: Oh, for heaven's sake, hold it steady, if
you don't want to start again from the beginning.
DAISY: Do these biscuits go up?
MRS PATMORE: No, I put them out for the fairies.†

....

* Edith seems almost to be winning for once, but I'm afraid Robert has the response which is so disappointing when you find it in a parent. He assumes Edith will be a spinster because he thinks her the least handsome of his daughters. He expects her to be the one who stays at home to look after them in their old age. Here, my sympathies are entirely with Edith. It is very draining when the people you live with assume that you're a non-achiever and no one should have to put up with it.

The casting of Edith was a challenge. Just as you would never cast a boring actor to play a bore, so, when you are casting a plain character, the last thing you want is a plain actress. It's a trick, really. You need someone who is attractive but in a different way, allowing the others to act as if she were plain. This will give the audience the sensation that they can see her inner beauty. But of course they're not looking at her inner beauty, they're looking at her outer beauty. Laura Carmichael is just as pretty as Michelle Dockery and Jessica Brown Findlay, but she's got that slightly more reserved English face. The characters act that she's the least fetching of the sisters, but she isn't. They are, all three, very beguiling.

† Here we have Mrs Patmore demonstrating that she is the downstairs Violet.

DAISY: Oh.

MRS PATMORE: Of course they're going up.

Daisy nods and puts it all on a tray.

MRS PATMORE (CONT'D): What's wrong with you? You're always dozy, but tonight you'd make Sleeping Beauty look alert.

DAISY: I was just thinking.

MRS PATMORE: Blimey. Batten down the hatches.

DAISY: I think I've let misself down.

MRS PATMORE: It can't be a new sensation.

William walks in, takes the tray from Daisy and goes.

42 EXT. RIPON MARKET PLACE. EVE.

The High Sheriff is reading the results. The crowd is thick below the window where he stands.

HIGH SHERIFF: The Honourable Joseph Gerald Ansty, for the Conservative and Unionist Party: 6,363 votes.*

The mob is getting more excited.

HIGH SHERIFF (CONT'D): Martin James Dillon, the Socialist Party: 2,741 votes.

There is an absolute howl of booing and shouting, met with an equally forceful cheer. Branson joins Sybil.

BRANSON: Can we call it a day, m'lady?

SYBIL: Don't be silly. This is the moment we've come for.

HIGH SHERIFF: Trevor Andrew Morgan, Liberal Party:

BRANSON: I don't like it. This lot's not interested in politics. They're spoiling for a fight.

SYBIL: They think some things are worth fighting for and I agree with them. So do you, really.

---

* The story is in the detail. The *Honourable* Joseph Gerald Ansty means that he is the son of a peer and so probably a member of one of the local great families. For a landowner's son to stand for Parliament was fairly typical. But here we also have the Socialist party canvassing almost 3,000 votes, which is a way of reminding the audience that Socialism was already becoming a force in the land. As for the numbers, this election is before universal suffrage so the polling figures would have been much smaller than today.

Across the square a door opens. Matthew Crawley emerges. He takes in the general rowdiness and turns to lock it. Then something catches his eye. He starts to move towards the crowd.

HIGH SHERIFF: 5,894 votes.

There is a roar of anger at the defeat of the Liberals.

HIGH SHERIFF (CONT'D): I hereby declare The Honourable Joseph Ansty has been elected to —

But the rest of his speech is lost in the tumult which has turned violent and ugly. We recognise the faces of the trouble-makers as they break windows and smash chairs outside a pub. Matthew fights his way through the chaos.

43 EXT. ANOTHER ENTRANCE TO THE SQUARE. RIPON. EVE.

A truck full of heavies pulls over. A big man shouts.

THUG: Out you get, lads!

They start to climb down. They are pretty frightening.

THUG (CONT'D): We'll wipe the smile off their bloody Tory faces.

They set off towards the crowd.

MATTHEW: Sybil! Branson!
BRANSON: Mr Crawley!

Branson has his arm round Sybil and he is trying to pull her clear. At which point, Matthew reaches them.

MATTHEW: What on earth are you doing here?
SYBIL: I couldn't miss this!
MATTHEW: Couldn't you? I could.

He's taken her arm, as the thug from the truck steps out.

BRANSON: Look, I'm on your side. Don't cause any trouble. You have to believe me!

But the thug pushes him away, and squares up to Matthew.

THUG: What's your problem, Mr la-di-da?
MATTHEW: My problem is you.

The thug lunges at him. Matthew hits him back and they are brawling. Sybil runs forward as Matthew punches the man.

SYBIL: Stop it! This moment!

As the thug falls, he catches her jaw. She goes down, gashing her temple on the edge of a table.

BRANSON: Oh, no. Oh, please God, no!

He takes her up in his arms, as tenderly as a father with his child. All of which is seen by Matthew.

MATTHEW: This way.

He clears a path through the seething crush, with Branson following in his wake, carrying the unconscious girl.

MATTHEW (CONT'D): Where's the car?
BRANSON: Over there! By the bank!

They push through the crowds. At last they get her into the vehicle. With Matthew tending to her, Branson drives away.

44 INT. DRAWING ROOM. DOWNTON. NIGHT.

Robert, Cora, Mary and Edith are together after dinner. Pharaoh is by the fire.

CORA: She ought to be back by now.
ROBERT: Those meetings can go on forever.
EDITH: What do you think I should wear next Friday? I thought about the green with the brown trimming, but it might be a bit wintery.
MARY: Are we really going to spend a week discussing your clothes?
CORA: You look very nice in the green.
EDITH: Then I wondered about the pink, but is it too grand for York?

During this, Mary is distracted by William, who is removing a cup and saucer from a side table. As he is doing so, he catches her eye and nods towards the door. She looks over. Gwen is waiting there. She signs for Mary to come.

MARY: I think I might go up.
CORA: It's very early.
MARY: I really can't spend the evening reviewing Edith's wardrobe.

She kisses her parents and walks out of the room.

45 INT. HALL. DOWNTON. NIGHT.

Mary is coming from the drawing room where she finds Gwen.
Gwen leads her away from the drawing room door.

> GWEN: I've fetched a coat.
> MARY: Why? What do I need a coat for?

Gwen just holds the garment open, as Branson steps forward.
Mary hadn't noticed him. He speaks in a low voice.

> BRANSON: I've come to fetch you, m'lady. We've taken
> Lady Sybil to Crawley House. In the village.

This strikes panic in Mary's heart although she, too,
whispers.

> MARY: What's happened?
> BRANSON: I took her to Ripon for the count. She got
> caught in a fight.

Mary raises her hand to her mouth in horror.

> MARY: Take me there at once.

Without another word, she hurries out of the front door.

46 INT. DRAWING ROOM. CRAWLEY HOUSE. NIGHT.

Mary enters and approaches the sofa where Sybil lies, a gash
at her temple and blood down the side of her face, which
Isobel, in a dressing gown, is just beginning to wash away
with hot water. There's a bottle of iodine on a tray.
Matthew is there. He glances up at Mary as she sees the
invalid.

> MARY: My God! Oh, my darling...
> MATTHEW: I didn't know what to do, so I had Branson bring
> her here.
> MARY: Quite right. Mama would have fainted if she'd seen
> her like this. As for Papa...

She rolls her eyes heavenward, as she kneels and takes her
sister's hand. Sybil is just about awake.

> ISOBEL: This will sting a bit. But it's stopped
> bleeding.

She puts iodine on the cut. She looks at Matthew.

ISOBEL (CONT'D): Did you know she was planning this?
MATTHEW: Of course not.
ISOBEL: Well, what were you doing there?
MATTHEW: I was working late. I'd forgotten it was election night or I wouldn't have stayed.
SYBIL: I'm so grateful you did.
MARY: I could wring Branson's neck.
MATTHEW: What was he thinking? I'm afraid it'll cost him his job.
SYBIL: No. I told him he was taking me to a committee meeting. When he realised what it was, he wanted to come straight back.
MARY: You'll have to stick up for him, because Papa will skin him alive.

Matthew crouches down to be on a level with the invalid.

MATTHEW: Are you feeling strong enough to go home?
SYBIL: I think so. If you'll take me.

As he bends to help her up, Mary looks at him, this strong man, but just as she feels herself admiring him, she notices a new look in her sister's eyes. It is one of hero worship. Isobel has seen the look too, and unconsciously glances at Mary. They both know what is going on.

MARY: Pull your hair forward and here, wear my coat to cover the blood. You'll look more normal.

Her tone is quite brisk. Matthew helps Sybil into the coat.

MATTHEW: Lean on me.

The other women stand back as they go out.

MARY: Thank you so much for this.*
ISOBEL: I hope your parents won't punish her too harshly.

....

* Mary is an interesting character to write because, to begin with, she has a fairly tough shell. She thinks of herself as a very superior person, she's good-looking and intelligent and the daughter of an earl. But the leaking of the Pamuk story has made her vulnerable, and with vulnerability comes a slight opening up. We never have total meltdown because that's just not who she is, but she is less careful, all of which Michelle mines very well.

MARY: Don't worry. Papa talks a good punishment, but he
seldom delivers... By the way, what happened to William's
mother?
ISOBEL: Not good, I'm afraid. She's at home but she's
very weak. Another attack should finish her.
MARY: And he still doesn't know?
ISOBEL: She's adamant. I've tried to explain how hard
it'll be on him, but she won't have him disturbed. To
hear her talk, you'd think he was a Cabinet Minister.
MARY: He's made her proud. There are plenty of children
in grander circumstances who'd love to say the same.

Something in her tone interests Isobel, but they go out.

47 INT. CARSON'S PANTRY. DOWNTON. NIGHT.

Carson has the vault open and he carefully places the
evening's silver inside. Mrs Hughes is in the doorway.

MRS HUGHES: I wish you'd tell me what's troubling you.
If it's this business with Mr Bates —
CARSON: It's not that. I'll get to the bottom of that.
MRS HUGHES: Well, I hope you'll do it soon. If there's
one thing I hate it's an 'atmosphere' and we've got a
real atmosphere going now.
CARSON: I'll see them all tonight. When the family's
gone to bed.
MRS HUGHES: Good. It's an unfair rumour which needs to
be scotched.
CARSON: It's very hard to hear the names of people you
love dragged in the mud. You feel so powerless.

Mrs Hughes is surprised at this turn of the conversation.

MRS HUGHES: Well, I respect Mr Bates but I don't know
that I love him.
CARSON: I wasn't thinking of Mr Bates.
DAISY (V.O.): Mr Carson, have you got a minute?

The King and Queen of below stairs look down at this speck.

MRS HUGHES: What is it, Daisy? Mr Carson's a very busy
man.
DAISY: I know he is. But I think he'll want to hear
this... I've told you something that wasn't true.
CARSON: Why would you do that?

DAISY: I did it as a favour to a friend. But I know now
he was wrong to ask it of me.

Carson and Mrs Hughes exchange a glance. She is delighted.

48 EXT. DOWNTON. NIGHT.

*Matthew is helping Sybil into the house. Branson stands
watching. Mary is also going in when Branson speaks.*

BRANSON: She's not badly hurt, is she?
MARY: I don't think so, no.
BRANSON: Thank God.

The force of his words is almost startling. She smiles.

MARY: Better be prepared. I'm afraid Lord Grantham will
hit the roof.
BRANSON: I never would have taken her there. I may be a
Socialist but I'm not a lunatic.
MARY: I'm not sure Papa knows the difference.

She smiles. The fact she is joking makes things better.

BRANSON: You'll let me know how she gets on? Please.
MARY: If you wish.

And she goes in, leaving the lovelorn chauffeur alone. *

END OF ACT THREE

....

* We are beginning to understand that Branson has fallen for Sybil. But
Mary simply doesn't register that he has any special interest in her sister. I
believe it is important in this sort of material to give characters attitudes and
responses that are compatible with their own time. Some modern film-
makers would allow Mary to be instantly sympathetic to the idea of a
romance between her sister and the chauffeur, but that's not really believable,
given what her conditioning would have been in the world of 1914.

ACT FOUR

50 INT.   SYBIL'S BEDROOM.   NIGHT.

Cora, Sybil, Mary and Edith witness Robert's fury.

ROBERT: How dare you? *How dare you* disobey me in this
way?
CORA: Robert, I'm sure —
ROBERT: Are you so knowledgeable about the great world
that my instructions are to be set as *nothing?*

49 INT.   HALL.   DOWNTON.   NIGHT.

Matthew looks up at the sound of Robert's roar.

50 INT.   SYBIL'S BEDROOM.   NIGHT.

SYBIL: Papa, I'm sorry I disobeyed you, but I'm
interested! I'm political! I have opinions!
ROBERT: Of course, I blame Branson —
MARY: I don't think that's fair —
ROBERT: We had none of this, *none of it*, before he set
foot in our house! I suppose I should give thanks he
hasn't burned the place down over our heads!
SYBIL: Branson didn't know anything about it, until we
arrived there.
ROBERT: He leaves tonight!
SYBIL: If you punish Branson, I will never speak to you
again. *Never!*

Robert hesitates. This isn't what he wants, which Mary sees.

MARY: I don't believe this is Branson's fault. Truly,
Papa.
SYBIL: Blame me —
ROBERT: I do blame you!
CORA: Robert, can we do this in the morning? Sybil needs
rest.
SYBIL: But if I find tomorrow that Branson is missing,
I'll run away. I warn you.

She is so definite that Robert is tempted to laugh.

ROBERT: Oh? And where will you go?

SYBIL: Well, I can't think now. But I *will* go and you'll
be sorry!

Robert is calm now as he looks at his anguished daughter.

ROBERT: I should be sorry. Very sorry, indeed.

52 INT. BEDROOM PASSAGE. NIGHT.

Robert, Mary and Edith shut the door. Pharaoh waits there.

MARY: We must go down. Matthew will think we're all
dead.
EDITH: Poor Papa. Sybil was terribly wrong to do what
she did.

As Robert walks to the stairs, Mary turns to her sister.

MARY: Stop meddling and go to bed.

53 INT. HALL. DOWNTON. NIGHT.

MATTHEW: How is she?

He is by the fire as they come down, followed by the dog.
Robert shakes his head with exasperation, so Mary speaks.

MARY: She'll be perfectly fine.
ROBERT: I gather you're the shining knight in all this.
MATTHEW: Not really. But I'm glad I was there.
ROBERT: So am I, by heaven. If it had been left to that
bloody fool, Branson... You should see what he reads.
It's all Marx and Ruskin and John Stuart Mill. I ask
you.
MARY: Papa prefers the servants to read the Bible and
letters from home.

Mrs Hughes has entered the hall.

MRS HUGHES: There are sandwiches for Mr Crawley in the
dining room, Lady Mary.
MARY: Thank you, Mrs Hughes.

The housekeeper leaves. This is a pleasant development.

MARY (CONT'D): We couldn't let you starve.
MATTHEW: You really didn't have to.

ROBERT: Mary, look after Matthew while I go up and revive your mother.

The young couple head towards the dining room door. Unaware that Robert smiles hopefully at the dog as he watches them.

54 INT. CARSON'S PANTRY. DOWNTON. NIGHT.

Thomas, O'Brien, Bates and Daisy are lined up on one side, facing Carson, Mrs Hughes and Anna.

CARSON: Do you stand by your story?

THOMAS: I don't have a story.

CARSON: You saw Mr Bates in here alone, hanging up the cellar key. To me, that is a story.

THOMAS: I only said I might have seen him. I suppose I was wrong.

CARSON: And Miss O'Brien, were you wrong when you thought you saw Mr Bates carrying a bottle?

ANNA: You wicked creature.

MRS HUGHES: Anna! You are here to watch, not to participate.

O'BRIEN: I don't think I was wrong, no.

CARSON: What do you say to that, Mr Bates?

He has addressed Bates, who speaks quite calmly.

BATES: I know this to be untrue because I have no need for it. Since I arrived at Downton, you have never seen me drink one drop of alcohol.

ANNA: He's right. He never touches it.

MRS HUGHES: I knew that. Why didn't I think?

CARSON: Let us say, then, that Miss O'Brien was mistaken.

ANNA: Mistaken, my eye.

CARSON: And Daisy, we all know the value of your contribution.

DAISY: Yes, Mr Carson.

She hangs her head in shame.

CARSON: But I must ask one thing, Mr Bates: how did you know the wine had been taken?

Thomas hears this as the death knell of his career at Downton. He looks at Bates but Bates does not look at him.

55 INT. DINING ROOM. DOWNTON. NIGHT.

On the table, Matthew sits at a place laid with sandwiches, fruit, a carafe of red wine, a jug of water and glasses for both. Mary's with him. He lifts the carafe.

MATTHEW: Will you have some? We can drink to Sybil's safe return.
MARY: Why not? I'll ring for a glass.
MATTHEW: Never mind that. Here.

He pushes the wine glass over to her, pours, and then slops some into the water glass for himself.

MARY: You're not very fastidious about doing things properly.
MATTHEW: Are you?
MARY: Less than you might think.

They raise their glasses.

MATTHEW: Are you at all political?
MARY: Yes. But with a hung Parliament, it's hard to get excited about a by-election. You know nothing will change, whoever gets in…

56 INT. CARSON'S PANTRY. DOWNTON. NIGHT.

O'Brien and Thomas and Daisy are leaving. Anna is following them, when Bates interrupts, shutting the door.

BATES: If I might keep you for a minute more, Mr Carson?
MRS HUGHES: If you'd like me to leave…?
BATES: No, I'd like you to stay Mrs Hughes. And you, Anna.

They wait for what is coming. And he is ready.

....

* Bates dislikes Thomas tremendously, but he would be uncomfortable betraying a fellow member of staff and thereby risking Thomas's job. He cannot do it, even to help himself. Once again, I hope the audience can see both points of view.

BATES (CONT'D): You have decided to take no action over the allegations Thomas has made against me because you believe them to be untrue.
CARSON: That is correct.
BATES: And you are right. There's no truth in them.

Which, to a degree, relaxes them.

BATES (CONT'D): But if you were to proceed with the matter, you would find them to be proven.

This is odd. No one speaks until Bates resumes.

BATES (CONT'D): Thomas has tried to convince you I'm a drunkard and a thief.
ANNA: Which we never believed —
BATES: Because you know no different. Until a couple of years ago, I was a drunkard. And I was imprisoned as a thief.

This could not be more startling if a bomb had gone off.

BATES (CONT'D): I have repaid your kindness very poorly. I masqueraded as a man of honour and integrity, but by any moral code, I am disgraced.
CARSON: Does his lordship know this?
BATES: No. He too, like you, has been my dupe. Which neither of you has merited. And I apologise.

His humiliation fills Mrs Hughes with pity.

MRS HUGHES: That can't be the whole story.
BATES: Perhaps not. But it's enough of it to demand my resignation.

Carson appears to consider this for a moment.

CARSON: Do you want to leave, Mr Bates?
BATES: No. But I feel I have no choice.
CARSON: You owe me a say in the matter, surely?
BATES: If you wish.
CARSON: Then I will consider the case and give my decision, when I've discussed it with his lordship. Until then, I hope you will remain in your post.

Bates gives a slight nod of assent.

CARSON (CONT'D): And now I think we should all get some rest.

Without another word, Bates and Anna leave.

CARSON (CONT'D): There's a question to ponder.
MRS HUGHES: What? How were we all taken in?
CARSON: No. How so fine a man was brought so low. Well, well. Let he who is without sin cast the first stone. I will not judge them lest I be judged.
MRS HUGHES: Them? Who else is there?
CARSON: Good night, Mrs Hughes.
MRS HUGHES: Will you use this to get rid of Thomas?
CARSON: How can I? What evidence do I have? If Mr Bates will not testify against his tormentor?

The painful interview is at an end.

57 INT. DINING ROOM. DOWNTON. NIGHT.

MARY: Thank you for coming to Sybil's rescue. You were very brave. She told me you knocked the man down.
MATTHEW: I hope I did my duty.
MARY: Are you a creature of duty?

He is taken aback, but she wants to find out some answers.

MATTHEW: Not entirely.
MARY: When you laugh with me, or flirt with me, is that a duty? Are you conforming to the fitness of things? Doing what's expected?
MATTHEW: Don't play with me. I don't deserve it. Not from you.

There is a moment of intensity between them, then...

MARY: You must be careful not to break Sybil's heart. I watched her tonight at your mother's house. I think she has a crush on you.

He looks at Mary for a moment, as she sips her wine.

MATTHEW: That's something no one could accuse you of.
MARY: Oh, I don't know.

She speaks quite carefully, looking from under her lashes.

MATTHEW: I assume you speak in a spirit of mockery.
MARY: You should have more faith.

MATTHEW: Shall I remind you of some of your choicest
remarks about me, when I arrived here? Because they live
in my memory as fresh as the day they were spoken.
MARY: Oh, Matthew. What am I always telling you? You
must pay no attention to the things I say.

*When they kiss, it is a long kiss, all the more passionate
for being delayed far longer than it should have been.*

58 EXT. KITCHEN COURTYARD. DOWNTON. NIGHT.

ANNA: Mr Bates.
BATES: Anna.
ANNA: Will you really leave?
BATES: I doubt if his lordship wants a thief in the
house. Now go to sleep and dream of a better man.
ANNA: I can't. Because there isn't one.

*He looks at her and on an impulse puts his arms around her
and kisses her. He does love her, as much as she loves him.**

BATES: There. If you want to know how I feel, then
that's how I feel. But I'm only telling you because I'm
going, and even you can see that nothing will come of it
now.

*The noise of the hall boys' arrival breaks them apart. Anna
walks away.*

59 INT. CORA'S BEDROOM. DOWNTON. NIGHT.

Cora is alone in bed, reading, when Mary comes in.

CORA: Has Matthew gone?
MARY: Yes.
CORA: Thank the Lord he was there. Of course your
father's right. We ought to sack Branson.
CORA (CONT'D): I hope you thanked Matthew properly.
MARY: I got them to make him some sandwiches.
CORA: It's not quite what I meant.
MARY: And he asked me to marry him.
CORA: Heavens! What did they put in them?
MARY: I'm serious. He proposed to me.

....

* In the filming, it was decided that their kiss should be interrupted, and so
the final speech was redundant. I think this was the right choice, in fact.

Cora sees that her daughter is indeed serious.

CORA: Oh, my dear. Have you given him an answer?
MARY: Only that I'd think about it.
CORA: Well, that's an advance on what it would have been a year ago. Do you want to marry him?
MARY: I know *you* want me to marry him.
CORA: What we want doesn't matter.

Then she hears her own words and disagrees with them.

CORA (CONT'D): At least, it's not *all* that matters. Do you love Matthew?
MARY: Yes. I think perhaps I do. I think I may have loved him for much longer than I knew.
CORA: Oh my darling. Let's not pretend this isn't the answer to every one of our prayers.

Mary stands and peers out at the stars.

MARY: I'd have to tell him.
CORA: Oh… Is it absolutely necessary?
MARY: If I didn't, I'd feel as if I'd caught him with a lie.*

Before Cora can argue, the door opens and Robert comes in, dressed for bed. Mary smiles.

MARY (CONT'D): I hope you know that *really* smart people sleep in separate rooms.
ROBERT: I always have the bed made up in the dressing room, so at least I *pretend* we sleep apart. Isn't that enough?
MARY: No. But never mind. Good night.

She leaves her parents alone.

....

* This statement, that Mary is determined to tell Matthew about Pamuk, for me defines her as a sympathetic character because I suspect that most women wouldn't feel the same, especially then. The simple truth that she is only prepared to enter the state of marriage honestly and without deception means we cannot dislike her. I think, anyway.

60 INT. SERVANTS' STAIRCASE. NIGHT.

Thomas and O'Brien are together. Mrs Patmore appears.

MRS PATMORE: Haven't you gone up yet? Blow this out.
You're the last. Good night.
THOMAS: Good night.

She climbs the stairs, painfully. The lamp flickers.

THOMAS (CONT'D): I'm going to bloody get him. I don't
care what you say.
O'BRIEN: What would I say? Everything comes to him who
waits.
THOMAS: Well, I've waited long enough.

He starts upstairs. O'Brien blows out the lamp.

61 EXT. DOWNTON. DAY.

Mary is dressed for riding. William is with her horse.

MARY: Does Carson know you're here?
WILLIAM: I heard you were going out, and I wanted to see
how he was walking.
MARY: Lynch is happy for me to ride him.
WILLIAM: Oh, yes. He's better. But I'll wait and see
what he's like when you're up.

She nods and would return to the horse, but…

MARY: William, are you planning to go home soon?
WILLIAM: Well, it's a bit far for my half day, but I can
maybe get the time to go in July, when the family's in
London. That's if I don't go with you, of course.

Mary hesitates then comes to a decision.

MARY: I think you should take a few days off and go now.
I'll fix it. I'll speak to father and to Carson. No one
will mind.
WILLIAM: But why, m'lady?
MARY: Your mother's not been well.
WILLIAM: How do you know?
MARY: I heard someone mention it in the village. I
forget who.
WILLIAM: I'd a letter and she never said.

MARY: I'm sure it's nothing. But I know it would cheer
her to see you.
WILLIAM: Well, if it wouldn't be a bother.
MARY: It won't. I'll arrange it as soon as I get back.
WILLIAM: Thank you very much, m'lady.
MARY: She ought to spend some time with the people she
loves.

*Before William can respond to this novel idea, Mary walks the
horse away.*

62 INT. CORA'S SITTING ROOM. DOWNTON. DAY.

Cora writes at a little bonheur du jour when Thomas enters.

THOMAS: The Dowager Countess.

Cora stands as Thomas shows Violet in. He closes the door.

VIOLET: Good afternoon, my dear.
CORA: Good afternoon.
VIOLET: There's no need to be so prim. I come in peace.
Shall I sit here?

She plumps down on to an armchair.

VIOLET (CONT'D): Now, I've been thinking. I confess I do
not know if I'd have had the strength, mentally or
physically, to carry a corpse the length of this house.

She pauses, gazing at her daughter-in-law.

VIOLET (CONT'D): But I *hope* I would have done.

Cora is astonished.

VIOLET (CONT'D): You were quite right. When something
bad happens, there is no point in wishing it had *not*
happened. The only option is to minimise the damage.*
CORA: Or try to. But if the Flintshires have got hold of
it —

....

* Violet's initial repugnance on hearing Cora's confession has been overcome
in what seems to me a truthful way. Once she'd had time to think about it,
she realised that scandal and the lowering of the prestige of the family would
be much worse than carrying a dead Turk.

VIOLET: I've written to Susan. I said it was a story made up by Mr Pamuk's enemies to discredit him. Even if she doesn't believe me, she won't tell in case it reflects badly on her. The Ambassador's dangerous, but how many people really go to the Turkish Embassy?

CORA: It only takes one.

VIOLET: Well, well. There's nothing to be done about that. We can't have him assassinated.

She hesitates.

VIOLET (CONT'D): I suppose.

CORA: Robert still doesn't suspect.

VIOLET: Oh, I should hope not. No, our only way forward is to get Mary settled as soon as possible.

CORA: I have news on that score. Matthew has proposed.

VIOLET: My, my. And has she said yes?

CORA: She hasn't said anything yet. Except that she's going to have to tell him about Pamuk.

VIOLET: For heaven's sake, why?

CORA: She thinks to keep it secret would be dishonourable.

VIOLET: She reads too many novels. One way or another, everyone goes down the aisle with half the story hidden.

CORA: But won't he —?

Violet flutters her hands dismissively.

VIOLET: There are a million ways round that! After all, she knew enough for there to be no baby.

Cora is rather miffed by this.

CORA: Or he did.

VIOLET: The question is, will she accept Matthew?

CORA: I'm not sure.

VIOLET: Well, if she doesn't, we'll take her abroad. In these moments, you can normally find an Italian who isn't too picky. We'll give her to the start of the grouse.

CORA: Very well. If she turns Matthew down, we'll take
her to Rome in the autumn.*
VIOLET: It's official. On the 12th August 1914, we'll
review the situation.

Cora has been quite moved by this encounter.

CORA: Thank you for not turning against her. I know you
have rules, and when people break them, you find it hard
to forgive. I understand that and I respect it.
VIOLET: In this case, Mary has the trump card.
CORA: What?
VIOLET: Mary is family.

Even Cora knows that Violet is an ally worth having.

END OF EPISODE SIX

....

* The acceptance of the ruling class's power depended on their maintaining a
strong sense of their worthiness, to show it was *right* they should occupy their
privileged position. This meant that the unworthy members of those families
had to be put away, and the so-called Remittance Men, sons and nephews
who were drunks or simply useless, would be sent to Africa or Australia with
an income as long as they never came back. But we forget about the girls
who went wrong because there certainly were some. If you look in the
Peerage and find the daughters of the fourth Earl of Somewhere and it says
(1) Lady Amelia married the second Viscount Wotsit, (2) Lady Cecily
married the Bishop of Peterborough, and (3) Lady Clare married Count
Luigi Barrasconi Lupigi from Naples, you can be sure that she was the one
who was having too much fun. The foreign marriage got her out of sight and
out of mind in a reasonably respectable way. There's no account of how the
great ladies of Naples responded to these slightly *déclassée* English girls
arriving in their midst, but, either way, it was vastly preferable to an
unsuitable marriage in England as that kept her in full view. The clean
solution was to send her off to be moderately happy in foreign climes.

EPISODE SEVEN

ACT ONE

1 INT. DRAWING ROOM. DOWNTON. DAY.

Mrs Hughes sweeps in. Gwen is placing some flowers, and other maids are finishing off the room. In all of these early scenes, there is a sense of hurry and fluster.

MRS HUGHES: Come on, come on! You should be done here! They'll be back from the station any second now!

The young women hurry with the final details.

2 INT. KITCHEN STAIRCASE. DOWNTON. DAY.

Mrs Hughes and Carson descend together into more bustle.

MRS HUGHES: How was London?
CARSON: Much as usual. Dirty, noisy and quite enjoyable.*
MRS HUGHES: There was no need for you to come back a day early. I'm perfectly capable of getting the house ready.
CARSON: Of course you are. But I like to have the heavy luggage back and unpacked, before they get here.
MRS HUGHES: I suppose… Steady, William. This isn't a race.

William slows down as they walk past the buzzing kitchen.

MRS HUGHES (CONT'D): Poor lad.
CARSON: But did he see her? I was worried when I took him to King's Cross.

....

* Carson's coming back with the Granthams at the start of the episode is to show that certain servants travelled with the family to London, but others did not. Some great dukes kept fully staffed houses at both ends, but it was much more normal just to have a skeleton staff turning the house over unless the family was in residence. As a rule, there was a housekeeper at both ends and, in London, she would have a couple of maids who stayed even when the family was away and kept the place clean. But there wouldn't be any butler or permanent footmen in London, because when the family was not there, there was nothing for them to do. So when the Crawleys went up for the Season they would take the footmen, as well as the lady's maids and the valet. The under housemaids and so on would stay at Downton and the London staff would be increased with temporary workers while the family was there.

MRS HUGHES: Yes. He had time to say goodbye.

CARSON: How is he now?

MRS HUGHES: Well, you've only got one mother, haven't you?

Gwen runs up.

GWEN: They're here, Mrs Hughes.

The rustle and scrimmage increase.

3 EXT. DOWNTON. DAY.

July 1914. The car has arrived with suitcases. Bates, O'Brien, Thomas and Anna, in hats and coats, supervise as a groom and the hall boys carry things round the back. Robert, Cora, Edith and Sybil, still in their travelling clothes, are with Carson and Mrs Hughes. William stands at the entrance to Downton.

ROBERT: Hello William. It's good to have you back.

4 INT. HALL. DOWNTON. DAY.

ROBERT: What a relief to be home.

CORA: Don't listen when his lordship pretends not to enjoy the Season.

ROBERT: When in Rome…

MRS HUGHES: Will Lady Mary be back soon?

ROBERT: She's just staying on with my sister for a week or two.

MRS HUGHES: So Grantham House is closed?*

....

* If you just ran up to London for a short visit it was much easier to go to your club – they all had accommodation for valets. It was a bit more complicated for women but if they just wanted to pay a visit or go to a dressmaker, it was usually easier to take their maid and stay with a relation or a friend. This avoided the massive upheaval of opening the house. Those London palaces are interesting to me because they were built for entertaining, not for house parties. They had huge drawing rooms and even ballrooms, but there were not many bedrooms. There's a book by Lord Claud Hamilton, a younger son of the Duke of Abercorn, who describes how their London base was incredibly splendid, but they were absolutely shoe-horned into the bedrooms, with children sharing, and some even on the servants' floor at the top of the house. Nobody wanted people to come and stay.

CORA: It will be by the end of this week. Dear Mrs Hughes, I hope you've had some time to yourself while we've been away.
MRS HUGHES: I've tackled a few jobs that get forgotten when the house is full.
ROBERT: Any local news?
MRS HUGHES: The main topic here is the murder of the Austrian Archduke.*
CARSON: Here and everywhere else.
ROBERT: I'm afraid we haven't heard the last of that… And how is William?
CARSON: Bearing up.
ROBERT: Poor chap. He has our sympathies.

Bates, O'Brien and Anna now emerge from the servants' staircase. They have changed out of their own overcoats and hats, and start to help the family with theirs.

ROBERT: I think I'll wash the train off before dinner.
BATES: Very good, m'lord. I can unpack while you're bathing.
ROBERT: I'll see you up there.

Robert goes to the main staircase, Bates to the servants'.

CORA: Oh, Mrs Hughes, have you had any thoughts about the garden party for the hospital? We've scarcely a month, from soup to nuts.

....

* It is part of the style of *Downton Abbey*, that we make references to these world-shaking events without usually having anyone of historical significance come to the house. Here, we wanted to show how the assassination of a largely unknown prince and his morganatic wife was going to affect the lives of everyone at Downton and beyond, from the Granthams to the most modest agricultural worker. It was a happening that gradually grew in significance until it became clear that the Austrians were being encouraged by the German Kaiser's government to use the murder as a challenge to Tsarist Russia, once and for all. Russia had been trying to extend her influence in that part of the world and now the Germans and Austrians bonded together and decided to draw a line in the sand. Of course no one knew then that the fire they had lit would end by consuming almost the entire Old World.

MRS HUGHES: I've started on it, but there are things we need to talk about.*

CORA: Oh, dear. That sounds like trouble. I'll take my hat off.

SYBIL: Anna? Can I have a bath, too?

O'Brien and Anna set off, carrying coats and scarves.

CORA: Sybil?

The girl turns on the stairs.

CORA (CONT'D): You were a great success in London, darling. Well done.

EDITH: You never say that to me.

CORA: Don't I, dear? You were very helpful. Thank you.

5 INT. MRS HUGHES'S SITTING ROOM. DOWNTON. DAY.

Carson is with Mrs Hughes.

MRS HUGHES: I hate to spoil her homecoming but what are we going to do about Mrs Patmore? She's worse than when you left. Much worse.

He raises his eyebrows in acknowledgement of this.

MRS HUGHES (CONT'D): Oh, and I meant to ask: Is there a decision? About Mr Bates leaving?

CARSON: Oh, not yet. His lordship wants the facts, and Bates won't give them.

He goes to the door, then he pauses.

CARSON (CONT'D): So, what are you going to say to her ladyship about Mrs Patmore?

MRS HUGHES: I don't want the poor woman sacked, but things cannot go on as they are.

....

* This is the first mention of the garden party. As you can see, we make it a charity party, raising funds for the local hospital but, while there were charity bazaars and so on at the time, I'm afraid that making this one into a charity fund-raiser was a sop to modern sensibilities. In real life, the party would not have been for charity. It would simply have been a garden party that people expected the Granthams to give once a year. The thinking was that giving it a charitable purpose would render it more fragrant to modern eyes and ears. But I wasn't completely convinced.

6 EXT. HYDE PARK. LONDON. DAY.

Lady Rosamund Painswick is walking with her niece. She lacks
her brother's warmth. To say the least. *

ROSAMUND: There's nothing like an English summer, is
there?
MARY: Except an English winter.

....

*This is when we first meet Robert's sister, Rosamund. To be honest, I felt
(and feel) her image here is too 1870s in her hair and her clothes. It seems as
if we have suddenly gone backwards in time. The costume and hair
departments had pictorial evidence, so I imagine there was a revival of that
kind of look – the chignon with a tiny hat that one thinks of as very 1875 –
but it is an example for me of why things don't only have to *be* true in a
costume drama. They also have to *look* true.

Rosamund is very much her own creature; she is brisk, she is tart, she is
unsentimental (Samantha Bond gets all this very well), so Mary comes to her
for the unvarnished aristocratic viewpoint. We learn later that Rosamund's
husband, Marmaduke Painswick, was immensely rich but not tremendously
well born, being the grandson of the man who made the money. Rosamund
has made the decision to marry this immensely well-off fellow, with the
understanding that she would knock off any rough edges but, in my
experience, the unequal marriage is often accompanied by an absolute
determination, on the part of the grander member of the couple, to
re-educate their partners and not to surrender any of their own rank, in other
words not to pay any price for their choice of spouse. This often colours their
ambitions for their children. I knew one couple, where the man was
extremely nice but he was quite an ordinary chap, and the mother was much
grander. As a result she filled her children with this notion of how important
they were, pumping up their sense of social prominence, and I have to say it
paid off. They all became rather important.

This over-consciousness of position is what shades Rosamund's opinions
and it explains why she misleads Mary here. She was no great fan of the
Matthew marriage anyway. To her, Matthew is an obscure person. She's
polite to him but she doesn't see that Mary necessarily has to marry him.
Sadly, Mary's doubts are only strengthened by that foundation.

ROSAMUND: I'm sorry you haven't received more invitations. But then, after four Seasons, one is less a debutante than a survivor. My dear, is there anything you're not telling me?

MARY: No.

ROSAMUND: Only one hears stories…

MARY: There's nothing, Aunt Rosamund.

ROSAMUND: So, have you decided whether or not to marry Cousin Matthew?

Mary looks slightly surprised. Rosamund smiles.

ROSAMUND (CONT'D): Oh, there's no secret that Cora can keep for more than a month.

MARY: You'd be surprised! I've told him I'll give him my answer the day I get back.

ROSAMUND: Well, it would be very *tidy*. At least we can say that.

7 INT. SERVANTS' HALL. DOWNTON. EVE.

The servants are at tea. Bates and Anna are there. And O'Brien, who reads a letter, then catches Thomas's eye.

O'BRIEN: Fancy a smoke?

THOMAS: Don't mind if I do.

They slip out. William snorts.

WILLIAM: There they go. Guy Fawkes and his assistant.

GWEN: Which is which?

Which makes everyone laugh. Anna hands William a black armband she's been sewing. She turns back to Bates.

ANNA: Surely if his lordship hasn't done anything until now, it means he doesn't want to take it any further.

Before Bates can answer, Carson enters.

WILLIAM: Anna's made me an armband, Mr Carson. For my mother. Can I wear it?

CARSON: I dare say. Not when we're entertaining, but otherwise.*

8 INT. HALL. DOWNTON. EVE.

Robert walks in from taking the dog out, to see Clarkson coming downstairs, with his bag.

ROBERT: Hello, Doctor. I didn't know you were here.

CLARKSON: No, Lady Grantham sent a message.

ROBERT: Why? She's not ill, is she?

CLARKSON: Not 'ill', exactly...

ROBERT: Would you mind waiting in the library?

Robert makes for the stairs. Cora appears in her dressing gown on the landing at the top.

CORA: Robert, would you come up for a moment? Doctor Clarkson, can I ask you to wait in the library?

Clarkson goes to the library as Robert goes upstairs.

ROBERT: This is very mysterious.

....

* I like the mourning armband. For a long time, everyone observed the total mourning of the Victorians, with men and women submerged in black crêpe for months and years on end, but after the death of King Edward VII, things started to calm down. Mourning went on into my lifetime, but it wasn't very long by then, although one of my grandfather's relations, a darling woman whom we called Cousin Frances, chose to stay in half mourning colours for the rest of her life. It wasn't a harsh sacrifice. Lavender and violet and mauve are prettier than black, so it was an attractive token of her love for her late husband more than a gloomy reminder. The armband was part of this more moderate mourning but even that would soon prove too much for modern taste. I remember that when my mother died in 1980 we wore armbands for a month. But when my father died in 1999, we didn't. We were in black ties and morning coats at his funeral and his memorial, but the armband had gone. That twenty-year gap finished it off.

Carson tells William 'not when we're entertaining', because it is impossible for him not to put the interests of the family first, but we expect that. In Carson's defence the good servant is essentially invisible, and there shouldn't be anything about them that makes you follow them with your eyes and ask a question. That's what he would have been afraid of.

9 INT. CORA'S BEDROOM. DOWNTON. EVE.

Robert is thunderstruck.

ROBERT: *Pregnant?*

CORA: You needn't be quite so shocked.

ROBERT: Give me a moment. You haven't been pregnant for eighteen years.

CORA: And I'm pregnant now.

ROBERT: I don't understand what we've done differently.

She holds up her hand.

CORA: Stop, right there. If you want to know more, go down and offer the doctor some whisky.

ROBERT: I can't take it in.

CORA: But you're pleased?

ROBERT: *Of course.* Of course I'm pleased.*

10 EXT. KITCHEN COURTYARD. DOWNTON. EVE.

Thomas smokes as he reads the letter.

THOMAS: I didn't think she'd do it.

O'BRIEN: I told you she would. I could see she was interested. And I was speaking as one lady's maid to another. That means something, you know.

THOMAS: 'Course we thought we had him before but he's a slippery devil.

....

* This kind of thing was not uncommon in an era when girls married at eighteen or nineteen and had all their babies by the time they were twenty-six. So it follows that they were often fertile for twenty years after the birth of their last child. We had to make it clear that if the unborn child is a boy everything changes for everyone. I was a little bit worried at the time that the audience wouldn't understand this, but I was wrong. After all our nervousness, they grasped the concept of the entail, i.e. that in these families women had no rights, and so they did understand that if Mary had a legitimate brother then the whole game would be different. Where it gets, for me, enjoyably complicated, is that of course Robert would have loved a son. He loves Matthew, quite genuinely, but he would have loved a son.

11 INT. LIBRARY. DOWNTON. EVE.

Robert and Clarkson are drinking whisky.

CLARKSON: It's unusual, obviously.

ROBERT: Unusual? It's biblical.

CLARKSON: Not quite. You understand women go through a certain… change.

ROBERT: Thank you. I know quite as much as I need to about all *that*.

CLARKSON: Well, sometimes it can result in a surge of… fertility, for want of a better word. It might have been what happened with St Elizabeth.

Robert is not interested in discussing St Elizabeth.

ROBERT: But the child will be healthy?

CLARKSON: Oh, there's no reason why not.

ROBERT: How long has she…?

CLARKSON: Hard to be precise. Things had become irregular, but…

ROBERT: Please!

CLARKSON: I'd say she's about four months gone. It'll begin to show soon.

ROBERT: And I don't suppose there's any way of knowing if it's a…

Clarkson does not answer. The door opens. Mrs Hughes stands in the doorway.

MRS HUGHES: I do beg your pardon, m'lord. I thought you were alone.

CLARKSON: Please come in, Mrs Hughes. I'm just leaving.

Mrs Hughes turns to the open door and calls gently.

MRS HUGHES: William!

ROBERT: Well, thank you, Doctor… I'd better start writing some letters

William appears in the doorway.

MRS HUGHES: Show Doctor Clarkson out.

The others go and Robert and Mrs Hughes are alone.

MRS HUGHES: I didn't want to bother her ladyship, if she's not well…

ROBERT: She's resting, but tell me anyway.

MRS HUGHES: It's Mrs Patmore, m'lord. The time has come when we really have to make a decision.

12 INT. CARSON'S PANTRY. DOWNTON. NIGHT.

Carson is with Thomas and O'Brien. He's reading the letter.

THOMAS: Now do you believe me?
CARSON: Careful, Thomas. Your position is not a strong one.
O'BRIEN: Don't punish *us*, Mr Carson. It's Mr Bates who's wanting here.
THOMAS: Tell me, Mr Carson, do you think it right, a man like *that* should live and work at Downton?

Carson is floored. Thomas and O'Brien share a quick look.

13 INT. LADY ROSAMUND PAINSWICK'S DRAWING ROOM. LONDON. DAY.

Mary is sitting by the window when the door opens and the servant announces Mr Evelyn Napier. Evelyn comes into the room.

SERVANT: Mr Napier, m'lady.
MARY: What a surprise. I'm afraid you've just missed my aunt.
EVELYN: I know. I watched her leave.

Mary gestures for him to sit. He lays his hat on the floor.

MARY: How are your wedding plans going?
EVELYN: Not very well... In fact, we've decided to call it off.
MARY: Really? It seemed quite fixed at Sybil's ball. What a shame! Please.

She motions him to sit down.

EVELYN: It'll be better in the long run.
MARY: Perhaps. I know what high hopes you have of the institution.

She is cold. This is a man who effectively turned her down.

EVELYN: The thing is, Lady Mary, I am here today because I needed to tell you something, face to face, before you went to the country.

MARY: 'Face to face'? Gracious me.

EVELYN: I've recently heard gossip about the time when I came to Downton with Kemal Pamuk. Gossip that I believe has made life difficult for you. I've also heard it said that I am the source of these stories.

Mary just looks at him. She will not help.

EVELYN (CONT'D): It is *very* important to me that you should know I am not. From that day to this, I have never spoken one word on the matter.

MARY: Then who did?

EVELYN: It seems to come from the Turkish Embassy, from the Ambassador, himself, in fact. And his wife.

MARY: But who told them, if not you?

EVELYN: This is the hard part. When I discovered the answer, I debated whether I should relay it, but in the end I feel you ought to know.

MARY: The suspense is killing me.

EVELYN: It was your sister, Lady Edith, who wrote to the Ambassador. That is why people accept the story.

MARY: *Edith?*

EVELYN: It's very hard to believe.

MARY: Harder for you than for me.

14 INT. THE SERVANTS' CORRIDOR. DOWNTON. DAY.

Carson is with Mrs Hughes.

MRS HUGHES: I love the thought of a baby in the house, but if it's a boy…

CARSON: It'll be very hard on Mr Crawley.

He has completed her sentence. She is surprised. He nods.

CARSON (CONT'D): I know. I was no great champion when he first arrived. But it seems to me he's tried his best, and he's done the decent thing.

MRS HUGHES: I can't see that coming off.

CARSON: You don't mean the engagement?

MRS HUGHES: But it's not an engagement yet, is it?

CARSON: She'd never throw him over!

MRS HUGHES: Mr Carson, Lady Mary Crawley does not deserve you.

His shocked expression has made her smile.

15 INT. DRAWING ROOM. DOWER HOUSE. DAY.

Violet is with Cora.

> VIOLET: And she hasn't been in touch with Cousin Matthew?
> CORA: Not that I've heard.

Violet nods. She doesn't want to comment on this bad sign.

> VIOLET: Wonderful news, of course. You must look after
> yourself.
> CORA: Don't worry. O'Brien has me wrapped in silk and
> feathers.
> VIOLET: You're lucky. I have a horrible feeling Simmons
> is about to hand in her notice. She's looking very
> fidgety, lately, and I saw her hurrying to meet the
> postman.
> CORA: You poor thing. Is there anything worse than
> losing one's maid?
> VIOLET: I mean, why would she want to leave me? I've
> been as gentle as a lamb.

Cora says nothing.

> VIOLET (CONT'D): *Most* of the time.

16 EXT. THE PARK. DOWNTON. DAY.

Robert is walking with Matthew, in front of the house.

> ROBERT: I want to say I'll make provision for you, if
> it's a boy and you're pushed out —
> MATTHEW: Don't worry. I know you can't. If any man
> living understands the strength of the entail, it's me.
> ROBERT: I can give you Crawley House for life, if it's a
> help.*

....

* In real life, if this situation happened in a normal family, Matthew would simply have been demoted to the position of a younger son, despite being much older than the new heir. In other words, he would always have been welcome at the house, he would have had all the shooting he could handle, and lots of contacts and introductions and promotions. But he would have been expected to make his own way. Sometimes enormously rich people were able to set up their younger sons as country gentlemen, but most younger sons were on their own. They just had to get on with earning a living, and I think that's what would have happened here.

MATTHEW: Have you heard from Mary?
ROBERT: No. Have you?

Matthew shakes his head. They know this is significant.

ROBERT (CONT'D): By the way, I want to ask a favour.
What's the name of your cook? The one you brought with
you from Manchester?
MATTHEW: Mrs Bird.

17 INT. KITCHEN. DOWNTON. DAY.

*Daisy is loading William's tray, while Mrs Patmore is
draining some vegetables. She is very clumsy.*

DAISY: I'll get it, Mrs Patmore!

She darts in and saves the boiling saucepan.

MRS PATMORE: Oh! Don't fuss me!
WILLIAM: Is that everything?
DAISY: Yeah. How are you feeling?
WILLIAM: Well, most people's parents die before them, and
so they should…
THOMAS: Oh, give it a rest.

He has also come down to load up his tray.

THOMAS (CONT'D): Your mother knew how to drag it out.
I'll say that for her.
WILLIAM: *What?*
MRS HUGHES (V.O.): Thomas! Get up to the servery!

She's arrived as Mrs Patmore screams. She's burned herself.

MRS PATMORE: You gave me the wrong cloth! Ow!
MRS HUGHES: Here, sit down, Mrs Patmore.
MRS PATMORE: I can't sit down. I've got the luncheon to
finish!
MRS HUGHES: It was not a suggestion… *Sit!* Daisy and I'll
finish the luncheon.

18 INT. DRAWING ROOM. CRAWLEY HOUSE. EVE.

ISOBEL: So he'll give us this house for life, will he?
How generous!
MATTHEW: It *is* generous. He doesn't have to. But it's
made me think. You must stay here if you want but I

wonder if it mightn't be better all round, if I went back
to Manchester.*
ISOBEL: It may not be a boy.
MATTHEW: Really, mother. You never approved of it all in
the first place. If it *is* a boy, you should see it as a
release, not a disappointment.
ISOBEL: What does Mary say?
MATTHEW: Nothing yet.

They both know they should have heard. The door opens.
Molesley enters with a grim-looking woman. Mrs Bird.

MOLESLEY: You wanted to see Mrs Bird, sir.
MATTHEW: Yes. Mrs Bird, Lord Grantham has rather a
favour to ask of you.
MRS BIRD: I'm surprised Lord Grantham knows that I exist,
sir.

19 INT. DRESSING ROOM. DOWNTON. EVE.

Bates is laying out Robert's tails, when Carson appears.

CARSON: I'm sorry to disturb you.
BATES: Quite all right.
CARSON: Mr Bates, it's about your somewhat startling
confession. As you'll have surmised his lordship has yet
to come to a decision…
BATES: His delay is generous.
CARSON: However, it will be no surprise to you that Miss
O'Brien has been unwilling to let things drop. It seems
that, when we were in London, she made a new friend. A
lady's maid in the house of a colonel of your former
regiment.

He hands over the familiar letter for Bates to read.

CARSON (CONT'D): Please tell me that this account is
false, at least in part.
BATES: I wish I could.

....

* Matthew doesn't want to stay at Downton as a hanger on, having been the
heir, and I agree with him. I've never really understood lingering at the scene
of your former glory, like those people who sell their family house and move
into a farmhouse that's half a mile away. I couldn't do that. Once it had come
to an end, I'd be off and good luck to whoever comes after.

CARSON: I'll have to show it to his lordship.

BATES: Of course you will.

CARSON: I do not like to play the part of Pontius Pilate, but I'm afraid I must. Lord Grantham will decide what's to be done.

He goes to the door but then he stops.

CARSON (CONT'D): Mr Bates, I hope you don't feel I have treated you unjustly.

BATES: On the contrary, Mr Carson, I am astonished at your kindness.

Which, if anything, makes Carson feel even worse.

END OF ACT ONE

ACT TWO

20 INT. LADY ROSAMUND'S HOUSE. LONDON. DAY.

Lady Rosamund and Mary are walking down the stairs into the hall.

ROSAMUND: Of all of you, Sybil might find joy in a cottage. But not you.

MARY: We don't know it'll be a boy.

ROSAMUND: Exactly. So ask Matthew to wait until the child is born. If it's a girl then wed him happily, and all will be as it was before.

MARY: If I delay, won't he think I'm only after him for his position?

Rosamund is not interested in this line of argument.

MARY (CONT'D): Besides, I'm not sure I want to put him off, even without the title. We get on so well, you know. And he's terribly clever. He might end up Lord Chancellor.

ROSAMUND: And he might *not!* Come along, Mary, be sensible. Can you really see yourself dawdling your life away as the wife of a country solicitor?

*The problem is Mary can't quite picture this, either.**

21 INT. LIBRARY. DOWNTON. DAY.

Carson is astonished, which does not surprise Robert.

> CARSON: But why would we ever want a telephone at
> Downton, m'lord?
> ROBERT: Well, they have their uses. You could speak to
> the housekeeper in London. That'd be helpful surely?
> CARSON: I hope I've not failed in my management of the
> recent move?
> ROBERT: Not at all. But the telephone is here now, and
> the girls got used to it while we were in London.
> Besides, none of us know what the next few months will
> bring.
> CARSON: Because of the Archduke's death?
> ROBERT: The Austrians won't get what they want from
> Serbia. And now Russia's starting to rumble… Well,
> there's not much we can do about that… So, will you take
> care of the telephone man?

Carson is about to go, when he changes his mind.

> CARSON: Hmm. Oh, about Mr Bates, m'lord. I expect
> you've had time to consider the contents of that letter?
> ROBERT: Yes. Though I find it very odd. Regimental
> silver? I could more easily see Bates as an assassin
> than a petty pilferer.
> CARSON: I agree. And while the letter is hard to argue
> with —

....

* The key to Mary is that, despite her superficial snobbery, she has true
emotions and one of them is ambition. She loves Matthew for being
Matthew, but she also likes the fact that he will give her a position from
which she can do things. As the Countess of Grantham, she can lend her
social muscle to this interest and that charity, she can entertain the county,
she can promote a political candidate, a painter, a new novelist, she can have
a life. But for women of her class, because of the way the system was loaded,
if their husband did not provide them with a podium, it was incredibly
difficult for them to have any kind of career. Even though she's an earl's
daughter, as the wife of a lawyer, she would be unlikely to be a major player.
She would get invited to things and she'd go to them, but she wouldn't be a
power. And she wants to be a power. She feels she could acquit herself well.

Robert looks up, waiting for him to complete his thought.

CARSON (CONT'D): I wouldn't put anything past Thomas or
Miss O'Brien.

22 INT. DRAWING ROOM. DOWNTON. DAY.

Cora is relieved they are just family.

SYBIL: So, what did we miss?

MARY: Nothing much. Although you'd have had more
invitations than I did.

VIOLET: Have you thought about Matthew?

MARY: Of course, but Aunt Rosamund…

VIOLET: She's written to me. I should pay no attention.

EDITH: But, Granny, she has got a point. Mary can't be
completely naive.

MARY: I don't need your help, thank you.

She says this with a malice that makes Edith recoil.

VIOLET: Mary, listen to me. If you take Matthew now when
his whole future is at risk, he will love you to the end
of his days.*

SYBIL: Why, Granny! You're a romantic!

VIOLET: I've been called many things but never that.

EDITH: And what happens if the baby is a boy and Matthew
loses everything?

VIOLET: Mary can always change her mind.

MARY: I couldn't do that to Matthew. It's not how we are
together… I'm going upstairs to help Anna unpack.

Clearly, she doesn't want to continue this. She stands.

SYBIL: I'll come with you.

CORA: Edith? Why don't you go, too?

It's an order. Edith walks towards the door.

VIOLET: Sir Anthony Strallan was at Lady Wren's party.
He asked after you.

....

* A key factor of Violet's character is that she is not stupid about people. She
understands what makes them tick.

Edith flushes with pride, and shuts the door.   Violet sighs.

CORA: Is she really serious about him?

VIOLET: Any port in a storm… By the way, I was right about my maid. She's leaving to get married. How *can* she be so selfish?

CORA: I do sympathise. Robert's always wanting me to get rid of O'Brien, but I can't face it. And anyway, she's so fond of me.

VIOLET: Well, I thought Simmons was fond of *me*… What *am* I to do?

CORA: Why don't I put an advertisement in *The Lady*? It's always the best place to start.

VIOLET: Oh, that's so kind, thank you. Now, I really must be going.

But a new thought strikes her.

VIOLET (CONT'D): Don't let Mary wait for the baby before she gives Matthew her answer.

CORA: I'm sure it's another girl.

VIOLET: I know those men of the moral high ground. If she won't say yes when he *might* be poor, he won't want her, when he *will* be rich.

23 INT. SERVANTS' HALL. DOWNTON. DAY.

Thomas is reading the paper, during the servants' tea.

DAISY: Maybe we should knit something.

O'BRIEN: Oh yes, I'm sure they'd love a pair of bootees knitted by *you*.

WILLIAM: Or what about a christening mug?

THOMAS: They can buy their own silver.

GWEN: Anything in the paper, Thomas?

THOMAS: They've arrested this Princip fellow and his gang. All Serbian and members of the Black Hand.

O'BRIEN: 'The Black Hand'? Ugh. I don't like the sound of that.

BATES: I don't like the sound of any of it. War is on the way.

WILLIAM: Then we'll have to face it. As bravely as we can.

THOMAS: Thank you, Mr Cannon Fodder.

GWEN: Don't you think a war's coming?

THOMAS: Oh, there'll be a war, all right. And it's time
to prepare for it.

ANNA: The country, do you mean?

THOMAS: No, me.

BATES: You never disappoint.

Before this can develop, Carson looks in.

CARSON: Daisy, run and find Mrs Patmore. His lordship
wants to see her, in the library.

DAISY: His lordship wants Mrs Patmore to go up to the
library?

CARSON: That's what I said. And Anna, you're to come,
too.

The company is stunned. Daisy leaves the silent room.

O'BRIEN: And we thought the assassination of an Archduke
was a surprise.

24 INT. LIBRARY. DOWNTON. DAY.

Robert's at his desk.

CARSON: Mrs Patmore, m'lord.

He stands as Carson brings the cook and maid in.

MRS PATMORE: Your lordship, I know things haven't been
quite right for a while, but I can assure you —

ROBERT: Come in, Mrs Patmore.

MRS PATMORE: I *promise* you, m'lord, if I could just be
allowed a bit more time —

ROBERT: Mrs Patmore, I have not asked you here to give
you your notice.

MRS PATMORE: Haven't you?

ROBERT: No. Now, I understand you've had trouble with
your sight —

MRS PATMORE: That's just it! I *know* I could manage
better if only —

ROBERT: *Please*, Mrs Patmore!

ANNA: Let him speak! Beg pardon, m'lord.

ROBERT: Don't apologise. Now. On Doctor Clarkson's
recommendation, I'm sending you up to London to see an
eye specialist at Moorfields. Anna will go with you and

you'll stay with my sister Lady Rosamund Painswick, in Eaton Square.*

The news is like a thunderbolt. Mrs Patmore staggers.

MRS PATMORE: I'm afraid I'm going to have to sit in your presence, m'lord.
ROBERT: Of course.

Anna gets a chair under her in the nick of time.†

MRS PATMORE: But how will you get on here?
ROBERT: Well, Mrs Crawley is lending us her cook, Mrs Bird. She's coming over tomorrow. You'll be good enough to show her how things work.
MRS PATMORE: And are the Crawleys to starve while I'm away?
ROBERT: They'll eat here every evening. Now, my sister's butler will look after you. He's very nice. Anna, you won't mind a visit to London?
ANNA: No m'lord. It'll be an adventure.
ROBERT: One with a happy ending, I hope.

....

* Unfortunately, in the filming Robert referred to his sister as 'Rosamund', which would never have happened when speaking to the cook, and I had about fifty letters because of it. Quite rightly. Unfortunately I didn't pick it up in the rushes and I didn't see the edit in time to take it out. The correct speech is reproduced here. They also invented the fact that her house was 'new' when we learn later that Rosamund and Montague bought it when they married. So this whole speech in the televised episode is cock-eyed.

† The absolute rule was then that no servant should ever sit in the presence of a member of the family. I remember when I was about twelve my elder brother Rory, who was about fifteen or sixteen, was left alone in the house. My mother and I had been away and when we returned he was talking about having a talk with a housemaid we employed then. He described this conversation and my mother said to him: 'Do you mean she sat in your presence?' I can recall her utter incredulity as she said the words. Nowadays, you can hardly credit it, can you? The phrase planted itself in my boyish brain and that's why Mrs Patmore says it here. At that time, it would have been absolutely impossible for the cook to sit in the presence of the Earl of Grantham, unless she was actually going to faint, which is what is happening here.

25 EXT. GARDENS. DOWNTON. DAY.

Matthew is with Mary. He is angry.

MATTHEW: Let me get this clear! At Sybil's ball you said you'd give me your answer the day you got back, and now you say you will not!

MARY: Why do we have to rush into it? I need to be sure, that's all.

MATTHEW: But you *were* sure.

She will not answer this challenge, which angers him more.

MATTHEW (CONT'D): Shall I tell you what I think has altered you? My prospects! Because nothing else has changed!

MARY: No —

MATTHEW: Yes! If your mother's child is a boy, then he's the heir and I go back to living on my wits, and you'd rather not follow me there!

MARY: Oh, Matthew, you always make everything so black and white.

MATTHEW: I think this is black and white. Do you love me enough to spend your life with me? If you don't, then say no. If you do, then say yes.

MARY: I want to…

But she hesitates. Old habits die hard. She tries to joke.

MARY (CONT'D): Granny told me I should say yes now, and then withdraw if you lost everything.

MATTHEW: To make that work, you have to be a good liar. Are you a good liar?

MARY: Well, not good enough to try it, apparently.*

26 INT. DRESSING ROOM. DOWNTON. EVE.

Bates is dressing Robert for dinner.

ROBERT: How could you not have realised they'd discover the loss at once? And to keep them in your house… But you only served two years?

BATES: That's right, m'lord.

ROBERT: So clearly the judge thought there was some mitigating factor.

*Bates has fetched the tail coat from the bed. He helps
Robert into it and brushes the shoulders, without comment.*

ROBERT: Bates, we've come a long way together. I owe you
a great deal, some might say everything.
BATES: Please, your lordship. Whatever debt you think
you owe me, is long since paid in full.
ROBERT: I just want to know the truth.
BATES: I cannot speak of it, m'lord. You must decide
whether I stay or go on the basis of the evidence before
you. I will respect that.

27 INT. KITCHEN PASSAGE. DOWNTON. DAY.

ANNA: I'm sorry. I don't believe it.

Bates and Anna are talking together, softly.

BATES: How can you say that? When I confessed to the
crime?
ANNA: Well, his lordship obviously doesn't think that's
all there is to it, and I don't either.
BATES: Suit yourself.
ANNA: I will suit myself.

Mrs Hughes arrives down the passage.

....

* Matthew is very wounded by Mary's retreat. I like this situation because it
contains a variety of moral positions. Mary would despise herself for lying in
order to keep him, with a secret plan to dump him later if things didn't turn
out well. She'd feel this would be very dishonourable. On the other hand,
Matthew feels it is dishonourable in her to refuse him because he may lose
everything. So they have both defined Mary's honour differently, though
their difference doesn't make either of them dishonourable, in my opinion.
That is my hallmark, really. In writing this storyline, I never disliked Mary
for being troubled by what she had promised. She had accepted a man who
was going to give her everything, but now it may all be lost. She knows she
will be judged harshly for not wanting to go on with it, but not by me.
Personally, I think it would have been more reasonable of Matthew to
suggest adjourning the discussion of the marriage until the child is born. If
he'd done that, she probably would have married him anyway. So I am
sympathetic to Mary even though she's made a mistake, which turns out a
big mistake. I can see her point of view.

MRS HUGHES: Anna, are you set for the nine o'clock train tomorrow?

ANNA: All packed and ready.

MRS HUGHES: You'll be met at King's Cross by Lady Rosamund's chauffeur which I think is generous, but after that you're on your own... Right. I must get back. I'm acting referee for Mrs Patmore and Mrs Bird.*

BATES: Best of luck.

With a laugh, she is gone. Anna turns to the valet.

ANNA: Will you miss me?

BATES: Try not to miss me. It'll be good practice.

28 INT. KITCHEN. DOWNTON. DAY.

Mrs Patmore and Mrs Bird are evenly matched.

MRS PATMORE: I expect it'll be hard adjusting to this kitchen after the one you're used to.

....

* As always, I try to resist over-sentimentalising these things. It is completely believable that Robert would ring up his sister, tell her that the cook is coming up for an operation at Moorfields, and ask her to put up a maid. But in a sentimental version of the story Rosamund would look out for the maid and ask after the cook, and so on, which would be very unlikely. There is a moment before the servants' ball in the Christmas Special of the second series, where Robert and Matthew are having a drink beforehand to get their nerves up, before they have to go and face the ordeal. I was being interviewed for Australian radio and my charming hostess said she was shocked that they would have to fortify themselves, or that they wouldn't be looking forward to the ball, as they were such friendly people. I explained that the Crawleys must belong to their own time. For Robert Grantham, trying to make conversation with Mrs Patmore is not something he would be looking forward to for months. I don't think he hates it. Certainly he knows he's got to do it and he does it with good grace, but you can't ignore a character's real context.

† I feel this exchange has truth because cooks were notoriously bad tempered and they could find a quarrel in a bramble bush, if necessary. This was because their work day was endless with almost no labour-saving stuff at all. But also they were always in the heat of those great boiling ranges. Although many kitchens had very high ceilings to take the heat up, nevertheless the cooks were basically sweating from morning until night.

MRS BIRD: Not to worry. I'm sure I can have it cleaned up in no time.

MRS PATMORE: *Cleaned up?*

MRS BIRD: I'm not criticising. With your eyesight, it's a wonder you could see the pots at all.†

Mrs Hughes deems it time to intervene.

MRS HUGHES: You've met Daisy and the others?

MRS BIRD: I have. Though what they all find to do is a mystery to me.

MRS PATMORE: Are you not used to managing staff, Mrs Bird?

MRS BIRD: I'm used to getting it done with one kitchen maid, Mrs Patmore, but I suppose, in a house like this, you expect to take it easy.

On the edge of the room, Anna has joined Molesley.

ANNA: Do you think we should erect a ring and let them fight it out?

MOLESLEY: She's all right, Mrs Bird. She's more of a general than a trooper but, you know, you need that in a cook.

ANNA: Mrs Patmore's the Generalissimo.

They laugh together. Molesley likes this Anna.

29 INT. DRAWING ROOM. CRAWLEY HOUSE. DAY.

Isobel is indignant as she listens to her son.

ISOBEL: Well, I'm very sad. I thought Mary was made of better stuff.

MATTHEW: Don't speak against her.

ISOBEL: Of course she's taken advice from someone with false and greedy values.

MATTHEW: Oh, Mother —

ISOBEL: And we don't have to go too far to know who *that* is! I've a good mind —

MATTHEW: Mother! You are not to go near Cousin Violet. That is an order.

But Isobel shows clear signs of resistance.

30 INT. CORA'S BEDROOM. DOWNTON. EVE.

Robert is dressed for dinner. Cora's at the dressing table.

ROBERT: Something's not right about it.

CORA: I agree. Having a silver thief in the house does not seem right at all. Even if he could walk.

ROBERT: But Carson isn't keen to get rid of him, either, and he normally comes down on this sort of thing like a ton of bricks.

CORA: What's his reasoning?

ROBERT: He blames Thomas and O'Brien. He says they've been working against Bates since he got here.

CORA: So I should sack O'Brien instead?

ROBERT: You'll hear no argument from me.

O'BRIEN (V.O.): This should do the trick, m'lady.

O'Brien is in the room, walking towards them. She carries a sash which she starts to tie. But when did she come in?

31 EXT. KITCHEN COURTYARD. DOWNTON. EVENING.

Thomas is with O'Brien who is smoking furiously.

O'BRIEN: Ten years of my life! That's what I've given her! Ten bloody years!

THOMAS: But did she say she'd sack you?

O'BRIEN: It's obviously what *he* wants.

THOMAS: So when will they tell you?

O'BRIEN: When they've found a replacement! Heaven forfend she should have to put a comb through her own hair! And if I'm going, you won't be far behind.

THOMAS: Oh, so what? Sod 'em. There's a war coming and war means change. We should be making plans.

O'BRIEN: What are you talking about?

THOMAS: Well, put it like this. I don't want to be a footman any more, but I don't intend to be killed in battle, neither.

He winks, throws away his cigarette and goes back in.

32 INT. KITCHEN PASSAGE. DOWNTON. EVENING.

Thomas strides along, passing Mrs Patmore and Daisy.

MRS PATMORE: I'm not saying poison them. Just make sure they don't find her food all that agreeable.

DAISY: By poisoning it?

MRS PATMORE: Will you stop that!

DAISY: You don't want it to taste nice.

MRS PATMORE: I want them to be glad when I get back.
That's all.*

33 INT. HALL. DOWNTON. DAY.

Carson is with Mr Bromidge, from the telephone company.

CARSON: This will be for the family and the one in my
pantry is for the staff. Or more precisely, me.

BROMIDGE: We don't normally provide two.

CARSON: Then perhaps we should find another supplier.

BROMIDGE: Hold your horses. All right. Where do you see
this other telephone?

CARSON: Here. In the outer hall.

*There is, at that moment, a ring of the bell. Carson opens
the door to reveal the form of Sir Anthony Strallan.*

STRALLAN: Good afternoon, Carson. Is Lady Edith in?

EDITH (V.O.): I am! I most certainly am!

She's come downstairs with Sybil. She hurries towards them.

STRALLAN: I was just driving past…

EDITH: Yes?

STRALLAN: I thought you might like to come for a spin.
If you're not too busy.

EDITH: Wait 'til I get my coat!

She darts away. Mr Bromidge has been held up long enough.

BROMIDGE: Is it all right if I make some notes?

SYBIL: I'm so sorry, Mr…?

....

* If you lost your job in middle age, that was usually the end. You were not
going to get another. And there wasn't much of a safety net in those days,
some sort of parish payment was usually about it, so I think one has to have
some sympathy for Mrs Patmore, caught in this spot. After the First World
War, many landlords decided they no longer needed or wanted to pension off
endless servants, and so they began to pull down cottages. They didn't want
the maintenance, and they couldn't see them as a source of income until the
1960s and 70s. The truth is, they just didn't think financially at all.

CARSON: Oh, this is Mr Bromidge, m'lady. He's here about the telephone.

SYBIL: Oh, please make your notes, then Mr Bromidge. We're so looking forward to it. What an exciting business to be in!

STRALLAN: You must be expanding every day.

BROMIDGE: Oh, we are, sir, but that brings its problems. Training up men for the work, when many have no aptitude. I can't even find a secretary who can keep pace, at the moment.

SYBIL: What?

BROMIDGE: It's hard with a new concept. Too old, and they can't change. Too young, and they've no experience.

SYBIL: But have you filled the post yet? Because I know just the woman.

BROMIDGE: Well, she must hurry up. We'll close the list tomorrow night.

SYBIL: You'll have her application. I promise.

END OF ACT TWO

ACT THREE

34 INT. HOSPITAL ROOM. MOORFIELDS. LONDON. DAY.

Mrs Patmore is there, with Anna who carries a suitcase.

ANNA: Oh, this isn't bad at all, is it?

MRS PATMORE: I don't know… No one told me there'd be an actual operation.*

....

* I went onto the Internet to learn about the first cataract operations, and I discovered that they started years earlier than I'd thought, going back, in Europe, to the eighteenth century. I hoped they had come in before 1914, but it was much earlier. Moorfields, the eye hospital, has been going since 1805. That said, it was fairly crude and you had to wait until the cataract had formed. Even in my time, I remember my grandmother having a cataract operation in about 1970 and they wouldn't perform it until the tissue had formed a sort of crust. Golly.

ANNA: What did you think? They were just going to make magic passes over your eyes?

Mrs Patmore sits, as a doctor looks in, with his notes.

DOCTOR: All right, Mrs… Patmore?
ANNA: She'll be fine, thank you.
DOCTOR: And you've been sent to us by… the Earl of Grantham?
ANNA: That's it.
DOCTOR: Very good. You can leave her now. We'll keep her in for a week. You can collect her next Friday.
ANNA: I'll be in to visit every day.
MRS PATMORE: What about the rest of the time?
ANNA: Oh, don't worry about me.

35 EXT. DUKE OF YORK BARRACKS. LONDON. DAY.

Anna walks towards the great building.

36 EXT. OFFICE. DUKE OF YORK BARRACKS. DAY.

Anna is talking to an NCO.

NCO: Bates, you say?
ANNA: John Bates. He must have left the army about eight years ago.
NCO: Wait here, please.

She nods and sits on a bench.

37 INT. KITCHEN. DOWNTON. DAY.

Mrs Bird is with Daisy and the other kitchen maids.

MRS BIRD: Have you finished the soup?
DAISY: I think so, Mrs Bird.
MRS BIRD: And the sauce for the fish?
DAISY: Yes.
MRS BIRD: Well, then put them in the warmer.

She walks away. Daisy grabs a jug and pours water into the soup, then she sprinkles green powder, and orange powder into the sauce. She picks up the tray and scurries off.

38 INT/EXT. MOTOR CAR/DOWNTON. DAY.

Sybil comes out of the house and runs into the car.

SYBIL: Go! Quickly!

BRANSON: Where's the fire?

SYBIL: I have to put Gwen's letter through their door, and be back in time to dress for dinner.

BRANSON: I think it's terrific, m'lady. What you're doing. I think *you're* terrific.

He turns as he says this, and since she is leaning forward, their faces are only a few inches apart. For a moment, they are just a young couple, flushed with excitement. Then she remembers herself, lowers her lashes and sits back.

SYBIL: I don't want to be terrific. I want to be successful.

39 EXT. DUKE OF YORK BARRACKS. DAY.

The man returns, carrying a heavy ledger.

NCO: You don't mean John Bates who went to prison? For theft?

ANNA: That's correct.

NCO: Well, I know who *he* is right enough. That was an odd business.

ANNA: Why 'odd'?

NCO: Never mind. So you're his cousin and you'd like to be in touch?

She says nothing but waits. At last he nods.

NCO (CONT'D): Very forgiving. Well, I've got no address for him or his wife.

Naturally, the word comes as something of a blow.

NCO (CONT'D): But I have got one for his mother which should still be good. I've written it down for you.

ANNA: Thank you for your trouble.

40 INT. GALLERY. DOWNTON. EVE.

Mary is waiting in the shadows, but when Edith arrives, she steps out and starts downstairs with her, speaking softly.

MARY: Is it true you wrote to the Turkish Ambassador, about Kemal?

Edith nearly jumps out of her skin. She regains control.

EDITH: Who told you?
MARY: Someone who knows that you did.
EDITH: Then why are you asking?
MARY: Because I wanted to give you one last chance to deny it.
EDITH: And what if I did? He had a right to know how his countryman died. In the arms of a slut.

She walks away towards the library, as Mary gasps for air.

41 INT. DRAWING ROOM. DOWNTON. EVE.

It is after dinner. The family, plus Violet, Isobel and Matthew are there. Carson dispenses coffee and drinks at a table, with the help of William and Thomas. The latter takes a plate of sweets to Cora, sitting on a sofa with Violet.

VIOLET: How's that advertisement getting on? For the new maid?
CORA: Well, it's only just come out.

Thomas hears this. He walks back to Carson who beckons him.

CARSON: William and I can manage here now. Go and tell Mrs Bird we'll have our dinner in twenty minutes.

Thomas nods and leaves, as Cora sees Edith sitting alone and stands. On her way to her daughter, she passes Carson.

CORA: Carson, be sure to say to Mrs Bird the dinner was really delicious.

She has now joined Edith and takes the chair next to her.

CORA (CONT'D): So? How was your drive?
EDITH: Oh, it was lovely. Only…

She gives a breathless, excited glance at her mother.

CORA: Yes?

EDITH: Well, he said he had a question for me. He told
me he'd ask it at the garden party. And he hopes I'll
say yes!

CORA: You must think very carefully about what your
answer will be.

MARY: Yes, I should think very carefully about a lot of
things.

*They had not noticed she was listening. Mary walks on.
Matthew watches her, but looks away when she glances over.
He is with Robert, Violet and Isobel by the fire.*

MATTHEW: Do your neighbours have one?

ROBERT: Yes, they do, in London anyway.

MATTHEW: It seems very wise to get a telephone now. If
there is a war, it may be hard to have one installed in a
private house.

ROBERT: Well, let me show you where we're going to put
it?

Robert leads Matthew away and out of the room.

VIOLET: First electricity, now telephones. Sometimes I
think I must be living in an H.G. Wells novel. But the
young are so calm about change, aren't they. Look at
Matthew. I do admire him.*

ISOBEL: Do you?

Her tone and her look are not warm. Violet sighs.

VIOLET: What have I done wrong now?

ISOBEL: Oh please! Don't pretend Mary's sudden
reluctance can't be traced back to you.

VIOLET: I shall pretend it. I told her to take him.
Your quarrel's with my daughter Rosamund, not me. So put
that in your pipe and smoke it.

William reaches for her cup, bringing matters to a close.†

42 INT. KITCHEN PASSAGE/CARSON'S PANTRY.
DOWNTON. NIGHT.

*Molesley opens the door to find Thomas taking a wallet from
Carson's change coat. Thomas starts.*

THOMAS: Mr Moseley, what are you after?

MOLESLEY: I wanted a word with Mr Carson. I'm here to
have my dinner.
THOMAS: You don't want much, do you?
MOLESLEY: What were you doing?
THOMAS: Mr Carson dropped his wallet in the passage. I
was replacing it.

He dares Molesley to disagree with him.

43 INT. DINING ROOM. DOWNTON. NIGHT.

Robert and Matthew are alone, drinking port.

ROBERT: But everything seemed so settled between you, at
Sybil's ball.

....

* In many ways, this decade, from 1910 to 1920, effected what would come to
be seen as the change from the Old World into the New. Of course there had
been earlier inventions, different forms of heating, more efficient kitchen
ranges and so on, but not much had altered fundamentally in the way life was
lived in these houses for two centuries at least. You could say gas lighting was
a big modernisation, but the difference between a gas lamp and a candle is
only really one of maintenance. They both involve flames that must be lit
and, more importantly, safely extinguished. And anyway, you never had gas
lighting for everything. You still took a candle to light you to bed and many
places had no gas lighting upstairs. There were also paraffin or oil lamps but
these were too dangerous to carry around, when lit. A common mistake in
films and television is when we see an unlit paraffin lamp sitting on a table
during the day, as we might have a lamp that is turned off in a modern sitting
room. This never happened. Paraffin lamps were removed from the room,
either at night or first thing in the morning, when the family was not there,
and taken to a lamp room, where one of the footmen's duties was to clean and
refill them. They would not then be brought back into the drawing room
until it was time to light them. In this first series we have electricity in the
main rooms on the ground floor, but not in the bedrooms, which changes in
the second series. The table at the foot of the stairs with the candles for the
family and guests to carry upstairs went on in some places until the Second
World War, but in a lot of houses it was gone after the First.

† In this sort of narrative almost every scene has to play more than one role.
They have to deliver beats in two, three or even four storylines. This is
particularly true of a drawing-room scene where you have several members of
the family. In those big groups, about four or five different strands will be
served.

MATTHEW: Things have changed since then.

ROBERT: Not necessarily. I don't seem to be much good at making boys.

But Matthew is too worn down to joke about this.

MATTHEW: Any more than I'm much good at building my life on shifting sands.

There is something ominous in this, which saddens Robert.

ROBERT: You do know I should be very proud to have you as my son-in-law, whatever your prospects.

MATTHEW: Unfortunately, sir, your daughter is more practical than you.

44 INT. SERVANTS' HALL. DOWNTON. NIGHT.

The servants are seated as the hall boys serve the soup. Mrs Bird is hovering as Molesley enters.

CARSON: Will you join us, Mrs Bird?

MRS BIRD: I don't mind if I do.

DAISY: I'm not sure Mrs Patmore would like that, Mr Carson. Cook always eats separate, that's what she says.

MOLESLEY: Not in our house. There's only the four of us.

Thomas comes in and sits next to O'Brien. They whisper.

THOMAS: Well, you're going any minute. She's advertised for your replacement.

O'BRIEN: That filthy, ungrateful cow.

Mrs Hughes addresses Mrs Bird.

MRS HUGHES: Let the kitchen maids have theirs on their own. You stay with us.

CARSON: Her ladyship said to tell you that the dinner was delicious.

DAISY: *She can't have!*

CARSON: Daisy? Does that surprise you?

They have started to eat the soup but without enthusiasm. Now Mrs Bird takes a spoonful. And spits it out.

MRS BIRD: What have you done with this, you little beggar? I *knew* you were up to summat! That's why I said it was for upstairs. Come on. Tell us what's in it!

DAISY: Just water and a bit of soap.

She is crying now. The others stop drinking the soup.

MRS BIRD: And you've put something in the fish sauce as well?
DAISY: Only mustard and aniseed.
MRS HUGHES: Why, Daisy? Why would you do such a thing?
DAISY: Mrs Patmore was worried that they'd prefer Mrs Bird's cooking, and they wouldn't want her to come back.
CARSON: Is it likely? When they've taken so much trouble to get her well?

Daisy is really sobbing now.

DAISY: I'm sorry.

At last, Mrs Bird takes pity.

MRS BIRD: There, there. There are worse crimes on earth than loyalty.
BATES: Well said.
MRS BIRD: Dry your eyes, and fetch the beef stew I was making for tomorrow. You've not had a chance to spoil that, I suppose.
DAISY: I was going to mix in some syrup of figs. But I've not done it yet
THOMAS: Well, at least we'd all have been regular.

He's too vulgar for Mrs Hughes and Carson. The rest laugh.

45 INT. HALL. DOWNTON. DAY.

A workman is kneeling, surrounded by telephone wiring. Mr Bromidge is with him, with a notebook, when Sybil appears.

SYBIL: Carson said you were here.
BROMIDGE: Ah! Just checking that everything's being done right, m'lady.
SYBIL: Only we never heard back — that is, Miss Dawson never heard back from you. About an interview?
BROMIDGE: Ah, yes… We got the young lady's letter. But the trouble is, she didn't have any experience of hard work, that I could tell, so…
SYBIL: But she's a very hard worker!
BROMIDGE: Oh, I couldn't find any proof of it. And she gave you as a reference when you don't run a business, m'lady. Well, not that I'm aware of.

Just then Sybil hears movement…

> SYBIL: Lily, can you find Gwen. Tell her to come to the
> hall, now.
> LILY: Yes, m'lady.

The maid above hurries away. Sybil turns back to Bromidge.

> SYBIL: The reason Gwen didn't give any more details is
> because she works here, as a housemaid.
> BROMIDGE: And you thought that'd put me off?
> SYBIL: But she's taken a postal course, and has good
> speeds in typing and Pitman shorthand. Test her.
> BROMIDGE: I will, if I like the look of her.

Gwen emerges from the back staircase, rather breathless.

> BROMIDGE (CONT'D): So, young lady, you thought I'd turn
> up my nose at a housemaid?
> GWEN: I did, sir.
> BROMIDGE: My mother was a housemaid. I've got nothing
> against housemaids. They know about hard work and long
> hours, that's for sure.
> GWEN: I believe so, sir.
> BROMIDGE: Right. Well, is there somewhere we could talk?

He looks at Sybil, who sees the open library door.

> SYBIL: Gwen, take Mr Bromidge to the library. I'll see
> no one disturbs you.

*The two of them go into the room, as Robert enters from the
hall, and heads for the library.*

> SYBIL (CONT'D): Sorry, Papa, you can't go in there.
> ROBERT: Why on earth not?
> SYBIL: Gwen's in there with Mr Bromidge. She's being
> interviewed.
> ROBERT: I cannot use my library because one of the
> housemaids is in there applying for another job?
> SYBIL: That's about the size of it.*

46 EXT. A LONDON STREET. DAY.

Anna approaches a modest, tidy house in a row.

47 INT. MRS BATES'S SITTING ROOM. LONDON. DAY.

Anna is perched on a chair in her hat. Mrs Bates, a kindly woman of seventy, is facing her. A table holds tea things.

> MRS BATES: So, you're not trying to find John, Miss Smith?
> ANNA: No. I work with him. At Downton.
> MRS BATES: You're not, by any chance, Anna?
> ANNA: I am, yes. Why? Has he mentioned me in his letters?

Mrs Bates just smiles in reply, and starts to pour.

> MRS BATES: So what is it you want to know?
> ANNA: I want to know the truth about the case against him. I want to know why the sergeant thought it was 'odd'. I want to know what Mr Bates isn't saying.
> MRS BATES: Because you don't believe him to be guilty?
> ANNA: No, I don't. I know he's not.

This pleases the older woman as she gives Anna a cup.

> MRS BATES: Well, you're right of course.
> ANNA: Then, who was it? Who was the thief?
> MRS BATES: His wife. Vera.

END OF ACT THREE

....

*This exchange was designed to define Sybil as a strong personality. She is not just a vaguely rebellious teenager, but a serious critic of the system who is trying to get things done. This characterisation seems right for a time of change when quite a lot of young people were showing they did not want to go on with things as they were. Jessica Brown Findlay made a good job of it, and her performance pays off even more in the second series, so here we are laying the ground for the woman she becomes later.

ACT FOUR

48 INT. CARSON'S PANTRY. DOWNTON. DAY.

William, Daisy and Gwen are staring at the telephone.

WILLIAM: Who do you call if no one you know has got one?

GWEN: But they will have. You'll see.

CARSON (V.O.): Might I enquire why my pantry has become a common room?

WILLIAM: Sorry, Mr Carson. But do you know how it works?

CARSON: Of course I do.

DAISY: Will you show us?

CARSON: Certainly not! A telephone is not a toy, but a useful and valuable tool. Now get back to your work.

They file out. Carson closes the door. He takes down the earpiece and squints at it, upside down and right way up, as he blows into the speaking tube. He hasn't got a clue.

49 INT. MRS BATES'S DRAWING ROOM. DAY

MRS BATES: She worked at the barracks sometimes, helping at big dinners and so on. That night her opportunity came and she took it. They knew it was her. Someone even saw her with a big carry-all.

ANNA: The one that was in his quarters.

MRS BATES: Sitting right there. I knew he'd put it out to take back in the morning. But he never said.

ANNA: Why not? But why did he confess?

Mrs Bates sighs wearily. This is the hardest part for her.

MRS BATES: Well, John wasn't the same man in those days. The African war had shaken him up and made him angry. He'd been wounded, and he drank a lot, more than was good for him…*

....

* The important element of this exchange is for the audience to be aware that Bates was a drunk and a nasty drunk at that. In other words, he behaved very badly to his wife. Because I don't think you can understand his character without that knowledge. We already know he used to be a drunk because he's told Carson and Mrs Hughes. But we don't know that he was bitter and cruel. Consequently Bates blames himself for what his wife has become, and the audience needs to know that, to make this plot work.

ANNA: Was he violent?

MRS BATES: No, not violent, but he could be hard at times with a tongue like a razor. He felt he'd ruined Vera's life, Miss Smith. That she'd never have gone wrong but for his treatment of her.

ANNA: Do you agree with him?

MRS BATES: No. I thought she was a nasty piece of work. And her behaviour since has proved me right. But that's why he took the blame.

ANNA: Surely, if everyone knew he was innocent…

MRS BATES: But he confessed. It wasn't their fault. There was nothing anybody could do, once he'd confessed.

50 INT. HALL. DOWNTON. DAY.

THOMAS: I hope everything's going well?

Doctor Clarkson is being seen out by Thomas. He nods.

CLARKSON: Oh, yes. I think so.

THOMAS: Could I ask you something, sir? Only… I get the feeling that a war's on the way.

CLARKSON: I'm afraid we all do.

THOMAS: And when it comes, I want to be really useful to my country.

CLARKSON: How heartening!

THOMAS: So I've been thinking. What could be more useful than what you do? Bringing people back to health. Back to life.

CLARKSON: I see. Well, we are looking for volunteers to train for the Territorial Force hospitals if that's what you mean.

THOMAS: It's exactly what I mean.

CLARKSON: Will you not be missed here?

THOMAS: Maybe. But we'll all be going, won't we? The younger men anyway.

CLARKSON: As you wish. I'll make enquiries.

THOMAS: Thank you very much, Doctor.

Clarkson goes. Thomas has got himself out of the trenches.

51 INT. ROBERT'S DRESSING ROOM. DOWNTON. EVE.

Carson is with Robert, who is in evening dress.

CARSON: Mr Molesley walked in and there he was, bold as brass, taking my wallet out of my change coat. Mr Molesley would have no reason to make it up, m'lord. He doesn't know Thomas. Why would he lie?*

ROBERT: So Thomas has been caught red-handed. Well, we knew he was a thief, didn't we?

CARSON: And now we have unimpeachable proof. I'm afraid he has to go.

ROBERT: I hate this sort of thing. With Lady Grantham's condition and everything. Can we at least leave it until after the garden party?

CARSON: Very well, your lordship. But then, I think we must act.

52 INT. SERVANTS' HALL. DOWNTON. DAY.

Mrs Patmore, in dark glasses, is surrounded by the others.

MRS HUGHES: How long will you wear them?

MRS PATMORE: A week or so. But I can see much better already, even with them on.

MRS HUGHES: Thank heaven. Now we need to talk about the garden party. Mrs Bird and I have made some lists and —

MRS PATMORE: *Mrs Bird?* I think we can manage without any help from Mrs Bird.

MRS BIRD: Can you? Well, if you want your garden party to be run by Blind Pugh, that's your business.

MRS HUGHES: Mrs Patmore, there's a lot to be done and you're only just up on your feet. We really cannot manage without Mrs Bird.

MRS PATMORE: If you say so.

MRS HUGHES: Now, I've been checking the stores and I think I've ordered what you'll need for the baking.

....

* Butlers and footmen often had an informal cotton coat to wear when they came downstairs or into the servants' territory. They would take off their morning coat or livery, to protect them from being marked, but they would have a coat to change into so that they would be respectably dressed. This was called a change coat.

MRS BIRD: That's very kind, Mrs Hughes. But I believe we should check the stores. When it's convenient.

What? This is music to Mrs Patmore's ear.

MRS HUGHES: Mrs Bird, at Downton Abbey, the housekeeper manages the store cupboard, but…
MRS BIRD: I've never not run my own store cupboard in my life. Separate the cook from the store cupboard? Where's the sense in that?
MRS PATMORE: How long have I been saying this, oh Lord?
MRS BIRD: We're the ones who cook it. We should be the ones to order it.
MRS PATMORE: Mrs Bird, I shall be very glad of your help with the garden party. I'm sure we can manage it easily between the two of us.

53 INT. CARSON'S PANTRY. DOWNTON. DAY.

Carson takes the telephone earpiece reverently, and speaks.

CARSON: Hello. This is Downton Abbey. Carson, the butler, speaking.

He reviews his own performance and tries again.

CARSON (CONT'D): Hello. This is Mr Carson, the butler of Downton Abbey. To whom am I speaking?

To his amazement there is someone at the other end.

CARSON: What? I am not shouting! Who are you? Oh. Mrs Gaunt. No, I don't want to place a call… I was practising my answer… Well, I dare say a lot of the things you do sound stupid to other people!

He slams it back down. The telephone is not a friend.

54 INT. CORA'S BEDROOM. DOWNTON. EVE.

Violet is with Cora, who lies on the daybed in a tea gown.

VIOLET: I've written to your mother. She's very anxious, naturally. She suggested coming over —
CORA: Oh, God.
VIOLET: Well, that's what I thought. So I've put her off for now and told her to come and admire the baby.

There is a knock and O'Brien enters, carrying some clothes.

O'BRIEN: I'll just go and run your ladyship's bath.
CORA: Thank you, O'Brien.
VIOLET: Now. Have you had any answers about the position?
CORA: Quite a few.

O'Brien hears this as she shuts the bathroom door, fuming.

VIOLET: I shouldn't be making you do this in your condition.
CORA: Don't be silly. It gives me something else to think about.
VIOLET: So what do they sound like?

Behind them the door opens softly. O'Brien stands there.

CORA: There's one I think has real possibilities. She learned to do hair in Paris, while she was working for the Ambassadress.

O'Brien's face is a mask of cold hatred.

55 INT. LIBRARY. DOWNTON. EVE.

Robert is writing when the door opens.

ROBERT: Carson, I've been meaning…

It is not Carson. It is Anna.

ANNA: Your lordship.

She stands before him.

ROBERT: Oh, Anna, you're back safely, then?
ANNA: Yes, thank you, m'lord. And Mrs Patmore's fighting fit again.
ROBERT: Fighting fit's the phrase.

Which doesn't explain what Anna's doing here.

ROBERT (CONT'D): Is something the matter?
ANNA: I wanted to see your lordship because…
ROBERT: Please.
ANNA: I learned something about Mr Bates.
ROBERT: Not bad, I hope.
ANNA: No. Not bad at all. I'd have told Mr Carson but I thought you might like to hear it from me first.

ROBERT: Go on.

ANNA: You see, I went to call on Mr Bates's mother...

56 INT. CORA'S BATHROOM. DOWNTON. EVE.

Cora is lying in the bath. O'Brien is arranging a towel.

CORA: O'Brien, how long do you think it takes a lady's maid to settle in?

O'BRIEN: Depends on the maid, m'lady.

CORA: Of course it does. Thank you. Oh.

She has dropped a bar of soap. O'Brien stoops to pick it up and sees it has broken in two. Almost instinctively, she only picks up one half and leaves the other on the floor. As she stands, she nudges the wet soap so that it is no longer under the bath. She hands the broken soap back.

O'BRIEN: The other half's under the bath.

CORA: Never mind. Thank you.

O'BRIEN: I'll just go and sort out your clothes, m'lady.

CORA: Thank you.

She goes, leaving the door ajar behind her.

57 INT. CORA'S BEDROOM. DOWNTON. EVE.

O'Brien is laying out a dress when she stops. She stares at her own face in the looking glass for a moment.

O'BRIEN: Sarah O'Brien, this is not who you are.

She makes a decision, and turns resolutely, striding back towards the bathroom door. She's clearly changed her mind.

O'BRIEN: M'lady, if you could just wait —

But there's a splash and a scream and a crash and the sound of dripping water. O'Brien repented of her sin too late.*

....

* Here we have another mind-changing *Downton* moment, where, just when O'Brien is at her nastiest, exacting this horrible revenge on the luckless Cora, she is suddenly gripped by the horror of what she has done and she tries to stop it, but she is too late. Hopefully, this makes the audience feel slightly reluctant to condemn her absolutely, while still being on Cora's side over the unprovoked malice of the deed.

58 INT. DRESSING ROOM. DOWNTON. EVE.

Robert is alone, looking out of the window. Bates comes in.

BATES: The doctor's gone, your lordship. But he's coming back after dinner. Lady Mary's with her now.

ROBERT: Thank you.

BATES: I don't suppose you'll want to change. But is there anything else I can do to be useful?

At last, Robert turns towards him. His eyes are red.

ROBERT: It was a boy.

But his voice breaks and his eyes fill again. He wipes them dry with a handkerchief. Neither man moves.

ROBERT (CONT'D): I'm sorry. I don't mean to embarrass you.

BATES: I'm not embarrassed. I just wish you could have been spared this.

ROBERT: I know you do. Thank you.

Clearly there's nothing for Bates to do. He starts to go. *

ROBERT (CONT'D): By the way, Anna's told me what she learned in London.

BATES: Has she? She's not told me.

ROBERT: Oh! Well, the good news is you won't be leaving Downton. And I need some good news today.

....

* I find this scene between Bates and Robert moving, another illustration of the contrast in the relationship between master and servant when they are in public and when they're in private. Because they are alone together, Robert's guard is down and he does not hide that he is weeping for his dead son. It is a key moment between them, and a reminder of how little you could hide from a valet or a lady's maid. When Robert says, 'I don't mean to embarrass you,' and Bates replies 'I'm not embarrassed,' the moment was probably inspired by my late mother who used to say that embarrassment is the only unproductive emotion, which I agree with. Because of her, I strongly reject embarrassment and here Bates's statement of support, by also rejecting embarrassment, is important. It is a rare opportunity for him to show his affection for Robert.

59 INT. SERVANTS' HALL. DOWNTON. NIGHT.

The household sits about in shock. Branson is there.

MRS HUGHES: That poor wee babe.

ANNA: How's her ladyship doing?

MRS HUGHES: I'll take her up a tray in a minute, but I dare say she won't touch a bite.

WILLIAM: What about you, Miss O'Brien?

O'BRIEN: What about me?

WILLIAM: That must have been quite a shock.

O'BRIEN: Yes. Yes, it was.

She is very subdued.

CARSON: I think you'd better dine with us, Mr Branson. We can't know if you might be needed later.

BRANSON: I'm to go for the doctor at ten.

THOMAS (V.O.): What a long-faced lot!

Thomas is back among them.

CARSON: Kindly show some respect.

THOMAS: Come on, Mr Carson. She'll get over it. They're no bigger than a hamster at that stage.

BATES: Will you shut up?

MRS HUGHES: I quite agree. What's the matter with you, Thomas?

THOMAS: I don't know. I suppose all this makes me feel… claustrophobic.

He helps himself to a biscuit on the table.

THOMAS (CONT'D): I mean I'm sorry, 'course I am, but why must we live through them? They're just our employers. They're not our flesh and blood.

DAISY: Thomas, don't be so unkind.

WILLIAM: Is there nothing left on earth that you respect?

THOMAS: Hark at him. Blimey, if he carries on like this for the unborn baby of a woman who scarcely knows his name, no wonder he fell to pieces when his old mum snuffed it.

With a roar, William leaps out of his chair, seizes Thomas by the lapels and starts to punch the daylights out of him.

CARSON: William! Thomas! William! Stop that! That is enough!

But Thomas is badly beaten by the time William is pulled off by Branson, Carson and Bates. Thomas storms out as the others subside. By the door, Mrs Hughes whispers to Carson.

MRS HUGHES: And if you punish him for that, I'll punish you.

Carson doesn't put up any resistance.

60 EXT. GARDENS. DOWNTON. DAY.

An open-sided marquee shelters some of the colourful crowd, while others stroll around the lawns in groups. Carson supervises as William, Thomas, both looking rather bruised, and all the maids, serve at tables in the tent or walk among the guests with tea, sandwiches and cakes. Molesley is helping, too. Trays of used crockery are taken out and given to waiting kitchen maids at the side of the house, who in turn give over newly washed china and glass as well as fresh supplies of food. A string quartet plays. Thomas arrives at Doctor Clarkson's side, carrying a plate.

CLARKSON: Thank you. Oh, Thomas. I've done as I promised.

He takes an envelope from his pocket and hands it over.

CLARKSON (CONT'D): General Burton is commanding the Division at Richmond and I think I have a place for you there, under Colonel Cartwright. These are the papers. When you're ready, report to the local recruiting office and they'll take it from there. As a matter of fact, I'm being drafted back in as a Captain, so I'll try to keep an eye on you.
THOMAS: That's very kind of you, Doctor.

CLARKSON: With any luck, there may be some advantage in your having volunteered so early.*

THOMAS: Yes. That's what I thought.

Which doesn't sound quite right. William meets Daisy who has a tray of cakes. They're foxed. How can they exchange the two trays?

WILLIAM: Hang on a minute.

He transfers his own tray to one arm.

WILLIAM: Now give me yours and take this one at the same time.

It looks as if both will fall. With a squeal, Daisy rescues things and at last both hold the desired tray. They laugh.

DAISY: William, I'm sorry I've been so unkind to you, lately.

WILLIAM: Oh, that's all right.

DAISY: No, it's not all right. I don't know why I said those things.

WILLIAM: You were under an evil spell.

She knows what he means and blushes.

DAISY: I'm not under it now.

WILLIAM: I'm glad.

DAISY: Friends?

WILLIAM: Always friends.

He goes back to the party. She goes to the kitchens.

....

* I confess I like Thomas. He knows he's about to be sacked, he knows that everyone dislikes him, that they'd all be glad to see the back of him, and so like someone about to fall he jumps first. Of course he is a loner, with little interest in the opinions of others, but as I've said before, being gay at that time was very difficult, so he has some excuse for feeling alien and isolated. And what I like is that he doesn't sit about. Whether he's a deserter or a thief, he is always precipitating the next change in his life, which, for me, is essentially sympathetic. He is not passive and I suppose the people I do not admire are the ones who let life happen to them, as opposed to taking the wheel. Thomas always takes the wheel.

61 INT. KITCHEN. DOWNTON. DAY.

Mrs Patmore, looking more normal, is supervising. Mrs Bird is with her. All round the other maids carry, wash and dry.

MRS BIRD: I think we should start the ices now. If you agree, Mrs Patmore.
MRS PATMORE: Certainly, Mrs Bird.

There is the unfamiliar sound of a telephone ringing.

MRS PATMORE: Oh, my Lord. Listen to that. It's like the cry of the banshee.

Branson appears in the doorway.

BRANSON: Mr Carson's telephone is ringing. Isn't someone going to answer it?
MRS PATMORE: I wouldn't touch that thing with a ten foot pole.
BRANSON: Well, I will then.

62 INT. CARSON'S PANTRY. DOWNTON. DAY.

Branson is on the telephone.

BRANSON: No, Mr Carson's busy but can I take a message?

63 EXT. GARDENS. DOWNTON. DAY.

Branson comes tearing round the house. He sees Sybil and races up, rather surprising the others with her, including Edith.

BRANSON: I've got news, m'lady!

She listens and then looks round for Gwen. She sees her walking round the house with a full tray and hurries over.

SYBIL: Mr Bromidge has rung! You've done it, Gwen! You've got the job!

Gwen screams so that one or two guests look over. She turns to a passing maid to get rid of her tray.

GWEN: Take it! Take it!

She and Sybil and Branson hold each other and laugh and spin round. The guests do not see, but Mrs Hughes does.

MRS HUGHES: Something to celebrate?

GWEN: I've got the job, Mrs Hughes! I'm a secretary! I've begun!

MRS HUGHES: I'm very happy for you, Gwen. And we'll celebrate. *After* we've finished today's work.

GWEN: Of course, Mrs Hughes.

She hurries back into the throng, as Mrs Hughes turns away. Sybil and Branson are left holding hands. For a moment, they stare at each other. Then Branson speaks quite softly.

BRANSON: I don't suppose —

MRS HUGHES (V.O.): Lady Sybil!

The young couple look round. The housekeeper has come back.

MRS HUGHES (CONT'D): Her ladyship was asking after you.

Sybil drops Branson's hand and hurries away.

MRS HUGHES (CONT'D): Be careful, my lad. Or you'll end up with no job *and* a broken heart.

BRANSON: What do you mean?

But Mrs Hughes knows what she means. And so does he. Meanwhile Mary strolls with Sir Anthony Strallan.

STRALLAN: I don't seem to be able to find your sister.

MARY: I wonder where she is. Of course, she may have been cornered. I know there was some old bore she was trying to dodge.

This is disturbing to Strallan.

STRALLAN: Who was that?

MARY: I'm not sure. He's simply ghastly apparently, but he'd promised to propose today. I can't tell you how funny she was when she acted it out. She ought to go on the stage.

STRALLAN: Really? Ah, how amusing…

Carson has joined Mrs Hughes by the side of the house.

CARSON: Well done, Mrs Hughes. Beautifully executed as always.

MRS HUGHES: The key is in the planning.

They are interrupted by Thomas.

THOMAS: Mr Carson, this probably isn't the moment, but I've just heard from Doctor Clarkson I've been accepted for a training scheme for the army medical corps.
CARSON: Have you, indeed?
THOMAS: Yes. And I want to do it. So I'll be handing in my notice. I'll serve out the month, of course.
CARSON: Thank you, Thomas. We can talk about it, later.

Thomas goes and Mrs Hughes leans in.

MRS HUGHES: And you couldn't have planned that any better, either.

Edith's with Strallan but he does not seem anxious to talk.

EDITH: You can't be leaving yet!
STRALLAN: I'm afraid I must. Please make my excuses to your mother.
EDITH: But —

It's no good. He hurries away. As Edith follows the wretched man with her eyes, she sees Mary smirking at her. Cora lies on a chaise longue. O'Brien arranges the shawls.

O'BRIEN: I wish you'd come inside, m'lady.
CORA: No. People mustn't think I'm really ill. I don't want to cast a dampener on the party.
O'BRIEN: Very well. But are you sure you have everything you need, m'lady?
CORA: Dear O'Brien. How sweet you are.

As O'Brien walks away, Violet leaves Rosamund to catch her.

VIOLET: O'Brien. Can I have a word? I need a favour and I don't want to bother Lady Grantham with it.
O'BRIEN: Certainly, m'lady.
VIOLET: She's been helping me find a new maid and we've had quite a few answers to her advertisement, Can you find where she's put them, and get Branson to bring them to the Dower House?
O'BRIEN: Her ladyship was helping you find a new lady's maid?
VIOLET: Yes. We should have asked you, really. You might take a look at the letters if you've a minute. There was one we liked the sound of who'd been trained in Paris.

O'Brien is almost in a trance. Violet is a little puzzled.

VIOLET (CONT'D): Do you know where she might have put them? The answers?
O'BRIEN: Oh, yes, m'lady. There are only two or three places they could be.
VIOLET: Dear O'Brien. You're a treasure. Thank you.

Anna is carrying a tray for the kitchens, when she sees Bates.

ANNA: I didn't know a garden party was a spectator sport.
BATES: Pretty, though, isn't it? Hard to believe the clouds are gathering on a summer's day like this.
ANNA: Mr Bates, I know you think I was wrong, to call on your mother…
BATES: I don't think that. She likes you, by the way.
ANNA: I had to find out the truth.
BATES: But, you see, you don't know the whole truth, even now. You know my mother's truth.
ANNA: But not your wife's… Where is she, now?
BATES: Couldn't tell you. So, for all your efforts, everything remains quite unresolved.

But there is a smile on his lips that belies his words.

ANNA: I'd better get back.

As she hurries away, Molesley walks up to Bates.

BATES: You're here, Mr Molesley? I didn't know that.
MOLESLEY: Just helping out.

Together they watch as Anna walks towards the tent.

MOLESLEY (CONT'D): Nice girl, that Anna. Do you know if she's got anyone special in her life?
BATES: I'd like to say she hasn't. I would, truly. But I'm afraid there is someone.
MOLESLEY: And do you think he's keen on her? Or is it worth a go?
BATES: Well, he keeps himself to himself and he's very hard to read at times. But I'd say he's keen. I'd say he was very keen, indeed.

Mrs Patmore passes him, puffing along with a full tray of ice cream set out in little dishes, speaking as she goes. She hurries up to Daisy in the serving tent, who is arranging another tray of cakes.

MRS PATMORE: Daisy! I said ices, not iced cakes! Now, unclog your ears and get these to William before they turn into soup!

Meanwhile, Mary and Matthew are on the edge of the lawn.

MARY: But I don't understand. Nothing's changed.

MATTHEW: Everything's changed.

MARY: You can't be sure I was going to refuse you, even if it had been a boy. Because I'm not.

MATTHEW: That's the point. I can't be sure. Of you. Or of anything, it seems. The last few weeks have taught me that.

MARY: But you can't leave Downton.

MATTHEW: I can't stay. Not now.

MARY: What will you say to Papa?

MATTHEW: That I'm grateful for what he's trying to do, but the experiment is at an end. I'm not a puppet. I must take charge of my own life again.

MARY: Until you inherit.

MATTHEW: If indeed I ever do.

MARY: Would you have stayed, if I'd accepted you?

MATTHEW: Of course.

MARY: So I've ruined everything.

MATTHEW: You have shown me I've been living in a dream, and it's time to return to real life. Wish me luck with it, Mary. God knows I wish the best for you.

As he walks away, Violet is watching with Rosamund.

VIOLET: Well, Rosamund. I'm afraid your meddling has cost Mary the only decent offer she'll ever get.

ROSAMUND: I'm sorry, Mama, but you know me. I have to say what I think.

VIOLET: Why? Nobody else does.

Mary is weeping in the shadows, when Carson approaches.

CARSON: Are you quite well, m'lady?

She answers defiantly but the tears course down her cheeks.

MARY: Of course! You know me, Carson. I'm never down for long.

But she can't stop crying, and so Carson takes her in his arms, patting her back gently as she cries on his shoulder.

CARSON: I know you have spirit, m'lady. And that's what counts. It's *all* that counts, in the end.

Isobel has found Violet. They look across at Matthew.

ISOBEL: So Mary is to be denied her countess's coronet, after all?
VIOLET: Don't crow at me. I think she was very foolish not to take him when she could. And I told her so.
ISOBEL: Well, if I'm perfectly honest, I wonder if Matthew isn't making the same mistake, right now.

This is a kind of truce, as they stroll on. Robert is standing by Cora, with her hand in his.

ROBERT: Are you warm enough?
CORA: I am when you're holding my hand.

Carson approaches. He carries a telegram.

CARSON: Your lordship? This has just arrived for you.
ROBERT: Thank you.

He takes it and would open it, but…

CARSON: I'm happy to tell you that Thomas has just handed in his notice. So we'll be spared any unpleasantness on that score.
ROBERT: What a relief.

He opens the envelope and his face falls. He turns to the company and makes a sign to silence the band.

ROBERT (CONT'D): My lords, ladies and gentlemen, can I ask for silence?

As the band ceases to play, the curious crowd does indeed fall silent. The members of the family, Violet, Cora, the three sisters, plus Isobel, Matthew and Clarkson, look towards him. And so do the servants we know, Carson, the footmen, Bates, Molesley, Anna and Gwen, and, in the serving area at the back, the kitchen maids, the hall boys, Daisy and Mrs Patmore crane for a view of him.

ROBERT: Because I very much regret to announce… that we
are at war with Germany.*

Which is a terrifying and sobering thought.

END OF SEASON ONE

....

* The wording of this telegram comes from a story in my own family. My
dear father was born in July 1912, thus in the summer of 1914 he was two.
For some reason he and his parents were staying with his grandmother that
August at her home in Hampshire. There was a garden party at a house
nearby called Hurstbourne Park, which was lived in by the Countess of
Portsmouth, to which the whole Fellowes family was invited. All Pa's life he
could clearly remember standing with his nurse at the heart of the great,
chattering throng when a man walked out of the long windows of the
drawing room on to the terrace and asked for silence. There was a hush and
he said in a loud voice: 'I very much regret to announce that we are at war
with Germany.' And that was Daddy's first memory. I asked him why he
thought it had remained so vivid and he replied that he could only suppose
the announcement created such a tense vibration of emotions through all the
people present, all the adults, all the servants, everyone, that even a childish
brain could realise something extraordinary was happening. I nearly put a
little boy into the scene to have him being Pa looking up at the speaker, but
then I thought it was too private a joke. There was another irony in the tale.
My twenty-nine-year-old grandfather was there too, with his young wife.
He would be dead in less than a year.

CAST LIST

Robert Bathurst	Sir Anthony Strallan
Samantha Bond	Lady Rosamund Painswick
Hugh Bonneville	Robert, Earl of Grantham
Jessica Brown Findlay	Lady Sybil Crawley
Laura Carmichael	Lady Edith Crawley
Jim Carter	Mr Carson
Charlie Cox	Duke of Crowborough
Jonathan Coy	George Murray
Brendan Coyle	Mr Bates
Michelle Dockery	Lady Mary Crawley
Kevin Doyle	Mr Molesley
Bill Fellowes	Joe Burns
Siobhan Finneran	Miss O'Brien
Joanne Froggatt	Anna
Bernard Gallagher	Bill Molesley
Nicky Henson	Charles Grigg
Thomas Howes	William
Theo James	Kemal Pamuk
Rob James-Collier	Thomas
Allen Leech	Branson
Rose Leslie	Gwen
Christine Lohr	Mrs Bird
Phyllis Logan	Mrs Hughes
Elizabeth McGovern	Cora, Countess of Grantham
Sean McKenzie	Mr Bromidge
Sophie McShera	Daisy
Lesley Nicol	Mrs Patmore
Fergus O'Donnell	Mr Drake

Brendan Patricks	Evelyn Napier
David Robb	Dr Clarkson
Cathy Sara	Mrs Drake
Maggie Smith	Violet, Dowager Countess of Grantham
Dan Stevens	Matthew Crawley
Jane Wenham	Mrs Bates
Penelope Wilton	Isobel Crawley

PRODUCTION CREDITS

Writer & Creator	Julian Fellowes
Executive Producers	Julian Fellowes
	Gareth Neame
Series Producer	Liz Trubridge
Producer	Nigel Marchant
Director (Episodes 1, 6 & 7)	Brian Percival
Director (Episodes 2 & 3)	Ben Bolt
Director (Episodes 4 & 5)	Brian Kelly
Production Designer	Donal Woods
Directors of Photography	David Katznelson DFF
	David Marsh
Editors	John Wilson A.C.E
	Nick McPhee
	Alex Mackie A.C.E
Costume Designer	Susannah Buxton
Make-Up & Hair Designer	Anne 'Nosh' Oldham
Casting Director	Jill Trevellick CDG
Music	John Lunn
Writer (Episode 4)	Shelagh Stephenson
Writer (Episode 6)	Tina Pepler
First Assistant Directors	Phil Booth
	George Walker
	Howard Arundel
Second Assistant Director	Charlie Reed
Third Assistant Directors	Dannielle Bennett
	Gayle Dickie
Script Supervisors	Sarah Garner
	Heather Storr
Location Manager	Richard May
Assistant Location Manager	Mark 'Sparky' Ellis
Unit Manager	John Prendergast

Production Manager	Sarah Dibsdall
Production Accountant	Sarah Lucraft
Production Co-Ordinator	Bettina Lyster
Assistant Production Co-Ordinator	Jonathan Houston
Assistant Accountant	Davina Pem
Camera Operators	Xandy Sahla
	Paddy Blake
Focus Puller	Anna Benbow
Clapper Loader	Gabriel Hyman
Grips	Simon Fogg
	Rupert Morency
Gaffer	Otto Stenov
Best Boy	Aaron Walters
Supervising Art Director	Charmian Adams
Art Director	Mark Kebby
Production Buyer	Fiona Haddon
Set Decorator	Gina Cromwell
Standby Art Director	Pippa Broadhurst
Assistant Art Director	Lucy Spofforth
Sound Mixers	Mark Holding
	John Rodda
	Peter Eusebe
Prop Master	Mike Power
Dressing Props	Tom Pleydell Pearce
	Charlie Johnson
Standby Props	Damian Butlin
	Andy Forrest
Special Effects	Jason Troughton
Stunt Co-ordinator	Andy Bradford
Assistant Costume Designer	Caroline McCall
Costume Supervisor	Dulcie Scott
Costume Assistants	Jason Gill
	Vicky Salway
	Hanne Cauwenbergh
Make-Up & Hair Supervisor	Christine Greenwood
Make-Up & Hair Artists	Elaine Browne
	Sally Collins
	Gerda Lauciute
Historical Advisor	Alastair Bruce
Script Editors	Sam Symons
	Claire Daxter
Production Executive	Kimberley Hikaka

Business Affairs	David O'Donoghue
Unit Publicity	Milk Publicity
Post Production Supervisor	Moira Brophy
Post Production Assistant	Ilana Epstein
Assistant Editors	Al Morrow
	Sascha Dhillon
Colourist	Aidan Farrell
Online Editors	Clyde Kellet
	Barney Jordan
Re-Recording Mixer	Nigel Heath
Sound FX Editor	Adam Armitage
Dialogue Editors	Alex Sawyer
	Jessica Ward
Titles	Huge Design

ACKNOWLEDGEMENTS

I would like, first and foremost, to acknowledge the contribution of Gareth Neame. He had the idea in the first place, of making a series about a country house, dealing with the lives of a family and their servants, and since then, he and our producer, Liz Trubridge, have consistently improved the scripts at every stage. We are essentially the triumvirate at the heart of the show. I would also like to thank Ion Trewin who has been bottomlessly patient in editing this book, Doctor Alasdair Emslie, FFOM, for his matchless resourcefulness in supplying medical conditions that will answer the narrative requirements of a plot, my agents, Cathy King and Jeremy Barber, and of course my wife, Emma, and my son, Peregrine, who read the script before anyone else and so weeded out the worst bits. I am very grateful to them all.